TOM MURRAY

# DEADLY BY DESIGN

## THE SHOCKING COVER-UP BEHIND RUNAWAY CARS

MARK ADVERTISING
Sandusky, Ohio

*Deadly by Design: The Shocking Cover-Up Behind Runaway Cars*
by
TOM MURRAY

Published by
MARK ADVERTISING
1600 Fifth Street
PO Box 413
Sandusky, Ohio 44870
sales@markadvertising.com
*Book Design: Bryan Fleck*

Price at retail: U.S. $14.95



ISBN, print ed. 978-0-615-92153-2
Printed in the United States of America
Library of Congress Catalog-in-Publication Data

**TOM MURRAY**
***Deadly by Design: The Shocking Cover-Up Behind Runaway Cars***
**ISBN: 978-0-615-92153-2**
**Library of Congress Control Number: 2012905760**

www.deadlybydesign.com

*Dedication*

*To Ann Murray, my beloved wife of fifty years,*
*without whose unstinting support,*
*this book would not have been possible.*

# CONTENTS

# PROLOGUE

**VIRGINIA STATE TROOPER RONALD CAMPBELL WILL NEVER FORGET** the summer day in 1991 when his training in evasive driving saved his life. It was a Saturday, and he was doing chores outside his home in Southwest Virginia when his wife, on returning from grocery shopping, stopped their Mercury Grand Marquis near the entrance to their home. After helping his wife unload the groceries, Campbell decided to move the car about 80 feet out of the hot midday sun to a shaded area near the end of the driveway, something he had done countless times before. But this time his training was about to be tested beyond anything he could have imagined.

After seating himself behind the wheel of the Grand Marquis, he placed his right foot lightly on the brake pedal, shifted into drive, and then removed his foot from the brake pedal to let the car move at idle speed down a slight grade to the shaded area. But as he would later testify, the moment he completed shifting, the car "suddenly accelerated abruptly with the engine racing." He quickly applied the brakes, but "there was no effect." With the car now rapidly bearing down on the trees at the end of the driveway, Campbell's training kicked in and he "cut the car sharply to the left" hoping to maneuver it through "an open gate leading to our pasture... where I would have time to stop it safely." The car missed the trees, but the sharp turn on the grassy surface put the car into a spin. The quick-thinking Campbell somehow maneuvered the car between a guy wire and a utility pole near the gate to the pasture. "The front bumper just touched the utility pole and the car continued to turn around." But to his horror, the car was now headed straight at a propane tank in their yard. "At that moment, I literally thought I was going to die right there if I didn't get this vehicle stopped." Campbell "jammed the gear selector from drive to park" bringing "the car to a stop just like that . . . "

"I was emotionally frightened; I was weak, literally sick at my stomach; I was so weak, I didn't think I could even stand up. That is how badly it scared me. I turned the engine off. It took me several minutes before I got out of the car . . . . "

Although Campbell's quick thinking saved him, thousands of people, lacking his training, have been injured or killed because they were unable to stop a runaway car. Some of the most destructive occurrences have happened in closed areas with little time or space for maneuver, like a driveway, parking lot, or crowded street where a runaway car has often crashed into a residential dwelling, garage, storefront, or other automobiles. Some victims suffered a horrifying death in a matter of seconds; others lingered in agony before succumbing; many others were left permanently paralyzed, comatose, or crippled; still others recovered from fractures and internal injuries that would plague them for years; and those lucky enough to escape physical injury were often left with the trauma of a brush with death etched forever in their memories. The most heart-wrenching cases involved a child or spouse of the driver being crushed to death in a driveway or garage, leaving the driver with an unbearable sense of guilt at having failed to prevent the death of a loved one. Many people refused ever again to drive the car.

The first reports of this terrifying automotive behavior surfaced in the late 1970s, and by the early 1980s were being referred to as "sudden acceleration." Because it was like a mysterious illness with symptoms never before seen, pundits were soon referring to sudden acceleration as an "automotive plague." But the mystery didn't end with the event itself. When the engine was turned back on, it performed normally; when the car was inspected, nothing was found to explain what had caused the car to spontaneously speed out of control; and when the brakes were inspected, they were invariably found to be in good working order.

In the early 1980s, the National Highway Traffic Safety Administration, or NHTSA, began investigating this phenomenon, but couldn't find a defect. One of the first investigations involved Volkswagen of America's Audi 5000, which initially blamed reports on a jammed floor mat and possible misalignment of the brake and accelerator pedals. When that fell flat, the company tried a double-barreled strategy that was soon adopted by the entire industry: (1) insist that any defect capable of sending a car out of control would leave evidence detectable during a vehicle inspection; and (2) shift the focus from the car to the driver by insisting that unless the brakes were defective, they would have safely stopped the car. These assertions implied that the cause had to be the driver.

The industry's strategy worked like a charm on NHTSA, which opened and closed dozens of investigations during the 1980s without finding a safety defect. Consumer organizations like the Washington, D.C.-based Center for Auto Safety, the New York Public Interest Research Group, the Florida Public Interest Research Group and others were incredulous, and demanded that the government do something to stem the growing carnage. Runaway car disasters, however, did not gain wide public attention until November of 1986 when CBS's *60 Minutes* aired a story entitled "Out of Control" about the Audi 5000, which created public pressure for a government solution. In late 1987 NHTSA retained a Boston-based government-funded company to conduct an industry-wide study of the phenomenon, by which point there had already been at least 50,000 sudden accelerations in the United States, resulting in about 20,000 accidents, 10,000 injuries, and 1,000 fatalities, making runaway cars one of the most destructive problems in automotive history.

Although thousands of drivers of all ages and differing levels of driving experience told NHTSA they had tried unsuccessfully to stop the car by braking, they were shocked when the agency concluded in January 1989 that the likely cause of most sudden accelerations was "driver pedal error." This armed carmakers with a government report they could use against people who sought compensation for their injuries and damages. By the point this book was completed in August of 2013, there had been at least 500,000 runaway car occurrences just in this country, resulting in about 100,000 injuries and 5,000 fatalities; and yet, over the years very few people have been compensated for their injuries.

This is the untold story behind these appalling statistics. It poses two overarching questions: what basis did the federal government have for blaming drivers; and if drivers were not the cause, why has this devastating automotive behavior continued unabated for more than three decades? While the book's title and subtitle hint at how it answers these questions, it took fifteen years of grueling litigation inside and outside courtrooms throughout the United States to assemble the evidence presented in these pages in four novella-length parts that tell the story from distinctly different angles.

Part One, entitled "Man or Machine", begins with a sudden acceleration of a Ford Crown Victoria from the driveway of a Cleveland minister, Leon Manigault, that eventually crashed into a neighbor's house, leaving Mr. Manigault in a permanently comatose condition. Although I was approaching my sixtieth birthday when I accepted the case, I was intrigued by this deadly automotive mystery and moved by how the Manigaults' adult children were caring for their stricken father in his home. Few product liability cases in U.S. history have had more twists and turns, or made a greater impact on product liability law than *Manigault v. Ford*. Part One ends with a dramatic turn of events in the case, which doesn't reach its surprising conclusion until later in the book.

Part Two, entitled "Trailing a Killer," focuses on how my legal associate Molly O'Neill, paralegal Jo Ellen Seiler, ever-faithful secretary Janet Raifsnider, and I fought a series of legal battles with the Ford Motor Company to uncover the truth behind this often lethal automotive behavior. This part of the story ends with a landmark decision by the Second U. S. Circuit Court written by Sonia Sotomayor, now a Justice of the United States Supreme Court. Readers who enjoy stories about the trials, tribulations and triumphs of courtroom lawyers should find this section particularly interesting.

Part Three, entitled "The Color of Corruption", examines why NHTSA didn't put an end to this automotive disaster many years ago. While the title suggests the answer, I suspect that readers will nevertheless be shocked by what emerges in these chapters.

The final section of the book entitled "Toyota and the Unraveling of a Cover-Up" focuses on Toyota's runaway car problems after it made a fundamental change in its throttle control electronics. After fending off government inquiries for several years, everything changed for the Japanese carmaker following media coverage of a frantic 9-1-1 call from a runaway Lexus driven by a California State Patrolman and his family who died moments later when the car crashed and incinerated its occupants. The final chapters contain good news and bad news for anyone concerned about automotive safety.

While each novella-length section has eye-openers of its own, the biggest surprise may be that the story's importance exceeds the sum of its many revelations.

PART 1

# MAN OR MACHINE

CHAPTER 1

# SHATTERED LIVES

### DRIVER, WIFE HURT AS CAR HITS HOUSE

A 67-year-old Cleveland man was critically injured when the car he was driving struck the back of a house in the 9700 block of Adams Ave. last night. Leon Manigault of Kempton Ave. . . . was driving forward out of his driveway about 9:30 p.m. and continued across Kempton Ave., went up the driveway of the house across the street and continued on until his car hit the back of the house on Adams, according to police. Manigault was listed in critical condition with head and chest injuries at Mt. Sinai Medical Center. His wife, Virginia, 63, who was a passenger in the car, was in guarded condition at Mt. Sinai. Two grandchildren riding in the car were not hurt. William C. Graham, the owner of the Adams Ave. house, said the car traveled through a fence before crashing through the wall of his pantry. No one in the house was hurt.

Cleveland *Plain Dealer*, April 4, 1993

**THE MOMENT HE SPOTTED THE SLEEK BEIGE AND BLUE 1987 CROWN** Victoria at a Ford dealership, Leon Manigault fell in love. It was exactly what his wife, Virginia, and he had been looking for. They had never owned a new car. As the sole breadwinner of a family of six, Leon's earnings had been too meager for that. Now, with their children grown, and Leon recently retired, their plans called for a new car.

Leon and Virginia were the children of poor black South Carolina sharecroppers. Leon liked to tell his children their mother was "the prettiest girl I'd ever seen, and the most graceful." Virginia remembered Leon as a "serious young man, a real go-getter" who she knew "would better himself." Their life had not been easy. After their first son was born, they moved north where Leon found work in Cleveland's booming construction industry as a pipe fitter and soon earned a reputation as a hard worker, turning up for work even on bitterly cold days. Leon eventually saved enough to buy the home on Cleveland's east side they had occupied for the previous seven years. Leon was especially proud to have helped his daughters Evelyn and Jacqueline earn college degrees.

Leon and Virginia had been raised by deeply religious parents. As children, they had regularly attended services at a small, rural Pentecostal church where everyone, no matter how meager their circumstances, came to church in their best finery and joyfully expressed their faith in song and proclamations of gratitude to their Creator. These memories never left Leon, and as he grew older he dreamed of service in the church after his retirement. Soon after he turned 50, he began taking bible study courses in the evening, and eventually helped start a small Pentecostal church in an abandoned one-story building in East Cleveland several blocks from his home, where he eventually became pastor. In 1986, at age 67, Leon left pipefitting to begin full time service in their church.

Virginia had come up with the idea of starting a foster home, where they could care for neglected children, victims of the poverty, joblessness, teen pregnancies, and despair that permeated sections of Cleveland's east side. Virginia reckoned they could fill the bedrooms once occupied by their own children, an idea Leon took to immediately. The Manigaults were granted a license to start a foster home. Now all that remained was to find a car that could be used to bring hot meals prepared by Virginia to shut-ins, sick children to the doctor, and transport foster children to and from school activities. "We need a car we can trust," Leon insisted.

In early January of 1987, they found what they were looking for at Mullinax Ford, one of Cleveland's largest dealerships. "When Leon saw that car," Virginia recalled, "he couldn't take his eyes away from it. He kept looking at it for the longest time. I knew right then we would own that car." Pointing to the Crown Victoria, Leon had told the salesman that he would "come back tomorrow for that car; we just need to do some figuring tonight."

That evening the two Manigaults spent hours at their kitchen table discussing how they could afford the car. The next morning they accepted the dealer's trade-in offer on a ten-year-old Chevrolet they had purchased used, Leon signed the necessary papers, and they drove off the lot in what, except for their home, was the biggest investment of their lives.

Leon and Virginia were soon caring for several foster children, ranging in ages from five to 12, while ministering to the needs of the sick and elderly in their congregation. Virginia remembered it as, "Our golden years, when Leon just seemed to grow every day in his love for the Lord and everyone he met, especially children." Later she would tell people, "That man never spent one minute thinking of himself. He never complained. He just tried to help people any way he could."

Their work did not go unnoticed. A story in the Cleveland *Plain Dealer* featured their foster home as an example of compassion in action. Without intending it, the Manigaults became important people in their community.

As they greeted departing church members following services on the evening of April 3, 1993, Leon and Virginia had much to be thankful for. Their church was flourishing; the six foster children in their care had heartwarmingly taken to calling them "Mom" and "Dad"; and their son, John, healthy and fit from construction work, was studying bible courses in the hope of one day following in his father's footsteps. Evelyn and Jackie were doing well in their nursing and teaching careers. Before them was a quiet evening with family—dinner at home, followed by a visit to Evelyn's nearby home where she and Jackie had offered to feed four of the foster children. But fate had turned the hourglass of their golden years on its head the moment Leon signed the papers for the Crown Victoria.

Before leaving for home, Leon and Virginia spent a few minutes enjoying a fresh breeze off nearby Lake Erie. After the short drive home, Leon backed the Crown Victoria into their driveway. When they returned to the car for the short drive to Evelyn's place, Virginia made herself comfortable in the right front passenger seat, while Leon strapped two foster children in car seats before sliding behind the wheel and turning on the ignition. At that moment, the last grains fell to the bottom of the glass. Virginia would later describe the next terrifying seconds to a jury: "The moment Leon put that car in gear, it just took off like a jet. There wasn't time to be scared. We were going too fast. Leon steered that car with both hands. I don't know how he missed those houses or that tree, but then there was nowhere to go. That man saved my life."

The evidence would later show that when Leon shifted into drive, the car shot forward from the driveway directly toward a house on the opposite side of the street. As he pushed desperately on the brake pedal, Leon deftly steered the car to the only space available, a narrow driveway running between two houses. Somehow he missed the houses, but at the end of the driveway a large tree loomed directly in his path. Leon missed it by quickly steering to the right, only to find the car heading for the rear of a two-story frame house. With no more room to maneuver, he tried to steer away from the house, but the car crashed into the structure, shattering the windshield as it burrowed under the cinderblock foundation until the A-pillar of the driver compartment struck the bottom edge of the structure. Leon's head was driven violently forward into the building "shattering his skull" and, as one doctor put it, "tearing the covering of the brain so that . . . there was blood coming out of his ears . . . . " In his final conscious act, Leon had turned the car just enough that Virginia's head stopped short of the structure, sparing her a fate like his.

John Manigault, who had stayed behind to watch a movie, knew something was wrong when he heard a frantic knocking at the door and a foster child's urgent cry, "Come quick, John, come quick; Mom and Dad are hurt real bad!"

As he ran toward the crash site, John noticed that the brake lights on the car were illuminated. Several neighbors were already gathered around the Crown Victoria trying to help the occupants trapped inside. Someone had called 9-1-1 and, within minutes, ambulances and a rescue squad with the Jaws of Life were at the scene. Inside the tangled wreckage, Leon remained slumped over the steering wheel, unconscious, as Virginia squeezed his motionless hand and prayed, "Please, Lord, don't take Leon from us. We all need him so much!" But as she watched the blood streaming from his ears, she feared she had lost her sun, moon and stars. Cut and bleeding from facial lacerations and gripped with pain from a fractured hip, she continued holding Leon's hand until the Jaws of Life tore away the car roof and rescue workers lifted him into a waiting ambulance.

The Manigaults were rushed to nearby Mt. Sinai Hospital where doctors worked feverishly to stem the hemorrhaging in Leon's brain. After the doctors removed the windshield fragments they could find and stitched up her facial cuts, Virginia was admitted with multiple fractures in her right hip. Jackie and Evelyn, who had hurried to the hospital, huddled with John and waited to learn if their father would survive. Shortly after midnight, they were told that Leon's brain damage was so extensive he would never regain consciousness. Without life support, he would die a peaceful and painless death. If he lived, he would remain in a vegetative state in need of constant care in an extended care facility. The three Manigaults told the doctors they would consult with their mother, who would have the final say.

Virginia was shocked to have to choose between letting her husband go or having him institutionalized to be cared for by strangers for the remainder of his life. Throughout the night, Evelyn, Jackie and John had agonized over what to do. By morning, they had decided that if their father survived, they would care for him at home. Virginia was deeply moved and concurred in their decision. Their instructions to the doctors were unambiguous: they would not consent to having the feeding tubes removed from Leon.

Because it was open to the living room where most family activity took place, the Manigaults decided the dining room would be Leon's permanent care facility. Evelyn, drawing on her nurse's training, found a hospital bed equipped to move a comatose patient for bathing and skin care. A TV set was placed near the foot of the bed where, they hoped, it would provide stimulation to their father. Evelyn, John, and Jackie were soon caring for their father in shifts, while their mother, crippled by her injuries, looked helplessly on.

CHAPTER 2

# AN IRRESISTIBLE INVITATION

**ACCIDENTS LEAVE TRAIL OF SUSPICIONS BUT, SO FAR, NO CURES**

"On Thursday, March 19 . . . ," [Mary Erickson testified], "I left the school my children attend, walked to my 1986 Mercedes 560 SEL, opened the door, got into the car, put the key into the ignition, turned the car on, and the car immediately accelerated in reverse at an alarming rate of speed. There was a car parked 30 feet behind me, the driver was sitting in his car. My car hit his and immediately accelerated forward, back through the parking space, over a concrete courtyard between two buildings. This entire incident took between 10 and 15 seconds."

*The Detroit News,* December 14, 1987

**IN THE EARLY AFTERNOON OF OCTOBER 23, 1995, MY TRUSTED** secretary of many years, Janet Raifsnider, aka JR, asked me on the intercom, "Time to take a call about a referral?"

"Who's the caller?"

"It's Mr. Zelvy."

"Did you tell him I'm about to leave for the airport?"

"Yes, but he said it will only take a few minutes. He said it's important."

Although most of my cases come from referrals, Bob Zelvy had never referred a case, so my curiosity was piqued.

"Have you ever heard of something called sudden acceleration?" Zelvy began.

"Sure," I replied. "Wasn't there a story about it several years ago on *60 Minutes*?"

"Right. Have you handled such a case?"

"No. Why do you ask?"

"Because I represent two people who were badly injured when their Ford Crown Victoria took off and crashed into a neighbor's house. The driver, a minister named Leon Manigault, has been in a coma for more than two years."

"Who was with him?"

"His wife, Virginia. She says he was fighting the car all the way. She's a great witness. And guess what, the same thing happened once before, but Leon was able to get the car stopped by turning off the engine. It scared the hell out of him, and he had the car towed to the dealer who sold it to them."

"What did the dealer do?"

"Fiddled with the idle controls. The service records are in the file. Leon had regular maintenance done on the car, so it was in good condition."

"Look Bob," I said, glancing at my watch. "I'm getting ready to leave for a meeting in Seattle with a toxicologist in a defective drug case. Why don't we meet and discuss this next week?"

"Could you meet the Manigaults this afternoon, on your way to the airport?"

"Where do they live?"

"On the east side, not far from the Cleveland Clinic."

"No way, Bob. I have less than an hour to spare if I'm going to make my flight."

"That's too bad," said Zelvy. "I have an extra ticket for tonight's Series game. Great seats, upper deck directly behind home plate. Perfect place to watch Maddox and Hershiser duel it out."

The Cleveland Indians and the Atlanta Braves were scheduled to play Game 5 of the 1995 World Series that evening. Several years earlier, Zelvy and I had represented separate clients in a trial in Pittsburgh, and while there, had attended a play-off game between the Pirates and Braves. He knew I loved baseball and, as I learned later, had convinced his wife to give up her ticket as an inducement to get me to meet the Manigaults that evening.

"Wait a minute, Zel," I said, using a nickname I'd coined during the Pittsburgh trial. "If you're messing with my mind, you're doing a good job. That second ticket is mine. I'll reschedule my meeting in Seattle."

An hour later I met Zelvy at the Case Western Reserve Law School, where I had taught in the 1970s. We went to an empty classroom where he opened a file and showed me a Polaroid of a boy about nine or ten standing between a strikingly handsome couple. The man, immaculately dressed in a creased white suit and wearing a grey bowler hat with a black band, appeared wiry and fit.

The woman, in a light blue summer dress with a pleated skirt, had a comely face that was a picture of serenity.

"The Manigaults?" I asked, picking up the photograph.

Zelvy nodded affirmatively.

"Who's the boy in the middle?"

"He's one of several foster children they were caring for when this was taken."

"When was that, Bob?"

"A few months before this happened."

"How old was Mr. Manigault at the time?"

"I think he was about 66."

I continued studying the photograph. "Remarkable!" I finally said. "He could pass for someone in his forties. There isn't an ounce of fat on him. I assume they had to put him in a permanent care facility."

"That's the amazing thing. Their children wouldn't hear of it. They are caring for him at home. Their son John and daughter Jackie are waiting to meet you there. It's only about five minutes from here. Their other daughter, Evelyn, who's a registered nurse, had to work and couldn't be there, but she's the one who provides most of the nursing care for her father."

"So they have been caring for this comatose man for more than two years?"

"It's a remarkable story. Every several months an ambulance takes him to the Cleveland Clinic for a checkup. One of the doctors told Evelyn he has never seen a bedridden patient in better condition."

Zelvy's admiration for the people I was about to meet was contagious. "Bob," I said, pointing at the thick file he had brought with him, "my expert in Seattle moved our meeting back a day, so I can read this on the flight tomorrow. We can save time if you drive me to the Manigaults' home; I don't want to miss the first pitch."

On the way, I asked Zelvy how the case had come to him. It was a bizarre story. The Manigaults had immediately hired a Cleveland lawyer, who did an initial investigation before referring the case to a prominent Cleveland law firm, whose founder, Fred Weisman, is a longtime friend. After placing the Crown Victoria in a secure storage to protect it as evidence, the firm filed a suit accusing

Ford of making an unsafe car and the dealer of negligently failing to repair the car following the sudden acceleration five months earlier. The case was progressing well when it was discovered that the damaged Crown Victoria had apparently been stolen. This was a serious blow. The law requires a party with custody of evidence to protect it from alteration or destruction—known as "spoliation"—under pain of sanction, including possible dismissal of the case, if the evidence is important enough to warrant the ultimate penalty. Because neither defendant had inspected the car, they announced they would ask the court to dismiss the case. That would put Fred Weisman's firm in a bind, and he decided the ethical thing to do was to withdraw from the case.

We had arrived at the Manigaults' home, so I postponed my additional questions.

Before going inside, we walked along the driveway on the opposite side of the street along which Leon had desperately steered the Crown Victoria. Even in the gathering dark, it was obvious that without skillful maneuvering, the car would have crashed into the front of a house directly in line with the Manigaults' driveway, and could never have stayed on the narrow driveway with barely two feet to spare. "How could anyone keep an out-of-control car from missing these houses?" I asked Zelvy.

"John Manigault says his father was an excellent driver with quick reflexes. He had prevented a crash after the car had suddenly accelerated from their church parking lot."

"How did he do that?"

"John said he shifted into neutral and turned off the engine. He thinks that his father was so busy this time trying to avoid hitting something that he didn't have a chance to disengage the engine before he ran out of space."

"Is John sure the brake lights were on when he came out of the house?"

"Absolutely sure. As you are about to find out, he is an impressive young man."

"How far did the car travel before it crashed?" I asked.

"According to a diagram prepared by the lawyer who referred the case to the Weisman firm, it covered almost 200 feet. He took some good pictures a couple of days later that are in the file. So what's your impression of the case so far?"

I had expected the question, and as we stood in the descending darkness near the tree the Crown Victoria had barely missed, I was struggling to grasp what could suddenly turn an automobile into an uncontrollable missile. We had started walking toward the Manigaults' home when I responded to Zelvy's question.

"Bob, it's obvious something went terribly wrong inside that car. After I study the file, I'll let you know my thoughts. Right now, I want to meet the Manigaults, and get to Jacobs Field."

I liked the Manigaults immediately. Jacqueline, in her early thirties, had a strong, attractive face, lively eyes, and a gentle manner. John, who had taken on the role of the man in the family, appeared tired and care-worn. Zelvy was right about Virginia, a shadow of the stately woman in the picture he had shown me earlier. As for Leon Manigault, his eyes were open as if he might at any moment join the conversation. I explained that we were sure that something was dangerously wrong with the Crown Victoria, but I first had to convince my partners to accept the case. I promised to let Mr. Zelvy know their decision as soon as possible.

"Can we win without the car?" Jacqueline asked.

"I don't know," I replied. "That's a question I will need to answer for my partners. Your case, however, is unusual, because a Ford dealer inspected your car after this happened at your church, but didn't do anything to correct the problem. That, by itself, might be enough to get a settlement from the dealer."

As we were about to leave, Virginia said, “Mr. Murray, the Lord sent you to us, and we know He won’t let us down.”

I was moved. “Mrs. Manigault,” I replied, “please keep praying. We will need all the help we can get.”

Returning to the law school parking lot following the game, I asked Zelvy to complete the story of how the case had come to him. After the Weisman firm withdrew, a friend of the Manigaults recommended Zelvy to the family, and he was so taken with them he agreed to help them find a lawyer who would handle the case. “I told them,” Zelvy insisted, “that I couldn’t handle the case myself because of the upfront costs.”

“Fair enough, Zel, but there are plenty of experienced trial lawyers in Cleveland. Why go slumming in Sandusky?”

“I was impressed with the way you handled that case in Pittsburgh, and I thought I’d give you a try at another tough case.”

“Come on, Zel,” I chortled. “How many lawyers turned you down before you went to the bullpen 60 miles away?”

“OK, you’ve got me,” Zelvy laughed. “I called several firms, but nobody would even agree to meet the Manigaults.”

“Why? Did you tell them the car had been stolen?”

“I mentioned it, but they were more put off by a government study that blamed drivers.”

“When was that done?”

“The report came out in 1989, and since then car companies have been clobbering anyone who sues them with it.”

“Have any of these cases been won?”

“A few, but in those cases they apparently found a mechanical problem. I have to be honest with you, Tom, several lawyers told me that the government report has made it so difficult to win these cases that lawyers who do product liability work have given up on sudden acceleration.”

I couldn't help being amused. "So after being turned down by every law firm you could think of in Cleveland, you offered me a chance to take on both Ford and the government. With friends like you, Bob, I need to rethink my enemies."

When he responded, Zelvy was subdued. "Tom, I remember a talk you gave in Cleveland. You said anyone can win easy cases. But the tough cases define who the real trial lawyers are. I assume you meant it."

I remembered the talk, and had meant every word. In fact, our law firm had earned a reputation for taking on difficult cases that other firms turned down. From what I had learned so far, I was beginning to wonder about the reliability of the government report Zelvy had mentioned. How many times had a car done what the Manigaults' Crown Victoria did twice? Although I was troubled at the thought of a government report being used against a defenseless Leon Manigault, whose quick-wittedness had prevented an earlier disaster, I needed to make Zelvy aware that Fred Weisman was a personal friend. "Bob, if my partners decide to take this case, it will be on the condition that no claim will be made against the Weisman firm because of this lost car business. I don't see how they could have done more to protect it."

"Will you explain that to the Manigaults?" Zelvy asked.

"No; that's your responsibility. But the first question my partners will ask is the name of the judge assigned to this case."

"It's Anthony Calabrese. Do you know him?"

"No. What's the book on him?"

"He's a Republican, but that doesn't matter. He doesn't care whether it's a big corporation or people like the Manigaults; he's fair to everybody. He has a deep respect for the jury system, so he's slow to throw cases out for technical reasons. He hires bright law clerks, so his legal rulings usually hold up on appeal. In my opinion, he's an ideal judge for this case."

I was encouraged. If the Manigaults had drawn a judge known to dismiss cases on narrow, legalistic grounds such as the unintentional loss of evidence, it would have been difficult to convince my partners to accept this case.

"Who represents Ford?" I asked.

"Elizabeth Wright, who regularly defends Ford. Do you know her?"

"I know she's with Thompson, Hine, and Flory," I replied, referring to one of Ohio's largest firms (now Thompson Hine). "She has a reputation as one of the better corporate defense lawyers around. Have there been any settlement discussions?"

"That's another thing I forgot to mention. Wright said with the car gone, Ford will never voluntarily pay a penny. Those were her exact words."

"That's almost as good as having the case assigned to a fair-minded judge."

"You're joking."

"I couldn't be more serious."

"Why?"

"Because there's nothing worse than taking on a case like this, putting up a couple hundred grand to prepare it, and then have a defendant dangle a settlement offer that the client would otherwise need to consider were it not for legal fees and preparation costs. That forces us to choose between cutting our fee for hundreds of hours of work and eating preparation costs, or making the client go to trial and risk coming away with nothing. But the case against the dealer is different because negligently failing to repair a car is not the same thing as selling a dangerous automobile. Who represents the dealer?"

"The Reminger firm, which usually makes a good faith effort to settle cases. We didn't get into specifics, but I got the impression that they might make a decent offer."

At the law school parking lot, Zelvy retrieved the file he had shown me earlier. "There's a ton of information about sudden accelerations in here, and there is a report from an expert the Weisman firm hired, who thinks the problem is in the idle controls. I suggest you start with the folder labeled 'Ditlow petition.' Clarence Ditlow is the Director of the Center for Auto Safety started by Ralph Nader. He tried to get the feds to take action against Ford two years before the Manigaults bought their car. His petition to the National Highway Traffic Safety Administration will open your eyes."

As we parted company, I remarked, "Ford would be taking a huge risk by taking this case to trial."

"Why is that?" Zelvy sounded surprised.

"Two words, Bob: the Manigaults. Any jury will have to think twice before turning them down. Maybe the Indians won't be able to take this Series from the Braves, but beating them tonight might be a good omen for this remarkable family."

CHAPTER 3

# AGATHA CHRISTIE REDUX

### MOTORIST IS KILLED IN PLUNGE, HEROIC RESCUE EFFORT

> A Mercedes-Benz plunged into the East River yesterday, killing its driver despite a dramatic rescue effort as the car sank deeper and deeper into the murky water. The driver was identified as Isaac Yorkowitz, 67, an employee in the cashier's department of the *New York Post*. The episode began about 2:40 p.m. The car was parked in a lot under the FDR Drive, near the Brooklyn Bridge. Yorkowitz started the car, but instead of backing onto the street, the Mercedes sped straight ahead into the river, passing over a six-inch-high curb.
>
> *New York Daily News*, October 25, 1997

**WHEN, DURING THE FLIGHT TO SEATTLE, I BEGAN READING CLARENCE** Ditlow's 1985 petition to NHTSA, I suddenly realized how little I knew about runaway cars.[1] The petition began:

> The owners of 1.4 million 1984-85 Ford full and mid-size cars are subject to sudden acceleration and engine surging defects which may result in death and serious injury. The sudden acceleration condition occurs spontaneously and without warning, causing cars to shoot forward at a high rate of speed from a standstill. The engine surge causes cars to suddenly speed up and race down the road when the owners are driving at normal highway speeds.

Ditlow next turned to Technical Service Bulletins Ford had sent to its dealers:

> The danger posed by the conditions described in these bulletins is evident from the reports received by the Center for Auto Safety and NHTSA: The sudden acceleration problem usually occurs without prior warning and with frightening consequences. As numerous complaints indicate, the acceleration condition causes loss of control; the increase in speed occurs so rapidly that drivers simply cannot react in time. Even when they do, the acceleration is so great that applying the brakes is ineffective. The reports indicate these cars can spontaneously accelerate in a variety of situations but most frequently . . . after the engine is turned on and the vehicle's transmission is put into drive, or while idling at an intersection . . . .

My nagging doubts about NHTSA's decision to blame drivers increased when I read these reports:

> Many sudden acceleration accidents have occurred just after the vehicle was started . . . . Paul Tuttle, of Portland,

---

1. *Clarence Ditlow is the Director of the Washington, D.C.-based Center for Auto Safety, a branch of Public Citizen, founded by Ralph Nader.*

Maine, reported that after he started his 1984 Mercury Marquis and shifted into drive, the car "accelerated out of control for a couple of minutes" in a parking lot, hitting two cars and injuring a woman. According to Mr. Tuttle:

> "My brakes did not stop my car until I was on the opposite side of a large parking area."

An equally terrifying experience was reported by Mary Hartledge of Louisville, Kentucky, who wrote the following about her 1985 Mercury Grand Marquis:

> "As I backed up to leave, I bumped into a steel pole in the parking lot—backing into it. Immediately upon contact, my car took off forward at great speed. I drove through a chain link fence and stopped only when I hit a concrete wall over the side of a drainage ditch. I'm not exactly sure what happened; I was so busy steering to avoid cars parked in the area."

Ms. Hartledge fortunately escaped serious injury.

While Edward Carner of West Orange, New Jersey, was not injured when his 1984 Grand Marquis accelerated through his driveway, the vehicle caused an accident resulting in extensive damage. According to Mr. Carner:

> "I got into the car, turned on the key to start. Suddenly the motor raced, and within an instant the car spun its wheels on the concrete floor and I was flying out of the garage in reverse. I attempted to hold the car with the floor brake but it wouldn't stop. The car continued to spin its wheels, and didn't stop until it backed into a pickup truck in the driveway and pushed the pickup truck into a large tree."

A story in *The San Francisco Chronicle* on February 24, 1986, about Clarence Ditlow's attempts to convince NHTSA "to widen its inquiry, tracing more than 75 deaths and more than 1,000 injuries to sudden accelerations," strengthened my appreciation of his work. But it was a five-part series about runaway cars in *The Detroit News* in December 1987 that left me stunned. Entitled "Unexplained Acceleration Plagues Auto Industry," the first paragraphs opened my eyes:

> It is the auto industry's most baffling problem. It has made people afraid of their cars and turned homemakers into consumer activists.
>
> It threatens to drive one import to extinction in the American market, while thousands of other complaints involve U.S.-made cars.
>
> The phenomenon is sudden acceleration, also known as the runaway car syndrome. One official calls it the AIDS of the auto industry; there is no known cause and some fear the list of victims could reach epidemic proportions.
>
> Reports grow more troubling all the time. So far, sudden acceleration is blamed for 56 deaths and more than 2,000 injuries.
>
> The 5,804 U.S. complaints on file tell roughly the same story. A driver starts a car and shifts the automatic transmission from park or neutral into drive or reverse. Suddenly, and without the driver's foot on the gas pedal, the engine surges to full power, and the car speeds off. The driver applies the brake, to no avail.
>
> Frequently the car is stopped only after hitting a garage, tree, car or pedestrian or when the ignition is turned off. After the incident, the car returns to normal.

Since these figures were based on drivers' reports to the National Highway Traffic Safety Administration (NHTSA), I was sure carmakers had known about many more similar occurrences, although I could never have guessed it was about ten times as many. Moreover, these reports "told roughly the same story." They began at gear engagement; braking was ineffective; and, after the ignition was turned off, the car "returned to normal." My mind was racing. The 1989 NHTSA report had concluded that the cause was "driver error"—that the drivers had pressed the wrong pedal. Why would thousands of drivers in a stopped car suddenly push the gas pedal to the floor? Why, if they did make such a bizarre mistake, would they keep the pedal depressed until their car crashed into something? It also seemed strange that there was no mention of a driver having admitted pushing the accelerator pedal to the floor by mistake. Wouldn't at least some people, I wondered, admit to having made such a mistake? The more I thought about it, the more dubious the government's conclusion seemed.

Zelvy was right; I have never turned down a meritorious case because it was difficult. But I was approaching 60, and I wondered if there was enough gas left in the tank to take on a case as challenging as this one. Somewhere over the Rockies, I recalled an Agatha Christie mystery about a murder committed with an icicle, which had long since melted away when the corpse was discovered. Was something that couldn't be found by looking inside the car causing this often lethal automotive behavior? Was it possible sudden acceleration was the "perfect tort," with victims numbering into the thousands? It was an astounding thought, and yet everything I was learning pointed to that possibility.

Since we were about to land in Seattle, I decided to read the rest of what Zelvy had given me during the return flight.

CHAPTER 4

# LETTERS PLAINTIVE

### SHERIFF FAULTS CAR FOR HIS ACCIDENT

> Sheriff Joe Arpaio insists this is not interesting. That the citizens of Arizona won't care to read about how he totaled his county-issued car at a Fountain Hills drugstore. How he says the car lurched forward uncontrollably, ramming over a curb and a giant boulder before mercifully coming to rest inches from a busy street . . . . That impact blew out the front tires and broke the drive shaft . . . . He says his wreck was caused by something mechanical . . . . "It lurched and I couldn't stop it and I just kept going," Arpaio said.
>
> *Arizonarepublic.com,* May 30, 2005

**ON THE RETURN FLIGHT, I FOUND MYSELF AGAIN OVER THE ROCKY** Mountains, this time pondering the heartrending stories in the file Zelvy had given me. The following letters to *The Detroit News,* in particular, had stuck in my memory:

Two people were killed Oct. 17, 1984, when Sheila Daar's Datsun accelerated out of a parking lot and collided with another car in downtown Chicago. Daar, then 50, was charged with reckless homicide. Here is an account of the incident, taken from a 1985 letter by her lawyer to the National Highway Traffic Safety Administration.

> THE LETTER: "Mrs. Daar's vehicle surged forward upon shifting the gear selection lever from park to drive when exiting a parking lot even though she did not depress the accelerator, and she could not control the sudden acceleration.
>
> "As a result of the occurrence, an indictment was returned against Mrs. Daar in the Circuit Court of Cook County, Ill., charging her with reckless homicide.
>
> "Newspaper and television coverage of the occurrence resulted in our receiving numerous telephone calls and letters from other owners and drivers of Datsun 280Z and other substantially similar Datsun vehicles who experienced sudden acceleration while driving their Datsun."
>
> POSTSCRIPT: A Cook County Circuit judge found Daar not guilty of reckless homicide after defense lawyers presented a case based on a sudden acceleration defect in her car. Daar is being sued by the families of the people killed. She, in turn, is suing Nissan, maker of the Datsun 280Z . . . .

A second letter was no less poignant:

A school crossing guard in Melrose, Mass., was killed Sept. 5, 1985, when Joseph Silva, then 71, lost control of his 1984 Oldsmobile Cutlass Supreme. Silva pleaded not guilty to vehicular homicide and claimed his car suddenly accelerated and his brakes failed. Silva's daughter, Linda Bertolami, made the following plea in a letter last Jan. 1 to consumer advocate Ralph Nader.

> THE LETTER: "I am writing to you about sudden (unintended) acceleration in cars with automatic transmission. Could you please help fight this important safety hazard by speaking out publicly?
>
> "As these accidents continue to occur, there will be more victims and more people like my father who will face criminal charges and the resultant legal ordeal. People have said this is a terrible thing for someone my father's age to go through.
>
> "Actually, it's a terrible thing for anyone at any age. My father does not have another 30 or 40 years to live with this, but there are people, given a normal life expectancy, who do."

We learned later that Joseph Silva was one of many drivers who has faced criminal charges following a runaway car accident, some of whom have gone to prison because no one believed them.

Bob Zelvy mentioned during the ball game that the Weisman firm had found a lawyer in Erie, Pennsylvania, named Jack Potter, who had unsuccessfully tried a sudden acceleration case against Ford. The case involved a Ford Tempo that had accelerated from a driveway, plunged down an embankment and crashed. Potter had found a mechanic named Alan Orringer, who believed that a malfunction in the idle control electronics had caused the accident. According to Potter, Orringer was an experienced mechanic who made a good witness. But Ford overwhelmed them with experts who insisted that the idle controls could not possibly have caused the accident. Orringer, who had inspected the Manigaults' Crown

Victoria without finding evidence of a defect, nevertheless noted in this report that when he tested the highest speed the idle air bypass could generate, the Manigaults' Crown Victoria had registered 2750 rpms. "It is this high idle setting," he wrote, "that is of particular interest here. It is not necessary for the throttle to be opened at all for the engine to reach 2750 rpms."

Orringer concluded that there were two mechanical problems in the Crown Victoria. "The first defect is in the idle air bypass system, allowing the computer the authority to generate 2750 rpms of unloaded engine idle, that I duplicated. The second defect makes it possible for the engine to experience this level of idle without recording any type of fault codes from a computer-monitored circuit. In my opinion, this level of idle control is well in excess of any demands that may be required by the subject vehicle. As always, the degree of danger surrounding an unwanted acceleration incident, such as this one, is relative to both the time and distance available to the operator."

Relying on Orringer's report, the Weisman firm sued Ford and the Manigaults' dealer on July 14, 1994, in the Common Pleas Court of Cuyahoga County. The suit accused Ford of selling a defective car with "flagrant disregard for safety . . . . " and the dealer for negligently failing to diagnose "a defective condition in the plaintiffs' Crown Victoria." Although no one, least of all the author, could have predicted it, *Manigault v. Ford* was destined to become one of the most protracted and bitterly fought product liability cases in U.S. history, with more twists and turns than ten miles of bad country road. When it finally came to a surprising conclusion more than a decade later, the case had set in motion events that would help expose the truth about runaway cars, make new product liability law, and contribute to exposing NHTSA as a dangerously corrupt bureaucracy. But that lay well in the future. As for the Manigaults, their quest for justice had barely begun.

CHAPTER 5

# FIRST STEPS

### AT CAR WASH, JEEP TAKES OFF, PINS AND INJURES EMPLOYEE

A Jeep Grand Cherokee that apparently accelerated spontaneously at a Westside car wash Saturday morning pinned an employee against a cabinet, sending him to University Hospital with a broken pelvis. A similar incident involving the same model vehicle occurred three years ago at an Octopus Car Wash. The accident occurred when the Jeep came off an automated conveyor belt in neutral and a worker got into it to move it to the drying station. The worker shifted the car into drive and it "took off like a missile," he says. The employee swerved to avoid a car in front of him but the Jeep hit an employee standing by the car's open driver's door and pinned him in front of a work cabinet.

*Wisconsin State Journal*, Sunday, August 2, 1998

**"I THINK WE'RE ONTO SOMETHING BIGGER THAN I REALIZED," I TOLD** Zelvy when I called to discuss the materials he had given me.

"Will your firm help me?"

"I hope so, but we need to do something before I present the case to my partners."

"Such as?"

"Hightail it to Pittsburgh ASAP to find out more about Orringer's theory. My partners will want to know if we have a credible expert."

Alan Orringer's home was in a quiet residential neighborhood where he had marked off a 200-foot stretch on the street in front of his house. To simulate what he believed had caused the Manigaults' Crown Victoria to go out of control, he had contrived a device to hold the idle air bypass open in a Ford car with the same idle controls. When I asked about safety, he assured me he had run the test several times, and was able to bring the test car safely to a stop. Reassured, I climbed into the passenger seat. I recall vividly what happened next.

When Orringer activated the idle controls to a fully opened position with his contrivance, the test car slowly picked up speed until it leveled off at about 25 mph at the 200 foot mark, where Orringer brought it to a to stop with no apparent difficulty. He repeated the test with Zelvy in the passenger seat. We then conferred out of Orringer's hearing.

"Are you thinking what I am?" I asked. "A herd of turtles could have given the car a run for the money. It must have taken 20 seconds to cover the distance the Crown Victoria did in a fraction of that time before it crashed."

"Not only that," Zelvy added, "but the Crown Victoria had to be going much faster, because Virginia says the car 'took off so fast she didn't have time to be scared.'"

We quickly agreed that Orringer had easily stopped the test car with what seemed like normal braking action, and that for his theory to work, "the brakes on the Crown Victoria could not have been applied prior to the crash."

"And don't forget," Zelvy pointed out. "John Manigault saw the brake lights illuminated seconds after it crashed."

We also agreed that if Leon Manigault, for whatever reason, had pushed the gas pedal to the floor and kept it there, the car would have been going so fast when it hit the house that neither Manigault would have survived. We concluded, therefore, that the idle controls could not have caused the Manigaults' disaster.

When we told Orringer this, he politely thanked us for coming to Pittsburgh, and then surprised us by recommending that we talk to an electrical engineer he knew who had a theory he was sure we would "find interesting."

"Where does he live?" Zelvy asked.

"About fifteen minutes from here," replied Orringer. "In fact, he said he'd be happy to drop by and tell you about what he has been doing."

Twenty minutes later, Orringer ushered into his living room a stockily built man in his middle forties with a neatly trimmed salt and pepper beard, who was introduced as Sam Sero. It turned out that Sero had earned a degree in electrical engineering from Carnegie Institute, then become a troubleshooter in the electrical power industry, where his skill in diagnosing electrical failures earned him several promotions. Sero had eventually started his own consulting business, whose clients initially were insurance companies, suspicious about the cause of fires they were being asked to pay for. His reputation as a forensic engineer had grown until he was being asked by lawyers to evaluate a wide range of accidents calling for expertise in electronics and physics. A

New York City firm had eventually asked him to investigate a sudden acceleration in a new Ford Aerostar that had taken off on a private driveway in the Catskill Mountains and crashed. The driver, a social worker named Kathy Jarvis, insisted she had applied the brakes, first with one foot and then by pumping with both feet. I asked Sero what he thought had sent the Aerostar out of control.

"In my opinion, it had to be the cruise control electronics."

Zelvy was incredulous. "You said the Aerostar took off from a stop. How could it be the cruise control?"

There was a pause as Sero collected his thoughts. "Alan may have told you that I have investigated several cases involving a stopped Ford car that shot out of control at gear engagement. All the drivers insisted that the brakes wouldn't stop the car, and the evidence supported them. Therefore, unless drivers are pushing on the wrong pedal, as the car companies claim, the cruise control electronics are being tricked into pulling the throttle open even when the car is stopped."

"How is that possible?" I asked, struggling to understand.

"Let's start with basics. There are only two cables attached to the throttle plate. One is connected to the accelerator pedal, the other to an electromechanical device called the servo that holds the throttle open when the cruise control is engaged. So if a car takes off while the gas pedal is not depressed, it means the servo pulled the throttle open. There is no other possibility."

"Does it have to be the electronics," asked Zelvy. "Why couldn't it be something mechanical?"

"Mechanical things can cause the throttle to become stuck so the car won't decelerate when pressure on the gas pedal is removed. But we are talking about cars that spontaneously and rapidly accelerate from a dead stop. That can only happen if something first activates the two electrical switches that control the vacuum and vent functions when the cruise control is engaged or disengaged."

"Hold on, Sam," I pleaded. "You're talking to lawyers, not automotive mechanics."

Sero laughed. "The servo is a fairly simple device that uses vacuum inside a canister to hold the throttle open when the cruise control is engaged."

"Where does the vacuum come from?" asked Zelvy.

"From the engine manifold. The idea is to allow vacuum in the servo to hold the throttle open when the cruise is engaged, and to let air into the servo when the system is disengaged."

"Is this accomplished electronically?" I wanted to know.

"Yes. But now you're getting into technical stuff we can talk about later if you decide to retain me in your case. Just keep in mind that if a car suddenly accelerates from a dead stop, either the driver pushed the accelerator pedal to the floor, or something electrical caused the cruise control servo to pull the throttle wide open."

Zelvy was still struggling. "I can see how this could happen on the interstate when the cruise control is engaged. But the Manigaults' car took off from their driveway."

"Making cruise control the culprit might seem counter-intuitive, but the evidence strongly indicates that the two electrical switches that control the creation and release of vacuum in the cruise control servo can be tricked into making it suddenly pull the throttle wide open."

"Do you have any ideas or theories about how that could happen?" I asked.

Sero was thoughtful. "I haven't seen an electrical diagram for this system, but I have a hunch there is something about the design that makes the system susceptible to failure during shifting. Why else would this happen so often in stopped automobiles? That's why it's so amazing that the car industry has been able to put the blame on drivers."

"And the federal oversight agency backed them up." The indignation in Zelvy's voice struck a chord.

"I had the same reaction," I interjected, "when I read news stories about runaway automobiles. It boggled the mind that the federal agency bought the idea that drivers were the problem. What's your take on this driver error business?"

"What struck me is that the people who did that study all had close ties to the industry."

"Did they consider the cruise control electronics?" Zelvy asked.

"Yes," replied Sero. "But the way they went about it showed they were way over their heads. In fact, they said some pretty stupid things in their report."

Coming to a question that was troubling me, I asked, "If the problem is in the cruise control, why don't inspections ever find it?"

"Without getting too technical, there are all kinds of things that can go wrong in the electronics that an inspection won't find. Do you have a PC?"

"Yes," nodded Zelvy.

"Has it ever shut down for no apparent reason?"

"Sure, doesn't everybody's?"

"That's right. Do you think if you looked inside you could find what made it suddenly go down?"

"So you think the same thing happens inside the cruise control electronics?"

"As far as I can tell, that's the only explanation that makes any sense. And don't forget, just like your computer that returns to normal after it crashes, so does the engine when it's turned back on after one of these events."

"Do electrical engineers know what makes this happen in a computer?" I asked.

"The general term is 'noise,' which has many other names, like 'electromagnetic interference,' 'radio frequency interference,' 'transients,' 'intermittents,' you name it. The important point is that it's often impossible to identify by inspecting components or parts of the system that malfunctioned. That's the nature of the beast."

"In our case," observed Zelvy, "Alan did a thorough inspection of the car, and ruled out a cruise control malfunction. My question is, how in hell do you prove a defect that can't be found?"

Although I was amused by Zelvy's outburst, I was wrestling with the same doubts, and hoped that Sero might quell them. "I recall reading that cars started taking off when they introduced automatic transmissions. Could that be a clue?"

"I know some people have made that association, but I suspect it's the fact that automatic transmissions and electronic cruise control happened at about the same time that is the real clue. The most important clue, however, was the rapid rise in sudden acceleration reports that began about 1983 or 1984."

"You'll have to explain that, Sam," I urged.

"We know that every company introduced basically the same electronic cruise control system during the early '80s. Now ask yourself why reports suddenly shot up around 1983 if all the companies had basically the same cruise control electronics?"

"You're obviously suggesting this big jump was caused by something other than a change in the cruise control electronics," I observed. "Any idea, Sam, what it was?"

I could see Sero was enjoying himself. "My theory is pretty simple. As electronics become more complex, they are more difficult to control. That's because electronics are highly interactive, so more interactions cause more fluctuations with failure potential in the electrical current. Therefore, if sudden accelerations are caused by something in the electronics, one would expect to find a correlation between electronic complexity and the failure rate."

"That makes sense," I remarked. "But if it wasn't increased complexity in the cruise control electronics, where did this increased complexity come from?"

"I think that's fairly obvious," replied Sero. "During the eighties, car companies continually added to their engine electronics, while their cruise control systems stayed basically the same. That tells me this surge in reports was caused by more complex interactions with the cruise control electronics. I know correlation doesn't prove causation, but in this case I'm not aware of any other possibility."

"If I understand you, Sam," I remarked, "we need to look for evidence that sudden accelerations always happen in cars with both electronic engine and cruise control systems."

"That's exactly what I'm suggesting," Sero replied. "If you can make that historical connection . . . . "

"We'd make you a national hero," Zelvy needled.

"And make you a bundle off this *Manigault* case, so you can buy a big yacht like some hot shot lawyers do."

"Touché!" retorted Zelvy. "Anyway, Sam, I keep coming back to how are we going to prove the Manigaults' cruise control went berserk and turned their car into a monster."

"I have a suggestion," said Sero. "I told Philip Morrell, the lawyer in the *Jarvis* case, that I could build a table model with the cruise control electronics in the Aerostar on which I could experiment. He said his firm would pay half, if I could find someone to bankroll the other half."

"Let me guess the rest," I laughed. "Alan here told you about us and you're wondering if we might put up the rest of the money."

Sero shrugged, "Why not? The facts of the two cases seem almost identical."

"Are the cruise control systems the same?" asked Zelvy.

"As far as I know they are. I work with a man who can quickly get that information, so it won't take me long to find out."

"What will a model cost?" I asked.

"About $10,000."

"How long will it take?"

"A couple of months."

"It's a deal," I said. "Tell Mr. Morrell he has a partner."

On the way home, Zelvy asked if my commitment to share the cost of the model meant my firm had agreed to accept the Manigault case.

"No," I confessed. "But I find this sudden acceleration business so interesting that I'm willing to risk $5,000 of my own to find out whether Sam Sero has cracked this dangerous riddle."

Zelvy was somber. "Even with Sero's model, how do we prove there's some kind of dangerous ghost behind these malfunctions that Ford should pay for?"

"That's what intrigues me," I replied. "Do you remember Agatha Christie's icicle murder story?"

"No, but what's the point?"

"Just this. If someone is found stabbed to death with a gaping wound, but there is no weapon to be found, it doesn't mean you can't prove a homicide."

"I understand the comparison, but a stab wound is obvious evidence of a crime. Orringer inspected the Crown Victoria and found no evidence indicating a malfunction in the cruise control. Even if we had the car, there would be no evidence that a crime, or in this case, a tort, was committed."

"Doesn't that overlook that if an automobile begins at point A and moves rapidly on its own for 187 feet before crashing, the culprit has to be something like an icicle that melts away in a stabbing victim? Even if the Agatha Christie analogy limps a little, the behavior of the vehicle is still evidence of a dreadful malfunction, in the same way her fictional stab wound was evidence of a homicide."

"In other words," Zelvy mused, "even if their car had not been stolen, the Manigaults would still have to rely on circumstantial evidence to prove their case, because there would have been no evidence of a cruise control malfunction inside the car."

"That's the way I see it until someone proves me wrong. In fact, the more I learn, the more obvious it becomes that something is happening in the electronics that can't be found by inspecting components, or even by the kind of simple testing they do at dealerships."

"If you're right, we might be able to use some leverage on the Manigaults' dealer to learn something that will help us against Ford."

"I hope you're right. If the dealer knows that a malfunction in the cruise control can make this happen, then it's in hot water because it did nothing about it."

Finishing the thought, Zelvy added, "And if Ford never told Mullinax about this possibility, the dealer might be the best witness against Ford. So are you ready to present this case to your partners?"

"I understand your impatience, Bob, but there's one more thing I need to do. If that pans out, it should clinch the deal with my partners."

There was a tinge of impatience in Zelvy's voice. "Is it a secret?"

"Actually, I do need to be circumspect about what I have in mind. I've been calling some lawyers around the country who handle product liability cases for suggestions that might help us. One lawyer, who asked that I not mention his name, told me about a former FBI agent who has made a specialty of investigating suspected automotive defects for law firms. He said the guy is so good one company has him on a large annual retainer to keep him from investigating suspected defects in its cars. I've arranged to meet him."

"Can you tell me his name?"

"When I called him, the first thing this guy did was insist on anonymity. I know that sounds a little mysterious, but I trust the judgment of the lawyer who made this suggestion, and I promised to keep any dealings with this former FBI agent in strictest confidence."

"That's fine," replied Zelvy. "But don't forget I'm on the hot seat with Judge Calabrese to find someone to take the lead in this case."

CHAPTER 6

# MR. X

### SUV HITS CROWD AT BAKERY, KILLING ONE

A sport utility vehicle backed into a crowd outside a New Jersey shore bakery Sunday morning, killing a woman and injuring five people—at least one critically, police in Wildwood Crest said. A preliminary investigation found that Dorothy Burke, 51, of Bensalem, Pa., was trying to parallel-park outside Britton's Gourmet Bakery when her Ford Explorer suddenly accelerated, backing over the curb and striking people on the sidewalk.

*The Atlanta Journal-Constitution*, Monday, August 25, 2003

**MOST OF THE ACTION IN MODERN LITIGATION HAPPENS OUTSIDE** the courtroom, during discovery designed to help parties obtain relevant evidence. These procedures include depositions, questioning witnesses under oath; interrogatories, written questions an opposing party must answer under oath; and formal requests for documents, such as internal studies, technical reports, memoranda, and the like. Each side must surrender relevant evidence, even if it would not be admissible at trial, so long as it might lead to evidence that is admissible.

Because a verdict against a product maker can bring adverse publicity that, in turn, can generate more litigation, discovery and product liability cases are often contentious. The stakes are especially high if a company has successfully defended its product, in the past, as Ford had done in these cases up to this point in our story. For example, one Ford lawyer boasted to *Bloomberg News* in the late '80s that the company "had won 500 straight sudden acceleration cases."

As I mulled over the *Manigault* case in the fall of 1995, I hoped to avoid protracted discovery battles with Ford with a strategy I had recently described to the *Ohio Lawyers Weekly*:

> **Q:** What is your litigation philosophy?
>
> **A:** . . . [Y]ou have to have some imagination in your approach to the facts. Many lawyers in the modern era have fallen into the trap of becoming litigators rather than trial lawyers. They get involved in an endless, expensive and time-consuming battle in the discovery phase of trial, when the best way to get to the bottom of many cases is to do your own peripheral, extralegal discovery.

I had "extralegal discovery" in mind when I contacted the former FBI agent I had mentioned to Zelvy. When he answered the phone, the man I will refer to as "Mr. X," came directly to the point. "I use contacts I made as an FBI agent to find retired people who know their former employer's secrets."

"Do you know anything about something called 'sudden acceleration'?" I asked.

"Sure, it's when a car takes off and causes an accident. I've seen newspaper stories about bad accidents caused by whatever makes this happen."

"In our case," I explained, "we found an electrical engineer who thinks the problem is in the cruise control electronics. Can you find a retired Ford engineer floating around out there who could confirm this?"

"I am sure I can. Every car company has offices around the country with people trained to know everything that can go wrong in a car. I'm sure there are retired Ford engineers who know what causes sudden accelerations. But I don't believe in using deception."

"Neither do I," I replied. "In fact, I want everything completely above board. That rules out anyone who is currently employed with Ford, since it would be unethical to contact them without first putting the company on notice."

"I've worked for some good lawyers, so I know the ground rules. If it comes up, do you want me to disclose who I'm working for?"

"Absolutely. I'll send you a letter describing what happened to this family. Tell whoever you talk to that I'm trying to help this family without getting tied up in legal battles that could delay a trial for years. I need to know if the case has merits before my firm accepts it. So what are your terms?"

"I work for a flat retainer, plus expenses. If I come up empty, I refund everything but my expenses. I'll mail you a simple contract, but my name won't be on it or the envelope. It requires you to pay 25% up front, to cover expenses. If I strike out, you won't owe me anything. Mail the signed contract and retainer to the P.O. Box listed on the contract."

"How long," I asked.

"A month, max. Probably less."

"Done," I said. "Send me your contract."

"One more thing," interjected Mr. X. "I prefer to deliver my report face to face. No phone calls, faxes or letters. If I deliver, that's when you pay the balance of my contract. I usually deliver; that's how I get clients."

I laughed. "I feel like I'm dealing with James Bond. How will I know when you're ready to report?"

"That's the one call you'll get from me. I'll identify myself to your receptionist as someone working on this case, nothing else. Just make sure I get through to you."

About a week later, Mr. X called. "I have to be in Pittsburgh next week; I'll drive to Sandusky when I'm finished. I found what you're looking for, so have a check ready." Before I could respond, "James Bond" hung up.

A week later, looking like an FBI agent from central casting, a well-built, neatly attired middle-aged man appeared in my office and announced he was ready to make his report.

"Sit down," I said, after shaking hands. "And don't keep me in suspense."

"I found a retired engineer who worked for many years in one of Ford's district offices and who remembers investigating at least two sudden accelerations, one he is sure involved an Aerostar. He claims every engineer in Ford's district offices knew the problem was in the cruise control electronics. When they investigated a case, they filed something called a service investigation report that went directly to corporate headquarters. He thinks there must be hundreds of reports stashed away somewhere in Dearborn."

"Would he be willing to testify?"

"No."

"Is he believable?"

"You'll have to take my word. All my clients are lawyers who have relied on my judgment, and I haven't been wrong yet."

This was more than I had hoped for, and I handed Mr. X a check with the comment, "I only wish my other investments were doing as well."

At this point it would have been possible to file a formal discovery request for all sudden acceleration-related service investigation reports in Ford's possession. But my instincts told me this would set off a protracted discovery battle, so I decided to stick with extra-legal discovery. The first place I intended to look for incriminating reports was Jack Potter's office in Erie, Pennsylvania.

CHAPTER 7

# POTTER'S TROVE

**DRIVER KILLED WHEN HE LOSES CONTROL OF CAR HE JUST BOUGHT**

Just after purchasing a brand new Mercury Grand Marquis, the driver of the vehicle sped through the dealership lot and an adjacent bowling alley lot, across five lanes of traffic, and hit another car in the street. The driver of the Marquis was killed instantly, and the driver of the other vehicle was seriously injured. In all, the Marquis traveled more than 150 yards. Customers and employees in the dealership saw a car suddenly begin speeding past them and then heard a loud crash . . . . Police believe that the driver's accelerator may have gotten stuck, causing the vehicle to continue speeding without being able to stop.

*St. Petersburg Times*, March 4, 1986

**THE MORNING AFTER MY PARTNERS ACCEPTED THE *MANIGAULT*** case, Bob Zelvy and I piled into his Chevy van and headed for Jack Potter's office in Erie, Pennsylvania, to find out what he had learned about sudden accelerations during his case against Ford. Potter, an angular, well-spoken man in his early sixties, ushered us into a large conference room where several rows of bankers' boxes were stacked along the walls. Gesturing toward the boxes, he remarked, "This is a good example of how big companies make us waste time and money looking for needles in a haystack."

Trial lawyers refer to this tactic as "dump truck" discovery, and Ford's version had turned out to be a so-called "Sudden Acceleration Reading Room" in a dingy little building in Dearborn, full of boxes stuffed with paperwork in no particular order. "When we served them with discovery requests," Potter explained, "they cordially invited us to this hole-in-the-wall."

"Did you find anything helpful?" Zelvy asked.

"We had a law clerk and two paralegals there for three days. We ended up with about 35,000 documents at 17 cents a copy that were basically a bust."

Zelvy sounded let down. "So you didn't find any smoking guns—or maybe I should say smoking documents?"

"No, but just about everything we picked out shows that Ford has had huge sudden acceleration problems since at least the early eighties."

"Jack," I interjected. "I've had some experience with 'dump truck' discovery tactics. Their lawyers weed out anything harmful and everything else gets dumped in boxes. If we complain, they piously proclaim how open they've been about discovery."

"Have you seen their privilege log?" Zelvy asked, referring to a record corporations are required to maintain for documents they claim are beyond the reach of discovery because, for example, they involve privileged communications between lawyer and client.

"We thought about going after the privilege log," responded Potter, "but we knew Ford would fight us document by document, every step of the way. As you know, these battles can tie you up for months or even years, and since they are hard to win anyway, we decided it just wasn't worth the time and effort."

When I asked about his case, Potter described his client, Joe Pierotti, as a healthy middle-aged man with a spotless driving record whose 1987 Ford Tempo was parked in his driveway, facing away from his house. "When he shifted into drive, it took off along the driveway and plunged down an embankment."

"Is it possible he made a pedal error?" Zelvy asked.

"I've asked myself the same thing a hundred times," Potter responded wistfully. "Anything is possible, I suppose, but there was a witness who saw brake lights and the front wheels locked up before the car went over the embankment."

"Can you summarize Ford's trial strategy?" I asked.

Potter thought for a moment before observing, "They have given these cases a lot of thought. They understand that if they only deny there's a problem with the car, they will get hammered with all kinds of circumstantial and eyewitness evidence that the car malfunctioned. They have figured out that if they hit you with that damn NHTSA report blaming drivers, they can keep hitting you with a one-two punch, the first being that they thoroughly inspected the car without finding anything that could explain what happened."

"I assume the second punch is the government study," snorted Zelvy.

"Yes. But they also claim that if the brakes were working they would have stopped the car; and since there is no evidence of mechanical brake failure, the cause had to be driver error. It's diabolically clever, but very effective."

"Who were their experts?" asked Zelvy.

"Their main guy was an electrical engineer named Victor Declercq, who ran a big test facility for about ten years where they bombarded prototype cars with huge amounts of radio frequency interference."

"Let me guess." Zelvy's tone was caustic. "With all their testing, they never got a car to do what your client said his Tempo did. So Pierotti must have caused his own accident."

"That's it in a nutshell."

"Who was Ford's other expert?" I asked.

"I'm not sure I would call him an expert. He's a manager in the Customer Service Division headquarters who supervised a special project for several years that investigated hundreds of sudden acceleration reports in great detail."

"Let me guess again," interjected Zelvy. "They never found anything that could possibly make a car suddenly accelerate on its own."

Potter laughed. "You must have read the transcript. But you're right. This guy, Alan Updegrove, insisted that Ford literally turned almost 3,000 cars inside out without finding anything that could send a car out of control from a dead stop."

"Would it be possible for us to borrow these boxes long enough to make copies?" I asked.

"I was worried you might never ask," Potter chuckled. "I had these boxes hauled out of storage so you could take them with you and keep them. We really don't have space for them, so if you don't want them, they'll end up in our dumpster."

An hour later, with Zelvy's van crammed full of boxes containing 35,000 documents, we were on our way back to Ohio with renewed appreciation of "extralegal discovery".

"So what's the next step?" Zelvy asked as we headed west on the Ohio Turnpike.

"I have a hunch there are some important needles in Potter's haystack. We just need to find them."

"How do you propose to do that?"

"The first step is to find a place to store these boxes where the documents can be spread out, studied, and organized. If Ford can have a reading room, so can we."

"Do you have space in your office to do that? I certainly don't in mine."

"No," I replied. "But there are several buildings near our office with space for rent. I'll have my paralegal, Jo Ellen Seiler, look for a place."

"Who's going to read all this stuff?"

"Jo Ellen is extremely busy, but it won't take her long to figure out how to organize all this paperwork. I doubt if she will have time to read everything, so I may have to hire somebody to help her."

"Do you think there are other firms that might be happy to get rid of their files?"

"I suspect a lot of law firms have gone through the same meat grinder Potter's did, and have a load of documents they'd gladly part with. But let's not get ahead of ourselves. How would you like to become the proud owner of a 1987 Crown Victoria?"

"Don't tell me you're the guy who stole the Manigaults' car," Zelvy laughed impishly, "and you want to unload it on me."

"Close. Actually I believe we can turn the tables on Ford by taking the initiative and proving Leon Manigault could not possibly have caused what happened at their church or home."

"I assume you are thinking about an accident reconstruction in a car similar to the Manigaults' Crown Victoria."

"Not exactly. I'm thinking of tests to make an accident reconstruction more persuasive."

"Such as?"

"We can test how fast the car would have been going with an open throttle without braking when it crashed."

"You mean by keeping the gas pedal depressed for 187 feet?"

"That's one way. Sero says he can cause a sudden acceleration by using a device he made from Ford's troubleshooting guide for the cruise control."

"OK. But how do we show Leon Manigault was pushing on the brake pedal?"

"By estimating the crash speed from government test data. That's a standard part of many accident reconstructions."

Zelvy was skeptical. "Do you really think these tests will be enough to prove Leon Manigault could not have made this happen?"

"Look at it this way, Zel. Ford will try its best to pin this on Leon. We should welcome the chance to defend a man who can't defend himself, even if that means taking on a burden that's technically not required of a plaintiff."

"Such as?"

"Such as proving that Leon didn't cause this accident."

Zelvy was incredulous. "Are you saying we should forget all the stuff we learned in law school about the defendant having the burden of proving that an accident was caused by the plaintiff?"

"You got it, Bob. In the brave new world of automotive electronics, we need to adjust our thinking or we'll keep getting our tails kicked in these runaway car cases. In fact, I suspect many of these cases are being lost because lawyers are unwilling to assume the burden of proving the driver didn't cause the accident."

Zelvy was subdued. "Ya know, Tom, some people think you're crazy, and I'm beginning to think they're right."

"Crazy, or crazy like a fox. If you're patient, you'll find out which soon enough."

This last retort was cocky, and I would soon come to regret it. In any event, we had arrived in Sandusky, and it was time to unload Potter's trove. Before we parted, I reminded Zelvy he needed to find a 1987 Crown Victoria ASAP.

CHAPTER 8

# MAKING OF A DREAM TEAM

## DRIVERS BLAME SUDDEN ACCELERATION FOR CRASHES

Marian Armstrong has been fighting Nissan over sudden acceleration for more than a decade. She says the problem caused her 300 ZX to crash in a parking lot in 1992. She hit a building and a pole, putting her in a hospital. She sued Nissan, claiming a defect caused the accident and that the company knew about it. Armstrong won her lawsuit. A Houston appeals court approved the verdict, saying evidence showed Nissan had recorded numerous reports of similar accidents and did not tell the government or its customers. The case is in its final appeal. A Nissan spokesman said the company believes it was driver error and not a defect.

*KIROTV.com*, May 5, 2004

**AS A STUDENT AT THE UNIVERSITY OF VIRGINIA LAW SCHOOL IN** the early 1960s, I wrote appellate briefs for my father's cases. Fortunately, I enjoyed the work, because it would be many years before our family law firm could afford associate lawyers or law clerks to help with our briefs. Shortly before we accepted the *Manigault* case, two juries had awarded my clients substantial damages and the verdicts were being appealed. I needed help.

The first time I heard the name Molly O'Neill was at a wedding reception not long after Bob Zelvy and I met Sam Sero. My wife, Ann, and I were seated next to long-time acquaintances, Dr. Steve Damko and his wife, Joanne. Over dessert, Joanne, a good-looking woman with a disarming manner, asked, "Are you by chance looking for a really smart and experienced lawyer?"

Surprised, I replied, "We're always on the lookout for talent that fits our practice. Why do you ask?"

"I have a niece who just moved here from New York City where she had been working in the corporate counsel's office representing the city in court. She's smart, attractive, talented, and she's looking for a position in this area."

"Sounds like a role for Julia Roberts. Why here and not New York?"

"She was married to a New York City lawyer. After they divorced, she decided to start a new life near Willard where her mother and father, my brother Dick, have been living since he retired."

"Why do you say she's so bright?"

"She breezed through Smith and then law school in Boston."

"Why law school? And why Boston?"

"She met her ex-husband in college. After he took a job in Boston, she got a law degree, hoping to practice with him, but he had other ideas. They moved to Atlanta for a while. He eventually started a firm of his own in New York City, and she got a job representing the city."

"Where is she living now?"

"She just bought a place near the lake."

"How do you know she has legal talent?"

"I just know she was responsible for representing New York City in court, so I assume she's good at her work. Would you like to meet her?"

"I could use someone who knows how to research and write appellate briefs. First, however, I'd like to see a few samples of her work. If she's interested in our firm, have her send me some writing samples, and we'll see what happens."

In the mail the following Monday was a large envelope containing several briefs and a note from Molly O'Neill thanking me for my interest in her work. When I read the briefs that evening, I recognized the work of a first-rate legal mind, and remarked to Ann, "Joanne Damko's niece is an impressive writer. She could be manna from heaven with all this appellate work piling up."

A short time later, we hired Molly O'Neill as my legal assistant who, happily, got along so well with my outstanding secretary Janet Raifsnider, and my excellent paralegal Jo Ellen Seiler, that I was soon referring to these three talented women as my "dream team".

CHAPTER 9

# BRASS TACKS

### SEVEN DEAD AFTER SUV CRASH ON MAINE HIGHWAY

Carmel, Maine—Seven people died when their rented SUV veered out of control and went airborne while passing other cars on Interstate 95. It was one of the deadliest highway crashes in Maine history. Two women and a child were fatally thrown from the Ford Explorer, while its other four occupants . . . died inside. Three of the dead were children under the age of 10 . . . . Troopers quoted witnesses as saying one car was in the travel lane and another was passing it in the passing lane when the Explorer came up quickly from behind. Skid marks from the out-of-control SUV were visible across the roadway in both lanes, he said.

*USA Today*, May 9, 2004

**EVERYTHING I WAS READING LEFT NO DOUBT THAT SUDDEN** accelerations in stopped cars were not just similar, they were overwhelmingly so. They began at gear engagement. When the engine was turned back on, it performed normally. Inspections never turned up evidence of a defect in the electronics, and there was invariably no evidence of a mechanical brake failure. Although this fact pattern was completely consistent with what had happened twice in the Manigaults' Crown Victoria, the disappearance of the car from storage made a case that would have been difficult with the car especially daunting. Therefore, when the dream team and Bob Zelvy met with me to discuss our strategy, Molly began by explaining how Ohio law viewed the loss or destruction of evidence.

"Ohio law gives the trial court broad discretion to craft a remedy that protects the rights of a party potentially disadvantaged by the disappearance of partial destruction of evidence.

The decisions talk about factors that a court may consider, such as whether the spoliation was intentional or inadvertent, the importance of the evidence and so on. In fact, this seems to be the approach in most jurisdictions. Ford will ask for the ultimate sanction, dismissal of the case, even though there is no evidence of intentional wrongdoing. But there is no Ohio law that supports dismissing a case under our circumstances. Therefore, unless Ford can show there is no other remedy to protect it from irreparable prejudice, the court should simply tell the jury a vehicle inspection found no evidence of a defect. I don't see how the defendants can ask for more than that."

Zelvy couldn't resist a quip. "Tom said you were smarter than both of us combined. He was half right; you're obviously smarter than he is."

Molly's rejoinder was instant. "He told me, Bob, that your witticisms will compensate for shortcomings in your legal scholarship."

"Zel," I laughed, "you better not match wits with a New Yawker!"

"I'll be more careful in the future," chortled Zelvy, adding, "so, Great Leader, how do we win this case after Molly wipes up the floor with their spoliation motion?"

"OK," I said. "Fasten your seatbelts. First, we need to stop worrying about the disappearance of the car. If the damn thing was in our parking lot, we would still have to admit that nobody found evidence of a defect in the electronics. But that shouldn't be fatal because the car was towed to the dealer five months earlier after a similar sudden acceleration. They made some repairs to the idle controls, but, according to the service records, they never considered the cruise control. Zel, why don't you summarize what happened at the church parking lot?"

"According to John Manigault," Zelvy began, "he and his father left the Crown Victoria there facing 102nd Street while they did some work inside. When they finished, John went to open the parking lot gate while Leon started the car. The next thing John knew, the car shot past him, the engine racing, along Columbia Avenue, which is directly opposite the church parking lot. John ran after the car and saw brake lights before it finally came to a stop about a block away. When he got to the car, Leon was standing in the street, trembling all over, with the ignition key in his hand. John says he kept saying, 'The only way I could stop it was with this.'"

"What did they do with the car?" Jo Ellen asked.

"They were only a couple of blocks from home, so Leon turned on the engine, kept his hand on the ignition key, and let the car creep along to their home."

"What happened when they got there?" asked JR.

"According to John, the dealer sent a tow truck for the car, but, as Tom mentioned, the service records show they never looked at the cruise control."

"When did that happen?" asked Molly.

"In late November, 1992."

"That should help our case against the dealer," Molly observed. "But I'm not clear how it helps us against Ford."

I had anticipated Molly's question. "As I see it, either the dealer was clueless because it was in the dark, or the dealer negligently failed to correct the problem. Ford is on the hook either way as far as I'm concerned."

Molly was not convinced. "I see a fly in that ointment. We have to prove the dealer knew what happened at the church. And since there's nothing in the service records that describes that event, John Manigault is the only proof we have that the dealer was notified, and the defendants will cry hearsay if we ask John what his father said on the phone."

Molly was referring to out-of-court statements that, with some exceptions, are inadmissible during a trial because the declarant—in this case Leon Manigault—cannot be cross-examined about what he or she said.

"Assuming we can't find the person who took Leon's call, there's usually a way to get around hearsay objections. John Manigault can certainly describe how his father called the dealer, how animated he was during the conversation, and how a tow truck from the dealer showed up a short time later. Before we ask John what he saw, we should ask him what he heard, and make Ford create the impression they don't want the jury to hear what Leon said."

It was Jo Ellen's turn. "It's just common sense that anybody would report something like that to the dealer, so the jury will know Mr. Manigault told the dealer what happened."

Over the years I have come to rely on Jo Ellen's intuition about the common sense of juries, and I decided to put her instincts to the test.

"Do you have any gut feeling, Jo Ellen, how the loss of the car will play with the jury?"

"I think they'll believe it's a big deal unless we can prove that an inspection wouldn't have made any difference."

"I agree with Jo Ellen," Zelvy remarked. "You're our guru, Tom, so how do we do that?"

"Do you want a short lecture," I chided, "or a quick and dirty explanation?"

"The quicker the better," Zelvy rejoined.

"OK. We tell the jury straight off that the car was thoroughly inspected by a qualified mechanic, Alan Orringer, and didn't find anything in the cruise control because the problem wasn't something that can easily be found during an inspection."

There was a deafening silence until Jo Ellen spoke up. "If you present it the way you just said, the only thing the jury will hear is that the inspection showed there was nothing wrong with the car. I think you need to go back to the drawing board."

"I agree with Jo Ellen," Molly interjected. "Ford will stress to the jury in its opening statement that the federal government has concluded that if an inspection doesn't turn up evidence of the cause, it was probably driver error. Therefore, if we try to make Orringer's inspection favor our case, Ford will turn it around and make the issue Orringer versus the federal government."

"OK, guys," I sighed. "Since I flunked Trial Advocacy 101, what do you suggest?"

Molly passed around copies of a three-page letter from NHTSA to Ford dated December 31, 1986, addressed to the director of the company's Automotive Safety Office.

"Jo Ellen found this in Potter's files. We think it will help us turn the tables on Ford." After a pause, she continued, "You'll notice that NHTSA 'identified 439 consumer reports which cite 193 accidents, 106 injuries, and five fatalities relating to alleged sudden acceleration . . . in 1983-through-1986 Ford vehicles equipped with 3.8 and 5.0 liter engines and automatic transmissions . . . . '"

"That's interesting," intoned Zelvy. "But how do we use it in our case?"

"I found an appellate decision by the appellate court for Cuyahoga County that found this same agency letter was admissible to show that Ford was on notice of a possible defect. Why not make notice of a defect the issue, and use this decision to make Ford explain why the two occurrences in our Crown Victoria were not caused by the same defect?"

Zelvy was skeptical. "Is there a specific reference to cruise control in the government's letter?"

"No, but the case I just mentioned involved a cruise control malfunction. And, as Tom keeps reminding us, this is an either/or case. If we prove Leon Manigault was pushing on the brake pedal, that means it was the cruise control."

"I don't want to be the skunk at the family picnic," responded Zelvy, "but my experience is that the jury will want to know what made this happen twice, and this NHTSA letter won't cut it when Ford brushes it aside by claiming that the same government agency two years later decided the problem was driver error."

Although I was taken with Molly's analysis, I could also see Zelvy's point.

"Look, gang," I said. "I know some of you think it was a World Series ticket that got us involved in this case. It's a wonderful rumor that nobody here should squelch. However, it wasn't Sandy Zelvy's ticket that did it. Bob reminded me that I once gave a talk about how tough cases like this one separate real lawyers from the pretenders. I don't know how we are going to win this case, but I know something was dangerously wrong in that Crown Victoria, and I know this remarkable family desperately needs our help. That's enough for me, and I hope it's enough for you. So let's roll up our sleeves and get to work."

CHAPTER 10

# DISCOVERIES IN PITTSBURGH

**FIVE PEDESTRIANS STRUCK BY SUV**

> The driver of an SUV lost control of the vehicle, striking five people, a tree and a suburban hotel. The man behind the wheel said the accelerator on his Jeep Cherokee malfunctioned.
>
> *ABC Local News,* August 7, 2004

**AS PLANNED, WE DID A SERIES OF TESTS WITH A 1987 CROWN** Victoria Zelvy had found. Photographs taken three days after the Manigaults' car crashed into a neighbor's house showed there were no tire marks where the Crown Victoria was parked when it accelerated from the Manigaults' driveway. Since we knew Ford's defense was driver error, we wanted to know whether that would have caused tire marks on the driveway, so we had someone floor the gas pedal in Zelvy's Crown Victoria. As expected, the rear wheels immediately spun wildly, leaving four foot long burn marks on the pavement before they gained traction. We then repeated the test with a video camera recording what happened. Since there were also no tire marks where the Crown Victoria suddenly took off from the church parking lot, we had proof Leon had not suddenly floored the gas pedal on either occasion.

The next step was to find out if cruise control malfunction would have caused similar tire marks. To simulate a sudden acceleration, Sam Sero had developed a way of wiring the cruise control servo so that flipping a switch would cause the servo to suddenly pull the throttle wide open. He had also located a test site near Pittsburgh where our accident reconstructionist, Dr. William Berg, could experience for himself what happens during a sudden acceleration.

When we arrived at the test site, Sam Sero had placed orange traffic cones 187 feet apart—the distance the Manigaults' car traveled before crashing. With a video camera positioned immediately behind the test car and another one just beyond the traffic cone at the end of the course, Dr. Berg flipped the switch on Sero's device. The sudden, guttural roar of the engine was so frightening I felt my braking foot reflexively trying to find an imaginary brake pedal. I was not alone. Dr. Berg was so startled that, he quickly flipped the switch to shut down the servo, causing the car to coast to a stop. What happened next is etched in my memory.

Dr. Berg, looking shaken, walked back to where we were standing, and said simply, "I panicked."

Then he added, "Now I know why people say this is the most terrifying thing that ever happened to them."

"And you knew what was going to happen," Bob Zelvy observed.

After Dr. Berg assured us he was OK and wished to continue, we did nine test runs. Each time, Dr. Berg shifted into drive before instantaneously activating the cruise control servo with Sero's device. When none of the test runs left tire marks on the pavement, we were exultant. In fact, I recall remarking to Sam Sero that absence of tire marks "should be enough to win any sudden acceleration case."

His response surprised me. "That depends on whether the malfunction occurs before shifting is completed or, as in this case, after the car is already in gear."

"You'll have to explain that, Sam. I'm thoroughly confused."

"Do you recall when we discussed our test protocol, I told Bill Berg to flip the switch *immediately after* he shifted into drive? That was because you told me the Manigaults' car took off immediately after your client shifted into drive. I've also tested what happens if the servo is activated before shifting is completed, and the wheels left tire marks as if I had suddenly floored the gas pedal as you did during your test in Sandusky."

"Do you mean that when you flipped the switch before shifting was completed, the wheels spun and left burn marks?"

I could see that Sero was amused by my question. "Do you know how long it takes the throttle to go wide open when a fault bypasses the normal controls?"

"Honestly, Sam, I've never thought about it."

"The throttle flies open in just a little over one second. As a teenager, did you ever pop the clutch in a manual transmission car by shifting into first gear while you were goosing the gas pedal, making the wheels spin and squeal and burn rubber? If you were good, you could shift into second and then into third gear about the same time the tires gained traction, and if you were really good, your girlfriend might even reward you."

"Sam, I think you've been watching too many James Dean movies. Now tell me what that has to do with our case?"

"Believe it or not, as far as tire marks are concerned, popping the clutch was no different than having the cruise control servo pull the throttle open before shifting is completed. If the

Manigaults' Crown Victoria had left tire marks on their driveway, it would have been just as easy to connect it to a cruise control malfunction by having Bill Berg flip the switch before he shifted our test car into drive."

"So tire marks or no tire marks depends on whether or not the throttle is open before shifting is completed."

"Exactly," was Sero's response.

"This will probably cost me, Sam, but you're one hell of a forensic engineer."

Before leaving the tests in Pittsburgh, it is worth mentioning that during each test run, Dr. Berg observed that the speed, after 187 feet, was about 47 mph. Since government crash data showed the Crown Victoria's speed when it crashed was about 25 mph, we now had compelling evidence that Mr. Manigault was pushing on the brake pedal during the final terrifying moments of his conscious existence.

CHAPTER 11

# THE CALM BEFORE THE STORM

**SUV PLOWS INTO STUDENTS OUTSIDE MIDDLE SCHOOL**

> Belmont, California (AP) A sport utility vehicle jumped a curb outside a middle school Wednesday afternoon, plowed into a group of children waiting for a bus and rammed into a tree, trapping several students underneath, police said.
>
> *CNN.com*, May 3, 2007

**FOLLOWING OUR TESTING IN PITTSBURGH, THERE WAS THE USUAL** run of depositions that produced few surprises. Sam Sero described how supplying power to the cruise control servo at ignition made it possible for non-detectable faults to bypass the control logic and trigger an open throttle acceleration. Ford's expert, Victor Declercq, acknowledged that the switches for the servo were powered at ignition, but insisted that *at least two independent hardwire faults had to occur simultaneously* to make the servo, as he put it, "stroke." The chance of that happening, he insisted, was virtually impossible, and, in any event, such faults would leave detectable evidence Orringer's inspection would have found. For good measure he added that NHTSA's 1989 study supported his conclusions. It was a mark of my naîveté that I finished questioning Declercq in less than half the time I usually take with an opposing expert.

A high point in our discovery came when I deposed Carl Whelpley, the service manager on duty when the Manigaults' car was towed to their dealer following the occurrence at the church. Whelpley, who struck me as honest and conscientious, said he had never heard of sudden acceleration, and was unaware of anything that might have caused the Crown Victoria to take off on its own. If that was true, Ford was keeping dealers in the dark to cover up its negligence, which explained why there was no mention of the cruise control in the service records.

"No wonder their dealer stuck the Manigaults with a $700 bill for fiddling with the idle controls," Molly fumed. "The service people couldn't think of anything else because the fat cats in Dearborn know that if they tell dealers the truth, the company will have to compensate people like the Manigaults, and the shareholders would start scrutinizing their year-end bonuses. If I were the dealer, I would try to stick it to Ford."

Shortly after the deposition, the dealer made a settlement offer. Since we felt Whelpley was a credible witness who would help our case against Ford, we advised the Manigaults to accept the offer. Because the settlement didn't begin to cover the Manigaults' losses, Zelvy and I waived our fee and applied it to the cost of going forward against Ford.

There was another bright spot during the run-up to the trial. Molly's brief-writing ability paid off when the court declined to dismiss the case because of the lost car. All in all, I felt we had a strong circumstantial case against Ford, and I looked forward to a trial presided over by a fair-minded and compassionate judge.

I met the Honorable Anthony O. Calabrese for the first time at the final pretrial conference in our case. He began by asking each side how long it would take to present its case. I said we needed about seven days, and Ford's lead counsel, Elizabeth Wright, estimated the defense would take a week.

"So," observed the Judge, "if we add time for motions, final arguments and jury deliberation, we are looking at a three-week trial." There was a pause as the Judge studied his trial calendar before announcing, "Let's start jury selection on June 10, 1997."

Before we adjourned, Judge Calabrese broached the delicate matter of settlement. "Folks, this is an interesting case, but giving up three weeks for a civil case presents a real problem because our Supreme Court rules say the criminal docket takes precedence over civil cases. Is there any chance the parties can resolve this before you spend time and money trying this case?"

Wright responded first. "Your Honor, the disappearance of the car has severely prejudiced Ford, and we are confident a verdict for the plaintiffs would be reversed on appeal. Therefore, Ford is unwilling to make a settlement offer."

The Judge turned to me. "Mr. Murray, the court has accepted your argument that the loss of the car can be remedied by a jury instruction. But Ms. Wright has a point. The loss of the car is a serious matter, and there is no guarantee my ruling will be upheld on appeal. As a practical matter, wouldn't it be better to let the Court of Appeals decide the spoliation issue before going through a three-week trial?"

It may surprise non-lawyers that a judge, having decided the lost car issue in our favor, would suggest reversing that decision to facilitate an appeal. Actually, it was a thoughtful suggestion by an experienced trial judge. If a verdict for the Manigaults was reversed after a lengthy trial, it was my firm that would bear the cost of having gone to trial prematurely. In fact, we had considered asking the court to do what the judge had suggested.

"Your Honor," I began, "we have discussed the possibility you suggest, but it has now been four years since this happened, and the Manigaults desperately need to have this resolved. The settlement with the dealer helped, but it didn't begin to cover their losses. If we get a verdict, there will be an appeal and, given the issues involved, there's a good chance the case will end up in the Ohio Supreme Court. Since that could take several years, we must respectfully decline the court's thoughtful suggestion."

"Very well," replied the judge resignedly. "We will see you at 9 a.m. on June 10 to start jury selection."

"Do you think we did the right thing not having the spoliation issue decided first?" Zelvy asked on the way to the courthouse parking lot.

"Why the second thoughts?" I responded.

"You told me Jo Ellen and Molly haven't had time to read through Potter's files. What if there are some smoking documents, and we lose this case? I know how desperate our clients are, Chief, but I'd be more confident if we knew what was in Potter's files before going to trial."

"I understand your concern, Zel, but I doubt there is anything in Potter's files that could add much to what we already know. All the evidence says the car went crazy, not once, but twice.

"And don't forget that Jack Potter and a lot of other good lawyers have rounded up thousands of Ford documents, gone to trial, and lost. Let's not fret about documents, and come at Ford with both guns blazing."

These words were as brave as they were simplistic, for I had glossed over questions that had long ago bedeviled industry outsiders. If failures were electronically induced, why didn't inspecting and testing components find the cause? If failures left no detectable evidence, why should Ford, or any car company, be blamed for not correcting an undetectable problem? Why hadn't the brakes stopped the runaway Crown Victoria before it crashed into a neighbor's house? Finally, since to err is human, was it possible, after all, that NHTSA was right that negligent driving was behind this automotive phenomenon?

While I had given scant thought to such questions, Ford had long ago thought them through, and, as *Pierotti* and many other cases showed, had developed a seemingly impregnable strategy to exploit overly confident opponents. Ironically, my overconfidence would tempt Ford to overreach, and set in motion events that over the next decade would inexorably expose how terribly vulnerable the legal system is when a giant industry believes it is better to hide its mistakes than to admit them, and a federal agency turns a blind eye to the concealment.

CHAPTER 12

# STORM CLOUDS

### TOYOTA DRIVER: "ABC NEWS VIDEOS HELPED SAVE MY LIFE"

Kevin Haggerty says he brought his runaway Toyota under control by using what he'd learned on-line and on-air.

*ABC News*, Jan. 21, 2010

**INCLUDED ON THE EXHIBIT LIST WE FILED TWO WEEKS BEFORE THE** Manigault trial was to begin, was NHTSA's December 31, 1986, letter to Ford. Although it never mentioned cruise control, I was unperturbed because Sero could verify that all Ford models with cruise control had the identical system. I felt certain that making the jury aware of hundreds of sudden accelerations would force Ford to explain how so many reports could be squared with NHTSA's 1989 report blaming drivers. Our strategy seemed so elegantly simple I wished I had thought of it instead of Molly.

The wake-up call came with a motion *in limine* to bar any mention of NHTSA's notification in the presence of the jury.

*In limine* is a Latin term meaning "on the threshold" or "at the outset". *In limine* motions, therefore, allow the court to streamline a trial by ruling in advance on the admissibility of evidence.

Molly was fit to be tied. "The *Babb* case is crystal clear that this notice is admissible to show Ford had notice of a possible safety defect."

"Maybe they smelled our strategy," I replied, "and decided to give up the 1989 NHTSA report in exchange for keeping the jury in the dark about other reports. They certainly can't bar NHTSA's notice, and still beat us over the head with that 1989 report."

"How should we respond to their motion?" asked Molly.

"My gut feeling is to stick to our guns, and take our chances with the 1989 study."

Molly wanted more. "We don't have much time. Should I try to get a written response filed before trial?"

"Yes, but make it brief! We have more important things to do! Besides, I doubt if Judge Calabrese will look favorably on a last-minute motion to keep out a document the Court of Appeals for this county has ruled is admissible as notice of a defect. Just be on top of the *Babb* decision if the court asks for oral arguments before ruling on Ford's motion."

As we were to learn, last-minute motions to block important evidence are routinely used by Ford to overwhelm opponents with work on the eve of trial. This was no ordinary motion, however, because keeping NHTSA's notice from the jury would allow Ford to portray our case as an isolated occurrence in a six-year-old car that, to boot, had disappeared. Nevertheless, I was confident the *Babb* decision would convince Judge Calabrese to admit our certified copy of NHTSA's notice.

Then, out of the blue, two days prior to jury selection, the case was transferred to the Honorable Thomas Matia, a judge on senior status, with no previous connection to the case. Such last minute reassignments are common in busy courts where, as in Cuyahoga County, Ohio, the regular docket is clogged with criminal cases that, by law, take precedence over civil matters.

Over the years, in fact, I have had several cases bumped from the regular docket by a criminal matter and assigned to senior judges, who have proven to be outstanding jurists. But I knew nothing about Judge Matia, so I called my old friend, Fred Weisman, who I was sure would have the "book" on our new judge.

"Sure, I know Tom Matia," Weisman answered immediately. "He's one of the old timers. He's a kindly gentleman with a good judicial demeanor, and he tries hard to be fair to everybody. In fact, I'd take him for most cases."

"Why not any case, rather than most cases?" I asked.

There was a pause as my friend gathered his thoughts. "Tom Matia is getting up in years, his health is shaky, and he's always been more of a seat-of-the-pants judge than a legal scholar. With no law clerk to help him sort out legal questions, and no familiarity with your case, I'm afraid you'll be at a disadvantage, especially with Elizabeth Wright on the other side. She's plenty sharp, and her firm makes a point of knowing judges. I would be surprised if Judge Matia doesn't know her fairly well, so . . . . "

"So," I interrupted, "what are you doing next week? I need you on this case—lost car or no lost car."

"Tom, I would join you in a heartbeat, but I have a case coming up that I need to focus on."

After thanking my friend for his read on Judge Matia, I made a prediction that was to prove prescient. "Fred, I have a gut feeling that this case will have to be tried more than once and, sooner or later, you will be part of it."

CHAPTER 13

# MORE UNPLEASANT SURPRISES

> On 4-10-86 Lydia Sramek was reportedly driving the vehicle. She allegedly was operating the vehicle very slowly with her foot on the brake about to park in a parking lot when the car "suddenly accelerated to a high rate of speed, jumped over a curb and down a ditch and hit two condominiums" and injured a pet dog. Lydia Sramek alleges that she was injured in the alleged accident, but the nature of the injuries were not specified. The central office file contained no unprivileged information specifying the nature and degree of property damage.
>
> *Ford's submission to NHTSA*, March 13, 1987

**WITH JURY SELECTION SCHEDULED TO BEGIN AFTER LUNCH ON** Wednesday, June 11, 1987, Zelvy, Molly, and I arrived about a half hour early at the old Lakeside Courthouse where senior judges preside. Shortly after we ensconced ourselves at the table nearest the jury box—the traditional place for plaintiffs—Elizabeth Wright and her associate, Mike Smith, entered the stately old high-ceilinged, oak-paneled courtroom and took their places at the defense table. A tense silence ensued, as we waited for the judge, who soon sauntered in with an amiable "good afternoon," followed by a cheerful inquiry to no one in particular.

"Well, what do we have here? I'm told this is a product liability case of some kind." Wright was on her feet immediately. "That's right, Judge, and we have some matters we'd like to take up with the court before jury selection begins."

"Certainly, Ms. Wright," the judge answered with a smile, adding, "it's been a while since I've had the pleasure of having you in my court."

"Thank you, Judge. I'd like to introduce my associate, Mike Smith, and plaintiffs' counsel, Mr. Murray, Mr. Zelvy, and Ms. O'Neill."

This was skillful gamesmanship, and I admired how gracefully Wright had exchanged pleasantries with the judge, been granted her request to argue Ford's last-minute motion *in limine,* and taken control of introducing everyone else to the newly assigned Thomas Matia. It was clear Elizabeth Wright would be a formidable adversary.

In chambers, Wright's associate, Smith, summarized why we should be barred from even mentioning NHTSA's December 31, 1986, notification in the presence of the jury. The government letter, Smith argued, was "inadmissible hearsay" that did not qualify as a "public record" because the "information . . . came from consumer complaints." The plaintiffs, therefore, were attempting "to create guilt by association that this letter substantiates their cruise control defect theory" that was never mentioned in the notification. Therefore, the "probative value" of the letter "is substantially outweighed by the danger of unfair prejudice and the danger of misleading the jury."

Although Ford had made the same argument in its written motion, Judge Matia's expression showed it was new to him. The record reflects what happened next:

**The Court:** All right. Mr. Murray.

**Mr. Murray:** Molly, would you respond to this?

**The Court:** Ms. O'Neill.

**O'Neill:** Your Honor, taking the easiest of the three points first, namely, the issue of authentication, we intend to offer a certified copy of this public document from the federal agency, and, as such, it should be deemed self-authenticated under Rule 902, subdivision 4 of the Ohio Rules of Evidence.

But addressing myself now to the hearsay point, as we set forth in our memorandum in opposition, the *Babb* case . . . supports our position here. We are not offering this letter to prove that sudden unwanted acceleration events, in fact, occurred. We are instead offering this notice to show that there were consumer complaints of unwanted acceleration. Mr. Smith brings out the fact that this letter does not mention cruise control. Well, of course, it does not. These are consumer complaints.

These are from consumers who do not have the sophistication to ascertain what the cause was. And indeed, Mullinax itself, Ford's own dealer, could not ascertain the cause. So I believe the point Mr. Smith brings out regarding no mention of cruise control does not diminish the document's relevancy whatsoever . . . .

***

Molly was right. While "consumer complaints" were hearsay, they were admissible as notice to Ford of similar occurrences, indicating a possible defect. Ironically, the same objection applied to NHTSA's 1989 report, which we assumed would be a lynchpin of Ford's defense. The government report, in fact, was filled with hearsay, but, as a government report, was nevertheless admissible as a public record. The *Babb* case made the consumer complaints referred to in NHTSA's notification admissible because, as Molly had explained, they were not being offered to prove the existence of a defect but, rather, notification to Ford of vehicle behavior that put the company on notice of a possible safety problem. Therefore, a judge familiar with the case would almost certainly have overruled Ford's motion. But Judge Matia's position was similar to that of a general surgeon suddenly called upon to perform an operation he had never done before and Smith's rebuttal took full advantage:

> **Smith:** Once again, Judge, there is nothing in this letter to tie the letter to the cruise control defect theory that the plaintiffs are espousing in this case. We don't even know if any of these consumer complaints contained a car that had a cruise control. We don't even know that.
>
> **The Court:** All right. Defendants' motion *in limine* is granted.

***

I was dumbstruck. Our trial strategy assumed that Ford would rely on NHTSA's 1989 report blaming drivers, and that we could put Ford on the defense by making it explain why hundreds of drivers would report similar vehicle behavior to the federal government. But it was now clear that Ford recognized that the 1989 report was a double-edged sword because it opened the door to correspondence between the agency and Ford leading up to the government's investigation. While I was relieved that we would not have to deal with the government report Ford had consistently used with great success, the court's ruling put Ford in a position to portray our case as an aberrational occurrence in an old car it had never had a chance to inspect. But we had unexpectedly been given the means of preventing Ford from isolating the *Manigault* case.

On the eve of trial, Bob Zelvy called to say he had located a lawyer in Little Rock, Arkansas, named Chris Brinkley, whose firm had recently tried a sudden acceleration case against Ford and won. Given all the reports we'd heard about Ford's unbroken success in these cases, this was big news.

"Did they base their case on a defect in the cruise control electronics?" I asked.

"Unfortunately for us, they found something wrong in the idle controls so they relied on the same theory Orringer proposed."

"Maybe the jury made the right decision for the wrong reason. What happened to the people in the car?"

"The driver and passenger—both women—were killed. The verdict, I guess, was niggardly but, according to Chris, they made some amazing discoveries that he thinks will help our case."

"Such as?"

"His senior partner and Chris deposed the guy Potter told us about—I think his name is Updegrove—who supervised an investigation of several thousand sudden accelerations. Chris said there's some great stuff in the deposition, and I asked him to send us a copy. He promised to mail it to your office as soon as he can get it copied and, if we need him, he will testify."

Since Jack Potter had left us with the impression that Updegrove had been an effective witness for Ford, the possibility that his testimony might help the Manigaults was intriguing, and we immediately added Chris Brinkley's name to our list of potential witnesses. The impression we were on to something grew when, after the court's exclusion of NHTSA's December 31, 1986 letter, the following occurred on the record:

**Ms. Wright:** As to Mr. Brinkley, we learned of his identity yesterday. He's a lawyer in Little Rock who advised us that, after one and a half years of discovery attempts, he learned of the existence of an unintended acceleration reading room in Dearborn, and that he had obtained sanctions for Ford's discovery abuses in not revealing this fact.

He advised us that he visited this room; that it contains several thousand documents, some 52 boxes full of complaints regarding sudden accelerations, unintended accelerations.

Obviously, your Honor, we are not in a position at this point to tell you that we know the contents of those boxes. But since we only learned of the identity of this lawyer yesterday, we want the opportunity to *voir dire* [question a witness] him in your Honor's presence at the appropriate time. We aren't going to mention his existence on opening statement. But in light of the issues in this case, we've asked for that opportunity at the appropriate time.

**The Court:** That's acceptable. Let's discuss this matter in chambers at the time of adjournment today, to figure out if we're going to set up a time for this.

**Ms. Wright:** Your Honor, we also realize that we would move for a continuance—to the extent that issue was even held in abeyance and they decide to bring somebody in midway through the trial, we would move for a continuance of that as well.

**The Court:** I understand that. Your motion is denied.

***

The possibility that Updegrove's testimony might help our case raises the question of why I had not concurred with Wright's request for continuance. The reason requires a brief digression.

When I began trying cases in the 1960s, modern discovery was still in its infancy, and trial lawyers like my father did most of their discovery by cross-examining opposing witnesses in the courtroom. Our firm was founded in 1931 by my father, Thomas, and his older brother, Emmett. It would be many years before the firm had the resources to engage in costly discovery battles with law firms representing insurance companies and big corporations. Thus was born the practice of "extralegal discovery" that continued long after many of our contemporaries were spending large sums of money on formal discovery; and because postponements usually favor the defense, we were loath to have a case continued if it could be avoided. As a result, by the 1970s we were trying more civil cases to juries than any other firm in Ohio. During one year, in fact, I set a record by trying 26 jury trials to a verdict.

This habitual mindset kicked in when Wright suggested a continuance to Judge Matia, and I passed up an opportunity to buy time until we knew for sure what Updegrove's deposition would reveal.

Since it was now too late to impanel a jury, we adjourned for the day.

CHAPTER 14

# THE BEST LAID PLANS

### NO NEED FOR ADDITIONAL SPEED: THE ISSUE OF UNINTENDED ACCELERATION RETURNS TO THE SPOTLIGHT THANKS TO HIGH-TECH ADVANCEMENT IN VEHICLES

Carol Mathews, 60, has been driving since she was 12 years old on a South Dakota farm. So when her 2002 Lexus ES 300 ran into a tree as she pulled into a restaurant parking space last fall, she was pretty sure she wasn't the problem. She says it was the third time the car lurched forward without her help.

*Edmonton Sun,* April 15, 2004

**THAT EVENING WE HUDDLED TO REASSESS OUT TRIAL STRATEGY.** Although Molly was upset that the court had not followed the Babb decision, Zelvy saw a silver lining.

"Doesn't the court's ruling strengthen our case for presenting the testimony of Chris Brinkley?"

"I think you're right, Bob," I replied. "So let's decide how to play it tomorrow morning before we start jury selection. If Wright claims there have been no occurrences similar to ours, it would be an outright fraud. With Chris Brinkley in the wings, how do we make Judge Matia aware of what is going on?"

"Why not state on the record straightaway that it would be fraudulent to claim there have been no occurrences similar to ours?" Molly suggested.

I was dubious. "I'm afraid being that blunt might spook Judge Matia more than he already is. After he learns more about our case, we'll have plenty of chances to use the 'F' word."

At this point, Zelvy made a suggestion that carried the moment. "Why not make Wright admit what she intends to do, and explain to the court why it would be fraudulent?"

I was intrigued. "Any idea how we can do that, Bob?"

"Why not turn the tables by arguing that Ford should be barred from suggesting that we are required to produce evidence of similar occurrences. If she agrees, and I think she will, you can cite Goose v. Gander. If we can't mention other occurrences, then Ford should not be allowed to say there have not been other similar runaway car crashes."

I took Zelvy's suggestion, and prior to jury selection the next morning I pointed out to the court that, "It would be highly prejudicial for defendant to suggest that we have some burden of proving other cruise control-related occurrences. I don't see how Ford can have it both ways."

This provoked the response Zelvy had predicted:

**The Court:** Let me interrupt you. Is there any question about that?

**Ms. Wright:** I'm not suggesting that it's his burden to prove other instances. But the lack of any other car where there's been a documentation of this particular defect is highly probative as to whether there is a defect in this design. There are millions and millions and millions of cars on the road with this system, and I ought to be permitted to tell the jury they are not going to hear about another instance documented where this happened.

**The Court:** You don't have any objection to that do you?

**Mr. Murray:** I certainly do . . . .

***

Wright's claim that we couldn't prove that "this particular defect" had caused a sudden acceleration in "any other car" was a clever example of a calculated ambiguity. The linchpin of our case was that powering the cruise control servo at ignition made the system vulnerable to a sudden acceleration at gear engagement. However, since it was undisputed that the servo was powered at ignition, it was clear that "this particular defect" was not the point of Wright's argument. I now saw that Ford had devised a trial strategy as clever as it was devious. Having blocked us from using reports to NHTSA to show Ford was on notice of a possible defect, Ford had decided to argue that we had the burden of proving that the "particular defect" that caused the Manigaults' injuries also caused other similar uncontrolled accelerations. At the time, however, I simply didn't know enough about electronics to fully grasp how shrewd Wright's argument was. While Ford had decided to forego the benefit of NHTSA's 1989 conclusion that multiple and detectable hardwire faults were prerequisites for a sudden acceleration, its new strategy would allow the company to have it both ways by having Victor Declercq make the same claims contained in the government report. Moreover, since the disappearance of the car before Ford inspected it left us no choice except to concede there was no evidence of hardwire faults, Wright was bent on convincing Judge Matia that Ford should be permitted to "tell the jury they were not going to hear about another instance documented where this happened."

But it seemed strange that Ford would elect not to clobber us with the 1989 report. Had this change in strategy, we wondered, been influenced by the appearance of Chris Brinkley's name on our witness list? Was it possible that Updegrove's deposition, rather than confirming the industry's position, showed that the 1989 report was wrong? If so, was it a mistake to pass up an opportunity to do further discovery by opposing Wright's request for a postponement? Adding to our doubts was the fact that Judge Matia was struggling to grasp exactly what we were arguing about. Therefore, I pointedly told Wright that what she intended to tell the jury would be intentionally misleading. This provoked a sharp rebuke:

> **Ms. Wright:** Tom, I'm sorry. You missed the boat totally. Number one, just because there are complaints by a consumer about sudden acceleration does not mean that any of those sudden accelerations relates to cruise control. There is not even a notice issue.
>
> **The Court:** Stop. Do you agree to that?
>
> **Mr. Murray:** I absolutely do not agree with that.
>
> **Ms. Wright:** I have every right to make that argument. The jury is not going to hear about another incident in another vehicle in which it was verified there is a cruise control problem under these circumstances.

***

Although Wright had repeated the argument that we couldn't prove something we were not required to prove, I could tell from his expression that Judge Matia was bewildered by these exchanges. Although I repeated my charge, Wright persisted:

**Ms. Wright:** Tom . . . what I'm going to say is that the plaintiffs are not going to present any evidence of another incident. That's what I'm going to say. I'm not saying you have the burden to prove it. I'm simply going to point out that you're not going to present any evidence on that fact.

**Mr. Murray:** You're not going to imply that somehow that's relevant?

**Ms. Wright:** Of course, it's relevant.

**Mr. Murray:** That's like . . . .

**Ms. Wright:** Tom, one cruise control, one vehicle with cruise control that's a problem in all the millions and millions of vehicles, not only Fords, but GMs and Chryslers and everything else.

**The Court:** Which is the one?

**Ms. Wright:** Pardon me?

**The Court:** Which is the one?

**Ms. Wright:** No, I mean all of them. Oh, this one. I mean their one claim.

**The Court:** Oh, their one claim.

***

It was now so painfully obvious that the court was struggling to grasp what was happening that I decided it was time to put the "F" word on the record:

**Mr. Murray:** Well, Your Honor, I can just respond this way. If she makes that statement, I will guarantee you . . . we will put into the record every document we can find to show that we've been prejudiced by that remark. And we will claim . . . that there's been *fraudulent concealment* and we will make our record, I guarantee you.

> **Ms. Wright:** What fraudulent concealment are you going to try to claim, Tom? Because I'm insulted. I'm going to tell you right now. [Emphasis added.]

***

Although my accusation of "fraudulent concealment" was to prove shockingly accurate, that is to outpace our story. At that time, I couldn't think of anything more we could do to convince Judge Matia, so I ended on a note of resignation:

**Mr. Murray:** Well, your Honor, I've made my motion . . . . I've made my argument.

**The Court:** Motion denied. Note your exception.

***

Having lost our motion, we could only hope that what remained of our strategy would carry the day.

CHAPTER 15

# GROUNDS FOR SUSPICION

### DRIVE-THROUGH HORROR

A car veered across a dual carriageway in rush-hour traffic . . . smashing through a fence before slamming into a packed McDonald's restaurant . . . . Customers looked on in horror as the Mitsubishi Shogun demolished the wall of the fast food outlet, just a few feet from where they were sitting . . . .

*Hartlepool Mail (UK)*, August 15, 2008

**AFTER I OUTLINED OUR CASE FOR THE JURY, WRIGHT TOLD THE JURY,** "There will be no evidence from anyone that this has ever happened in the real world." After dismissing Sero's table model as "jerry-rigged," she promised to call an expert, Victor Declercq, "who knows more about cruise control than anybody who's going to talk to you."

I could see Wright had made a strong impression, so I hoped our first witness, John Manigault, would recapture the momentum. Standing next to models of the church parking lot and the Manigaults' driveway to the crash site, John recalled both events. Although he appeared nervous, I felt his sincerity and the clarity of his recollections should convince the jury there was something terribly wrong with the Manigaults' Crown Victoria.

Our next witness, Dr. Berg, took the jury step by step through the various steering maneuvers Leon Manigault must have made to avoid a crash before he ran out of room to maneuver. Citing government crash data, Berg explained that, without braking, the Crown Victoria at impact would have been going twice as fast. On balance, I felt we were off to a good start and could hardly wait to read Updegrove's deposition, which I knew from JR had arrived in the day's mail.

That weekend was as exhilarating as it was sobering. As Zelvy had predicted, Updegrove's 400-page deposition with dozens of exhibits contained many surprising revelations. Shortly after NHTSA announced its industry-wide study, for example, Ford had recalled a small group of previously retired employees to investigate sudden accelerations using an exquisitely detailed format that was attached to Updegrove's deposition. But the recalled employees had been ordered not to express an opinion regarding the cause of the events they were investigating. We knew from Mr. X, however, that engineers employed in district offices investigating sudden accelerations at the time were required to record their opinion regarding the cause in a service investigation report, or SIR. Why, I wondered, had Updegrove's team been forbidden to do the same? Had Ford, perchance, decided to cut off incriminating field reports, while also steadfastly maintaining that its investigators were unable to find a cause? The more I read, the more suspicious it all seemed.

I was particularly struck by several exhibits with Updegrove's deposition. For example, a Secret Service agent gave Ford's investigator this written description of the event:

> With my right foot on brake, I started the engine . . . ; I pulled the transmission from park position to drive. At that point, the engine went wide open throttle. With the rear wheels spinning, it jumped forward at high speed. I finally was able to stop the car by pushing very hard on the brakes. Once stopped, I put the transmission in park and then turned the key off.

Another Secret Service agent described a sudden acceleration in a 1992 Crown Victoria:

> As I put the transmission into reverse, the car suddenly accelerated at a very high speed, squealing the rear tires. My foot was on the brake, but had little slowing effect. The car hit the railing with a loud bang and I then turned off the ignition which stopped all rearward motion.

There were also letters like the one from an officer of Dollar Rent-A-Car describing his investigation of a sudden acceleration. The writer, William Felberg, told Ford about an event in a 1990 Lincoln that began when "the car was shifted into reverse and . . . took off rapidly increasing in speed in the reverse direction." Felberg pointed out that a passenger in the car observed the driver pushing on the brakes throughout the event, and that "the car was literally out of control and screeching rubber was heard throughout the lot because of the conflict between the acceleration and the brake action." The driver, he added, was an officer of his company "who was only 43 years old, in excellent health and an individual with a blemish-free driving record." This and similar information made the pedal error hypothesis appear increasingly absurd.

I was also struck that about two-thirds of the more than 2,877 occurrences investigated had begun at gear engagement *in a stationary vehicle.* This finding was so universal, in fact, that Ford gave these events a special category, defined as "where the customer enters the vehicle, starts the engine, pulls the vehicle into gear, and has what he would suggest to be an uncontrolled rpm response." Since witnesses often corroborated the driver's description of the event, I was puzzled as to why Ford had added "what the drivers would suggest" to this definition. We learned eventually that the company had a special vocabulary regarding safety issues we came to call "Fordspeak".

By the following Monday, I was convinced that the data collected by Ford's investigators was the key to finally unlocking the decades-old mystery surrounding runaway cars. While it was an exhilarating prospect, the immediate challenge was to convince Judge Matia we were entitled to present Updegrove's deposition to the jury. If we lost that argument, we would almost certainly lose the *Manigault* case.

Before going on the record the following Monday, I pulled Judge Matia and Wright aside to announce that we were prepared to show that Ford's opening statement was "false and misleading." Judge Matia, who looked stunned, asked, "You can't be serious that the Ford Motor Company would intentionally mislead this Court?" To which I responded, "Your Honor, that is exactly what I'm saying."

The record reflects what happened next:

**The Court:** Have you read these depositions?

**Mr. Murray:** I have, your Honor, I have read them.

**The Court:** Do they refer to the cruise control?

**Mr. Murray:** Absolutely. Sure they do, absolutely.

**The Court:** Are they just complaints?

**Mr. Murray:** They are much more than complaints. They are a description of what Ford did . . . [that] . . . includes the Crown Victoria.

***

Judge Matia then asked Wright on the record:

**The Court:** Have you seen what he's talking about?

**Ms. Wright:** No, I haven't seen those depositions, but I've heard about them. Those depositions do not say what you're claiming happened in Mr. Manigault's car with a defective cruise control in the manner in which you are claiming it having anything to do with anything discussed in those depositions, Tom, and you know that.

***

Wright's rejoinder caused the court to ask if the deposition mentioned cruise control. Since the investigative format showed Ford had specifically focused on the cruise control electronics, I stated emphatically that the investigation had included the cruise control. In fact, I was about to read from the deposition itself when Wright suddenly changed the subject by pointing out, correctly, that the deposition from Arkansas could not be presented to the jury because it was not an authenticated copy.

Her objection meant that the two court reporters who recorded Updegrove's testimony on separate days would have to appear in court to authenticate the transcript. While this was the first time an opposing lawyer had invoked this hypertechnical objection to block the use of a deposition copy, I knew Wright had little choice. If the verdict went against her client, Ford would be exposed to a flood of similar lawsuits.

During the noon recess, I placed a call to the reporting firm, Patricia Murray & Associates, who had recorded Updegrove's testimony. When I reached Ms. Murray (no relation), I summarized our predicament and asked if she and her colleague Susan Parrish, who had recorded the second part of the deposition, would be willing to authenticate the depositions. There was a heart-pounding pause as Ms. Murray, who recalled the depositions, pondered my plea. Finally, she said simply, "OK, but the only day available for us is next Tuesday."

"Beggars can't be choosy," I stuttered, heaving a sigh of relief. "Ford should rest on Tuesday, so we'll use the depositions in rebuttal. And by the way, Patricia," I added, "we may need your services in other cases like this one," a prediction that was to prove accurate in spades.

When I told Zelvy the court reporters had agreed to come to Cleveland, he asked whether we also needed Chris Brinkley's testimony.

"I can't think of anything he might add to the depositions," I replied. "In fact, since they based their case on an idle air bypass failure, his testimony might only confuse the jury. Why don't you thank him for his offer of help, and let him know the court reporters have made his appearance unnecessary."

CHAPTER 16

# DENOUEMENT

### MAN'S CAR ACCELERATES INTO CROWD IN ILLINOIS

The sudden acceleration of an Illinois man's car caused seventy-eight people, including sixty-five children, to be injured. Oddly enough, the man's engine actually began to race as he was applying his brakes. His vehicle sped onto a sidewalk and into the group of children. Federal officials stated that a cruise control problem prompted the recall of the vehicle to GM.

*Atlanta Journal and Constitution*, May 3, 1992

**FORD'S KEY WITNESS WAS VICTOR DECLERCQ, WHOM JACK** Potter had described as likeable and effective in front of a jury. His evaluation of Sero's testimony was scathing:

**Q:** And an engineer like you or Mr. Sero can come in and manipulate the system so it fails?

**A:** That's possible.

**Q:** Does the fact that an electronic system can be manipulated by an engineer mean it can happen in the real world?

**A:** Not necessarily.

**Q:** Just so we're clear, Vic, do you have an opinion to a reasonable degree of engineering certainty as to whether Mr. Sero's theory can happen in the real world?

**A:** I have an opinion.

**Q:** What is that opinion?

**A:** That can't happen. It just doesn't happen.

***

This testimony was the foundation of Ford's defense. Since Sero had manipulated wires on his tabletop model to demonstrate how supplying power at ignition to the cruise control servo made a sudden acceleration possible, Declercq was right that the demonstration had not replicated what could "happen in the real world." When we come to Toyota's current sudden acceleration problems in a later section, we will see how the Japanese carmaker attacked the testimony of another electrical engineer because "it couldn't happen in the real world." But, despite our suspicions, we simply didn't know enough about these electronics at this point in our story to counteract Declercq's criticism of Sero's work. Ironically, however, it was not Declercq's assessment of Sero's work that proved most damaging to our case but his testimony regarding a videotaped braking demonstration in an identical Crown Victoria. To simulate a sudden acceleration from a standstill, Declercq pushed the gas pedal to the floor with his right foot, waited about two seconds, and brought the car to a stop with the brakes in less than half the distance the Manigaults' car travelled before crashing. Although Declercq never mentioned how much force he applied to the brake pedal, he told the jury that *15 to 20 pounds of force* would have stopped the Manigaults' car. The jurors' expressions left no doubt they were impressed.

Moreover, it now struck me that we had been so preoccupied with Ford's electronics that I had not paid much attention to why the brakes had not stopped our clients' car.

Bob Zelvy must have been thinking the same thing because he whispered in my ear "I think we're in big trouble, Chief. What do you suggest we do?"

"I'll tell you at the next recess," I whispered back with a confidence that was rapidly evaporating.

At the recess, I reminded Zelvy that Updegrove's testimony showed that even Secret Service agents "had been unable to stop their cars with the brakes."

Zelvy wanted more. "Assuming the court reporters show up, how do you know the judge will let us read the deposition to the jury?"

"He may not, Zel," I conceded, "but that doesn't mean I can't confront Declercq with the fact hundreds of people, including these Secret Service agents, couldn't control their cars by braking."

Zelvy sounded skeptical. "Suppose Declercq says he doesn't know squat about the Updegrove investigation; what then?"

"Aren't you forgetting that we learned from Potter that both Declercq and Updegrove testified in his case? You can bet they spent a lot of time together, and were thoroughly coached to be sure they stayed on the same page. If Declercq pleads ignorance, we'll cry cover-up."

My optimism, in fact, was unrealistic. If Declercq was aware of what I had learned over the previous weekend, Ford could hardly rely on him to support its defense, a hunch that proved accurate:

**Q:** Do you know the results of [Updegrove's] investigation?

**A:** As a generalization.

**Q:** Did you discuss the results of his investigation with him?
**A:** No sir. I met with Mr. Updegrove one time and I've talked to him for perhaps two or three hours at the most, and this was not one of the things that we really talked about.

***

Declercq's acknowledgement that he knew about the Updegrove investigation "as a generalization," suggested a carefully coached witness. On the one hand, if I asked what he knew "as a generalization," I sensed he was primed to say Ford had found no evidence of a defect in its cruise control system. On the other hand, if I pressed the point further, he could politely suggest that I should question Updegrove. Rather than risk further damage to our case, I decided to lay a foundation for Updegrove's anticipated testimony:

**Q:** Well, Mr. Declercq, let's get right down to it. Do you know how many claims of sudden acceleration were being reported to Ford in that time period that involved exactly this complaint; that is, the driver got in the car, turned on the ignition, and the car took off at a sudden, rapid rate, identical to what Mrs. Manigault testified happened on April 3, 1993. Do you know?
**Mr. Smith:** Objection.
**The Court:** Overruled.
**Q:** Can you answer that question, sir?
**A:** I don't know that. I don't know the number at all. I couldn't even give you a ballpark number.

***

While my question was based on Ohio law governing notice to a manufacturer of a possible defect, we could only expose the falsity of portraying our case as an isolated and aberrational occurrence if the court allowed us to present Updegrove's testimony to the jury.

Since the court reporters were scheduled to appear the next day, I spent a restless night fretting over how Judge Matia would rule.

CHAPTER 17

# COUP DE GRÂCE

### TOYOTAS, DEATHS AND SUDDEN ACCELERATION

> As was routine, Ethyl Marlene Foster, 67, was picked up at her home by a friend for church. The two noticed that the car's gears stuck when the driver shifted from park into reverse. But it wasn't until the shift to drive that the car accelerated uncontrollably, plowing into a mobile home nearby . . . . The Camry crashed into the doublewide mobile home with such impact that it moved the structure a foot . . .
>
> . . . The accident injured the driver, and killed Foster, who was crushed by the impact.
>
> *Los Angeles Times*, February 28, 2010

**WHEN JUDGE MATIA ASKED IF PLAINTIFFS HAD REBUTTAL EVIDENCE,** I called the two court reporters to authenticate Updegrove's deposition taken on separate dates. To be admissible, rebuttal must specifically address opposing testimony or evidence. However, because Updegrove's deposition ran to 400 pages with dozens of attached exhibits, Judge Matia was faced with deciding a page at a time what was and was not proper rebuttal. This would have taken at least a full day while the jury was left to cool its heels. While I was tempted to suggest that the jury be sent home while we went over Updegrove's testimony, my instincts told me Ford would have a compelling argument on appeal that it had been prejudiced by the last-minute identification of a witness we could have deposed ourselves. Truth be told, the thought of defending against that argument caused a knot in my stomach.

On the other hand, I felt our position would be much different if we were appealing a verdict in Ford's favor, in which case I could accurately portray Updegrove's deposition as an attempt to protect the Manigaults against the court's erroneous exclusion of a government notice we had counted on to show Ford knew about a dangerous safety defect. Hence, I bit my tongue as the judge, without reading the now authenticated depositions, ruled that we could not present them to the jury. With that, we adjourned until final arguments the following morning.

It is the conventional wisdom of trial lawyers that by final arguments most jurors have probably made up their minds regarding who has the better case. If so, the way things had gone didn't bode well for the Manigaults, whose case would be decided by a jury that knew nothing about hundreds of virtually identical occurrences and that was being asked to reject the defense of an American icon based on the testimony of a lone electrical engineer, Sam Sero, who worked out of the basement of his home in Pittsburgh. After I did my best to appeal to the jury's common sense, Wright delivered the *coup de grâce*:

> The only evidence we have here is that this cruise control was in tens of millions of vehicles made by Ford alone . . . .
>
> And *this defect*, this occurrence that they are claiming happened once, maybe twice, even if you want to talk about their church incident, in a car with 113,000 miles, and not in any of these other hundreds of millions of vehicles, through billions of miles, doesn't meet the risk/benefit test . . . .
>
> So what do the plaintiffs come back to? They come back and ask you to tell us that we should have warned the Manigaults that this could happen. There is nothing to warn about. *It was a purely theoretical possibility. It had never happened. Ford had no duty to warn.* So what's the last fallback position? We should have told Mullinax how to look for it? You can't tell Mullinax to look for something that *doesn't happen in the real world* . . . . No evidence that this has ever happened in any other vehicle at any time. No evidence it happened here. No explanation for how this accident happened. [Emphasis added.]

With Updegrove's testimony excluded, Wright's declaration that "there was nothing to warn about," was devastating.

The jury took just three hours to find for Ford, with one of the eight jurors dissenting. As I walked to the elevators, I encountered one of the jurors who had voted against us and, after thanking him for his service, I asked, "Would it have made any difference if the jury had known there had been hundreds of sudden accelerations identical to this one?"

"Are you kidding?" he said, looking stunned.

"No," I answered. "And that is why I am confident we'll eventually get a new trial."

Still appearing surprised, our juror said simply, "I hope you do. Good luck!"

Zelvy and I went immediately to the Manigaults' home with the bad news. While Virginia, John, Jackie, and Evelyn Manigault sat around the bed in which Leon Manigault lay blessedly unaware, I explained what had happened, and promised we would do everything possible to win them a new trial. These simple, honest people listened with an air of dignified resignation. When I finished, Virginia Manigault spoke for the family.

"Mr. Murray, we have faith in you and Mr. Zelvy. We know God sent you to us, and we know He won't let us down."

I was moved to tears, and responded simply, "Thank you. We needed to hear that."

CHAPTER 18

# THE WORM TURNS

### 100 TOYOTA DRIVERS FILED COMPLAINTS BEFORE RECALL

Early one morning as she headed to work in her new Toyota Camry, Mary Pries-Morrison sped up a little to pass a white pick-up . . . . Pries-Morrison's Camry, which had about 6,000 miles on it, kept accelerating after she passed the truck and took her foot off the gas pedal. The car barely slowed down when she pressed the brake. "I could get it down to 60 mph, but that's it. The car wanted to go 80, or higher." . . . By the time she got the car stopped miles later—with the coaching of a 9-1-1 operator, she managed to turn the car off—smoke was filling the car. Her brakes were smoldering, and the tires had started to melt near the wheel rims.

*USA Today*, January 27, 2010

**LOSING A CASE IS PAINFUL ENOUGH TO DRIVE SOME LAWYERS** from trial work. The late Edward Bennett Williams, a celebrated Washington, D.C. trial lawyer, was so devastated by losing a big case it took him ten years to recover and start trying cases again. Lawyers who sue manufacturers for product liability must be willing to endure the agony of defeat, or give up these kinds of cases. For decades big business and insurance companies have been attacking plaintiffs' lawyers as predators who would drive up the cost of products and insurance rates, a campaign that has created a climate in which even the most meritorious cases are as likely as not to fail. One reason runaway cars have been destroying hundreds of lives every year, in fact, is that the ranks of lawyers willing to take on a car company have been decimated by these relentless attacks on trial lawyers.

Although I was vaguely aware of the difficulties product liability lawyers face, such cases until now had been a small part of my practice. As a result, I had approached the *Manigault* case with a naïveté that I was determined to correct. After Judge Matia overruled our motion for a new trial, we appealed the verdict to Ohio's Eighth Appellate District, accompanied by a motion to send the case back to the trial court pursuant to Ohio law, under which a losing party has a right to "relief from judgment" if, among other reasons, the verdict was a result of "fraud, misrepresentation or misconduct of an adverse party." Our motion was granted, and the case was sent back to the trial court to decide if the Manigaults had been defrauded of a fair trial. Then, in a surprise turn of events, the case was reassigned to Anthony Calabrese, the original judge. In the meantime, Molly and Jo Ellen pored over the materials Potter had given us. When Judge Calabrese scheduled a hearing to determine if the Manigaults had been cheated of a fair trial, we were ready.

We began by calling several people identified in Updegrove's testimony in Chris Brinkley's case. One was Virginia State Trooper

Ronald Campbell, who was so incensed by two occurrences in his 1991 Mercury Grand Marquis, that he agreed to drive to Ohio to testify. On September 8, 1991, Campbell, who at the time was a special agent with the Virginia State Police Bureau of Criminal Investigation, entered the Grand Marquis with the intention of moving it to a shady area on his property about 100 feet away. With the car standing on a slight incline, his intention was to let it "creep" at idle speed to the shaded area. But when he shifted to drive, with his foot "hovering above the brake pedal," the Grand Marquis "sharply accelerated as if it had been floor-boarded to wide open, and I was suddenly headed directly toward the trees a short distance away." Thinking his wife might have "placed something under the seat and it had rolled up against the accelerator," Campbell "glanced down quickly to see if anything was interfering either with the accelerator or the braking action," but saw nothing. As he continued to push on the brake pedal, he "immediately cut the vehicle to the left in the direction of an open gate to a pasture area. But the power to the rear wheels and the force of the turn" made the car "go into a slide and I began to lose control." When he "attempted to steer between a utility pole and the guy wire to the gate area, the car began to slide broadside . . . and the front bumper guard struck the utility pole as I slid past it and the vehicle continued on around with the front end turned opposite the utility pole."

As the car headed toward a propane tank, Campbell recalled thinking, "I'm going to die right here in my backyard. Fortunately, the good Lord just gave me enough sense to put the car in 'park,' and when I did that, it rocked back and forth and continued to run wide open."

Campbell's description of what happened next would be echoed by many people in the years ahead. "I cut the engine off, and continued to sit there for a little while. It scared me so badly that I was weak. I got out, checked again to make sure that there couldn't have been something in the interior of the vehicle that could have caused this problem, but I did not see anything, so I opened the hood. Although I'm not a mechanic, I know enough about the air filter and things like that, so I removed the air filter to see if there might have been something that could have mechanically obstructed the throttle, but I didn't see anything. I went in the house and told my wife what had happened, and contacted my father-in-law, who has some mechanical experience. He came over."

Campbell remembered restarting the car, while "never removing my hand from the ignition switch so that I could turn it off if I needed to, and pulled the car back around into the driveway. Then I went up and down the driveway several times trying to duplicate what had happened."

**Mr. Murray:** Did you duplicate the incident?

**The Witness:** No, I did not.

**The Court:** What does that mean, you didn't duplicate the incident? Do you mean the experience that you just described did not happen again?

**The Witness:** Yes, sir. I was trying to see if the vehicle would accelerate again unexpectedly.

**The Court:** It did not?

**The Witness:** No, sir, it did not.

***

We see here one reason these occurrences have long mystified people outside the auto industry. With rare exceptions, turning off the engine clears the fault, making attempts to replicate the malfunction futile. On the other hand, there were thousands of occurrences like the one described by Trooper Campbell that it should have made it obvious to NHTSA that drivers were not the problem. What happened next has also happened to many owners across the industry.

When their Grand Marquis was inspected by their dealer, the Campbells were told there was nothing wrong with the car. "I told them I respected their opinion, but due to the seriousness of the matter, I felt the vehicle was unsafe for my family and asked that it be checked out by somebody like an engineer from Ford, and they made arrangements for that to take place."

**Q:** Describe what happened.

**A:** [I] met a service engineer for the Ford Motor Company. It was my understanding that it was his job to investigate incidents like this. He questioned me in great detail and filled out a form several pages long. I was ushered into the dealership owner's office. We went over again and again what had taken place. I was asked to demonstrate how I normally started the vehicle, which I did, and then at a later point I was asked actually to go out with them observing me drive the vehicle, which I did.

When Campbell asked that Ford "replace anything that could cause this problem . . . as reassurance to me, my wife, and infant daughter who would ride in that car, they told me that it would be unlikely because Ford would be admitting liability . . . ; and I said, well, I'm not after who's liable, I just want to have the assurance that our vehicle is safe for our family and other people on the highway."

***

What happened next recalled the Manigaults' experience. On the morning of July 29, 1992, Campbell's wife left the house to take the Grand Marquis on an errand but, a short time later, "she suddenly came back in upset."

**Ms. Wright:** Objection to anything his wife said, your Honor.

**The Court:** Yes.

**Ms. Wright:** It's hearsay.

**The Court:** Sustained as to what she said.

**Q:** Now, Mr. Campbell, just tell us what you observed plus anything that you personally related to Ford Motor Company and what they told you.

**A:** I observed the car sitting at an angle in our driveway. The gravel behind the left wheel and the right wheel were disturbed by spinning marks. On the left side there was a six-foot spin mark. On the right side there was a two-foot spin mark . . . . [A]s a result, I contacted the Ford dealership . . . [and] . . . the vehicle was examined again. We would not drive the vehicle. It was left in the driveway, and we told them we refused to operate that vehicle any more.

**Q:** What did you tell [Ford's representative]?

**A:** We explained the situation . . . about unexpected acceleration again. He tested it, and I believe the term that he used was a star test on the vehicle. Again, no codes were found on it . . . . We had asked Ford to replace the parts on several occasions that could have caused it. When they would not do that, we asked that they replace the vehicle. I had an attorney write a letter to Ford on our behalf notifying them we felt the vehicle was unsafe . . . .

***

Like the Manigaults, the Campbells were told their car was safe to drive. But they were luckier than the Manigaults because the second occurrence happened in an area where Mrs. Campbell had time to disengage the engine before the car crashed into something.

Wright's cross-examination of Campbell was a caricature of the approach the car industry had used for decades:

**Q:** When Ford Motor Company looked at this vehicle, they told you they checked the cruise control, didn't they?

**A:** Yes, ma'am.

**Q:** And they told you there was nothing with the cruise control, correct?

**A:** That's correct.

**Q:** They never told you they found a nicked wire, did they?

**A:** No, ma'am.

**Q:** They never told you it was a bent wire?

**A:** No, ma'am.

**Q:** They never told you they found a short in the harness of the cruise control, did they?

**A:** No short.

**Q:** And they checked your brakes and they said those were operating correctly, didn't they?

**A:** Yes, ma'am.

**Q:** And when your friend at the dealership, Ernie Tanner, whoever he had look at it, he never told you it was a cruise control problem, did he?

**A:** No, ma'am.

**Q:** And he never told you it was a brake problem, did he?

**A:** No, ma'am.

**Q:** But when you expressed dissatisfaction to the Ford Motor Company and they looked at your vehicle a number of times and were unable to remedy the problem that you believed you were having, they replaced your vehicle, didn't they?

**A:** Yes, ma'am.

***

We also presented Judge Calabrese with a compendium of data covering 370 occurrences, resulting in 150 collisions, 76 of which had caused serious injury or death. In one case, for instance, a 1986 Crown Victoria driven by a police officer suddenly accelerated immediately following gear engagement and traveled nearly 100 feet before striking a building, injuring the officer.

Most damaging to Ford, perhaps, was its response to a letter from a Dr. Richard Swartzman to Phil Benton, Ford's president at the time. Dr. Swartzman described two sudden accelerations in his Lincoln, and asked Ford's president whether the company had received reports of similar incidents. Although Ford knew about hundreds of similar occurrences, it told Dr. Swartzman:

Currently we are not aware of the problem you have described occurring in other vehicles.

Ford called Declercq, who essentially repeated his trial testimony. Although eight months had passed since the trial, he had done nothing to learn about the results of the Updegrove investigation. Judge Calabrese was incredulous:

> **The Court:** Did you ever follow up to try to find out the results of the Updegrove . . . investigation?
>
> **Declercq:** No, I did not—at the time, and even . . . at the time of the *Manigault* trial. I did not follow up on the . . . investigation for the results.

***

While we were confident we had proved that the Manigaults were entitled to a new trial, Judge Calabrese's blistering ruling exceeded our expectations:

> It was fraudulent and unconscionable for Ford to represent to the jury that there is no evidence that a cruise control malfunction had ever caused a sudden acceleration event in millions and millions of cars equipped with this cruise control, in light of the fact that hundreds, and perhaps thousands, of similar incidents were occurring each month during the four-year period prior to the Manigaults' accident.

> It is clear from the exhibits discussed herein that, in fact, there have been injuries and fatalities under circumstances clearly demonstrating the possibility of a cruise control malfunction . . . .
>
> If as appears to be the case, Ford is intentionally engaged in a course of conduct *intended to conceal this fact from the United States government and from the courts,* it seems certain that further death and injury is likely to occur unless and until the truth about the cause of sudden acceleration events becomes public knowledge. [Emphasis added.]

The Court concluded there were "substantial grounds for granting plaintiffs both relief from judgment and the immediate right to conduct further discovery regarding the issues raised by the plaintiffs' motion."

The finding that Ford had been *concealing the truth from the United States government and the courts* had enormous implications. If that was true of Ford, it was probably also true of the entire industry. However, it wasn't clear whether NHTSA had been defrauded or had collaborated with the industry in a cover-up. In fact, the more evidence we uncovered, the more plausible the latter possibility became. But that again lay in the future. Our immediate concern was how to take advantage of Judge Calabrese's ruling. In addition to a new trial, the Manigaults had been granted the right to pursue discovery bearing on the issues of fraud and concealment.

But, as expected, Ford appealed Judge Calabrese's ruling, thus suspending further formal discovery pending completion of the appellate process. We could still pursue "extralegal" discovery, of course, which is exactly what we did.

CHAPTER 19

# A VISIT TO THE CENTER FOR AUTO SAFETY

### CONSUMERS CONFOUNDED BY SUDDEN ACCELERATION PROBLEMS

The victims of sudden acceleration all tell a similar tale. "I got into my car and turned on the ignition. I put the car in reverse. The car rocketed backward into a telephone pole." . . . Terri Moore from Seattle is one of the most recent. "I am yet another victim of sudden acceleration," she writes. "My Saturn Vue was parked in a parking lot. I entered the car, turned on the ignition and put the car in reverse. The car rocketed backward and hit a pole." After Terri's Saturn slammed into the telephone pole behind her, she said that she "put the car in drive to inch away from the pole I was wrapped around and the car rocketed forward, out of control . . . ."

*Consumer Affairs,* August 22, 2005

**IT WAS MOLLY WHO SUGGESTED A MEETING WITH CLARENCE DITLOW,** the Director of the Center for Auto Safety, a branch of Public Citizen founded by Ralph Nader. She thought Ditlow would know a great deal about the history of sudden acceleration, and she was right. Seated in a conference room in the Center's offices near Georgetown, Ditlow explained that Congress had created the National Highway Traffic Safety Administration in response to public concern over increasing traffic casualties during the 1960s. Highway safety advocates until then had focused mainly on preventing crashes by trying to change the behavior of "the nut behind the wheel." The focus changed from crash avoidance to crash survival after William Hayden, Jr., M.D., showed how public health principles could help identify a complete range of options for reducing crash injuries and other losses. Ralph Nader drew public attention to the lack of priority given to the safety of vehicle design with his 1965 best-selling book, *Unsafe at Any Speed: The Designed-In Dangers of the American Automobile.* When some states began issuing their own auto safety regulations in the early 1960s, the car industry decided that it preferred uniform national standards to a patchwork of state regulations. Congress responded with two laws bringing the federal government more directly into the traffic safety area: the National Traffic and Motor Vehicle Safety Act of 1966 and the Highway Safety Act of 1966.

President Lyndon Johnson appointed Dr. Hayden as the first Federal Traffic Safety chief. The 1966 National Highway Traffic Safety Act required the National Highway Safety Bureau—the predecessor of NHTSA—to develop vehicle safety standards that were initially based primarily upon those of the Society of Automotive Engineers. In 1967, the General Services Administration applied these standards to federal government vehicle purchases, and, in 1970, Congress took the agency out from under the Federal Highway Administration and renamed it the National Highway Traffic Safety Administration, or NHTSA.

There were numerous recalls prior to 1980 that were sometimes misleadingly associated with sudden accelerations. These usually involved defects detectable by inspection, such as an improperly installed throttle control spring, a kink in the accelerator cable causing throttles to become stuck open, and cracks in the soldered terminals for the cruise control computer caused by improper application of coding to the printed circuit board. Such problems differed in kind from a classic sudden acceleration: they were readily detectible by inspection, easily repaired at relatively low cost to the manufacturer, usually involved a particular model, and, rather than causing a sudden, rapid increase in speed, they usually interfered mechanically with the throttle closing when the driver's foot was removed from the gas pedal.

Ditlow explained that Joan Claybrook, who led NHTSA during the Carter administration, had been particularly effective in making car companies recall and repair safety defects. "Unfortunately, sudden accelerations surfaced shortly after Joan left NHTSA and came to Public Citizen."

"How would you grade NHTSA's handling of the sudden acceleration problem?" I asked.

"If the grading is based on results, NHTSA deserves an 'F.' However, there were some mitigating factors."

"Such as?" Molly inquired.

"For one thing, sudden acceleration hit the scene at the same time Ronald Reagan made deregulation a government policy. One of the first things he did, in fact, was cut NHTSA's budget almost in half. Unfortunately, after Joan Claybrook, administrators under both Democratic and Republican Presidents were less willing to vigorously pursue vehicle safety improvements."

“Do you believe the car industry is covering up the cause?” I wanted to know.

Ditlow didn’t hesitate. “Yes. And that will continue as long as NHTSA rolls over for the industry.”

“How has the industry been able to convince NHTSA there’s no need for a recall?”

“As I said, sudden acceleration came along during the early stages of the electronic revolution in automotives. Until then, NHTSA had been doing a decent job making manufacturers correct mechanical defects. But, the things that can go wrong in electronics are completely different from mechanical things that can usually be found during an inspection.”

“Are you saying,” I asked, “that automotive electronics caught NHTSA with its bureaucratic pants down?”

“It wasn’t that simple,” replied Ditlow. “Everybody knew that electronics presented new kinds of safety issues. What NHTSA should have done was hire electrical engineers in its Office of Defects Investigation. But that would have required an increase in its budget, so it never happened.”

Molly was incredulous. “Do you mean there are no electrical engineers at NHTSA?”

“Unfortunately, yes,” answered Ditlow.

“Do you know why Ford was one of the last companies to be investigated by NHTSA?” Molly asked.

“Yes. Car making is a notoriously copycat business, so all the companies came to market with pretty much the same electronics. Ford was just a little slower than some of its competitors.”

Recalling the many newspaper and magazine articles Zelvy had given me, I asked Ditlow if he knew whether there had ever been sudden acceleration reports prior to the introduction of electronic cruise control.

"I'm not aware of any, so that was one clue NHTSA should certainly have picked up on. There was also a pattern in these reports it either missed or deliberately ignored. In Ford's case, for example, there weren't many reports until about 1984, when they suddenly skyrocketed as if a mysterious disease had suddenly struck Ford models, causing an epidemic of uncontrollable accelerations. People were saying their car was possessed, or that it acted as if it had a mind of its own."

"Any ideas about why reports involving Ford suddenly shot up like that?" interjected Molly.

Ditlow, who has both engineering and law degrees, had obviously thought about the matter. "It wasn't just Ford that had sudden accelerations go through the roof. All the car companies were adding electronics as fast as they could during the early eighties. My guess is that all this new electronics was the reason for that pattern. I would make Ford tell you what changes in their electronics were going on during that period."

Looking at his watch, Ditlow indicated that he needed to leave for a board meeting.

"Before you leave, would you take a quick look at this ruling we obtained in our *Manigault* case?" I handed Ditlow a copy of Judge Calabrese's ruling, which I could see captured his interest. When he finished reading, he asked if the decision had received "much media coverage." When I told him there had been a short article in the Cleveland *Plain Dealer*, he responded, "This really deserves national coverage."

"What do you suggest?" I asked.

"I know a producer for NBC's *Dateline* program named Steve Eckert, who helped produce a story about sudden accelerations in the Audi 5000s for *60 Minutes*. That's what first made the public aware of runaway cars. There were all kinds of media stories back then, but after NHTSA published its 1989 report interest died out. Steve has convinced the powers at NBC that it's time to re-examine sudden accelerations. Would you be willing to talk to him about your case?"

"Sure," I replied. "If what Ford did to the Manigaults is any indication of how the car companies are treating people, I'd love to help expose the truth. So what's next?"

"I'll send Steve a copy of the *Manigault* decision and suggest that he give you a call."

CHAPTER 20

# NBC *DATELINE*: AN HOUR OF SURPRISES

### LOUISVILLE MAN CRASHES IN RECALLED CAMRY

A Louisville man remained hospitalized in intensive care Sunday after crashing his 2010 Toyota Camry—and the model he was driving is among those included in Toyota's most recent recall. Paula Allen says her husband, Todd, was pulling into a parking spot off Blue Lick and Preston in Okolona Saturday night when suddenly, for no reason at all, the car took off at a high speed. Paul says her husband tried to brake with both feet, but the car wouldn't stop.

*WAVE3 TV*, Louisville, KY, Jan. 31, 2010

**WHEN STEVE ECKERT AND HIS PRODUCTION TEAM ARRIVED AT OUR** office, I asked Molly and Jo Ellen to take them through the copious materials in our files. When I tuned into *Dateline* on February 10,

1999, I was surprised that the entire hour was devoted to Eckert's production, which began with the moderator, Stone Phillips, offering a historical perspective:

> There are new questions about a mystery that has plagued drivers and automakers for years—runaway cars that seem to take off on their own. "Sudden acceleration" first grabbed headlines in the '80s. The federal government investigated a variety of mechanical and electrical causes, but came to the conclusion that the most likely explanation was human error—drivers mistakenly hitting the gas instead of the brake.
>
> Now there's a new theory about what can cause sudden acceleration, and a judge's blistering criticism of one carmaker may force another look at an issue that hasn't gone away, and at accidents that have not been forgotten.

*Dateline* turned next to a disaster at the church picnic in Nokomis, Illinois, after a woman entered a Ford Aerostar to run an errand.

**A Witness:** I just looked up and heard this engine roar.

**Another Witness:** It just had this screaming noise to it, like it was going out of control.

Witnesses had watched in horror as the Aerostar plowed through a concrete bench, several picnic tables, and headed straight for a Sunday school teacher and mother of ten sitting next to a stroller.

"The front of the van crashed and killed the baby and the teacher," Phillips said, before adding that, "There was something about the accident . . . no one could understand. The woman driving the van said, under oath, 'her foot was on the brake—not the accelerator.' And there were four witnesses who confirmed it."

**Witness:** She had to have her foot on the brake, I saw brake lights.

**Mr. Phillips:** When investigators from Ford and the federal government examined the van, they *couldn't find any defects*. So, in spite of the brake-light witnesses, Ford concluded the driver must have made a tragic mistake—slamming the accelerator to the floor—instead of the brake, and a jury agreed.

It echoed the findings of a 1989 government report. Experts reviewed thousands of accidents involving all kinds of cars—not just Fords. Their conclusion: "pedal misapplication" by the driver was the most likely cause—that it was "virtually impossible" for electrical failures to cause sudden acceleration.

And that seemed to close the book on sudden acceleration. For years, car companies pointed to the government report, and won nearly every lawsuit against them, but lately there have been a few bumps on the road to blaming drivers.

***

NHTSA had apparently told *Dateline* that "experts had reviewed thousands of accidents involving all kinds of cars," a claim we learned later was false.

When the story turned to the *Manigault* case, it was apparent the production team had carefully reviewed our files.

**Mr. Phillips:** After the Reverend Leon Manigault led a Pentecostal church service in Cleveland, his family says his car suddenly sped out of the church parking lot. "My father said the car just shot off," says John Manigault, the reverend's son. He says his father's foot had to be on the brake because he chased the car down the street, watching the brake lights flash, until his father turned the key and killed the engine. Repair records show that the family complained to a local dealer that the car "accelerated by itself." And a few months later, they say it happened again with tragic consequences. Today, the Reverend Manigault is in a coma, after the same Ford Crown Victoria roared out of his driveway and into the back of a house. He suffered massive head injuries. His family sued Ford in a case that challenges the carmaker's claim that drivers are to blame.

***

The narrative now turned to Sam Sero who, viewers were told, had "developed a new theory" that the cruise control can cause some cars to take off without anyone hitting the gas.

**Mr. Phillips:** For years, investigators didn't think cruise controls could be much of a factor in sudden acceleration, in part, because they thought the system didn't get any power until you got up to speed and turned it on. But when Sero investigated, he found that in tens of millions of Ford-built cars and trucks, in some, but not all, models, from the mid-\`80s up until 1995, the cruise control is getting power *as soon as you turn on the engine,* even if you've never touched the cruise control button. [Emphasis added.]

***

Had NHTSA with all its resources missed a critical design feature that made runaway car disasters possible? The surprising answer came from Michael Brownlee, who until 1997 had served as the Director of the agency's Office of Defects Investigations:

**Mr. Phillips:** Although Ford says it was no secret, and should have been clear from the information it gave the government, Brownlee says there is an important fact about Ford's old cruise control design that he didn't know.

**Mr. Phillips (to Mr. Brownlee):** Were you surprised to hear that the cruise control in millions of Fords was getting power, even if it's off?

**Mr. Brownlee:** Yes, that is a surprise to me. And I don't think I was aware of that ten years ago and I don't believe our investigators were either.

**Mr. Phillips:** And if the problems are caused by vibration and water, as Sero claims, could that explain why they might go undetected? Does that make any sense to you?

**Mr. Brownlee:** Well, certainly. Water is present in the environment of a vehicle. Under the hood and elsewhere. Vibration is a fact of life in vehicles.

**Mr. Phillips:** So that could explain why the evidence could be hard to find?

**Mr. Brownlee:** Sure. It heals itself. The water can go away, the water will evaporate.

**Mr. Phillips:** While Ford still maintains Sam Sero's theory requires a combination of failures that is virtually impossible, Brownlee's not so sure. Is this a theory that you looked into when you were investigating this?

**Mr. Brownlee:** This is a simpler way for it to fail than what was looked at by the government at the time. From a technical standpoint, certainly it's plausible. And that's based not only on Sam Sero's opinion, but other electrical engineers I've talked to about this.

**Mr. Phillips:** Brownlee is not endorsing the short-circuit theory. But after reviewing some of the records *Dateline* found, he says he has a lot more questions he'd like to ask Ford.

**Mr. Brownlee:** It makes you think that there is something more substantive to Sam Sero's theory than just theory.

***

Although Brownlee had left NHTSA several years earlier, I felt that it took courage to admit before a national audience that a lone electrical engineer had discovered a critically important design feature his agency had missed, and which helped to explain automotive behavior that had destroyed thousands of lives. And what about those running the agency at the time the *Dateline* story aired? With runaway cars still destroying hundreds of lives every year, did they have the integrity to admit the agency's past mistakes, and take the steps necessary to end this automotive carnage? We'll see in the pages ahead.

*Dateline*, of course, had heard a much different story from Ford.

> **Mr. Phillips:** What did Ford say about all this? In court, the company argued that the Manigault family had changed experts and changed theories. Before Sero, another expert [Orringer] had offered an entirely different explanation because he didn't find any problems with the Manigaults' cruise control. And the fact is, Sam Sero didn't either, because before he or Ford engineers could inspect the car, it disappeared from a storage lot.
>
> Ford declined a *Dateline* request for an on-camera interview, but in a letter to *Dateline*, the company told us essentially what it told the jury, that Sam Sero's test was a "contrived stunt" with a "doctored vehicle". His demonstration was "junk science". According to Ford, if *real failures* caused an accident, *it would leave evidence* for investigators to find. [Emphasis added.]

***

This was straight from the trial playbook Ford and its competitors were using to deny countless people compensation for often-terrible injuries. It was at this moment in the *Dateline* story that I was suddenly seized by the thought that the federal government might have accepted this simplistic explanation as a way of protecting the car industry from its deadly mistakes. If that was the case, neither the industry nor NHTSA could countenance having an electrical engineer working out of his basement expose their devious designs. Was that the reason Ford had used *Dateline* as a mouthpiece to discredit Sam Sero?

> **Mr. Phillips:** Ford says Sam Sero was paid to come up with a problem. And a Ford expert testified that, although Sero's explanation is theoretically possible, in the real world, that can't happen. It just doesn't happen. And Ford showed the jury a test of its own, demonstrating that, even if those short circuits sent the engine "wide open" . . . the *brakes will still stop a runaway car.* [Emphasis added.]

***

On the screen as Phillips spoke was the videotaped braking demonstration Ford had used to convince the *Manigault* jury that 15 to 20 pounds of braking force would have stopped the car, but with a shocking difference. To my astonishment, a voice on the video could be heard saying, "*175 pounds!*"

"I'll be damned!" I bellowed, startling my wife and two of our children who were watching with us.

"What's wrong, Dad?" asked our youngest son, Bill, alarmed by my outburst. I waved him off with a curt, "I'll tell you during the commercials."

At the next break, I explained that the same videotaped demonstration had been shown to the *Manigault* jury, during which the Ford witness said that 15–20 pounds, not 175 pounds, of braking force would have stopped the car.

"Will you be able to make Ford give you a copy of the videotape with sound?" Ann asked.

"That's what discovery is for," I replied.

"Does that mean the Manigaults will get a new trial?"

"It should. We already have a strong ruling by Judge Calabrese in our favor, and now we have a doctored videotape. If that isn't enough to win a new trial, I can't imagine what would be."

When *Dateline* turned to Judge Calabrese's ruling, what Eckert's team had learned from Updegrove's deposition was on parade:

> **Mr. Phillips:** The record shows Ford was getting so many complaints—as many as 100 a month—it had launched its own internal investigation.
>
> But the judge in Reverend Manigault's case never allowed the jury to hear about that. What the jury did hear was a Ford lawyer say Sam Sero's ideas were "purely theoretical," and had "never happened" in the real world.
>
> When the Reverend Manigault's lawyer told a different judge [Calabrese] that Ford knew about thousands of sudden acceleration incidents, including ones with trained drivers who swear they didn't hit the wrong pedal, the judge issued a blistering ruling, saying Ford had "perpetrated a fraud upon the court" and may have misled the government.

***

The staggering implications of this ruling were still sinking in at this point. More than a decade after the federal government had exonerated one of the most powerful industries on the planet, a respected judge had found its conclusion suspect. If NHTSA was complicit in a cover-up, the implications were almost too shocking to contemplate. Yet everything we were learning suggested that NHTSA was either grossly incompetent or in the hip pocket of the car industry. Either way, it was a national scandal that countless lives were being destroyed by runaway automobiles while the best-staffed car safety agency in the world sat on its hands. That was enough to stoke the passions of any trial lawyer, and, while I was almost 60, thoughts of retiring were put on hold.

CHAPTER 21

# BATTLE BEHIND THE SCREEN

## FIVE-STORY FALL KILLS FOUR IN CAR IN VIRGINIA BEACH

On a hot summer day in Virginia Beach, tourists of the Sandcastle Oceanfront Hotel were shocked to see a car smash through a three-foot-high cinderblock retaining wall and plunge 41 feet from the top floor of the parking garage onto the walkway below. Four pediatric nurses from New York City were killed from the fall. Miraculously, no one was injured on the street below, on which thousands of tourists were celebrating a local festival. Police were puzzled as to what caused the horrific accident. Their investigation revealed that there were no skid marks leading to the wall that the 1999 Honda Accord plowed through and that drugs and alcohol were not involved. Those that saw the accident said that the car drove up the ramp at a normal speed, turned to the left, and then appeared to go straight into the retaining wall. Witnesses

> stated that they heard the car's engine revving just before it crashed into the wall.
>
> *The Washington Post*, September 25, 2000

**WE SENSED FROM THE *DATELINE* STORY THAT THERE HAD BEEN** extensive written communications between Ford and NBC. I could not have imagined how extensive, however, until a feature article appeared in *Newsweek* magazine about the program entitled "Battle Behind the Screen," with the sub-title "The TV News Magazines and Car Companies Go to War over Safety Stories." The piece began:

> On February 10, eight million households tuned into *Dateline* NBC and a parade of wrenching, now familiar images. A toddler killed at a church picnic, a comatose preacher—and a possible safety flaw in a car. Stone Phillips described how a series of glitches may make certain Ford vehicles accelerate out of control. "The alleged defect is just a theory," Phillips said, "unproved in the real world." But for Ford, which spends billions burnishing its image for safety-minded car buyers, the segment was a PR nightmare. In the broadcast, Ford's defense—a strongly worded letter—seemed mild. Behind the scenes, Ford was waging war.

*Newsweek* left little doubt Eckert had been under relentless pressure from Ford. The story described how the man in charge of "Ford's legal public relations, Jim Cain, a former Lehman Brothers vice-president, had become involved in a massive game of fetch" during the run up to the story. According to *Newsweek*, "Eckert and his team would submit a list of technical questions, and Cain would consult Ford lawyers and engineers to craft a response." The story said Cain had outlined Ford's case in a series of letters to *Dateline* that characterized Sero's theory as "junk science that's never occurred in the real world," and described NHTSA's investigation as proving "most of these accidents happen when a driver mistakenly stomps on the gas." The article also said Cain had described the television story as "one of the most heavily qualified pieces of journalism I've ever seen."

When we eventually obtained copies of the Ford-NBC correspondence, we were surprised to find page after page of letters from Cain to Eckert containing vitriolic attacks on Sero, Judge Calabrese, and the author. Here is a sampling:

- In our conversations and my letters, I have exposed Sero's theories as pure sophistry . . . revealed Murray's misrepresentations, and presented you with substantial evidence that Ford's speed control systems *are not the cause* of sudden acceleration.
- Does *Dateline* acknowledge that Tom Murray, the Manigaults' lawyer, Sam Sero, and other parties have a vested financial interest in discrediting the findings of four governments and the Ford Motor Company with respect to the issue of sudden acceleration?
- You and Sero have both portrayed your ignorance (or willful disregard) of a very elementary principle: the difference between allegation and fact. It's not enough to swear that your foot was on the brake pedal, and point to 100 other people who swear their feet were on the brake pedal, to prove sudden acceleration is caused by a vehicle defect.
- Judge Calabrese said the fact that Ford has received reports of sudden acceleration was "sufficient to place Ford on notice that sudden acceleration events are occurring because of malfunctions in the cruise control system." Rubbish! Reports of sudden acceleration are *not proof* that the speed control system was at fault.

- Will *Dateline* assure Ford that it will not broadcast footage of Sero's contrived stunt without prominently disclosing to its viewers that he had *rewired the vehicle* and is involved in pending litigation against Ford?
- If you had any journalistic integrity whatever, you would have recognized that NHTSA's report supports everything I told you and pretty much shoots the Sero theory straight to hell.
- Any statements that suggest Sero's stunt proves a safety defect in the cruise control systems of Ford vehicles would be unwarranted and inaccurate.
- I suggest [Stone Phillips] remove from his rolodex the business card of Sam Sero, your key source for the recent "*Dateline* investigation" of sudden acceleration in Ford vehicles.
- When last we spoke, you said you were sure that we would have the opportunity to work together again. I certainly hope not.

It was apparent Cain had been completely in the dark about the results of the internal Ford studies we are about to examine. Let me end with a bit of Cain's purple pique about Sero, Calabrese, and Yours Truly on November 25, 1998:

> For *Dateline* to provide a "full and fair account" of sudden acceleration, you must make some determination as to "who's right and who's wrong" *before* you broadcast. If Sam Sero, Tom Murray, Judge Calabrese . . . or anyone else made statements that can be proven to be demonstrably false, incorrect, misleading or hearsay, it is your professional and moral obligation as journalists to disclose it, excise it from your story or drop the segment altogether to avoid creating unwarranted concern over sudden acceleration. [Emphasis original.]

Cain had asked "who's right and who's wrong" about the cause of sudden accelerations. As we continued to gather evidence from law firms that had unsuccessfully battled a car company, the possibility that the federal oversight agency aided and abetted thousands of "perfect torts" loomed ever larger. At this point, however, our main concern was how to probe further into what Ford knew about the source of the problem while the *Manigault* case was on appeal.

PART 2

# STALKING A KILLER

CHAPTER 22

# ANOTHER SHATTERED LIFE

> Reportedly, on 7-21-85, Mr. Pickett entered the vehicle with his stepson, Charles Robert Jacob Riley, and began backing the vehicle from near the garage toward the street. The vehicle allegedly accelerated backward, made two complete circles onto the street, and then proceeded across the street a third time and crashed into a large pecan tree located across the street. The vehicle owner allegedly suffered "intense physical and mental pain and extreme mental anguish." Reportedly, the vehicle passenger, the owner's stepson, was fatally injured. No unprivileged information concerning the degree of damage to the vehicle was found.
>
> *Ford's submission to NHTSA*, March 13, 1987

**ABOUT A WEEK AFTER JUDGE CALABRESE'S RULING, I RECEIVED** a call from a lawyer named Alan Konigsberg, a partner in the

Manhattan-based law firm handling the *Jarvis* case. "Would you be interested in serving as co-counsel?" he asked.

"Are you looking for someone to work with Phillip Morrell?"

"He's left the firm, so now it's my baby. Unfortunately, it's been on the docket for five years, and the federal court wants it tried immediately or it will be dismissed."

"Why the delay?"

"I don't know the whole story, but apparently there was some stonewalling by Ford and Morrell couldn't get it worked out with the court."

"Why do you think I can help?"

"Sam Sero says you got a great ruling in Cleveland that will help our case. I'll have Kathy Jarvis fly here from Arkansas where she now lives. You can also meet her parents, who live here in Manhattan. You'll like them."

Kathy Jarvis, her parents, and a family friend, a Catholic nun, Sister Carmella, were already assembled in a spacious conference room when I arrived. For the next hour, Kathy and her father, Paul Jarvis, took turns recounting what happened.

In early July 1991, Kathy, who had two Masters Degrees and was working at the time for the Manhattan-based Advocates for Children, purchased a new Aerostar to transport children under her supervision to their activities. The following weekend, she drove her parents and recently adopted 12-year-old son, Paul Michael, to a wooded area in the Catskills where she and her parents had adjoining summer cottages. After Sunday morning mass, Paul Jarvis drove to nearby Boiceville for groceries. On the way, he tried unsuccessfully to engage the cruise control. Annoyed, he read the cruise control instructions in the owner's manual before leaving Boiceville, but was still unable to get the system to engage. On his return, he stopped the Aerostar on the driveway leading to the cottages, retrieved a power saw from a tool shed, and began cutting back foliage overhanging the driveway. A short time later, Kathy decided to move the van to the parking area by the cottages as a courtesy to neighbors who shared the lightly graveled driveway.

Kathy Jarvis, who had an unblemished driving record, would later testify that she "got into the van . . . , closed the door, and put the seatbelt on." With her right foot resting "lightly on the brake pedal," she turned on the ignition. Suddenly the Aerostar "just took off—V-R-O-O-M!!—in the direction of three people walking along the driveway toward a neighboring cottage. She pushed on the brake pedal, first with her right foot, "as hard as I could," while "steering slightly to the right off the driveway to miss those people." When the van kept going, she started "pumping with both feet," glancing down momentarily "to make sure I had both feet on the brake pedal." With a large tree now looming at a fork in the driveway leading one way to the cottages and the other way along a winding stretch toward the highway, Kathy instinctively steered away from the cottages. As the van approached a deep ravine beyond a sharp right turn, Kathy sensed the van was going too fast to make the curve, so she steered hard left up a tree-filled embankment. She heard the Aerostar "brushing against saplings . . . . Whoosh! Whoosh! Whoosh! The next thing I knew, it was black."

Paul Jarvis was startled when the Aerostar "started off at an unusually fast speed for Kathy." As it raced past where he was standing, he observed Kathy "holding onto the steering wheel, very tight." He watched as the van veered away from the pedestrians, and then to the left at the fork, where he lost sight of it. Moments later, he heard it "rubbing the brush. Then there was a crash."

As it moved up the embankment, the Aerostar had toppled onto its roof about 320 feet from where it took off. When he got to the scene, Paul Jarvis called out repeatedly to his daughter trapped in the overturned van:

**Q:** Did Kathy say anything?

**A:** Yes, finally she answered me . . . . I kept hollering to her, "Kathy, are you all right?" And she finally said, "Yes, Pop, I'm all right" and then she started screaming and just got hysterical.

As she was pulled from the Aerostar, Paul remembered Kathy saying, "'Pop, there is something wrong with the car! The brakes don't work.' She repeated that over and over."

Kathy suffered a severe brain injury that changed her from a productive, well-organized person into someone for whom even the simplest everyday tasks like grocery shopping, paying her bills, or helping her son with his homework, were a struggle. She returned to work, but was unable to do the job. Single, and fearful of becoming a burden to her aging parents, she relocated with her son to Fort Smith, Arkansas, to be near friends she hoped would help her start a new life.

Kathy struck me as warm, big-hearted, and sincere. While it was painfully obvious she had difficulty organizing her thoughts, she had a clear recollection of important details, and I felt she would make a good witness.

Paul Jarvis came across as the salty retired ship captain he was. His description of having twice failed to engage the cruise control reminded me that Sam Sero had explained how something as simple as a loose ground connection for the control module could make the system inoperable; and with a loose connection, a fault on a wire controlling the servo could suddenly send the throttle wide open. Compared to the *Manigault* case, it seemed to add up to a better set of facts.

As the meeting was about to adjourn, Sister Carmella, a handsome woman with sparkling eyes and salt-and-pepper hair, spoke up. "Mr. Murray, I've known Kathy for many years. She is one of the most caring people you'll ever meet. I hope you'll find it in your heart to help her."

Although I was touched, there was something about the relationship between Kathy and Konigsberg that I found troubling. Therefore, I promised to let Konigsberg know my decision after I consulted my partners. After the others left, Konigsberg took me to a storage area where dozens of boxes marked "JARVIS v. FORD" were stacked several feet high. Konigsberg explained that Morrell and a paralegal had visited Ford's Sudden Acceleration Reading Room in Dearborn, where they had "bought the store."

"Did Morrell," I asked, "ever depose a Ford manager named Alan Updegrove?"

"Yes," replied Konigsberg. "After he left, I remember seeing a deposition of someone named Updegrove in one of these boxes."

I was in a quandary. Should I take the time to read the deposition and catch a later flight back to Ohio? I looked at my watch, and decided that if I didn't join the case, I could still obtain a copy of the deposition later. But something still bothered me.

"Alan," I said, "before I leave for LaGuardia, I need to know what's up between you and Kathy."

Konigsberg explained that Kathy was already upset by the delays in getting to trial when Morrell left and he took over the case. Since then they had never hit it off. Although he assured me I would be lead counsel, I sensed that his tense relationship with Kathy spelled trouble. After discussing the case with my partners, I wrote Konigsberg that we declined the offer to participate in the case.

Several weeks later, however, I received a call from Paul Jarvis. "Mr. Konigsberg asked the court to let him withdraw from the case. Would you reconsider your decision?"

Suddenly everything had changed. With discovery in *Manigault* on hold while the case was on appeal, the stash of documents in Konigsberg's office could be a godsend. I explained to Paul that I needed to discuss a few matters with Konigsberg, and promised to get back to him as soon as possible.

Konigsberg told me Ford had offered $250,000 to settle the case, but Kathy had rejected his recommendation that she accept it. Since his firm already had $100,000 invested in the case, and there were legal fees to consider, Kathy's position was understandable. To make matters worse for Konigsberg, Ford had withdrawn the settlement offer, putting him in the position of having to go to trial soon or having the case dismissed.

"If I take the case, will you assert a lien for your costs?"

"No," Konigsberg replied. "My firm will waive any claim for compensation and will not seek reimbursement for our preparation costs." It was an extraordinary example of putting his client's interests first, and I told him so. I never saw Alan Konigsberg again.

I invited an old friend, George Tompkins, to serve as co-counsel. George sent a courier to collect the *Jarvis* files, and a few days later Molly, George, and I began sorting through the documents in the boxes retrieved from Konigsberg's office. We had barely begun when George received a call from the assignment officer at the federal court where the *Jarvis* case was pending. When he handed me the receiver, I heard an impatient male voice brusquely telling me to be ready for trial immediately, or the case would be dismissed.

"But, sir," I stammered, "we just received the file, and . . . . "

"I understand your situation, Mr. Murray," the voice interrupted. "But this case has had nothing but problems and postponements, and the court wants it tried or dismissed."

"Can we have 30 days to get ready?" I pleaded.

"Not unless you agree to have the case tried by Magistrate Buchwald. Ford's counsel have given their approval, and I need your answer today."

"May I call you back in about an hour? I need to consult with our New York co-counsel."

"Fine. I'll await your call."

Federal court cases are frequently handled by Magistrate Judges, political appointees who aspire to a full judgeship on the federal bench, and who perform most functions judges do. All sides, however, must agree before a Magistrate can preside over a trial. And because a party can veto use of a Magistrate, someone known to favor a corporation is unlikely to be accepted by a plaintiff in a product liability case. Ford's quick consent, therefore, was cause for concern.

When I told George about the court's ultimatum, he immediately conferred with several of his partners. "Buchwald's husband is a corporate lawyer; she's a former prosecutor, and very bright. But the book on her here is that we better have a damn good product liability case or she could be trouble." (As it turned out, Naomi Buchwald would be nominated by President Clinton and confirmed by the Senate as a federal judge while the *Jarvis* trial was in progress.)

"Do we have a choice?" I asked. "I'd hate to try this case without photographing the scene and doing some tests with a similar Aerostar. And don't forget, we need a crack at Updegrove. I'm convinced Ford is hiding something, and is scared stiff someone will dig into what the investigation actually found."

"Being on standby over there," George moaned, "means you have to be ready to start your case on two days' notice whenever there is an opening on the court's schedule. That could spell disaster for us."

Ten minutes later, I called the assignment officer. "We'll consent to Magistrate Buchwald on the condition we will be given time to prepare the case."

"Magistrate Buchwald will want to have a pretrial conference to become acquainted with the case. I'm sure she will be understanding of your position."

As it happened, the first hearing with Buchwald was not until several months later, which gave us time to develop a strategy. Although the court had closed further discovery, we felt Judge Calabrese's ruling was grounds for amending the order. Our first priority was to depose Alan Updegrove. However, since Philip Morrell had already done so, we needed a justification for a second deposition. When I read the deposition Morrell had taken, I knew we had the reason.

CHAPTER 23

# OBSTRUCTING JUSTICE

According to a police report, the wife of the vehicle owner entered the vehicle which was parked in a drug store parking lot and was attempting to back up when the vehicle allegedly "went out of control." According to the operator, she could not "slow it or stop same and the vehicle was erratically driving at a high rate of speed backwards." The subject vehicle struck vehicle #2 damaging the bumper and then impacted vehicle #3 damaging its bumper. The subject vehicle continued, striking vehicle #4 and pushing it into vehicle #5. Vehicle #4 was significantly damaged in the left side, and vehicle #5 experienced minor front end damage. The subject vehicle then struck the front of vehicle #6. All vehicles struck by the subject vehicle were unoccupied.

*Ford's submission to NHTSA*, March 13, 1987

**ALTHOUGH UPDEGROVE HAD TESTIFIED IN JACK POTTER'S *PIEROTTI*** case, Potter's files did not include either a transcript of the testimony or the investigative report. And while Chris Brinkley and his partner had questioned Updegrove extensively, they had focused heavily on the idle electronics, and their materials also did not include anything about the report. Consequently, I was intensely curious whether Phillip Morrell had pursued the matter of the report with Updegrove.

Morrell had deposed Updegrove on March 12, 1996, at the Manhattan offices of Ford's trial counsel, Howard Wexler. When Morrell asked Updegrove about a report, however, he immediately met resistance from Wexler:

> **Q:** Did your unit ever prepare any memoranda or other documents to other units of Ford . . . ?
>
> **A:** At the request of Ford's general counsel, I prepared a report.
>
> **Q:** What type of report did you prepare?
>
> **A:** Simply a memo that outlined all we had done and our findings, and it was done at the request of Mr. Robert Donnellan, Ford's general counsel.
>
> **Q:** When was it done?
>
> **Mr. Wexler:** For the sake of the transcript, that document is identified and I am now going to interpose an objection regarding the information. The information was prepared for the purposes of ongoing litigation for attorneys in assisting in litigation.

***

If Ford's general counsel, Donnellan, had requested a memorandum to assist the company's trial lawyers in litigation, it would be a privileged communication beyond the reach of discovery. It suddenly struck me, however, that if the results of this massive investigation supported Ford's position, there would be no reason for objecting to a memorandum summarizing those findings. Moreover, we knew from Chris Brinkley's case that events in litigation were *specifically excluded* from the investigation. Wexler's privilege objection was so brazenly false, in fact, I suspected he had been misled by Ford's General Counsel. To his credit, Morrell kept his cool.

> **Mr. Morrell:** Have you seen the document? I will explain to you my problem, Mr. Wexler. This document has never been revealed to us nor has it been listed as a privileged document.
>
> **Mr. Wexler:** I don't understand what your request is. He is stating it. You asked at this deposition a couple of questions ago, did this group prepare any reports and he indicated to you that he had personally prepared a document for the Office of General Counsel at the request of Robert Donnellan. I can state to you that Mr. Donnellan is an attorney.
>
> **Mr. Morrell:** I understand.
>
> **Mr. Wexler:** He works in the Office of General Counsel, which is the group of attorneys at Ford Motor Company.
>
> **Mr. Morrell:** I have met Mr. Donnellan. I understand what you're saying . . . . I am trying in general terms, without revealing any privileged information, to determine if a privilege does exist and what the document is, so that if we wish to make an application to the court, it can be made in a reasonable and proper fashion. That is all I'm doing, and that is not waiving any privilege.
>
> **Mr. Wexler:** I am stating to you on the record of this transcript that the document was prepared with respect to ongoing litigation to assist the Office of General Counsel in dealing with lawsuits then pending at Ford Motor Company.

***

Morrell was right, of course, that a report isn't privileged simply because it was requested by General Counsel. Moreover, he had a right in any event to know the specifics of the privilege claim. Nevertheless, Wexler continued to block Morrell's attempts to learn the basis for the objection, until he finally threw up his hands:

**Mr. Morrell:** Mr. Wexler, instead of trying to raise a problem, the simple question I'm asking—and there should not be an objection to it; it is an identification issue and it is based directly on what your claim is. All I want to know is whether the document pertains to specific cases or is a compilation of what his unit developed. That is all the question is.

**Mr. Wexler:** I don't understand what your question is. Define it.

**Mr. Morrell:** Mr. Wexler, I would ask at this point whether in the form of correspondence or a pleading, for an identification so that a ruling can be made as to whether it is indeed attorney work product. In addition, I would like any objection that you are making at this point and time to its disclosure.

**Mr. Wexler:** Your request is noted.

***

While it was hardly surprising that a company capable of removing sound from a videotape to deprive a comatose man of compensation would assert a false privilege claim, the only plausible reason for doing so was that Updegrove's report was so sensitive Ford was willing to risk severe court-ordered sanctions for discovery abuse. The more I thought about it, the more suspicious I became that Ford's investigation would expose a lethal cover-up. Suspicion, however, was one thing. Getting our hands on the evidence to prove it was a different matter.

CHAPTER 24

# NAOMI BUCHWALD

On 2-1-85 Nina Marcantonio was reportedly operating her vehicle, cognizant of icy road conditions, when allegedly the vehicle hesitated and then "surged forward at a high rate of speed" onto ice, causing her to lose control and strike a guardrail. The owner's son alleges that the throttle stuck, causing the accident. Ms. Marcantonio alleges that as a result of this incident she incurred head, neck, back and shoulder injuries. Damage to the vehicle was characterized as "not extensive" by Ford representatives, but the exact nature of the damage to the vehicle and the guardrail was not specified. Unprivileged documents in the central office file indicate that one other person was in the vehicle and "both occupants hit the windshield" but there was "no mention of injuries".

*Ford's submission to NHTSA*, March 13, 1987

**WE ARRIVED FIFTEEN MINUTES EARLY FOR OUR FIRST PRETRIAL** conference with Magistrate Buchwald on December 4, 1998. The windows of the spacious modern courtroom on the eighth floor of the federal courthouse at Foley Square looked out on the Twin Towers of the World Trade Center on one side, and the Empire State Building on the other, panoramas we would enjoy often in the months ahead.

My first impression of Naomi Buchwald was favorable. A slender woman with aquiline features in her middle years, she put everyone at ease by telling us she viewed *Jarvis* as an interesting case and looked forward to working with us. After noting that plaintiffs' counsel were also new to the case, she asked how much time we needed to get ready, and when we requested six months, it was granted. When Tompkins asked for leave to take a videotaped deposition of Alan Updegrove, Wexler, to our surprise, did not object. After disposing of several routine matters, the Court set a date for a final pretrial conference several months later.

It had been a well-run conference by a courteous judge with a sharp mind who seemed sincerely interested in presiding over our trial. If Naomi Buchwald had any leanings toward the defense side, she hadn't shown it. "She'll run a tight ship," Tompkins predicted, "but I think she'll be fair."

Before Molly and I headed back to Ohio, George predicted we had seen the last of Wexler. "Ford knows there is more at stake than paying damages to Kathy Jarvis, so they'll bring in one of their big guns." He was right. A short time later, the Buffalo-based Gibson, McAskill & Crosby replaced Wexler's firm, and Brian Crosby was soon substituted as Ford's lead counsel. Tompkins described him as "a veteran litigator with plenty of trial experience."

On December 18, 1998, we filed a memorandum asking leave to amend the pretrial order to include Judge Calabrese's evaluation of Sero's testimony:

> This record offers compelling proof that the fundamental design of the cruise control system in question alters the operational capabilities of any vehicle equipped with the system. The record leaves no doubt that, if there is an open connection in the speed amplifier, a short to ground in either the vacuum or vent lines is capable of immediately causing the throttle to go to a wide open position and cause the machine to suddenly and rapidly accelerate. If such an event occurs in close quarters under circumstances where human beings might be struck by the moving car, the possibility that serious injury or death may result seems obvious. The implications of this fact for public safety are far reaching. It is clear from the exhibits discussed herein that there have been injuries and fatalities under circumstances clearly demonstrating the possibility of a cruise control malfunction.

Our memorandum also expressed concern that Ford intended to use deceptive tactics in *Jarvis*:

> In its August 4, 1997, Pre-Trial order, Ford served notice that it intends to offer at trial the same false assertions it has made to other courts and to the National Highway Traffic Safety Administration (NHTSA)—that a cruise control defect can never cause a vehicle to suddenly and rapidly accelerate from a stopped position without driver input . . . .

Chris Brinkley's case showed the importance of letting the jury hear from people who experienced a similar occurrence, so George Tompkins prepared a motion requesting leave to call what are generally referred to as "other similar incident" witnesses. The court, despite Crosby's opposition, ruled that we could call five such witnesses, a decision that was to prove crucial to our case.

As anticipated, Ford asked for a so-called *Daubert* hearing to determine whether Sero's opinions were scientifically reliable enough to be heard by the jury. In a 1993 landmark decision, the United States Supreme Court had given guidelines for determining if proposed expert testimony is reliable and relevant. Regarding reliability, the Court laid down four criteria to guide the trial judge as the "gatekeeper" in winnowing out scientifically unreliable evidence:

1. Whether the theory or technique has been tested;
2. Whether the theory or technique has been subjected to peer review and publication;
3. The known or potential rate of error of the method used and the existence and maintenance of standards controlling the technique's operation; and
4. Whether the theory or method has been generally accepted by the scientific community.

*Daubert* made clear, however, that these factors are *guidelines*, not a "definitive checklist or test," and therefore should be applied as part of a "flexible" protocol tailored to the specific facts of the case.

*Daubert* was quickly embraced by business interests and tort reformers. On its face, at least, the decision can be seen as adding a layer of protection against what tort reformers like to call "junk science." And since it is indisputable that verdicts should not be tainted by bad science, it is hard to argue with the Court's basic logic.

Unfortunately, *Daubert* also conferred on judges unprecedented discretionary power to influence trial outcomes by unduly restricting expert testimony. This power has helped the car industry and the federal government suppress the truth about runaway cars. My first case in point is Ford's *Daubert* motion in *Jarvis.*

The law applies a much different standard, on the other hand, regarding the admissibility of government reports as evidence. Plaintiffs' lawyers are not only barred from challenging such reports on *Daubert* grounds, they are not even allowed to question people who participated in a government study to learn the basis for their findings and conclusions. Ironically, this has allowed car companies to use NHTSA's 1989 report with virtual immunity in defending their electronics and shifting the blame to drivers. In that regard, *Jarvis* is a good example of this lopsided legal equation.

CHAPTER 25

# SHOCK ABSORBING MARTINIS

> Mr. Thompson reports that on 9/3/86 he was attempting to back his vehicle into the garage from an alleyway at the rear of his home. Mrs. Thompson exited the vehicle and was standing near the rear of the car. Allegedly, when Mr. Thompson "touched" the accelerator, the car "shot" rearward striking Mrs. Thompson and passing over her body. Damage to the vehicle was not specified. Mrs. Thompson died allegedly as a result of injuries received from the accident.
>
> *Ford's submission to NHTSA,* March 13, 1987

**WE HAD REASON TO BELIEVE SAM SERO WOULD PASS HIS *DAUBERT*** test with flying colors. The plan was to have him demonstrate on his model how a loose ground connection for the cruise control module would explain why Paul Jarvis, despite reading the instructions, had been unable to engage the system. Sero would also demonstrate how a fault in a wire controlling the servo could, combined with a loose ground connection, cause the servo to suddenly pull the throttle wide open. Because NHTSA's 1989 report had acknowledged that this combination of faults could trigger a sudden acceleration, we saw no way the court could possibly exclude Sero's testimony.

However, when I met Sero for dinner at the World Trade Center Marriott the evening before the *Daubert* hearing, things took an unexpected turn. When I reminded him that Paul Jarvis had been unable to engage the cruise control, he made me choke on my vodka martini by announcing:

"I don't think that's what caused this Aerostar to go wild."

"Are you telling me that we don't have a case?" The panic in my voice made Sero smile. "Just the opposite," was the calm reply. "I think you have a better case than I originally thought."

Too flabbergasted to respond, I waited for Sero to continue.

"Do you recall during the meeting at Alan Orringer's house that either you or Mr. Zelvy asked me why inspections never turned up anything in these cases?"

"Vaguely."

"I told you that in my opinion electromagnetic interference was probably causing most of these sudden accelerations, but I needed credible evidence before I stuck my neck out in court."

"Now that you mention it, I do recall your saying that. So what's your new evidence?"

"A number of things. First, it occurred to me that the car companies have been using inspections to cover up the truth. Who else says you should always be able to find physical evidence if the electronics malfunctions?"

"The United States government for one," I retorted.

"But where did NHTSA get that idea? That report contains one stupid statement after another that can only have come from car companies trying to cover up the gamble they took by supplying voltage potential to the cruise control servo at ignition."

"What's the difference between voltage potential and power?"

"Power is a layman's term. Voltage is what moves the current from the positive side of the battery to the negative side. I prefer the term voltage potential because only the positive side of the switches that control the cruise control servo are energized at ignition. Something still has to happen to activate the switches before current can engage or disengage the cruise control."

"Something different from hardwire faults? How?"

"One difference is that EMI inside the controls can't be diagnosed by inspecting parts or components. Everybody knows that if a computer goes down, you aren't going to find the reason by looking inside the controls. That's just the nature of electronics."

I took a generous sip of my martini. "That's interesting, Sam, but the court is going to want to know the methodology and reasoning behind your analysis. I assume you've read the *Daubert* decision."

"I read it several times, and I don't understand what's the big deal."

"Do you remember the guidelines the court laid down for testing whether an expert's opinion is scientifically reliable?"

"Yes, and they all refer to whether an expert's theory is reliable. There's absolutely nothing theoretical about electromagnetic interference, which has been well known since electronics were invented. Do you know what would happen if you asked an electronics expert if EMI is a generally accepted failure mode? He'd laugh in your face. That's like asking a physicist whether gravity has been generally accepted by the scientific community."

"Hold on, Sam. Even if electromagnetic interference is a known fact, you will still need to explain why, in your opinion, it can cause the cruise control servo to seize control of the throttle."

There was a pause as Sero pondered the problem. "As I see it," he began, "we need to get three basic points across. First, the court needs to understand that the cruise control electronics operate within a predetermined voltage range. Second, there are fluctuations and spikes in the current going on all the time that are outside this voltage range. Finally, there is nothing in the design of these electronics to prevent a transient spike in the current from suddenly activating the servo, and causing it to yank the throttle wide open."

"Does that mean the controls can't distinguish between a signal that's within the voltage range, and one that isn't?"

"That's exactly the point. As far as the controls are concerned, a signal is a signal is a signal, and if it happens to be outside the calibrated voltage range, it's still just a signal. That's why it's ridiculous to say that if an inspection doesn't find the cause, the system didn't malfunction. That's like saying if you can't find what made your computer go down, you must have been imagining things."

"What you're telling me, Sam, makes sense, but we still need to convince the court that your analysis is scientifically reliable under the *Daubert* standards."

For the next several hours, I grilled Sero about the basis for his opinion that internal electromagnetic interference was behind this dangerous automotive problem. Because no expert, as far as we knew, had yet specifically identified internal EMI as the culprit, if Naomi Buchwald had leanings favoring Ford, the next day's hearing would probably reveal them.

CHAPTER 26

# BREAKING NEW GROUND

> Mr. Guilone reports that on 10/15/86, he was attempting to back out of a parking space putting the car in Reverse, with his foot on the brake. He alleges the car "lurched backwards at a high rate of speed, and then forward, and repeating this backward and forward motion each time with greater violence until the force was sufficient to cause the car to vault a concrete parking barrier and smash into a concrete wall". Damage to the vehicle was not specified. Minor personal injuries were reported.
>
> *Ford's submission to NHTSA*, March 13, 1987

**WE BEGAN THE FOLLOWING MORNING WITH A TUTORIAL** describing the various components of Ford's cruise control and their function. As Sero explained each feature on his model, Judge Buchwald's incisive questions left no doubt that she was grasping how Ford's electronics worked much faster than I had done. The crucial moment came when I asked Sero whether the design was reasonably safe. His response went directly to the heart of the matter: "The major inherent problem is a direct battery voltage path [to the servo] the moment you turn on the ignition, all it's waiting for is that you complete the circuit—fire the servo transistors, and the car will take off down the road."

> **The Court:** What do you mean when you say "fire the transistors"?
>
> **Mr. Sero:** Cause them to operate in a conductive mode. Instead of inhibiting the signal, it causes them to complete the circuit . . . , something you will never see after the event. After you kill the power and turn the key off, the power is gone. Unless it gets the same false signal again, it will never do it again. You will never find any evidence that it ever happened on that circuit board.

***

Looking back, Sero's response was the first breach in the industry's long-running claim that detectable hardwire faults alone could induce a sudden acceleration. That claim had persevered for two decades despite thousands of occurrences with the same fact pattern and the insistence of countless drivers, including police officers and Secret Service agents, that the accelerator pedal was never depressed. How remarkable, then, that Sero was the first electrical engineer outside the industry to pinpoint a "false signal" in the controls as the root cause of what has become a worldwide automotive disaster. Although it was a different story for industry insiders, that is to outpace our story. At the time, I was encouraged when the court asked "if there was a solution to the problem," and Sero answered, "The only way to eliminate this from happening is not to power the servo the moment you turn on the ignition switch. There's no need for doing that, absolutely none."

Because Sero's presentation was nearly flawless, we expected a lengthy cross-examination from Brian Crosby. We were surprised, therefore, when he asked just seven questions about the electronics:

**Q:** Sir, for your hypothesis to in fact work, you need two simultaneous wire failures, correct?

**A:** No, you need a fault to occur on a system that's going to cause the actual servo to be energized. That could come from any number of avenues, not just two simultaneous wires like you're talking about.

**Q:** Let's take the first. You need a loose or disconnected ground?

**A:** Yes.

**Q:** And you need a fault in one of the other two wires?

**A:** Yes.

**Q:** At the same time?

**A:** No, you need a fault to draw the vacuum or the vent to a zero potential. That does not necessarily mean you need the physical fault that you could see afterwards to occur. It just means somewhere on the circuit board . . . , due to contamination that evaporates or water, or whatever took it to a zero potential. That's what it means.

**Q:** The circuit board is the third one, isn't it?

**A:** No, sir. I included the circuit board in the first one as a means of getting that ground.

**Q:** But you have never been able to duplicate that on the circuit board?

**A:** I can ground it on a circuit board. I can do it for you now if you want.

**Q:** In a real car? A real car, in a real situation, you have never seen that happen, have you?

**A:** You will never see it. There is no evidence left after the fact.

**Mr. Crosby:** That's all.

***

Why had Crosby barely touched Sero's groundbreaking testimony? Molly thought it was the mark of an experienced advocate, who understood that challenging Sero would give him a chance to elaborate on the basis for his analysis. George Tompkins had a different view.

"Crosby's *Daubert* memorandum made the court aware that the basic premise of NHTSA's 1989 report is that testing should be able to replicate these malfunctions. In my opinion, that's why Crosby stopped after Sam acknowledged he hadn't been able to replicate a sudden acceleration in a car. He's betting that will be enough to keep EMI out of the case."

"Do you think the court will use the 1989 report to disqualify Sero on *Daubert* grounds?" Molly asked.

"Buchwald can't do that," George replied, "because NHTSA's 1989 report acknowledges that hardwire faults could cause a sudden acceleration. Anyway, Crosby doesn't care about hardwire faults, because Declercq inspected Kathy's Aerostar and didn't find anything. It's EMI Ford is concerned about. If we get a verdict based on EMI, it will be an absolute disaster not only for Ford but the entire industry."

I had a sinking feeling Tompkins was right. "So you think Crosby is rolling the dice that Sero's admission about not having replicated an EMI-induced failure in a car is enough to get it excluded under *Daubert*?"

George thought for a minute. "Let's not forget that Naomi Buchwald was a government prosecutor who is now part of the federal judicial establishment, and that her husband is a corporate lawyer. If she allows a lone ranger like Sam to blow the lid off the problem, that would make NHTSA look foolish, force car companies to start paying for their mistakes, and upset the tort reformers' apple cart. In fact, it might even prevent Buchwald from becoming a federal judge."

Molly was incredulous. "Crosby never laid a glove on Sero because he knows that EMI isn't a 'theory,' but a generally accepted fact about electronics. If the court does what you're suggesting, George, that would be an outright perversion of *Daubert*."

Tompkins was somber. "I can't argue with that, Molly. Unfortunately, big money has sold the idea that you guys on the plaintiff's side are driving up costs and making American corporations less competitive with your multimillion-dollar verdicts. From my days defending corporations, I also know how the threat of getting hit with big verdicts is helping to make cars, drugs, toys, and many other products safer. Unfortunately for our client, my gut tells me Naomi Buchwald doesn't have much sympathy for that side of the story."

CHAPTER 27

# A PREDICTION COME TRUE

> Mr. Cherrault reports that on 6/7/86, he started the vehicle and put it in Drive. He alleges the engine "raced" and the vehicle accelerated up his driveway and struck his garage. He further alleges he then put the transmission selector in Reverse and the vehicle "sped" across the street, onto a neighbor's lawn and struck the neighbor's central air conditioning unit. At this time, the vehicle stalled and came to rest. The vehicle sustained damage to the trunk and rear quarter panels. There was damage to Mr. Cherrault's garage door and his neighbor's shrubbery. The central air conditioning unit was not damaged. The driver and passenger allegedly sustained back injuries.
>
> *Ford's submission to NHTSA*, March 13, 1987

**GEORGE TOMPKINS HIT THE BULL'S-EYE DEAD CENTER. AS HE** had anticipated, the court ruled that Sero could testify how a combination of hardwire faults might induce a sudden acceleration. From there, however, it was downhill for Kathy Jarvis.

> Sero surmises that many kinds of electrical interference emanating from electrical components such as the alternator, variable speed sensor, generator, or even a CB radio, can cause the servo to activate. However, unlike his testing of the first two conditions, Sero has neither replicated this condition in a model nor witnessed it in real life prior to the hearing. Sero testified that he had been experimenting with injected signals for seven years and had not been able to replicate the condition he proposes can cause sudden acceleration.

Although Ford had not produced an electrical engineer, much less one with Sero's background and experience to challenge either his reasoning or methodology, Buchwald had used her power as a "gatekeeper" to rule out what he believed was the only reasonable explanation for thousands of runaway car accidents. We suspected, therefore, that Buchwald had been unwilling to countenance the possibility of an independent researcher on the frontier of electronics discrediting both the industry's position and government's 1989 report.

The ruling was softened somewhat by the Court's rejection of Ford's argument that NHTSA's 1989 report was enough to disqualify Sero. Noting that "several passages in the NHTSA report" showed that "the agency produced the report with the assumption that the cruise control could not operate at speeds below 30 mph," the Court concluded that, "in the absence of testimony, by deposition or affidavit," from the authors of the NHTSA report, the Court was unable to evaluate how NHTSA reached its conclusions. The Court, therefore, rejected "the argument that the report is sufficient basis to exclude Sero's expert testimony."

Although the court had rejected Ford's attempt to disqualify Sero on the basis of NHTSA's 1989 report, Ford would nevertheless be allowed to use the study both to defend its electronics and to pin the blame on Kathy Jarvis. With electromagnetic interference now out of the case, we needed a strategy to fend off NHTSA's 1989 report while convincing the jury that Ford's electronics, and not Kathy, had malfunctioned. To that end, we were counting on the testimony of Alan Updegrove.

CHAPTER 28

# A HOT DOC

**CARS THAT SPEED UP MYSTERIOUSLY SPARK BITTER DISPUTE OVER CAUSE**

In Melrose, Mass., 72-year-old Joseph Silva will go on trial later this year on the charge of vehicular homicide for fatally injuring a 57-year-old parochial-school crossing guard. He claims that his 1983 Oldsmobile Cutlass Supreme took off and he couldn't stop it. The prosecutor, R.J. Cinquegrana, the assistant district attorney for Middlesex County, says he has had the car tested and that there aren't any indications of problems with it.

*The Wall Street Journal*, Sept. 3, 1986

**TWO DAYS BEFORE I CONFRONTED UPDEGROVE IN FRONT OF A** video camera at a hotel near Detroit's Metropolitan Airport, Molly, quite unexpectedly, came across a one-page document in our expanding repository, entitled "Alleged Unintended Sudden Acceleration Overview," that began:

> Investigations of alleged unintended acceleration events were conducted by the Ford Parts and Service Division [FPSD], Service Engineering Office. These investigations were begun in early 1987 and concluded in December, 1992. These investigations were handled by a team in the Special Projects Unit of Car Service Engineering. Prior to and following the investigation actions by this team, cases were investigated by FPSD district offices.

Molly's excitement was palpable. "This has to be part of the memorandum Updegrove mentioned when Morrell questioned him. If so, it means Updegrove became involved immediately after NHTSA told Ford it was considering a recall."

"When was that?"

"Ford received the notice in early January 1987. Didn't Mr. X tell you Ford's district offices were doing these investigations during the 1980s?"

"That's right. In fact, he said the investigators were engineers trained to identify safety defects."

"Voilá!" Molly exclaimed. "These engineers were fingering the cruise control electronics, and so Ford had to find a new approach or Pandora's box would be opened. Therefore they sent out an S.O.S. to some good soldiers who were delighted to be recalled to active duty, and couldn't care less whether they were allowed to express an opinion about the cause. Why would Ford go through all these gymnastics unless these field engineers were raining on the company's claim that it couldn't find anything that could possibly cause a car to take off on its own?"

"Do we know if these reports from field engineers were turned over to the government?"

"That's something Jo Ellen and I will look into the first chance we get. Anyway, I think the next paragraph is just as important."

> A total of 2,877 cases were investigated. Cases involving private, fleet, rental and dealer owned vehicles were investigated. There were alleged cases for all vehicle lines. Each alleged event was initially assigned to a group (I, II or III) based on the type of alleged event. Attachment A contains a definition of the three groups. At the conclusion of the investigation, the case was closed and assigned a closing status. These are also defined in Attachment A.

"Didn't Updegrove testify about these Groups I, II and III in Chris Brinkley's case?"

"Not only that," Molly shot back, "he also said that two-thirds of the cases were Group I events, meaning they began at gear engagement. That fits exactly with Sero's belief that current spikes during ignition and shifting explain why that's when sudden accelerations from a standstill always begin."

"Did Updegrove admit to any kind of a safety problem in Brinkley's case?"

"Quite the opposite. In fact, he said Ford turned these cars inside out without finding evidence of anything that could make a car take off on its own, which is probably why they didn't ask Updegrove about a report that might support that claim."

It was the final paragraph of the document, however, that I found most intriguing:

> Attachment F is a description of the electronic file that contains summaries of the individual cases. The location of copies of the electronic file are identified, and instructions for accessing these files are included . . . . Attachments G - Q are copies of printouts from the electronic files; only

> a summary of the individual case file data is included in these reports.

"Where did you find this document?" I asked Molly.

"In one of Konigsberg's boxes. Since there's no page number, it must have been tucked away in Ford's sudden acceleration reading room in one of those boxes where they hoped nobody would notice it."

"So how do you propose I use this with Updegrove?"

"I'd start by getting him to acknowledge that he either authored it or knows who did. Then I would make him tell me specifically what is included in these electronic summaries. Once we know that, we can make Ford give us copies of the questionnaires, and that should be the ball game."

"Meaning?"

"Meaning that Ford wouldn't spend five years investigating every detail without learning what was turning cars into unguided missiles. That's just common sense."

"I agree, but do you have any other suggestions?"

"Keep in mind that the court put a five-hour limit on this deposition. My suggestion is not to get bogged down in discovery issues like Updegrove's report until you have squeezed from him as much information as possible about the investigation itself. If there's still time to ask about a report, go for it."

"That's good advice. I know it's been tedious, but the hours you and Jo Ellen have spent in our repository might be about to pay off."

"Does that mean I'm due for a raise?"

"Only if I hit a home run on Monday."

"Then get busy."

CHAPTER 29

# UPDEGROVE

### SUDDEN ACCELERATION—NEW STUDY MAY UNRAVEL MYSTERY OF ACCELERATION

"Had my foot on the brake, but was unable to stop." Julie Tatsugi says she was driving her 1986 Honda Accord LXi in a parking garage in Santa Monica, Calif., when it accelerated and slammed into a parked car. Tatsugi, 29, says her auto required $6,000 in repairs from the Sept. 18, 1986 accident .... "The car was at a complete stop, and then, I slowly lifted my foot from the brake, I then began to drive very slowly in reverse, when suddenly, the car made a loud revving type of sound, and began accelerating, at an increasing speed ... the car continued to accelerate backwards, and collided into a parked car. The impact of the collision then caused the first parked car to ram into a second vehicle parked to the side, thereby dragging the second vehicle for several feet. My car continued to accelerate, and then jolted forward, wherein it collided with a third vehicle, which in turn rammed into a fourth vehicle."

*The Detroit News*, December 17, 1987

**BECAUSE UPDEGROVE'S DEPOSITION WOULD BE VIDEOTAPED,** Jo Ellen and I arrived about thirty minutes early to meet the videographer and make sure the setting was suitable for the proceedings. As usual, Jo Ellen had taken good care of these preparations, and when Brian Crosby and Alan Updegrove arrived, we were ready to proceed. The first thing I did was give Crosby a copy of the document Molly had found, explained that we had found it two days earlier in a file turned over by the Konigsberg firm, and asked if he wished to discuss it with the witness before we began. He glanced at the document, showed it to Updegrove, and the two men briefly left the room.

There were good reasons for showing Crosby the document in advance rather than springing it on him during the deposition. Since it was not included on the amended exhibit list the Court had permitted us to file, Ford could object to the document. Moreover, lawyers of my vintage were taught that it was dishonorable to use underhanded tactics against an opponent, and Crosby, I soon learned, held the same view of our profession.

After Updegrove was sworn, I did not beat around the bush. Referring to the document Molly had found, I cut to the chase:

**Q:** Have you had an opportunity to review what has been marked as Exhibit 271?

**Mr. Crosby:** Prior to this morning?

**Mr. Murray:** Yes, prior to the beginning of the deposition.

**The Witness:** This appears to be part of a document that I prepared at the conclusion of our effort. I think it's the second page.

**Q:** Did you prepare this particular document, Mr. Updegrove?
**A:** I believe that I did.
**Q:** Does it refer to the investigation of sudden acceleration events?
**A:** It does.

***

Having established that Updegrove prepared the document, I followed Molly's advice and set about learning the details of Ford's investigation, beginning with the methodology:

**Q:** Who prepared the format, that is, who sat down and decided which questions were going to be put on this questionnaire?
**A:** I was largely responsible for that with the assistance from the Powertrain area, the Design Analysis area, and the Safety Office at Ford Motor Company.
**Q:** Did you have input from the Office of General Counsel?
**A:** At a point in time, we did. Throughout our efforts, the Office of General Counsel at Ford Motor Company was involved with us.
**Q:** You mentioned Design Analysis and Engineering. What is their function?
**A:** Design Analysis is, in my terms, the area of expert witnesses within the company.
**Q:** Are you familiar with Mr. Victor Declercq?
**A:** I am.
**Q:** Who is he, sir, to your knowledge?
**A:** Mr. Declercq is a member of the Design Analysis Department of the Ford Motor Company.
**Q:** Does he serve as an expert witness to your knowledge in sudden acceleration cases?
**Mr. Crosby:** Objection.
**The Court:** You may answer.

**A:** I believe Vic is now retired, and I'm not sure what his status with the company is.
**Q:** Do you know if Mr. Declercq has served as an expert witness for the Ford Motor Company in sudden acceleration cases?
**Mr. Crosby:** Again, I object.
**The Court:** You may answer.
**A:** Yes, he has.

***

The fact that the very unit that employed Declercq had participated in developing the investigative methodology was highly suspicious. We knew from Chris Brinkley's materials that the investigation focused heavily on the cruise control electronics. Nevertheless, Declercq had pleaded ignorance regarding the results when I questioned him in *Manigault*. The obvious question, therefore, was why Ford had been defending sudden acceleration cases with NHTSA's 1989 report, and not with the results of its own investigation. The mystery only deepened when I turned to the electronic summaries mentioned in the document:

**Q:** Is there a Supplement Q that contains the data obtained from this questionnaire regarding the Aerostars that were covered by this investigation?
**A:** At such point in time as we submitted this material to the archives, there was an attachment as indicated.
**Q:** It contained a summary as to each vehicle line, is that correct?
**A:** That's correct.
**Q:** Did that summary include the answers to the questions on the questionnaire used in the investigation?
**A:** Not in all cases.
**Q:** In most cases?

**A:** No. It was more an operating, or tracking file.

***

This response confirmed that we needed both the electronic summaries and the investigative questionnaires to unravel what Ford had learned. The next step, therefore, was to find out exactly what information was recorded in the electronic summaries, and what data could only be found in the questionnaires. Although this proved to be laborious and time-consuming, Updegrove's responses were to prove crucial. In fact, responses like the following strongly suggested that the key to what Ford had learned was the information contained in the questionnaires.

**Q:** Did you record information on the questionnaire indicating what the operator told you happened as far as braking was concerned or what the braking action was?

**A:** The questionnaire provided our investigators with an opportunity to annotate the response from the customer as regards his braking, so that's the information we got . . . .

**Q:** Do you recall whether operators reported hard continuous braking with one foot? Did some operators report doing that during the event?

**A:** In some cases there would have been that comment, yes . . . .

**Q:** Do you recall whether there were some cases involving Aerostars where there was a witness outside the car who was talked to or interviewed by the person filling in that questionnaire?

**A:** In some cases, I'm sure there were but I don't recall a specific number.

**Q:** In some of the Aerostar cases did someone outside the vehicle report that he or she observed brake lights during the event?

**A:** Whether it was with the Aerostars or others, we have had those kinds of comments.
**Q:** Was that considered key information in your inquiry?
**A:** All the information was considered key, which is why we were out looking at these incidents, or alleged incidents . . . .
**Q:** Do you recall whether you talked with any owner or operator of these Aerostar events who reported to you they had had a prior similar sudden acceleration experience or event in another Aerostar other than the one involved in the inquiry?
**A:** I don't recall.
**Q:** Did your questionnaire ask the owner or operator whether prior service had been performed on the vehicle for a prior sudden acceleration event?
**A:** I believe we addressed the issue of prior service.
**Q:** Would it have been considered key information if the owner or operator reported that he or she had taken the Aerostar in for service because of a prior sudden acceleration event?
**A:** That would have been considered to be a key bit of information.
**Q:** Do you recall whether any of the operators said they had taken the car in for prior service because of another sudden acceleration event?
**A:** I don't recall.
**Q:** Did you inquire of the owner or operator how far the vehicle moved during the event?
**A:** We did have a question of that nature.

***

Sam Sero had explained that the two cables attached to the throttle plate—one for the accelerator pedal and the other for the cruise control servo—worked in tandem. Therefore, if the accelerator pedal moved by itself to the floor, the only possible explanation was a malfunction in the cruise control electronics. When I pressed Updegrove on the point, here was the result:

**Q:** Do you recall how many times the operator—and specifically of Aerostars—reported that the pedal moved by itself?

**A:** I do not recall.

**Q:** If an operator reported that the pedal moved by itself, would that be considered a key piece of data in your investigation?

**A:** It could have been, yes.

***

Because my questioning had consumed the time allotted by the court, I had only touched on some of Updegrove's revealing responses. When we finished, I asked Crosby for a copy of Updegrove's report and the electronic summary for the Aerostar. He said he needed to discuss my request with his client, and would get back to me in a few days. Several days later, he called to say that Ford was unwilling to voluntarily surrender the report.

"What's the basis?" I asked.

"I'm told the report is in the reading room, and you would have gotten it had you been more diligent. It's too late in the day to reopen that kind of discovery."

"Are you aware that your predecessor, Wexler, claimed Updegrove's report was privileged?"

"I understand your position," replied Crosby, "but I've been instructed by my client not to surrender the report without a court order. Sorry."

There was something bordering on the surreal about Ford's behavior. NHTSA's industry-wide study had lasted just nine months, during which the investigators had inspected just one Ford car, a 1984 Mustang. On the other hand, the company's investigation had lasted nearly five years, during which investigators had not only inspected 2,877 models, but collected a wide range of detailed information indicating the likely cause of each event. Nevertheless, instead of relying on its own investigation, Ford had wielded NHTSA's 1989 report for a decade to blame drivers. In addition, if its own investigation confirmed NHTSA's conclusions, why hadn't Ford ended the uncertainties surrounding this phenomenon by simply publishing the results, instead of trying to hide them? Unfortunately, with the trial beginning in a week, Ford's stonewalling put us in a bind. Even if the pages of Updegrove's report were scattered throughout the company's sudden acceleration reading room, since we had not visited the site ourselves, we were in no position to prove we couldn't have found the report had we looked for it in Ford's repository. But Wexler's false privilege claim had given us an ace in the hole, and I drafted a letter to the court asking for an order requiring Ford to produce Updegrove's final report and the electronic summary for the Aerostar events.

When the court granted the request, I was so pleasantly surprised that I forgot to ask for a deadline. Consequently, we didn't receive the report and summary until a few days prior to jury selection. But I was so busy with final trial preparations at this point that I barely glanced at the materials, and put them aside until I could find the time to study them carefully.

CHAPTER 30

# TRIAL

### CAR CRASHES INTO PUYALLUP-AREA STORE, INJURING SEVEN SHOPPERS

A Lincoln Town Car crashed into the main entrance at a Puyallup-area Fred Meyer store last night, sending seven holiday shoppers to the hospital. The vehicle smashed through the store's glass doors while traveling in reverse at about 7:30 p.m., said Detective Ed Troyer, Pierce County sheriff's spokesman. It traveled about 116 feet inside the store before stopping. The driver of the car, a man in his 60s, told investigators that the accelerator of the mid-1980s Lincoln was stuck.

*Seattle Post-Intelligencer,* December 21, 2004

**THE TRIAL TOOK PLACE IN JULY 1999, AND LASTED NEARLY A** month. What follows are some highlights.

After we summarized our case in our opening statement, Crosby told the jury:

> The cruise control system in this vehicle is essentially the same design that's utilized in 80% of the vehicles that are on the highway, not just by Ford, but 80% of the cars on the road at that point in time. It's fundamentally the same as a General Motors, Chrysler, Mercedes, and Toyota system. It's not unique.

In *Manigault*, Ford's strategy had been to isolate our case by blocking both owner reports to NHTSA and Alan Updegrove's deposition. In *Jarvis*, however, that strategy became impossible when the court granted us leave to depose Updegrove. Hence, it came as no surprise when Crosby served notice that NHTSA's 1989 report would be a centerpiece of Ford's case.

> You will also hear proof that the federal government looked into this problem. They looked into claims by drivers lodged with the National Highway Traffic Safety Administration to see if this could occur, and they put together a team of engineers, one fellow from MIT, one fellow from the National Bureau of Standards, and so forth. They examined the claims of this sudden acceleration event that were reported by drivers and went out and looked at the vehicles . . . .
>
> **Mr. Murray:** Mr. Crosby, I apologize for the interruption. Please note an objection to this line of argument for the record?
> **Mr. Crosby:** This is an incident investigation, your Honor.
> **The Court:** I know, you may proceed.
> **Mr. Crosby:** Thank you. They looked at Fords. They looked at Chryslers. They looked at General Motors' vehicles;

> I believe they looked at Toyotas, Nissans, Volkswagens, same type of claims. Their conclusion was that these events don't occur because of anything wrong with the cruise control. Their conclusion was that you would have to have two independent intermittent failures. That could not occur without evidence of damaged parts left behind . . . . Their conclusion was that this type of event reported by drivers is as a result of pedal misapplication, or inadvertent pedal application.

***

Watching for the first time a jury learn about the federal government's conclusion that faulty driving was behind runaway car accidents made me realize why countless people have been denied compensation for catastrophic injuries, as befell Leon Manigault. Armed with the federal government's imprimatur on a report plaintiffs can challenge neither on *Daubert* grounds nor by cross-examining those who did the study, carmakers were able to portray NHTSA's report as a thorough and scientific analysis. Paradoxically, Crosby barely mentioned the Updegrove investigation, a sure sign he realized it was his client's Achilles heel.

As expected, Kathy Jarvis proved to be a persuasive witness with a clear recollection of details. Since she clearly recalled pushing on the brake pedal with both feet, we had photographs showing her with both feet on the brake pedal in an identical Aerostar, and several photographs demonstrating the impossibility of placing both feet on the gas pedal. Kathy also described how she had glanced down to be sure her feet were on the brake pedal. If the jury believed her, Ford's driver error defense would be dead in the water. We were not surprised, therefore, when Crosby attacked this crucial testimony:

**Q:** In this Aerostar, between the dashboard and the steering wheel, there is a large shroud behind the steering wheel, is there not?

**A:** A shroud—like a cover . . . .

**Q:** A cover, exactly.

**A:** I mean like a cloth.

**The Court:** It is a strange term.

**The Witness:** Use another word, please.

**Q:** There is a large cover made of plastic that surrounds the steering column immediately in front of the steering wheel, isn't there?

**A:** Well, but you can see through the holes of the steering wheel.

**Q:** There is a cover over the steering column, is there not?

**A:** OK, now I see what you're talking about, right here. OK.

**Q:** And you cannot see your feet by looking through the top of the steering wheel, can you, because of that shroud?

**A:** Sir, I tested that. You can in fact see through the two holes. There are two holes in the steering wheel . . . .

**Q:** Ma'am.

**A:** And I could see my feet on the brake.

**Q:** In order to see your feet on the brake, you would have to be looking through the bottom of the steering wheel, isn't that so?

**A:** Sir, all I can tell you is that I can see my feet, both my feet, on the brake through the hole.

***

Several minutes later, Crosby again tried to shake Kathy's claim that she had seen both feet on the brake pedal.

**Q:** You're telling us that the vehicle suddenly started, you became aware of it, you were trying to avoid the pedestrians on the left, the tree on the right in the distance of less than this room, and you took your eyes off the road?

**A:** I glanced down to make sure—you have to understand, I didn't understand what was going on. Yes sir, I did glance. My two feet were on the brake.

**Q:** Why did you look down if you already knew you had your foot on the brake?

**A:** Because I was incredulous. I never had a vehicle take off before like that.

**Q:** When you looked down, your feet were still on the brake?

**A:** My two feet were on the brake.

**Q:** So you started out with your foot on the brake. It took off. You put your other foot on the brake and pushed?

**A:** Immediately.

**Q:** And the vehicle still continued to increase in speed?

**A:** Yes, sir.

**Q:** With you putting all the pressure down on the brake, is that right?

**A:** Yes, sir.

**Q:** And I take it, since the pedestrians were coming up on you, getting closer to you, you were steering and pushing harder and harder on that brake; is that a fair statement?

**A:** Sir, I had to swerve to the right ever so slightly to miss these people. Ever so slightly. Because as you see, it is a very narrow road.

**Q:** You kept your foot on the brake putting the pressure down trying to stop the vehicle while you were steering; is that a fair statement?

**A:** Yes.

**The Court:** Mr. Crosby, I think we need to give the jury a little break. Let's take a five-minute recess.

***

When Crosby asked if the Aerostar "still continued to increase in speed . . . with you putting all the pressure down on the brake," he was resorting to a trick the car industry has used to confuse plaintiffs for years. Although braking *decreases the rate* of acceleration, the automobile gains speed until braking reverses the increase, stops the car or, despite braking, it crashes. A quick-thinking driver might disengage the engine by shifting into neutral or turning off the ignition as Leon Manigault did after his Crown Victoria took off from the church parking lot. In any event, when Kathy said the van continued to speed up, she was being entirely accurate. Crosby may have realized this because he renewed his attack following the break:

**Q:** Ms. Jarvis, to pick up where we were when we took our break, as you approach the pedestrians, you were steering to the right around them?

**A:** Yes, sir.

**Q:** Your vehicle actually went off the roadway onto the shoulder, isn't that so?

**A:** Ever so slightly, yes, sir.

**Q:** OK. And then you were steering back to get on the road?

**A:** Yes, sir.

**Q:** As you approached the pedestrians, over the distance of this room and the engine continues to roar, is that what you are saying?

**A:** Yes, sir.

**Q:** It never goes down in noise; the noise remains the same?

**A:** What I recall was a V-R-O-O-O-M!

**Q:** A continuous . . . .

**A:** V-R-O-O-O-M!

**Q:** Up and down or continuous?
**A:** Continuous, that's the word.
**Q:** So it was a continuous loud noise?
**A:** Yes.
**Q:** It didn't change?
**A:** Yes, sir.
**Q:** And the vehicle continued to go faster and faster?
**A:** Yes, sir.
**Q:** Now as you approached the pedestrians, did you blow the horn?
**A:** No, sir, I didn't.
**Q:** Why?
**A:** Because I couldn't move my two hands [from the steering wheel]. I was ever so close to them, ever so close to the trees; and I couldn't move my hands.
**Q:** You were concentrating so hard?
**A:** Yes, sir.
**Q:** But notwithstanding that concentration, you say at some point you took your eyes off the road, you looked down at your feet, and put your eyes back on the road?
**A:** Glanced down.
**Q:** And as you passed the pedestrians, they didn't just stand there, did they?
**A:** As I recall, they jumped out of the way . . . .
**Q:** So what you are saying is that from the time the vehicle started until you were past those pedestrians, you had your foot, both your feet, as hard as you could on that brake?
**A:** I was pumping.
**Q:** You were pumping?
**A:** Two feet on the brake, pumping, pumping.
**Q:** When did you start to pump the brake?

**A:** I told you that I had my right foot on the brake. And as the vehicle took off, I applied the second foot to the brake.
**Q:** You already had the first one on there?
**A:** Exactly.
**Q:** So then you put the second on?
**A:** And I started to pump.
**Q:** Let me stop you at that point.
**A:** Yes, sir.
**Q:** How far had the car gone at that point?
**A:** I don't really know sir.
**Q:** After you passed the pedestrians and you started to pull the vehicle back on the road, had you taken your foot off the brake at any time?
**A:** I was pumping like that.
**Q:** So you didn't keep pressure on the brake then?
**A:** My two feet remained on the brake pedal, pumping, that's how I'm answering your question, sir.
**Q:** When did you start to pump?
**A:** You are asking me in terms of feet?
**Q:** Yes, ma'am.
**A:** And I honestly have to tell you I don't recall.
**Q:** When you applied the brake and what you now say is pumping, how long did you keep it on the pedal?
**A:** I was going like this, I mean . . . .
**Q:** You were constantly going up and down on it, is that what you're saying?
**A:** Pumping, yes.
**Q:** You never heard a change in the sound of the engine?
**A:** No, sir, I did not.

***

Many judges would have sustained an objection to Crosby's cross-examination as repetitious and argumentative. I chose not to object, however, because I sensed that he was losing ground with the jury. Happily, Kathy never wavered, and when Crosby finally finished, I took less than two minutes to clarify a few points and sat down. During the next break, we congratulated Kathy on how well she had done against a forceful cross-examiner. It was not idle praise, for her testimony had set the stage for the testimony of other Aerostar owners who had come to New York to tell their stories.

CHAPTER 31

# OSI'S

> Ms. Rogers reports that on 12/18/85 she was attempting to leave a parking place. She started the car, with her foot on the brake, put the car in Drive and "touched" the accelerator. She alleges the vehicle "spun off like an airplane hitting and totaling one parked car, damaging another, finally hitting a building". Damage to the Rogers' vehicle was not specified. Ms. Rogers sustained unspecified personal injuries.
>
> *Ford's submission to NHTSA*, March 13, 1987

**BY "EXTRALEGAL DISCOVERY," WE OBTAINED THE FILES OF TAMPA-**based Dennis Diecidue, who had valiantly but unsuccessfully tried an Aerostar case against Ford. The files identified several Aerostar owners who had experienced a similar incident—or OSI—five of whom agreed to tell their story to the *Jarvis* jury. Like Kathy, the details were etched in their memories.

Jacqueline Gibbs' Aerostar suddenly accelerated at her son's farm in Illinois. When she pulled the gear shift into drive, with her right foot resting on the brake pedal, she heard a "horrendous noise and the Aerostar shot forward." She pressed on the brake pedal "as hard as I could," but the van kept going until she turned off the ignition. Fortunately, this occurred in an open area with plenty of room for maneuver because the van, as measured by Mrs. Gibbs and her son, had travelled 560 feet before she managed to stop it. Although we were not aware of it at the time, there have been hundreds of well-documented cases of a car travelling 500 feet or more until it finally crashed or the driver disengaged the engine by shifting into neutral or turning off the ignition.

David Morse, a former police officer, described his Aerostar experience at a gas station:

> **Q:** Did there come a time when you sought to move the car by putting it into drive?
>
> **A:** Yes sir. After the gentleman in front of me finished fueling his vehicle, . . . he began to move away from the fueling area. At that time I shifted—I put my foot on the brake, shifting the vehicle from park to drive.
>
> **Q:** And what happened?
>
> **A:** As soon as I began to release the brake pedal, it moved forward, the vehicle went to wide open throttle causing me to strike the car in front of me.

***

At that point, "the vehicles bounced apart from the impact. I struck the vehicle again, and I was holding on—I was pushing the brake for all I was worth, and I realized at that moment that wasn't going to work, so I reached through the steering wheel and turned the ignition off."

Theda Blackstone's Aerostar suddenly accelerated from a dealership in Florida. With her right foot resting on the brake pedal, she shifted into "drive and the vehicle absolutely roared and leapt out. I don't even know how to describe it. It just leapt forward. That's the best description I guess." After the Aerostar hit a parked van and another car, it continued out of control "into the eastbound lanes of a four-lane highway," where it was struck "broadside" by another car, and "continued into the median where it stalled momentarily, but then picked up momentum again . . . back into the eastbound lanes heading westbound and then it stopped." Ms. Blackstone insisted she had pushed on the brake pedal throughout this event:

**Q:** And during this time, where were your feet?

**A:** On the brake.

**Q:** Did you happen to look at your feet?

**A:** Yes, I did.

**Q:** At anytime during this event, did you put your foot on the accelerator?

**A:** No, I did not.

***

When Mary Moore shifted from park to reverse at a supermarket in Detroit, her Aerostar suddenly took off:

**Q:** Did you have your foot on the brake pedal when you started the car?

**A:** Yes.

**Q:** Was your foot at any time on the accelerator?

**A:** No.

***

When the van bounced off a wall into another car, the gear was knocked into neutral ending the event.

Linda Schmidt described how her Aerostar suddenly accelerated the moment she placed it in reverse, even though her foot was on the brake. The car accelerated backward more than 100 feet until it was stopped by telephone cables. When she attempted to push the gear lever into park, it wouldn't go, so she pulled downward toward neutral, but it went into drive. The van rapidly accelerated forward about 100 feet, even though she was now pushing on the brake pedal with both feet. She again attempted to jam the gear into park, but it "flew backward in reverse." Mrs. Schmidt described how the event ended:

**Q:** What happened when you got to the highway?

**A:** The car hit the embankment on the west side of the highway, and then it was airborne over the highway and it came down and hit on the east side of the highway, and it then kept going—it smashed into the embankment and it kept trying to go up the embankment.

**Q:** And what happened?

**A:** I could still feel the car surging, and I knew . . . where I was. I couldn't see it at the time, but I knew where I was. So I just simply opened the door and jumped out.

***

This testimony, following that of Kathy Jarvis, clearly made a strong impression on the jury. But would it be enough to carry the day?

CHAPTER 32

# DECLERCQ

### ACCELERATOR JAMS, CAR HITS 135 MPH

A motorist drove for 60 miles at speeds of 135 mph after the accelerator on his BMW car jammed and his brakes failed. Kevin Nicolle, 26, was on the A1 near Thirsk in North Yorkshire when the car started to accelerate. "I was in tears most of the time on the phone to the police—I could really see myself dying," he told the BBC. "I took my foot off the accelerator because it's automatic—but I wasn't slowing down at all. I hit the brakes. They were braking OK, they were keeping me at about 70 mph . . . . Then the brakes started burning out—I could see smoke coming from the brakes . . . . " He had to drive on the hard shoulder to avoid crashing but eventually lost control and hit a roundabout near Blyth, Notts, but escaped unhurt.

*BBC News*, March 11, 2006

**ONE OF THE MOST EFFECTIVE WAYS FOR A PLAINTIFF TO PROVE** a case is to obtain concessions from opposing witnesses before the defendant offers evidence of its own. This can be particularly helpful in a product liability case if the opposing witness happens to be the defendant's designated corporate representative during the trial. Hence we were pleasantly surprised to learn that Victor Declercq would be Ford's representative throughout the trial, which offered the chance to buttress the testimony of Sam Sero and other witnesses from the lips of someone authorized to speak for the Ford Motor Company.

On the other hand, unless it was done with care, calling an experienced witness like Victor Declercq could easily backfire. After weighing the risks among ourselves, we decided that the court's *Daubert* ruling and Ford's plan to clobber us with NHTSA's 1989 study justified the risk. What follows are key parts of my cross-examination:

**The Court:** Good morning, ladies and gentlemen, I am pleased to note that the air conditioning is now working just fine.

**Mr. Murray:** At this time, the plaintiff calls Mr. Victor Declercq for cross-examination.

***

After Declercq was sworn, I plunged in:

**Q:** How old are you, sir?

**A:** 63.

**Q:** I understand you recently retired from the Ford Motor Company?

**A:** That's correct.

**Q:** How long were you employed by Ford?

**A:** Nearly 28 years.

**Q:** What was your last position at Ford, Mr. Declercq?

**A:** My last position at Ford was as a Design Analysis Engineer.

**Q:** Does the Design Analysis Department provide expert witnesses to Ford in the defense of product liability cases?

**A:** That is part of our responsibility . . . .

**Q:** Was that part of your duties while you were working in that department?

**A:** Yes, it was.

**Q:** You have testified previously on behalf of Ford as an expert witness in sudden acceleration cases?

**A:** Yes, sir . . . .

**Q:** Do you hold a license in electrical engineering?

**A:** No.

**Q:** Mr. Declercq, do you consider yourself the most knowledgeable person at the Ford Motor Company regarding cruise control design and operation in general?

**A:** I think it would be very presumptuous for anyone to say that they were the person that knows the most about cruise control within the Ford Motor Company.

***

Declercq had not been so modest during a discovery deposition taken by Phillip Morrell:

**Q:** Do you recall being deposed in this case?

**A:** Yes, sir.

**Q:** Have you had an opportunity to review your deposition prior to today?

**A:** Yes, sir.

**Q:** Mr. Declercq, be kind enough to look at pages 53 and 54, beginning with the question at the bottom of page 53 and your answer at the top of page 54. Please read what it says.

**A:** The question was: "Are you the most knowledgeable person with regard to speed control systems at Ford?" And my answer was: "That for the stand-alone speed control system that we're talking about, I would say that I am the most knowledgeable person regarding the system . . . . "

***

By demonstrating early who held the whip hand, I hoped to keep control of the examination. After Declercq described the basic features of Ford's cruise control, I turned to the specific design feature on which our case rested:

**Q:** Is it a fact that the moment the operator turns the ignition on, power comes from the battery to the device that controls the throttle?

**A:** The power, as it comes from the battery, obviously, it goes through fuses and so forth. It goes through the ignition switch. It goes to this amplifier, and then from this amplifier, it does proceed and go on to the servo mechanism.

**Q:** So that there is voltage or what we laymen call power within a split second of ignition?

**A:** That's correct.

***

Although this particular design feature was not contested, electromagnetic interference being out of the case, we felt it was important to let the jury learn from Ford's spokesperson that the servo was powered without regard to whether the system was engaged. With that accomplished, the real challenge remained, namely, how, without mentioning electromagnetic interference, to gain an admission from Declercq that the system was vulnerable to a sudden acceleration. Since the court's *Daubert* ruling had limited us to hardwire possibilities, we had struggled over whether to confront Declercq with potential hardwire failures, or rely instead on the testimony of Paul Jarvis, our OSI witnesses, and Updegrove's testimony. Although we had no illusions about the difficulty of getting Declercq to admit anything which supported Sero's testimony, we felt the court had left us little choice but to try:

**Q:** Now, in terms of the operation of voltage potential in this system, you have heard the term "ground connection"?

**A:** Yes.

**Q:** What does "ground connection" mean to you?

**A:** The battery operates normally just slightly over 12 volts, if it's fully charged, and again, that's the positive side of the battery. The other side, which would be the ground side, is tied to the ground, which would be the zero volt side of the battery. So you have zero volts on one side of the battery, and you have 12 volts on the other side of the battery.

**Q:** That's the way it's supposed to operate?

**A:** That's the way a battery normally operates, at least in an automobile battery.

**Q:** Are you familiar with the ground in this system?

**A:** Yes.

**Q:** What does it mean in terms of the proper functioning of the system?

**A:** As I explained earlier, there is one independent wire tied to ground. That's the zero volts end of the battery. The other end is the 12 volts that comes from the battery. That's the +12 volt side of the battery. So, the ground would be the zero volt side of the battery.

**Q:** That's this voltage potential we talked about earlier?

**A:** Yes.

**Q:** Zero to 12 volts?

**A:** Yes.

**Q:** Does the term "open connection" mean something to you?

**A:** That means a broken wire or the wire is not capable of conducting any current. In other words, there's no ground.

**Q:** Let's suppose one of those grounds is broken so there is no connection.
**A:** OK.
**Q:** And I want to turn on my speed control system, will it turn on?
**A:** No. I would say no.

***

Although he had tried to equate "open connection" with a "broken wire," Declercq had conceded that without a ground connection, the cruise control system would not work. While this could explain why Paul Jarvis had been unable to engage the cruise control, Declercq could claim he would have found an open ground connection during his inspection of Kathy's Aerostar. Therefore, challenging him directly on this point would give him a chance to insist he would have found a loose connection. In a quandary, I asked for a moment to confer with co-counsel before continuing my cross-examination.

Huddling with my colleagues at our table, I asked Molly if she knew whether Ford had ever "tested what would happen if there was a fault in one of the wires to the servo, while there was also an intermittently loose or open ground connection to the controls?"

Sounding anxious, Molly replied in a low voice, "I don't think we know."

Turning to George, I whispered, "This damned *Daubert* ruling has us boxed in. If Ford never tested for this condition, it's a homerun; but if they did, it could backfire."

Sounding unfazed, George whispered, "Forget that old saw about never asking a question unless you know the answer. If they tested for this condition, Crosby will bring that out anyway when Declercq testifies during Ford's case. So take a deep breath and live dangerously."

I left our table, drew a deep breath, and took a step in the dark:

> **Q:** To your knowledge, Mr. Declercq, has Ford ever tested what would happen if you have an open connection in the speed amplifier, and a short to ground in either the vent or vac wire; has the company ever tested that?
>
> **A:** Have we tested whether there would be simultaneous failure of those two?
>
> **Q:** No. Has Ford simply tested what would happen if you have an open connection in the speed amplifier, no ground, and there is a short in either the vent or vac wire?

For the first time, Declercq appeared to hesitate, and I could feel the tension rising in the courtroom. Finally came the gift-wrapped answer on which we had rolled the dice:

> **A:** OK. So, that there are two. Now, we are talking about there are two failures, essentially, the open wire and then the shorted wire. I haven't looked at the failure mode and effects analysis on this amplifier for a long time, but to the best of my understanding and to the best of my knowledge, *we did not.* [Emphasis added.]

This was one of the rare occasions in my career when tossing aside conventional wisdom about cross-examination paid off. More importantly, we now had an argument that could carry the day for Kathy Jarvis.

CHAPTER 33

# FINAL ARGUMENTS

### CAR KILLS WOMAN AT MARKET

Five cars were smashed and a woman was killed in Syracuse when the driver of a Colony Park drove through a crowded market at over 40 mph. The driver remembers that his vehicle's accelerator seemed stuck and he could not slow the car down. Witnesses stated that the deceased woman flew an unbelievable 20 or 30 feet through the air after being struck by the Mercury, eventually coming to rest under another car. Bystanders attempted to lift the vehicle to help her, but were not able to save her life.

*Post Standard*, Syracuse, NY, May 15, 1992

**IN NEW YORK, THE DEFENSE ARGUES FIRST IN CIVIL CASES. THIS** means the plaintiff is able to respond without being rushed by the time constraints courts often place on rebuttal when the plaintiff argues first. Since I knew Crosby's argument would be well prepared and forceful, I was glad we were in New York. Not surprisingly, Crosby began by ticking off the elements of the industry's standard screed:

> On July 14, 1991, the evidence has shown there were not multiple, simultaneous, undetectable, independent electronic faults in the plaintiff's vehicle. There was not an inoperable dump valve in the brake system and the cruise control of that vehicle. There was not an inoperable set of brakes on the vehicle. There were not inoperable stoplights. There was not an inoperative transmission.
>
> The plaintiff has come to you and said that all of those things occurred simultaneously, and all of those things after the accident disappeared. And they have given you a theory. What they have not done, however, is give you any physical evidence to support any single portion of what they say goes into the mix to have caused the accident by a sudden, unintended rewiring in the speed control.

Listening to this argument, I was grateful to the Aerostar owners who had come to New York to describe their experiences, and surprised when Crosby began picking away at minor details. David Morse had been "wrong" about the location of the gear shift; if Jacqueline Gibbs had been "applying the brakes in reverse, the front brakes would have locked up . . . and you couldn't steer the vehicle"; Theda Blackstone "doesn't recall exactly what she did with the seat . . . [but] . . . she claims she got both feet on the brake . . . "; and Linda Schmidt was "the lady who said she had dinner, had a glass or two of wine, and then was driving her daughter up to their farm." None of these people's Aerostar, according to Crosby, had malfunctioned. Instead, "the very people they brought in here to tell you they've had a sudden acceleration event, I'm certain did. But they had a sudden acceleration event as a result of applying the wrong pedal."

Crosby's approach showed the bind he was in because of our OSI evidence, Updegrove's testimony, and the concessions we had gotten from Declercq. No matter the evidence, Ford expected its trial counsel to follow the strategy that had helped the company win one case after another for almost two decades. If that meant keeping a captive witness like Declercq in the dark, asserting a false privilege claim, removing sound from a videotape, or putting an unbelievable spin on the company's massive investigation, so be it. Hence this regarding Updegrove's testimony:

> Ladies and gentlemen, the only physical evidence is that the plaintiff applied her foot to the accelerator . . . . [T]here clearly had been people who had claimed these type of events with other Ford Aerostars. You heard that from Mr. Updegrove's deposition that Ford . . . looked at many, many vehicles. They actually went out and inspected them to see if there was anything wrong with them, or to see if there was any possibility that a wire was cut and so forth. And the conclusions were pretty clear: the overwhelming conclusion was that the cause of this type of incident, not only by Ford, but by the National Highway Traffic Safety Administration, found with every single auto manufacturer . . . that people were just putting their foot accidentally on the accelerator instead of the brake.
>
> You have heard about the number of complaints. You have heard that the complaints against Ford or against the Aerostar are virtually no different and less than many other vehicles . . . . If this is a mechanical problem, something in the speed control system, you should continue to get the same relative number of complaints every year, because it's not driver dependent. On the other hand, if it is driver dependent, and it's largely driven by people who are not

used to the car, you would have a high drop-off. And that's what happened.

Not surprisingly, Crosby ended with NHTSA's 1989 study:

These multiple failures were examined by the National Highway Traffic Safety Administration in detail. We've been through their report with you. They found that there is no evidence to support that concept. We have brought you those tests. They found that there was no basis for that. They found that there are as many claims in these types of vehicles that don't have cruise control as with cruise control. And they ultimately found that analysis of the circuitry shows that for nearly all controls designed in the last few years, and one of the designs they looked at was the one in this case, two or more independent intermittent failures would have to occur simultaneously to cause the throttle to open in a way that would be difficult to detect after the incident. The occurrence of such simultaneously undetectable failures is virtually impossible.

They go on to say, in any event, the brakes overcome the speed control. Ladies and gentlemen, there is *no evidence* here of a defect in this vehicle. There is *no evidence* here that simultaneous failures occurred at the same time that the brake system failed and that the dump valve failed at the same time. There is clear evidence here to suggest that Ms. Jarvis, on July 14, 1991, thought she was applying the brake and in an agitated state when, in fact, she was applying the accelerator.

Thank you.

**The Court:** Ladies and gentlemen, why don't we just take a brief break before we hear Mr. Murray? And I remind you to keep an open mind and not to talk about the case. We are getting to the point where you can talk. [Emphasis added.]

***

Since I had been scribbling notes during Crosby's presentation, I welcomed the chance to organize our response. Following the recess, I began my argument with Kathy Jarvis.

**The Court:** Mr. Murray?

**Mr. Murray:** Thank you. Your Honor, counsel, members of the jury: No evidence of a problem? No evidence of a malfunction in this new Aerostar? Just a theory? A woman in the prime of life, who's been described as responsible, careful, organized, gets in a brand new Aerostar with 400 miles on it. The next thing she knows, there is a sound as if a cowboy, a madman had pushed the accelerator pedal all the way to the floor. Everyone around hears a V-R-O-O-O-M, V-R-O-O-M as if something is terribly wrong. Eight or ten seconds later, it's in a ditch 320 feet away. And during those seconds, this responsible woman looked down and saw *both feet on the brake pedal.*

No evidence? You have the speed. There is no disagreement that the speed at the end of this terrible event was totally consistent with a woman fighting against the engine. If she hadn't been fighting to stop that Aerostar, it would have been going 45–50 miles an hour when it went up that embankment.

We have five responsible adults who had an identical experience that Ford describes as a Group I event. And we have agreement that there are only two ways something like this can happen. Only the driver's foot on the gas pedal or the cruise control can move the throttle to a wide open position.

Members of the jury, when something looks like a duck, walks like a duck, and quacks like a duck, we call it a duck; and what we have here is an event that when you reason it through is totally consistent with one conclusion and that is a malfunction in the machine. And there is only one system that can malfunction and cause such an event, and that's the cruise control.

I very much like Judge Buchwald's description of circumstantial evidence in the instructions of law you will be given when I'm finished. But my favorite example of circumstantial evidence—maybe some of you recall it—is the story of Robinson Crusoe stranded on an island. He thought he was all alone and doomed to remain alone perhaps for the rest of his life. And then one day, he came down to the beach. What did he see? He saw a footprint in the sand. He didn't see a foot; he didn't see a leg; he didn't see a person, and yet he knew with absolute certainty that he wasn't alone on that island. Ladies and gentlemen, every day in our lives from morning until night we make decisions based on circumstantial evidence. In this case, the surrounding facts and circumstances, together with Kathy's testimony, point to one conclusion, a malfunction in that machine . . . .

***

I turned next to Kathy's credibility:

You knew almost nothing about Kathy Jarvis's head injury when you first had a chance to gauge the kind of person she is, how trustworthy she is. You hadn't heard from Doctors Huisman, Chambers, and others. But you saw a woman who with every fiber in her being was trying to be truthful and tell you everything she could remember to

> the best of her ability. I now ask you on her behalf to give the same kind of effort, the same kind of commitment to getting it right that she gave to you when she was on that witness stand.

Having stressed the accuracy and reliability of Kathy's testimony, it was time to make the jury aware of what Ford had learned from investigating 2,877 sudden accelerations. Although the court had ordered Ford to produce Updegrove's final report and Supplement Q—the electronic summary of certain data regarding Aerostar occurrences—we hadn't received these materials until the eve of trial, by which point, as mentioned earlier, I was so preoccupied with other things I put off reading the materials until the evening before final arguments. Even then, I first had to review hundreds of pages of testimony. Consequently, I set my alarm for 4 a.m. and read Updegrove's report and Attachment Q when I was feeling rested. It was a decision that would prove the adage, "Better late than never."

By the time room service delivered breakfast at 7 a.m., I could hardly contain my excitement. Although Updegrove's report was couched in carefully guarded language, the information recorded in Supplement Q gave me a shot of adrenaline. The bad news was that by the time I finished poring over the electronically recorded data, there was barely time to jot down a few final notes, shower, shave, grab a cab, and make it in time for the opening of court. Now, with my heart pounding, I turned to what I had discovered in the wee morning hours about Ford's investigation:

> I want to come now, members of the jury, to what may be the most revealing document in existence regarding sudden acceleration . . . . Let's think back to the videotaped deposition of Mr. Updegrove. It was rather lengthy, but

> . . . you'll have a summary of what Ford did during this investigation that began in 1987 and was concluded according to his final report in 1992 . . . . What did he tell us about that investigation? We learned it was a concentrated, in-depth investigation using a format designed to recreate these events as well as they could. The format contained many questions for drivers. Did you brake? How did you brake? Did you brake with two feet? Did the accelerator pedal move by itself? They were the kinds of issues to help them learn whether they were dealing with a malfunction or driver error.
>
> They also created some definitions, so that as this information came in, they could decide what kind of event they were dealing with. One of the definitions was Group I, defined as an increase in engine rpms or vehicle speed upon engagement from park to drive or reverse. Notice it said "upon engagement from park to drive or reverse." Ladies and gentlemen, that's what we have here.

One reason it had taken hours to finally decipher Supplement Q was how the data was organized. Once I figured that out, I was able to calculate how many of the 560 Aerostar events, had begun, as in *Jarvis,* exactly at gear engagement. As I explained what I had learned, several jurors leaned forward in their seats.

> Mr. Sero told us that the moment when a fault or short is most likely to occur is when you put the vehicle in gear. That's when you call for extra energy into the system. In other words, there's an extra surge of energy . . . . There were 560 Aerostars in this investigation; and even though the investigation was winding down in 1992, they already had 167 events involving a 1991 Aerostar, 162 of which—that's 97%—occurred when the gear was engaged. If my

> mathematics is correct, about 92% of the 560 Aerostar cases also fell into that category.

The most startling discovery, however, had come just minutes before I had to scurry for the opening of court. Ford had assigned a causal category to each case indicating one of three possibilities: an electronic malfunction, a mechanical or hardware problem like a stuck throttle cable, or a pedal misapplication. Although Supplement Q identified the "causal" category for each event, it had taken me nearly two hours of frantic scribbling on a yellow pad to do the numbers. The result produced a jolt of adrenaline I was still feeling as I turned to Ford's causal conclusions:

> Neither Mr. Updegrove nor I had Supplement Q when he was deposed, but we have it now; and we know they created groups or categories they called "causal groups." One of the groups was called "inconsistent." I thought I might have a blow-up of this, but I decided there's so much data on each of these sheets that I would trust you to make the computations yourselves. You have across the top here different categories that include the name of the owner; and that is important because the people who came here to testify—Ms. Blackstone, Ms. Moore, Mr. Morse, Ms. Schmidt, and Ms. Gibbs—are all on here and are characterized as Group I or Group I-A. Among the causal groups is the term "inconsistent," which they defined as follows: "The allegation interview and vehicle investigation results are not consistent and/or not supported by tests on the customer vehicle or like vehicles." And guess what? All five of those people are listed as "inconsistent." In fact, ladies and gentlemen, if my count is correct, they put "inconsistent" after about 420 of the 560 Aerostar occurrences . . . .

> There was another category, ladies and gentlemen of the jury, they called "complete," which they defined as: "allegation, interview results and vehicle inspection results are logical, but no explanation for the event can be determined." The assignment of this causal factor was used in early cases only. If my count is correct, there are 96 completes for the Aerostar. Now if ever there was proof that Sam Sero is right that this is a difficult problem to diagnose, we have here plain language saying, "Yes, it's perfectly logical that it was a malfunction, but we couldn't find anything when we did our inspection."

Updegrove would later acknowledge that there was no practical difference between the causal groupings designated "inconsistent" and "complete", and that they had stopped using the category "complete" when the OGC intervened and ordered him to stop placing cases in that category. While that admission was in the future, not so for the devastating category the entire industry had been using for decades to evade paying compensation to people like Kathy Jarvis:

> Members of the jury, they have another category here; it's "misapplication". That's obviously misapplication of the pedals. And how many times do you suppose they felt justified in writing down misapplication of a pedal? *Less than one percent!* Is it any wonder that Mr. Declercq didn't want to rely on Ford's five-year investigation? The moment I got into it, you saw how he wrapped himself in NHTSA, NHTSA, NHTSA.

I had considered arguing that NHTSA should have seen through the industry's driver error strategy but had decided to keep both barrels on Ford:

Tragically for this woman, they didn't do a failure analysis, but turned control of the throttle over to chance events like a loose or open connection or one of the most common things in any electrical system, a short . . . . Members of the jury, the issues here are simple. The first has to do with negligence. Did they fail to use reasonable care in the design of this product? I'm sure I don't have to talk about how important a failure mode and effects analysis is. How can they possibly suggest they weren't under a duty to do that? This is so important, I want to take a minute to read from the trial transcript. When I called Mr. Declercq, as the corporate representative, for cross-examination during our case, let me read:

**Q:** Does the term failure mode effects analysis mean anything to you?

**A:** Yes.

**Q:** What does it mean?

**A:** Failure mode effects analysis is known—we abbreviated with an alphabet soup, FMEA—meaning that you examine all possibilities for component failures, open shorts and all these kinds of things to determine if there was anything that was related to safety that might be involved in the failure, and then you proceed and try to minimize or reduce or eliminate the possibilities.

First, you try to eliminate the possibility of any failure causing, you know, an adverse safety-related effect.

**Q:** To your knowledge, has Ford ever tested what would happen if you have an open connection in the speed amplifier and if you have a short-to-ground in either the vent or vac wire? Have you ever tested that?

> **A:** Had we tested whether there could be simultaneous failures of those two?
> **Q:** No. Has Ford ever simply tested what would happen if you had an open connection in the speed amplifier, no ground, and there is a short in either the vent or vac wire?
> **A:** OK. So, that there are two. Now, we are talking about there are two failures, essentially, the open wire and then the shorted wire. I haven't looked at the FMEA on this amplifier for a long time. But to my understanding and the best of my knowledge, we did not . . . .
> **Mr. Murray:** Ladies and gentlemen, to put a car that can do this on the road without doing the most basic kind of failure analysis of its design is negligence of the highest order.

***

Since I had now used most of the time the court had allotted for arguments, I turned to a brief discussion of Kathy's injuries and damages before ending with some final thoughts about how they had changed her life:

> This woman, who was described as once being able to have a dozen balls in the air at one time, today struggles; going to the grocery store is a struggle; it is a struggle to help her son with third grade math; she can't keep a checkbook. It is a struggle for her not to fall into the depths of depression and despair, and to just keep going. I can't begin to understand this, but somehow you have to find a way. The justice system demands that we find a way to compensate her justly, fully, and fairly. The losses here, ladies and gentlemen, are large; and, therefore, I suggest to you in

> conscience that the compensation must be proportionate to the enormity of that loss.

It had been an intense and often exhausting trial, and after the Court read the instructions of law to the jury, there was nothing left except to await the verdict.

CHAPTER 34

# VERDICT

### TERROR AS CRUISE CONTROL "JAMS"

A young driver thought he was going to die as his Ford Explorer hurtled along at 80 km/h on a major Melbourne freeway stuck in cruise control. Chase Weir, 22, . . . was travelling at the speed for about 30 minutes before he finally was able to stop his 2002 Ford Explorer . . . . Mr. Weir called Ford to ask for assistance and was told to pump the foot brake and turn off the ignition, neither of which had any effect. "I tried turning the ignition off, I tried changing the gear shift, I put my foot on the brake but the brake pedal became stiff and the car would only slow down to about 80 kilometres per hour and that's when I realized I had a bit of a problem," he said.

*Courier-Mail*, Melbourne, Australia, December 15, 2009

**AFTER DELIBERATING UNTIL 5:00 P.M., THE JURY NOTIFIED THE** Court it wished to adjourn for the day. The following morning it sent three notes to the judge that produced the following proceedings without the jury present:

> **The Court:** The first note that we received this morning, which is marked as Court Exhibit 3, reads: "We want to know which is Supplement Q, if we have it in evidence or not?" And I told you about that before, and counsel agrees that Exhibit Q or Supplement Q was Plaintiff's Exhibit 271 and we ascertained that the jury had it.
>
> The second note is: "Can we have a calculator?" And we gave them a tiny calculator, and that note is Court Exhibit 4.
>
> The third note is: "Supplement Q is hard to read. Please provide a better copy."

***

With a less conscientious jury, my decision to put Updegrove's report and Supplement Q aside until the evening prior to final arguments might have proven costly. Fortunately, several jurors had post-graduate degrees, and every member of the panel had shown a keen interest in the case. Since I had urged the jury to carefully study Supplement Q, the request for a calculator was encouraging. After some discussion with counsel, this occurred on the record:

> **The Court:** We have your notes and we have responded to some of them already. I think it's the third note that indicates you were having trouble reading Supplement Q. What I'm going to do, with the permission of counsel, is to give you another copy that I have in my files and that is going to be marked 271, Court Copy, and we will give you back the other one as well.

***

Waiting for juries is an almost unbearable time for trial lawyers, and since the jury was apparently just getting to Supplement Q, we knew we were in for a long wait. Over the next several hours, the jury sent several additional notes requesting information that seemed to indicate it was getting close to a verdict in favor of Kathy Jarvis. But it was not until it asked for "Dr. Markus's financial estimates" of her economic damages that we felt confident of the outcome. Shortly before 5 p.m., the jury returned a unanimous verdict finding that Ford was negligent and setting total economic and noneconomic damages at 1.1 million. After it was polled, the court thanked the jury before making a surprising announcement:

> I don't want you to all rise in fury when I tell you there's a possibility that I may need your services again, not tomorrow, not the next day. There's a possibility of another issue in the case that I may need to call you back for. If that happens, we would give you plenty of notice. We would try to accommodate your schedules and I know it would be a fraction of the time that we have given to this case until now.
>
> For now, I can only say thank you. You were terrific. You paid an awful lot of attention all the time. I didn't catch anyone napping, as sometimes occurs, and we worked very long days. I think we also worked hard to get you the evidence as quickly as we possibly could. We realize it was a tough schedule that we kept, but I hope you'll agree that it was better to do it in fewer days than more days. I thank you again for your verdict, and you are excused.

Since the court had ruled that punitive damages would be tried separately, we assumed that was the unresolved issue mentioned by the court. We were doubtful, however, that Buchwald would let the jury decide if punitive damages were warranted. By excluding electromagnetic interference, she had locked herself into a position entirely consistent with Ford's defense that a loose and undetectable ground connection at the speed amplifier and a shorted wire affecting the servo was a virtual impossibility. We had gotten the impression throughout the trial, in fact, that she was having second thoughts about having allowed Sero to opine that Ford's cruise control electronics were defective because of a possibility she correctly saw as remote. On the other hand, we were convinced that the totality of our testimony and evidence convincingly proved that Ford's electronics were negligently designed, regardless of whether the cause was hardwire faults, EMI, or some other condition.

While we were pondering what the court might do, Ford filed a motion to reverse the verdict for lack of evidence and to dismiss the case. We responded that the evidence supported the verdict and warranted punitive damages. As the weeks wore on, however, it became clear that a ruling upholding the verdict was the best we could hope for. When I asked George Tompkins what our chances would be if Buchwald dismissed the case, he pointed out that the federal circuit court of appeals for New York "has some of the best legal minds around, and there's some good New York law we can use to support our verdict."

A short time later, the court ruled we failed to prove our case, and dismissed the suit. While we were disappointed, we left confident the federal appeals court would reverse the ruling. Therefore, it was time to study the trial record and write our appeal. Meanwhile, the *Manigault* case took a dramatic turn.

CHAPTER 35

# HIGH DRAMA IN A HIGH COURT

### SUV WRECKS, PINS MAN AT RESTAURANT

A sport utility vehicle crashed into a downtown restaurant Friday afternoon, pinning a man against an outside wall, Charleston police said. Police said a Jeep Cherokee jumped the curb outside Doe's Pita on East Bay Street and struck a man having lunch at a sidewalk table. While other diners looked on, the Jeep pinned the man against the front of the restaurant for several seconds until the driver was able to put the vehicle in reverse, witnesses said . . . . The Jeep's driver told officers she was trying to park her vehicle when it suddenly accelerated and went over the curb. The woman told police she had her foot on the brake at the time . . . . After the initial impact, the Jeep continued to accelerate, "bucking" back and forth against the man and the wall. The injured man remained conscious the whole time, staring up at the vehicle as it came at him. The driver was "hysterical" and seemed unable to stop the car or put it in reverse.

*Post and Courier,* October 20, 2001

**AFTER BOUNCING AROUND FOR NEARLY THREE YEARS IN THE APPEALS** court for Cuyahoga County, the *Manigault* case finally reached the Supreme Court of Ohio. One of the questions we had asked the court to review was whether the removal of sound from Ford's videotaped braking demonstration deprived our clients of a fair trial. After I described how we had learned about the doctored videotape during the *Dateline* story about the *Manigault* case, Elizabeth Wright began her argument by describing the videotape as a piece of demonstrative evidence that had not prejudiced *Manigault.* At this point, Justice Francis Sweeney, a former professional football player and prosecuting attorney interrupted Wright:

**Justice Sweeney:** So what you're really saying is that whether the sound was on the videotape or not, it makes no difference because it wouldn't prove anything.

**Ms. Wright:** Justice Sweeney, those are two different issues, but you are correct. I would like to address the sound on the video.

**Justice Sweeney:** How did the sound happen to disappear?

**Ms. Wright:** Certainly, contrary to Mr. Murray's representation to this Court, he did not ask for the video. The video was a demonstrative exhibit . . . .

**Justice Sweeney:** Did you hear the question?

**Ms. Wright:** The video was a demonstrative . . . .

**Justice Sweeney:** Answer my question.

**Ms. Wright:** The video was a demonstrative exhibit used at trial. There were versions with audio and versions without. In this particular case, the one word . . . .

***

Justice Sweeney's expression showed he was incredulous at Wright's "no harm, no foul" argument.

**Justice Sweeney:** Who chose to send the one without the sound?

**Ms. Wright:** The client made two different copies, one with an audio and one without. Because the one with audio, the one word was on a test that was not being used at trial, the fourth test, it involved a gentleman other than the person who was going to be testifying at trial. As a demonstrative exhibit, it would have been hearsay and Ford was actually presented . . . .

**Justice Sweeney:** Who made the determination that it would be better for everybody if they sent the one without sound?

**Ms. Wright:** I don't know, Justice Sweeney, if anyone made a decision. It was simply a demonstrative exhibit.

**Justice Sweeney:** I want to know who made the decision to send the exhibit without sound.

**Ms. Wright:** That portion of the video wasn't going to be used, Justice Sweeney, so I don't . . . .

**Justice Sweeney:** Someone had to make the decision to send the video without the sound.

**Ms. Wright:** That portion of the video wasn't going to be used, Justice Sweeney, so I don't . . . .

**Justice Sweeney:** Someone had to make the decision to send the video without the sound.

**Ms. Wright:** I understand, your Honor.

**Justice Sweeney:** Who sent the video without the sound, who made that decision?

**Ms. Wright:** I don't know who made that decision.

**Justice Sweeney:** You don't know?

**Ms. Wright:** The video was a demonstrative exhibit, which had no sound on it for purposes of trial . . . . In fact, [the video] which Mr. Declercq testified about is in connection with another case where it was requested by Mr. Murray in 1999.

**Justice Sweeney:** So he finally got it in 1999.

**Ms. Wright:** Correct, but they had . . . .

**Justice Sweeney:** Why would you send it then?

**Ms. Wright:** It was in connection with another case where Mr. Murray's co-counsel requested it based on Mr. Murray's appearance on *Dateline* . . . .

**Justice Sweeney:** So we still don't know who sent the video without the sound.

**Ms. Wright:** The video at trial had no sound. The client had a video with the sound and a video without sound.

**Justice Sweeney:** Who decided to send the video without sound? Who would be responsible for that?

**Ms. Wright:** The client provided a video that had no sound on it.

**Justice Sweeney:** Ford decided not to send the one with sound?

**Ms. Wright:** I don't know Judge that there was a specific decision.

**Justice Sweeney:** In whose possession was the video?

**Ms. Wright:** In Ford's possession.

**Justice Sweeney:** I see, so if Ford sent the video anywhere else, it was their decision to send one without sound?

**Ms. Wright:** Yes, I mean, the bottom line is . . . .

**Justice Sweeney:** You've answered my question.

***

Because the court had focused almost entirely on the soundless video, its decision on October 9, 2002, was somewhat anti-climactic:

We cannot condone the manner in which the video evidence was handled. Ford gave *Manigault*, and showed the jury, a videotape without sound. Ford solicited testimony based on the videotape from an expert witness. It is possible, as *Manigault* alleges, that the expert's testimony was directly contradicted by his own words on the audio portion of the videotape. At the very least, the presentation of the video without audio was seriously misleading.

Section 16, Article I, of the Ohio Constitution provides that "every person, for an injury done him in his land, goods, person, or reputation shall have a remedy by due course of law." Based on the facts before us, the only way to ensure that the apparently misleading testimony did not unfairly affect the jury, thereby violating the Manigaults' right to pursue a remedy, is to order a new trial. We hold that a new trial is the appropriate remedy when an expert witness's testimony accompanying a videotape without audio is allegedly contradicted by a copy of the videotape with audio, even when the videotape with audio is not discovered until after the trial has been completed.

In its brief, Ford makes various arguments concerning the relevance of the video and the audio content. We will not consider them now. Ford will have ample opportunity to make them at the new trial.

Almost a decade had elapsed since the Manigaults' Crown Victoria had crashed into a neighbor's house ending forever the life they had struggled so long to build for themselves. Eighteen more months would pass before their ordeal would finally come to a stirring conclusion.

CHAPTER 36

# SONIA SOTOMAYOR

### RUNAWAY CAR KILLS THREE IN TEXAS

Tyler, Texas—A car that drove out of control for nearly a mile smashed into a busy intersection Friday, killing the driver, his wife and an infant whose car seat flew 20 feet into the roadway, police said. Police said it was unclear how fast the car was going, but witnesses reported that it was well above the speed limit when it struck nine cars, including one carrying the 8-month-old girl and two adults.

*Kentucky.com*, November 28, 2003

**WHEN WE ARRIVED FOR ORAL ARGUMENTS IN *JARVIS* WE LEARNED** that the presiding judge would be Sonia Sotomayor, later to become a Justice of the United States Supreme Court. After she was nominated by President Obama, pro-business tort reformers like Kentucky Senator Mitch McConnell were quick to label her as "a liberal activist." During her Senate confirmation hearings,

Sotomayor repeatedly emphasized that the core of her judicial philosophy was to apply the law to the specific facts of the case before the court. Her conduct in *Jarvis* is a good example of this approach. I had barely begun my presentation when then Judge Sotomayor began asking questions showing she had mastered the trial record. Because it takes many hours of hard work to prepare an appeal, there is nothing more discouraging than arguing to a panel that hasn't done its homework. While I have argued many cases in state and federal courts, including the United States Supreme Court, I have never had the pleasure of responding to questions from a judge so thoroughly familiar with the case. On February 7, 2002, the court reversed Judge Buchwald and reinstated the verdict for Kathy Jarvis.

Sotomayor's 51-page decision in *Jarvis* provides a valuable insight into why pro-business tort reformers like McConnell opposed her nomination. Here's how the *Washington Post* described Sotomayor's ruling in *Jarvis*:

> Her writings are full of details from the trial record . . . where she often meticulously analyzes witnesses' testimony. When she reinstated a verdict against Ford Motor Company in 2002 in a lawsuit of a woman who said her van suddenly accelerated without her touching the gas pedal, Sotomayor wrote that one witness's testimony "requires two simultaneous malfunctions in the cruise control circuitry. The first is an open ground connection to the speed amplifier, resulting from a loose or broken wire."

The *Post* contrasted Sotomayor's judicial approach with that of a Republican colleague on the Second Circuit who, in another case, wrote that "appellate courts are not fact finders; . . . I do not understand it to be our role . . . to engage in this kind of dissection of the empirical evidence cited by the district court." Fortunately for Kathy Jarvis, Sotomayor considered it her duty to "dissect the empirical evidence" cited by Naomi Buchwald in taking away the jury's verdict:

> The district court, meanwhile, failed to discuss the evidence in the record that weighs heavily against Ford's theory of driver error. Ford's theory that Jarvis had the parking brake on and applied her foot to the accelerator instead of the brake is irreconcilable with Jarvis's testimony that she began with her foot "lightly" on the brake and that the Aerostar's acceleration was sudden. If her foot was placed "lightly" on the accelerator instead of the brake, and the parking brake were on, the Aerostar would have accelerated slowly, if at all. Jarvis on the other hand testified that the Aerostar "took off."
>
> Another weakness of Ford's theory is that it assumes driver error not only as to which pedal Jarvis depressed but also to the effect of each stroke of the pedal. Under Ford's theory, Jarvis would have felt the Aerostar accelerate with each application of the pedal, and slow each time she lifted her foot on the pedal. Ford's theory asks us to believe that Jarvis repeatedly applied force to the pedal without understanding the effect of her actions.
>
> Finally, Ford's theory is unable to account for Jarvis's claim that she depressed the pedal with both feet. As part of the accident reconstruction, Jarvis was asked to sit in the Aerostar and to place both feet on the accelerator. She was able to do so only by placing one foot on top of the other. When asked to do the same with the brake pedal, she found that it accommodated both feet. The jury viewed photographs taken for purposes of this litigation showing Jarvis sitting in an Aerostar at the accident site. The photos

> also demonstrated that, when asked to put both feet on the accelerator, Jarvis had one foot placed over the other.
>
> In sum, we find the ultimate issue of Ford's negligence to be a jury question. Ford did not present evidence that conclusively demonstrated, as a matter of law, that Jarvis's accident did not occur because of a defect in the Aerostar's cruise control mechanism. Jarvis's testimony, the testimony of other Aerostar owners who had similar experiences, and the evidence of hundreds of other reported cases of sudden accelerations in Aerostars, combined with an expert scientific explanation of how the cruise control may have malfunctioned and of an inexpensive remedy, were all found admissible by the district court. Together, this evidence provided the jury with a sufficient evidentiary basis to reasonably conclude that the cruise control mechanism had been defectively designed.

I have only touched on the thoroughness of Sotomayor's analysis of the *Jarvis* record. Anyone interested in how she is likely to approach her work on the Supreme Court would do well to read the *Jarvis* decision.

Finally, it is worth mentioning that near the end of my oral argument, Sotomayor asked whether Ms. Jarvis would prefer to have her verdict reinstated or a new trial that included punitive damages. I replied that my client's circumstances were such that she desperately needed to be compensated for her losses as soon as possible.

Kathy's ordeal, however, was still not over. Ford asked the United States Supreme Court to review the case, and by the time its petition was denied, several more months had passed. Only then did Brian Crosby call to say that Ford was prepared to pay the judgment with accrued interest *if Jarvis would agree to have the judgment of the*

*Second Circuit vacated.* In return for having her groundbreaking case erased from the books, what was Ford offering? Absolutely nothing. If it didn't pay the judgment with interest, we could simply enforce it against Ford property or funds anywhere in the United States. My guess is that the Office of General Counsel had directed Crosby to try us out, on the principle that "there's no harm in asking." The maneuver was further evidence of corporate arrogance we had come to expect from Ford.

CHAPTER 37

# THE TRAIL GETS WARMER

### DRIVER CLAIMED SUDDEN ACCELERATION

> On May 22, 1994, Hal Eltiste and three passengers were driving 65 mph on Highway 67 near Peru, Neb. As they approached the intersection with Highway 75, Eltiste claimed that he tapped the brakes and turned off the cruise control when his Ford van suddenly accelerated and went through the intersection. It hit an embankment and soared about 60 feet before landing. The plaintiffs suffered serious injuries, including head trauma, vertebral compression fractures, broken ribs, pelvic and femur fractures and a crushed ankle.
>
> *Missouri Lawyers Weekly*, April 26, 2004

**FOLLOWING THE *JARVIS* VERDICT, I RECEIVED A CALL FROM TERRY** Mackey, a well-known Wyoming trial lawyer, who described how a Ford Cougar had suddenly accelerated out of control on a major artery near Casper and crashed into an oncoming vehicle, killing the driver and seriously injuring two of her children. When we were asked to join the case, I jumped at another chance to cross-examine Victor Declercq because, after *Jarvis,* he could no longer plead ignorance as he had done in *Manigault.* For example, he was now aware that Ford had classified less than 1% of 2,877 cases as a "pedal misapplication."

It turned out that following that trial, Declercq had asked the OGC's Robert Donnellan for a summary of the investigative results. His description of the encounter made my jaw drop. After establishing that he had asked Donnellan for a summary of the Updegrove results, the following exchanges ensued:

**Q:** When you made the request for a summary, was it your understanding that a summary of the investigation existed?

**A:** It was my understanding *after the conversation* I had with Donnellan that a summary did not exist.

**Q:** Did Mr. Donnellan . . . tell you that?

**A:** I can't say that Mr. Donnellan said that exactly. I remember that after the meeting and after the discussion that I walked away with the distinct feeling that—an understanding that—*a true summary did not exist.*

**Q:** Do you remember what Mr. Donnellan's exact words were?

**A:** No, sir.

**Q:** Do you remember what you asked him?

**A:** Again, I asked him pretty much the same thing that I just stated: Do you have a summary, is there a summary, of the Alan Updegrove—the results of the Alan Updegrove investigation?

**Q:** And you were told there was not?

**A:** That's my recollection, yes. [Emphasis added.]

***

Since Declercq knew from the *Jarvis* trial that Ford's electronic summaries contained the causal classifications assigned to each event, I was so stunned by his testimony I didn't follow up with the kind of questions readers at this point may be asking themselves. Why hadn't Declercq simply read Updegrove's report and Supplement Q during the *Jarvis* trial? Since he knew they contained the causal classifications, why hadn't he simply asked Donnellan to see the electronic summaries? If he had actually gone to Donnellan to learn the truth about the investigation, why hadn't he asked for a sampling of the questionnaires containing detailed information regarding each occurrence? Asking such questions of oneself, of course, is not unlike replaying missed golf shots in one's mind. In this case, fortunately, my unasked questions turned out to be harmless because Declercq was again Ford's corporate representative, and I was able to cross-examine him for two days during the presentation of the plaintiffs' case. After the jury returned a substantial verdict for our clients, the case was eventually settled on confidential terms.

The more we studied the detailed results of Ford's investigation, the more amazing it seemed that Ford could have concealed this massive investigation from NHTSA and the legal system. When we finally figured out how Ford pulled it off, Molly said it was "the mother of all deceptions in the history of runaway cars."

CHAPTER 38

# DISASTER IN MARYVILLE

### VAN CRASHES INTO MEDICAL OFFICE

Elaine Matke, an employee of Braidwood's Dew Medical Billing, had just walked away from the fax machine when she heard the screech of tires outside. Within seconds, those tires were slamming through the office's steel walls and glass entry door. Matke watched as the fax machine she had just used was crushed under the weight of a 2003 Ford Windstar van. Nearly the entire vehicle was inside the small office before the van finally stalled on some debris. "His wheels were still spinning as he was stopped in the building," Matke recalled.

*Braidwood Journal,* September 3, 2008

**ON A PLEASANT SUNDAY MORNING IN EARLY FALL 1994, MEMBERS** of the Rockford Baptist Church in Maryville, the county seat of Blount County just south of Knoxville, Tennessee, had gathered to chat on the front steps of the church following the morning worship service. Dan and Ann Emert had taught the Sunday school class and then sung in the choir; Thelma Henry had led a Bible class for senior church members prior to the service; others in the small group were Mark and Karen Lee, Ellen Wear, Judy Sauceman, and June Tipton. When she left the group, Tipton went to her 1991 Lincoln in the second row of the parking lot facing the church. Following her usual routine, she fastened her seatbelt, placed her right foot lightly on the brake pedal and turned on the ignition. Before shifting into drive, she paused to let several church members enter a Buick parked about two spaces to her left in the first row. As she shifted from park to drive, she removed her foot from the brake pedal to let the car creep forward. Instead, it suddenly shot forward with the engine racing. She instantly applied the brakes, but it was too late. The car jumped a curb, hurtled across a small lawn area, catapulted up the church steps onto the landing where, according to one witness, it knocked people down "like bowling pins." Ann Emert was crushed to death and several others were seriously injured.

As the engine continued to rev wildly and the right rear tire burned through the all-weather carpeting on the porch, Tipton crawled on hands and knees to the passenger side door. After she was helped from the car, Carl Cunningham and the pastor, Carlos Ownsby, observed the gas pedal near the floorboard as the engine continued to race. Cunningham then reached in and turned off the ignition. Tipton insisted she had never touched the gas pedal and that her foot had been on the brake pedal from the moment she realized what was happening until the car came to rest on the landing. Everyone agreed that no more than five seconds had elapsed from the moment they first heard the engine racing until the car landed on the church porch.

The event shocked Maryville, a close-knit picturesque college town of about 12,000 souls. In due course, the injured churchgoers and the Estate of Ann Emert retained lawyers, one of whom, Sid Gilreath, is a colleague of mine in the International Academy of Trial Lawyers. When Sid learned about our work, he came to Sandusky with Tim Priest, a well-regarded Knoxville-based trial lawyer who represented three of the families. Eventually, Sid and Tim asked us to join the case.

I knew from Jo Ellen that some of NHTSA's information requests to Ford were addressed to a man in the company's Automotive Safety Office named Edward L. Richardson. We knew from Mr. X that Ford's field engineers had investigated sudden accelerations during the 1980s. (See Chapter Twenty-Eight.) Therefore, my ears perked up when Jo Ellen told me NHTSA had asked for all sudden acceleration field reports.

"Who was the request addressed to?" I asked.

"Edward L. Richardson, whose name appears often in Ford's responses."

Although Richardson had retired in mid-1988, Ford agreed to produce him for deposition in the Tennessee case.

Molly believed that Richardson was an even more important witness than Updegrove. When I asked why, I quickly learned she wasn't shooting from the hip.

"Didn't Mr. X tell you these field engineers were trained to identify safety defects?"

"That's true, but . . . . "

Molly cut me off. "On the other hand, Alan Updegrove only has a degree in industrial engineering and the people he handpicked for the company's big investigation weren't even allowed to express an opinion regarding the cause. If these field engineers diagnosed a safety defect, their reports would incriminate Ford and every company with the same electronics. Furthermore, Ford was required to give them to NHTSA even if the agency didn't ask for them."

"Why? Because federal law mandates that car companies must report evidence of safety problems to NHTSA within a reasonable time."

A light switched on in my head. "Isn't it clear that Ford never gave these reports to NHTSA, or this problem would have been resolved years ago?"

"Exactly. That's why Richardson is a more important witness than Updegrove. If anyone knows what happened to these reports, it's Edward L. Richardson."

"Have you or Jo Ellen found any SIRs in our repository?"

"So far we've only found a handful, but they implicate the cruise control electronics. That should give you some leverage with Richardson."

Truer words were never spoken. Richardson turned out to be a sandy-haired, square-jawed Virginian with a rather sad demeanor, who seemed to loosen up when I showed him the field reports Jo Ellen had found:

> **Q:** This service investigation report, I take it, was a standard format used by investigators?
> **A:** A standard Ford form, yes, sir.
> **Q:** You would have seen service investigation reports during this period?
> **A:** I did indeed.
> **Q:** Did you see reports . . . where the customer said that when the gear was engaged, the vehicle went to wide open throttle?
> **A:** I have seen such reports.
> **Q:** Did you see reports where the driver also said that the brakes would not stop the car?

**A:** Yes, sir . . . .

**Q:** Were district engineers asked to get a history, make a diagnosis, and present a recommendation?

**A:** Yes. But one of the things I don't believe you mentioned was the purpose of SIRs, which is important. They were intended to convey back to the company engineers, whoever, what's being encountered in the field . . . and conveying that message back to the central headquarters, if you will.

**Q:** And at central headquarters, you said earlier, a reading committee would look over the SIRs for a pattern of facts that would point to a possible defect. Fair enough?

**A:** Yes; not necessarily a defect, but *some condition.* In fact, we solicited SIRs from the field simply to *define a problem* we hadn't seen before or didn't understand because everybody's got their own opinion, whether it's right or wrong. [Emphasis added.]

***

I felt like a kid in a candy store. The fact pattern for sudden accelerations from a standstill in SIRs mirrored exactly the findings of the Updegrove investigation; a major purpose of the SIRs was to keep corporate headquarters informed about safety investigations in the field; and a committee at corporate headquarters had studied the reports for a causation-related fact pattern. On top of that, the characterization of sudden acceleration as a "condition we hadn't seen before or didn't understand," implied that runaway cars first surfaced with the introduction of electronic cruise control. But Richardson was only getting warmed up:

**Q:** These district engineers were trained in Dearborn to go through various steps in analyzing a problem. They were required to render an opinion, were they not?

**A:** Yes.

**Q:** That was what they were trained to do?

**A:** Yes.

**Q:** Did you arrive at a profile of a classic sudden acceleration event; in other words, of the facts that seemed to define them?

**A:** Yes. The vehicle would *suddenly and unexpectedly accelerate* from a standing start to what apparently was wide open throttle. Simultaneously, the brakes wouldn't work, and in some cases the *steering wouldn't work.* Nothing worked, but the car was proceeding at a high rate of speed.

**Q:** Let's talk about these indicators that became part of the standard definition. First, the car accelerated at the moment of gear engagement from a stationary position.

**A:** That's part of it; it can be part of it, the moment of gear engagement. In some instances, the car was already in gear . . . .

**Q:** Mr. Richardson, the idea was that it took off at the moment of gear engagement from a stationary position?

**A:** Or it was already in gear; nevertheless it took off unexpectedly.

**Q:** In other words, sudden, unexpected acceleration?

**A:** Yes, sir.

**Q:** The second indicator was that "*the brakes didn't* stop the car." Am I correct?

**A:** That's another symptom, yes.

**Q:** And the third symptom you indicated was, at least in some cases, people said, "I couldn't steer the car."

**A:** Correct. [Emphasis added.]

***

Richardson's choice of the term "symptom" when referring to the fact pattern culled from field reports—I had used "indicator"—

was astute. As in medicine, where a patient's "symptoms" guide the doctor's clinical examination and choice of tests, Ford's field engineers *were trained to prod drivers and witnesses* about a malfunctioning vehicle's "symptoms." The vehicle history, in turn, determined the inspection and testing protocols they used to diagnose the car's "illness," and in prescribing a "treatment." The next step was to find out whether, as Mr. X had indicated, field engineers throughout the 1980s had fingered the cruise control electronics. Richardson didn't blink:

> **Q:** Do you agree that the service investigation reports prior to your retirement contained opinions as to the cause of the event?
>
> A: Yes sir. The field engineers were *required* to provide that opinion.
>
> **Q:** And you have *personally reviewed* many of those service investigation reports?
>
> **A:** Yes, sir.
>
> **Q:** You have already told us you had a committee doing multiple readings of those reports?
>
> **A:** Yes, sir.
>
> **Q:** Isn't it a fact that your people read *numerous service investigation reports* in which the speed control or one of its components was identified as the cause of a classic sudden acceleration report?
>
> **A:** Surely.
>
> **Q:** So these trained investigators in the field were reporting again and again . . . the conclusion that it was *something in the speed control*?
>
> **A:** Yes.
>
> **Q:** That's what they reported?
>
> **A:** They reported it.

**Q:** And they recommended that the speed control servo be replaced, did they not?
**A:** Yes, sir.

***

My head was still swimming when, strangely enough, I recalled how G.K. Chesterton's fictive detective, Father Brown, had solved a murder by remembering a dog that didn't bark. *If it turned out there were no SIRs implicating the driver,* they would be the pack of wolves that didn't howl. I decided to throw caution to the wind.

**Q:** Did you ever see a service investigation report involving a vehicle that reportedly took off from a stop where the field engineer concluded it was a pedal misapplication?
**A:** That wasn't the general belief. The general belief was that by default they had that conclusion. They could find nothing wrong with the car. That was not something we were even willing *to talk* about early on in the investigation, that *it might be people.*
**Q:** That was not my question; you certainly saw reports where they thought it was the speed control servo and recommended they replace it?
**A:** Or something.
**Q:** Or something in the car; I'm trying to find out whether *even one* engineer who investigated a sudden acceleration and applied the training he or she had received from the Ford Motor Company, ever filled out a report indicating that the problem, the cause, was the driver. Did you ever see that?
**A:** I can't point to one. [Emphasis added.]

***

When Molly read Richardson's testimony, she was irate. "NHTSA knew from long experience that Ford had field engineers who investigated accidents. Had it simply asked for every field report implicating a driver, the phony industry propaganda about driver error would have been exposed as a gigantic fraud. Furthermore, I was surprised that you didn't ask Richardson why Ford never even mentioned SIRs in its responses?"

"I guess it was an old trial lawyer's instinct not to ask a question I couldn't answer. Anyway, how could Ford get away with hiding so many SIRs?"

She was pensive. "I can't answer that right now. But if we can prove that's what happened . . . . " Her voice trailed off at this point.

"I know what you're thinking, Molly. If Ford covered up hundreds of incriminating reports, then other car companies must have done the same thing. And if we can prove that's what happened, we will have uncovered one of the most shocking and deadly cover-ups in U.S. history."

Years would pass before we finally pieced together how Ford had managed to conceal hundreds of incriminating field reports. At this point, however, the mystery surrounding SIRs only deepened during the trial in beautiful Maryville, Tennessee.

CHAPTER 39

# TRIAL IN MARYVILLE

**WOMAN DIES AFTER DRIVING THROUGH CAR WASH: CAR SUBMERGED IN WATER FOR MORE THAN 30 MINUTES**

Columbus, Ohio—An 82-year-old woman died Saturday, one day after she was trapped underwater in her car for more than 30 minutes. Ruth Ware, of Waverly, Ohio, was freed from the icy water of Paint Creek in Chillicothe on Friday. Ware was in line for a car wash at a gas station when she hit her accelerator. "I heard a big crash," said witness Holly Cyrus, who was working at a nearby Dairy Queen. "I turned around and looked and she hit the dumpster." Cyrus said that it seemed strange because she thought the woman looked like she was steering the vehicle.

*NewsNet5.Com,* February 22, 2004

**FOLLOWING RICHARDSON'S DEPOSITION, FORD OFFERED TO** produce him at trial in exchange for concessions on our part.

Because it was a chance to learn why, Ford never mentioned SIRs in its responses to NHTSA, I snapped up the offer. At first, Richardson was as forthcoming as he had been earlier. But that changed when I showed him the three SIRs we had discussed during his deposition, and asked if they had been disclosed to NHTSA:

> **Q:** Take a look, please, at what you sent to the government and tell us whether you can find any indication that your district service engineers were identifying the cruise control servo as the causal part, and were recommending that the servo be disconnected. Take your time. I would be interested in seeing anything in there that provided that information to the government.
>
> **A:** I don't particularly like the way you characterized that question. Other than the fact that they were certainly aware, and you were privy to that kind of information just as we were, and you have picked out three [SIRs] that happened to say that the speed control servo was what the field representative thought was the issue.
>
> If you will notice, all three of those were written immediately after that device was, or those devices were, implicated in a press release put out by the Center for Auto Safety and NHTSA's investigation, providing actually some words that come out of those petitions.
>
> And so, therefore, the servo being the only thing, the only device on the car that can actually move the throttle, the field engineer was left with little choice but to replace that . . . .

***

This rambling response surprised me. The press release by the Center for Auto Safety was *two years after* the dates on the SIRs Richardson had in front of him; what, I wondered, had provoked the testy suggestion that I had "picked out three reports" that implicated the cruise control; and since the servo was the only component that could activate the throttle without driver input on the gas pedal, Richardson's defensiveness regarding the device seemed painfully incongruent. His touchiness continued when I pressed him further about the apparent absence of SIRs in Ford's responses to NHTSA:

> **Q:** Would you mind showing us where in your response to the government's inquiry of December 31, 1986, you disclosed that service investigation reports were indicating a common fact pattern—gear engagement as the initiating event and a loss of braking effectiveness? Show us where you told the government this information was known to the safety office?
>
> **A:** Here it is. I can answer your question, as vague and confusing as it may be. It says here, Attachment 2A, which is not a part of this. It specifically says there are *copies of these, related to owner reports* as well as, so forth, in Attachment 2A, and that is where I would expect to find them.
>
> Also, there is some in Attachment 3, but I don't know what that is. It just says *some documents related to those reports.* In some cases, SIRs didn't have enough information for us to know where they belonged, so they are in there anyway. We gave them those as well. [Emphasis added.]

***

Because Richardson had already acknowledged the fact pattern mentioned in my question, his barely coherent response and pique—"I can answer your question, as vague and confusing as it may be"—suggested that he had been subjected to some intense coaching prior to his appearance in Maryville. But I sensed that the jury liked him and understood the position he was in, so I tried to remain non-confrontational:

**Q:** Are you telling us that you sent the government some service investigation reports?

**A:** I am certain that is what it says. And I know good and well if we left them out, we would have heard about it.

***

If Richardson was apprehensive that I might ask if the Safety Office had deliberately concealed incriminating SIRs from NHTSA, I had no intention of using such a ham-handed approach with someone in his position. Nevertheless, since his last response suggested that Ford had not been forthcoming with the agency, I couldn't afford to let matters rest there:

**Q:** Let's be real sure of ourselves on this point.

**A:** All right.

**Q:** I think you said you found there in the responses something indicating that *you did give the government* service investigation reports. Give me the Bates number, please?

**A:** Where it says, "Furnish owner complaints and reports."

**Q:** . . . Give us the line you are reading from.

**A:** I am reading just below the center of the page where the search located 94 [owner complaints].

**Q:** That refers to owner reports, right?

**A:** Yes.

**Q:** Is an owner report a service investigation report?

**A:** No sir.

**Q:** What is it?

**A:** It is a letter from an owner, a telegram, letter, whatever. And *20 other reports* concerning vehicles equipped with

3.8 and 5.0 fuel-injected engines submitted to their earlier inquiry. Apparently we submitted them, then, too.

***

Richardson's reference to the "20 other reports" seemed to imply that they included SIRs. It was also precious grist for the final argument taking shape in my mind:

> Ladies and gentlemen, the experts at Ford trained to help us understand what made Sally Tipton's Lincoln Town Car race out of control were the field engineers in 33 district offices throughout the country. We know there were 33 offices because they are listed on our Exhibit 20, the electronic summaries for the 2,877 sudden accelerations Mr. Updegrove described for you. You'll recall that about 2,000 of those occurrences began at gear engagement, exactly when Mrs. Tipton's car raced out of control. Mr. Updegrove's final report says that Ford began this investigation because the company's engineers in those 33 district offices were expressing an opinion regarding what was causing these cars to just suddenly take off at gear engagement. And what were these trained experts saying? We know the answer because we were able to locate three of their reports that you will have with you in the jury room as plaintiff's exhibits. They show that the field engineers in each case concluded that the cruise control electronics had caused the reported sudden acceleration.
>
> On the other hand, you've heard a great deal from Ford about a government report published in 1989 suggesting that defective drivers and not defective cars are behind these dangerous occurrences. But what happened when the National Highway Traffic Safety Administration specifically asked Ford for copies of sudden acceleration-

related field reports? Ford's response never mentioned them. You may recall that Mr. Richardson kind of implied that Ford's mention of '20 other reports' in its responses included SIRs. If so, where are they? If they support Ford's position, why hasn't it produced them? I hope you'll agree that the answer is pretty obvious. But even if each of those 20 reports was an SIR, they would represent only a small fraction of the field reports Ford knew about when it answered the government's request.

But, alas, this was a final argument I never made. Near the end of my cross-examination, I mentioned the same SIRs we had discussed earlier in his testimony, which caused Richardson to suddenly blurt "how did you happen to get them—SIRs—if we didn't hand them out?" It was a chance to end my cross-examination on a light note:

**Mr. Murray:** May I respond, your Honor?

**The Witness:** Sure.

**The Court:** I should admonish the witness not to interrogate the lawyers.

**Mr. Murray:** I would be glad to change places with the witness for a few minutes.

**The Witness:** I am always a little amused about how much you know about SIRs by *not ever having seen one.*

***

The jury's laughter told me they knew Richardson had hoisted a white flag. Ford may have thought so too, because it soon expressed an interest in settling and the parties reached a confidential agreement. While confidential settlements help corporate defendants conceal their negligence, in this case I felt the parties had achieved a fair and prudent resolution to a tragedy that had rocked this lovely community in the Tennessee heartland.

CHAPTER 40

# FROM THE HORSE'S MOUTH

### CAR'S ACCELERATOR GETS STUCK; WOMAN TAKEN ON SCARY RIDE

A 21-year-old Kent, Ohio, woman was taken on a wild ride when the accelerator on her car apparently got stuck in the down position—"It was just revving—I had no idea what was going to happen," she said. Her scary ride began in Independence and continued through several cities. After her car roared up to more than 90 mph, Craven was unable to stop the car because the accelerator was apparently stuck; the throttle was wide open. When her brakes burned up, she called 9-1-1 from her cell phone . . . . Craven finally got her car stopped, but not before nearly causing several accidents. It was a fellow driver that signaled her to turn off her car's ignition . . . . *News Channel 5* reported that all of the brake lines on her car were now blown and leaking

> fluid. The brake pads were also scorched, and the rotors were left scarred.
>
> *NewsNet5.com*, June 25, 2003

**ABOUT THE TIME OF THE TENNESSEE TRIAL, A CALIFORNIA** court ordered Ford to disgorge the records of its Technical Affairs Committee, or TAC, a senior management group that allocates corporate resources to technical aspects of designing and manufacturing the company's products. The California case involved malfunctions in an electronic component, the "thick film ignition module" that caused engine stalling. When the lead lawyer, Jeff Fazio, and I compared notes, we discovered that the pattern of failures in thick film ignition modules and in cruise control servos was strikingly similar. After Fazio guided his case to successful conclusion, he sent us the TAC records his firm had obtained by court order.

When Molly started wading through thousands of pages of TAC documents, she decided to take evening courses in electronics to help her recognize what was important. One day she announced she had found something "you should see before you leave for London," where I was traveling the next day. "It's a report to senior management in October 1986, when pundits were calling sudden accelerations an epidemic."

"Who prepared the report?"

"The Electrical and Electronics Division. When I started perusing it, I spotted something that blew me away." Molly showed me the bar graph in Figure 40-1.

"Do my eyes deceive me?" I asked, catching my breath. "If a speed control servo malfunctioned before 1984, they found the problem 80% of the time, but after 1984 . . . . "

Molly finished the thought. "They could find the problem only 20% of the time, which also means there were four times more

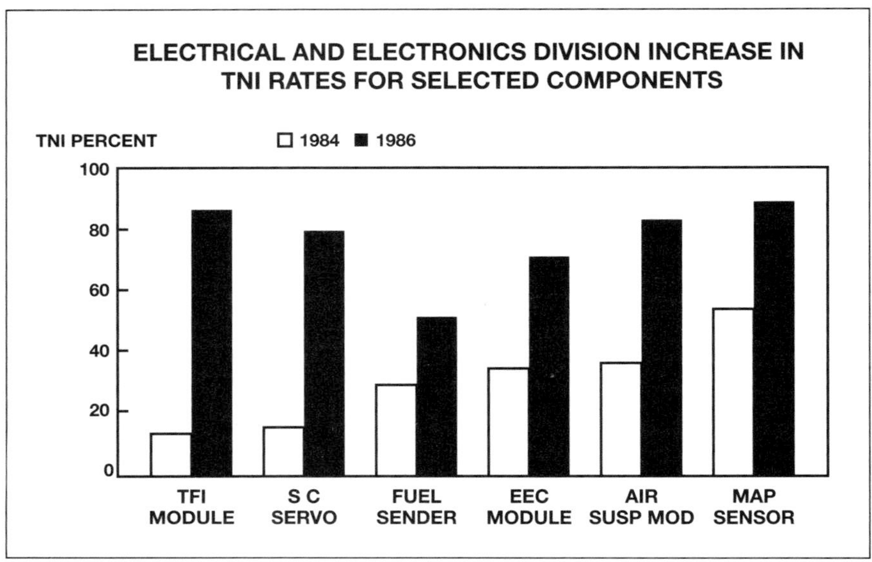


*Figure 40-1*

cruise control malfunctions after 1984, many of which must have been sudden accelerations."

"Does the report say what caused this incredible increase in just two years?"

"I've only glanced at it, but I assume it does. Why don't you read it during your flight tomorrow?"

The October 21, 1986 report was entitled "Electronics Systems Quality TROUBLE-NOT-IDENTIFIED With Field Return Components". By the time my flight landed in London, I realized that the report had changed forever our understanding of this automotive tragedy.

The report began with this definition of "TROUBLE-NOT-IDENTIFIED", or TNI:

> TNI COMPONENTS ARE PARTS REMOVED FROM VEHICLES THAT MEET ALL THE REQUIREMENTS OF ENGINEERING TESTS THAT WERE ESTABLISHED TO REFLECT DESIGN INTENT.

Since the entire report dealt with undiagnosed malfunctions in electronic components, including the cruise control servo, the implications of this definition were enormous. The entire industry at that point was busy palming off the notion that if the cause of a sudden acceleration could not be found by inspecting and testing cruise control components, the problem had to be driver error; and yet this highly sophisticated report never so much as mentioned the possibility that drivers might be influencing the 80% TNI rate for cruise control malfunctions. Quite the opposite, in fact, as shown by this description of how the company's alarming TNI rate needed to be attacked:

> ANY ATTEMPT TO IDENTIFY THE ROOT CAUSES FOR TNI COMPONENTS MUST LEAD TO INVESTIGATIONS OF AT LEAST THE FOLLOWING AREAS: COMPONENT DESIGN, MANUFACTURING PROCESSES, THE VEHICLE ASSEMBLY PROCESS, CUSTOMER EXPECTATIONS, SYSTEMS INTERACTIONS, SERVICE DIAGNOSIS, AND RETURN PARTS ANALYSIS METHODS.

After noting that there were "numerous potential root causes for TNI components," the report depicted what they were on the diagram shown in Figure 40-2.

Later we will see how this diagram helps to explain the slaughter runaway cars are still causing not only in this country but throughout the world. Here is how the EED report summarized what it showed:

> SYSTEMS INTERACTIONS
>
> ELECTROMAGNETIC INFLUENCES IN THE VEHICLE ENVIRONMENT MAY INDUCE A COMPONENT'S PERFORMANCE TO BE UNACCEPTABLE. WHEN

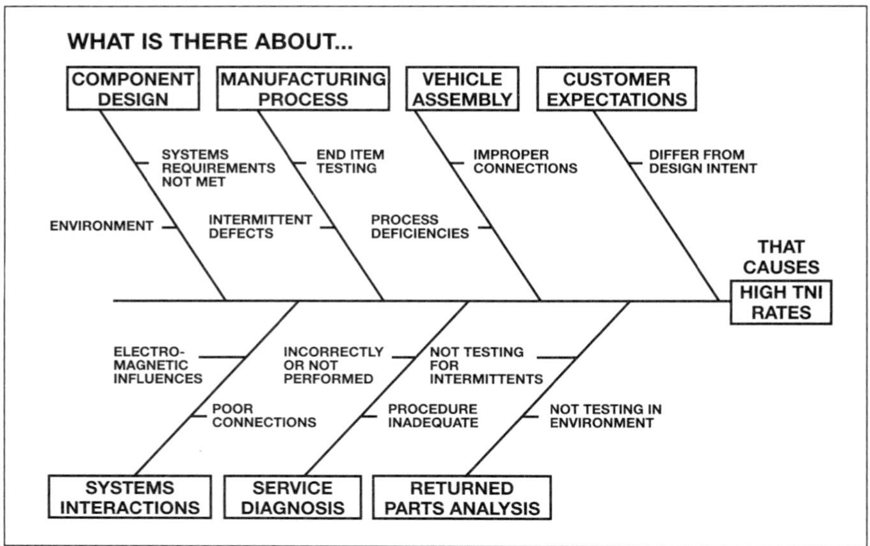


*Figure 40-2*

REMOVED FROM THE VEHICLE, THE COMPONENT WILL TEST GOOD.

THE TNI RATE FOR ELECTRONIC COMPONENTS HAS BEEN STEADILY INCREASING OVER THE PAST FEW YEARS. THIS HIGHER RATE HAS BEEN COINCIDENT WITH THE INCREASING COMPLEXITY OF ELECTRICAL SYSTEMS IN OUR VEHICLES . . . .

WHILE THE CURRENT TNI PROBLEM SPANS MANY SYSTEMS, WE'LL FOCUS PRIMARILY ON ENGINE ELECTRONIC COMPONENTS.

When senior management received this report in October 1986, three of Richardson's subordinates in Ford's Safety Office had been circulating summaries of SIRs to senior management for more than a year. There can be no question, therefore, that Ford's top management knew that field engineers were uniformly fingering the cruise control electronics without finding evidence of a fault in the system's components; and since Richardson had acknowledged that servos removed by field engineers had tested normal in the company's laboratories, this report also confirmed the unanimous conclusion of field engineers who were identifying the cruise control electronics as the core problem.

The more I pondered the EED's analysis, the pieces of a gigantic and perplexing jigsaw puzzle started to fall in place. After Ford roughly quadrupled its engine electronics in the EEC-IV, the TNI rate for cruise control servos and sudden acceleration reports simultaneously increased rapidly. In his final report, Alan Updegrove laconically described this connection between the EEC-IV and the sudden acceleration rate:

> NOTED INCREASE IN NUMBERS OF REPORTS WITH INTRODUCTION (1984) OF BROADLY APPLIED ELECTRONICS (EEC-IV).

It deserves mention that the EED report was submitted to senior management 13 years before Sam Sero tried to convince Naomi Buchwald that electromagnetic interference was behind most runaway car crashes; and while Ford knew it had not been able to replicate an EMI-induced malfunction in its laboratories, it had nevertheless used the fact that Sero had not replicated such a failure as a basis for excluding EMI from the *Jarvis* case. As for Naomi Buchwald, one wonders if it ever occurred to her that if these malfunctions could be replicated ex post facto, the cause would be readily correctable and sudden accelerations would long ago have become a thing of the past.

CHAPTER 41

# HOW NOT TO AVOID DISASTER

**ACCELERATION ISSUE STILL DOGGING FORD**

> All across the country, injured drivers are telling horrifying stories of crashes due to the unexplained acceleration of their vehicles. While automakers say drivers are at fault in every case, others say the evidence continues to mount regarding a fatal flaw with older-model Ford Explorers. Case after case of unexplained acceleration began surfacing back in the 1980s. A government report at the time dismissed those reports, and the issue faded. But did the problem really go away?
>
> *WFAA ABC 8*, May 11, 2005

**IN 1973, SIX YEARS BEFORE FORD SOLD THE FIRST CAR WITH** electronic cruise control, an engineer working on its development, William Follmer, published a paper that predicted the catastrophe that a decade later would overtake the car industry. The paper stressed the danger posed by "negative transients"—a form of EMI—"which result from the decay of inductive currents through the various electromagnetic actuators in the automobile." Sixteen years later, Ford's EED would describe this same phenomenon as "electromagnetic influences in the vehicle environment." Follmer listed many of the same design and environmental factors noted on Figure 40-2 in the previous chapter, and as the EED report would do years later, he emphasized that "to avoid disaster," it was imperative that these electronics include "failsafe" protection against potentially deadly failures. Perhaps the inexcusable aspect of the industry's behavior, it is that to this day most cars on the highway still have no failsafe protection against a sudden loss of throttle control that every year continues to destroy many lives. The question remains, however, why Ford or any company, would take such risk with people's lives and safety.

The disturbing answer appears in an internal Ford memorandum dated March 3, 1987 showing that when Ford began EMI testing for prototype models with the EEC-IV in 1976, the results had "grown progressively worse." Here's how the document described how the company trapped itself by disregarding the risk posed by EMI:

> 1976—electromagnetic compatibility was not noted as being a problem when the present speed control system was designed. Therefore, no special consideration was given to designing in electromagnetic compatibility immunity.

In other words, despite being warned three years earlier about the disaster that would follow if the cruise control electronics were not failsafe against EMI, Ford had not invested in a failsafe design. In fact, notwithstanding that this memorandum proposed modest changes to the printed circuit board that would have at least reduced the chances of a sudden acceleration, even these modest changes were rejected because they would have cost $2.99 per cruise control unit. Hence, fourteen years after Follmer's warning, Ford was unwilling to spend a few dollars per car to reduce the chances of a malfunction that, in a matter of seconds, could destroy peoples' lives. That Ford knew the gamble it was taking is crystal clear from the following entries in another Technical Affairs Committee document:

> In 1979, a corporate reserve of $75 million [roughly $150 million in today's dollars] was established to cover potential major recalls not provided for by the operations, including the controversy concerning unexpected movement of vehicles equipped with automatic transmissions.
>
> Accordingly, the reserve has been maintained at $75 million to provide for major recalls for potential problems such as *unexpected vehicle acceleration* (similar to the problem that the Audi 5000 is experiencing). [Emphasis added.]

It is worth pointing out that Ford established its reserve during the Carter administration, when NHTSA's Administrator, Joan Claybrook, vigorously enforced laws intended to protect the public from unsafe cars. Unfortunately, sudden accelerations didn't become a problem during Claybrook's tenure because she would not have hesitated to initiate the recall Ford's $75 million reserve anticipated. Sadly, however, Claybrook's successors at NHTSA would have none of her determination to make carmakers obey the law. One consequence of that attitude is revealed in our next chapter.

CHAPTER 42

# A SUDDEN ACCELERATION TASK FORCE

**RUNAWAY CAR HITS 100 MPH IN 75-MILE ORDEAL**

At first Angel Eck was just puzzled when her car suddenly began speeding up on its own. But bemusement turned to terror when the 20 year-old tried to brake and found that she could not slow down. Reaching up to 100 mph in scenes reminiscent of the film *Speed,* she narrowly missed smashing into a lorry and a vehicle full of children . . . . "It kept accelerating and my foot wasn't even down on the gas," she said. "It had a mind of its own."

*Guardian Newspapers,* February 2, 2004

**THROUGHOUT THE 1980S, CARMAKERS WERE UNWAVERING THAT** for a runaway car report to be credible, there had to be evidence of at least two simultaneous and detectable hardwire faults. We learned earlier that both Ford's field engineers and its Electrical and Electronics Division knew that these malfunctions rarely left evidence detectable by inspecting and testing components. We also learned that the EED had recommended to Ford's Technical Affairs Committee that an interdivisional team be established to learn how electronic interactions between the EEC-IV and the cruise control electronics were inducing the servo to suddenly pull the throttle wide open. It was Jo Ellen who found a memorandum showing that less than three months after the EED made this recommendation, Ford created an interdivisional team for that purpose. Dated January 12, 1987, the memorandum described the study's purpose:

> Task force mission is to look into unexpected acceleration, under either cold, warm, idle, or moving conditions. Study interactions between various electronic systems. The primary focus will be on vehicle electronics, idle speed control, cruise control, electronic engine control.

It is telling that this memorandum was prepared just days after NHTSA asked Ford to disclose all sudden acceleration-related "investigations and studies". Since electronic interactions, unlike hardwire failures, could not be found by inspecting or testing components, the mere existence of this study showed that the industry's position regarding prerequisites for a sudden acceleration is an outright fraud. That Ford was well aware of this is clear from the following entry on the memorandum:

> How do we document—any and all could be used in court, (i.e., video)—MLJ request

We knew from the TAC records that MLJ was a senior officer named Max L. Jurosek. That Jurosek was particularly concerned about a paper trail that "could be used in court," suggests that Ford considered the legal system a bigger threat than the federal government and, with good reason, as I hope this book demonstrates. While there is more to be said about Ford's interdivisional task force, it belongs in Part Three dealing with how Ford responded to a wide range of government requests during the months preceding NHTSA's fateful industry-wide sudden acceleration study.

CHAPTER 43

# GENERAL CONFUSION AT GENERAL MOTORS

## HI-TECH, COMPUTER-GENERATED AUTOMOBILES CAN GO AWRY

Today, cars can even parallel park themselves . . . . Newer model cars come equipped with high-tech, computer-generated electronic throttles, replacing the older mechanical throttle, and laser-controlled cruise control systems. But, owners of luxury vehicles, such as Lexus, Lincoln, Cadillac, and certain makes and models of SUVs are reporting that they have been involved in automobile accidents or near misses they say are caused by rapid unintended acceleration of their vehicle.

*Houston Community Newspapers,* February 11, 2004

**ON SEPTEMBER 6, 2000, CONSTANCE PETERS WAS** catastrophically injured when her 1993 Cutlass suddenly accelerated from her driveway and crashed. Peters' attorney, Mark Evans, told the *National Law Journal*:

> "We thought that the accident facts proved that it couldn't have been her foot, that it had to be the cruise control that accelerated the vehicle," . . . .
>
> Evans said that during trial he presented the jury with videotaped testimony of six other people involved in similar sudden acceleration accidents. Two additional witnesses testified in court, he said. GM attorney Rod Loomer of Turner, Reid, Dunkin, Loomer and Patton in Springfield, Mo., declined to comment on the case.
>
> "As far as we're concerned, it's a clear-cut case of pedal misapplication. She hits the accelerator instead of the brake," GM spokesman Jay Cooney said. "We don't think there is anything wrong with the vehicle." (January 7, 2003.)

A jury awarded Constance Peters who, like Leon Manigault, was rendered permanently comatose from massive head injuries, $30 million in compensatory and $50 million in punitive damages. After the verdict was reversed on technical grounds, the parties reached a confidential settlement agreement. Through discovery, Peters' lawyers obtained a memorandum dated March 30, 1987 from a Hughes Aircraft engineer named Walter Gelon in response to a request from GM for help with its sudden acceleration problems. Gelon, who was apparently aware that runaway car reports were at epidemic levels, described "sudden, uncontrollable vehicle acceleration as a modern plague in the automobile industry;" and he didn't mince words about the cause which he described as a "noisy car environment causing upsets in sensitive microelectronics . . . due to conducted or radiated *electromagnetic interference, or EMI.*" Gelon was equally clear how EMI was triggering these dangerous malfunctions:

> Upset problems in microelectronics have increased in frequency as device size and power decreases. Upsets could provide a major root cause for GM's (and other auto manufacturers') unwanted acceleration problems.

In other words, by adding more and more electronic functions to smaller and smaller microprocessors in an environment fraught with conditions conducive to EMI-induced "upsets", the sudden acceleration rate across the industry had naturally spiraled upwards. According to Gelon, Hughes had "offered its experience to help in searching out resolution of problems and eliminating any that may exist."

Two weeks after Gelon's memorandum, a meeting took place at General Motor's Technical Center during which Hughes engineers analyzed for GM engineers the reasons behind GM's growing runaway car crisis. Thanks to the diligence of attorney Mark Evans we also have a memorandum from the same Walter Gelon summarizing the gist of what GM learned from the Hughes engineers during this meeting. Here are some of the revealing comments in Gelon's second memorandum:

> It seems very clear . . . that General Motors vehicles have serious EMI problems which are triggering unwanted acceleration . . . .

It seems almost too obvious to ask why, if it was clear to engineers at an aerospace company that EMI was behind this deadly phenomenon, the auto industry found itself mired in elaborate denials and deceptions both to NHTSA and the American public. While sudden accelerations were increasing exponentially, carmakers were making their electronics increasingly complex, but with little regard for the fact that more electronics meant more interactions with potential for EMI-induced failures.

> Jim Clore of General Motors' Electrical Engineering Center was most eager to talk about his area of concern, which is cruise control . . . . Many clues seemed to point to a particular logic chip on the module being scrambled by electromagnetic interference.

GM's Clore saw that sudden accelerations were being triggered by interference at the "logic chip" controlling the vent and vac functions of the cruise control servo. His observation that "many clues point to the logic chip" implicitly recognized that an EMI-induced sudden acceleration could usually be diagnosed only by examining the effects on the vehicle's behavior, not by inspecting components as the industry claimed was where evidence of a defect, if it existed, would be found. In that vein, we've seen how Ford's investigation of 2,877 sudden accelerations, unquestionably the most exhaustive and scientifically valid investigation of this phenomenon yet undertaken, had focused heavily on the effects produced by the vehicle's behavior during the reported event.

> Jim Clore seemed to understand the System Engineering process [an interdisciplinary approach and means to enable the realization of successful systems] and its relationship to failure analysis. He was concerned with how the cruise control interacted with the other system components and recognized the importance of maintaining an open dialogue.

We've seen how six months prior to Gelon's second memorandum, Ford's Electrical and Electronics Division directly linked the quantum increase in cruise control malfunctions with the increased complexity of the engine control electronics in the so-called EEC-IV. We know, of course, the same thing was happening across the industry as carmakers added electronic features to their models; and since most of these added functions were connected by wiring to a central control unit, the wiring harnesses under the hood became increasingly complex. Here is how the Hughes engineers described the consequences of this industry-wide pattern:

> After studying the schematics and talking with their engineers, it is also my opinion that the electrical system harness on every automobile has evolved to such a confused state that it is impossible to eliminate many serious and expensive failures . . . . Hughes should provide GM with electrical systems engineering expertise and guidelines for proper harness layouts.

Although the entire industry desperately needed the kind of engineering expertise Hughes was offering, because car companies had rushed helter-skelter to get more electronic features into their models, they had created the potential for "many serious and expensive failures" with implications beyond anything the industry had previously faced. For one thing, since the core problem was not just wiring harnesses, but the design of the entire powertrain electronics, it could obviously not be corrected by a recall. There was also the specter of massive legal liabilities that would inevitably follow an admission of fault, particularly since owners had never been warned about the possibility of a sudden acceleration or instructed how to respond to such a dangerous emergency. But the greatest obstacle to a solution may have been a systemic industry problem that Gelon described this way:

> I am used to strong centralized system engineering management creating an environment for problem solving . . . . [T]he intermingling of disciplines often triggers the

> answer in unexpected ways. The team solves the problem. I found the GM culture of consensus management somewhat frustrating.

Compare that comment with the following description of Ford's corporate culture in the Electrical and Electronics Division's report to senior management about six months prior to Gelon's comments:

> THE TOTAL SYSTEMS INVOLVEMENT AND INTER-DIVISIONAL COOPERATION REQUIRED TO GET TO THE ROOT CAUSE IS CONTRADICTORY TO OUR CURRENT ORGANIZATIONAL STRUCTURE AND COMPONENT-ORIENTED WARRANTY RETURN ASSESSMENT SYSTEM.

Although thousands of lives have been destroyed in the decade since the first sudden acceleration reports surfaced, the two largest domestic car companies were only now awakening to how woefully unprepared they were to deal with serious problems in their electronics. Just how unprepared they were, is the subject in our next chapter.

CHAPTER 44

# TRUE CONFESSIONS

### FATHER CALLS DAUGHTER MOMENTS BEFORE HER OUT-OF-CONTROL EXPLORER FLIPS OVER: A DAUGHTER'S VOICE, A TERRIFYING INSTANT

She screamed, "I can't stop my car! I don't know what to do! . . . I'm on the tollway. My brakes don't work . . . . " And then she said "Daddy, what do I do?" They still don't know what caused the engine of the Ford Explorer to race out of control. Witnesses reported seeing Lauren try unsuccessfully to brake the vehicle on the tollway. She apparently talked to her parents moments before shooting down the Park exit ramp. She zoomed through the toll booth. Then, trying to avoid cars stopped at the light, she swerved into the empty U-turn lane. The racing vehicle hit the curb, rolled end over end and slammed into a concrete pillar beneath the tollway.

*The Dallas Morning News*, April 19, 2002

**ON OCTOBER 28, 1987, SHORTLY AFTER NHTSA ANNOUNCED AN** industry-wide sudden acceleration study, Ford's Technical Affairs Committee reviewed a report from the company's "electronics reliability studies team". While it parallels the observations and recommendations of Hughes engineers to GM, Ford's study contains a description of the industry-wide mistakes that led to what Gelon described as the "many serious and expensive failures . . . [that were now] . . . impossible to eliminate." The bitter irony is that despite the insightfulness of Ford's "Electronics Reliability Studies Team", it apparently never dawned on the policy or decision makers at Ford, General Motors, or their competitors that they had a moral and legal duty to face up to their miscalculations, and do what they could to protect the public from further automotive carnage. Here are the report's conclusions with selected comments of the company's senior managers:

> **Conclusion 1: Lack of Sufficient Problem Anticipation:** *Insufficient Availability of Technical Knowledge and Experience*
> Selected comments of TAC members:
> - Need more team approaches, less fragmented design responsibility, and more system analysis work.
> - Need more emphasis on technical competence of management.
> - Need to raise the average level of technical skills of engineers.
> - Need a plan for developing technical competence of engineering personnel.

This was an outright confession that the advent of automotive electronics had caught Ford with its corporate pants down, and with consequences that included:

**Conclusion 2: Sensitive Designs and Processes:**
*Products and Processes Not Designed for Changing Conditions or Not Immune to Excursions Within Tolerances (i.e., product robustness).*
Selected comments of TAC members:

- Need to quit putting high tech products in the low tech environments.
- Need to slow our new and unproven developments.
- Need to abandon our intoxication with new technology.
- Need to procure hardware only after thorough technical analysis and thorough design review, including manufacturing and review.

Design philosophies should be based upon problem prevention engineering rather than detection engineering, meaning more upfront analysis and verification before field release.

In other words, instead of cautiously embracing technology it barely understood, Ford plunged headlong where angels feared to tread with techniques that were untested and unproven; and with the horse already out of the barn because of this disastrous miscalculation, senior management were belatedly acknowledging that it was time to base the company's design philosophy "upon problem prevention engineering . . . [and] . . . upfront analysis and verification before field release." In short, people shouldn't be used as guinea pigs to test the safety and reliability of the company's electronics.

**Conclusion 3: Late Problem Detection:**
*Problems detected late in the design cycle due to: (1) late commitment/implementation of resources and, (2) problems with testing philosophy, specifically (a) using testing for inspecting the design, and (b) accepting low statistical confidence in verification test plans.*

Selected comments of TAC members:

- The vice-presidential team that had been established to address systems and resource issues in the electronics area has not yet reached any conclusions relative to the changes that should be made.
- Key resource needs are test facilities, models, and people with the right skills.
- Need to work with companies such as Boeing that have considerable experience in achieving high electronics reliability.

The recognition that Ford needed help from companies like Boeing is particularly poignant because it underscores how tragically unnecessary this automotive calamity was. Long before runaway cars became a national disaster, Boeing had evaluated 14 automotive designs for companies that included General Motors, Ford, and Volkswagen of America. Using a technique known as "sneak" analysis, these studies found a number of potential failure possibilities that could result in "loss of system functionality, and loss of the operator's life." Most important, Boeing found that car industry testing missed about 60% of these catastrophic failure possibilities. It is clear, therefore, that had carmakers turned to companies like Boeing and Hughes *before they began using unsuspecting customers to test their electronics,* readers would be doing something else at this moment. How ironic, therefore, that two decades after this report to Ford's senior management, the company turned to Boeing for a CEO, Alan Mulalley, to lead it out of the morass of problems neglecting electronic safety and reliability had created.

The report's final conclusion focused on four areas with particular relevance to our story:

**Conclusion 4: Technical/Other - Other observations:**

*System Engineering—Corporate organizations are too fragmented to address systems issues.*

*Circuit Analysis—No uniform procedures exist for circuit analysis.*

*TNI Field Returns—The 50% trouble-not-identified (TNI) rates are not understood for cause.*

*Electrical Transients—Transient problems continue to be evident.*

Selected comments of TAC members:

- We can no longer afford to make every mistake once and must find ways to head off most problems during development.
- Electrical/electronics are always late in the program. System is "put in car to see if it works."
- We need technology/products developed and on the shelf—we should not develop hardware in the car—we need prove out before applying to vehicles.

Throughout these pages we have seen how a lack of system engineering and procedures for circuit analysis—the first two shortfalls—helped make sudden acceleration a runaway freight train. For example, Ford's powertrain engineers in 1985 had pointed out that "existing FMEAs did not address system interactions or components which failed to meet design intent while operating within their dynamic range." This was precisely the kind of fatal oversight a company like Boeing could have recognized and connected before it was too late.

The report's final conclusion that "transient problems continue to be evident" meant simply that the core problem was the failure to adequately protect against electromagnetic interference that Follmer had warned in 1973 would invite "disaster".

Despite this splurge of mea culpas, the comments of Ford's decision makers read like a gathering of heavy smokers commiserating with each other, but with no clear idea how to kick the habit; and since the entire industry had backed itself into the same corner, carmakers faced a stark choice: confess their sins publicly and correct them, or continue subjecting people to a secret game of automobile roulette. The fact they chose the latter, however, doesn't answer what the federal government was doing to end the mounting injury and death toll runaway automobiles were exacting throughout the 1980s. First, however, let's find out what happened to the Manigaults after the Ohio Supreme Court granted them a new trial.

CHAPTER 45

# *MANIGAULT V. FORD* REDUX

## FORD'S EVIDENCE THREATENS CARMAKERS IN DEFECT LAWSUITS

Virginia Manigault will never forget what happened when her husband, a Pentecostal Christian minister, put his Ford Crown Victoria into gear to go visit their daughter. The car bolted out of the driveway and shot across the street. As Leon Manigault pressed the brakes, the car crashed into a neighbor's home in Cleveland, Ohio, according to a complaint filed in an Ohio state court. Manigault, 77, remains partially paralyzed and semi-conscious from the 1993 accident. The Manigaults lost their first lawsuit against Ford Motor Co. Now, internal Ford documents will be used in a second trial next year. Eleven other "sudden acceleration" complaints, citing the internal documents, are also on the docket for 2004.

*Detroit News,* December 3, 2003

**ON THE EVE OF THE SECOND *MANIGAULT* TRIAL IN FEBRUARY** 2004, things were much different than six years earlier. The judge was the Honorable Joseph C. Cirigliano, one of Ohio's most experienced and respected judges. John Coleman, whom we met earlier, was now Ford's lead counsel. Dr. Antony Anderson was ready to back up Sam Sero's assessment of Ford's electronics. We now have videotaped testimony of Alan Updegrove and Edward L. Richardson, as well as the internal Ford studies and reports discussed earlier. We also have Ford's videotaped braking demonstration *with sound* to prove why braking had not prevented the Manigaults' Crown Victoria from crashing into a neighbor's house; and my old friend, Fred Weisman, as I had predicted, had now joined our trial team.

Anyone unfamiliar with the case reading the transcripts of the first and second trials, in fact, might think they were different cases. In the first trial, for example, Ford had convinced a newly assigned trial judge to bar us from even mentioning the National Highway Traffic Safety Administration to the jury. Ford's opening statement this time around shows how much had changed during the intervening years:

> This theory that Mr. Murray refers to very vaguely as electromagnetic interference, EMI compatibility, transients, or what have you, are going to corrupt the speed control system, ladies and gentlemen of the jury. I assure you that the testimony is going to be that no one in the world, no one at Ford Motor Company, General Motors, Chrysler, none of the experts Mr. Murray may call, have ever been able to take some type of electromagnetic interference, transient signals, voltage spikes, anything like that and have the speed control system or cruise control system activate, no one. And you are going to hear that

> not only has the entire automobile industry studied this particular theory, and been unable to do this, but also the various safety agencies that are responsible for automobile safety in the United States, Canada, Japan, they have all looked at these things and no one has ever been able to get a system to activate like this.
>
> People do make pedal misapplications. There is no question about it. I mean in the course of the trial you are going to hear all kinds of publicity about it, or all kinds of papers about studies that have been conducted on pedal misapplications . . . . This publicity affects the whole automobile industry. In the meantime, in this period, we've got *60 Minute* programs, *Dateline* programs and governments, the National Highway Traffic Safety Administration, Transport Canada, and Ministry of Transport of Japan, all three of these safety agencies . . . look at the sudden acceleration phenomenon. And in 1988, Transport of Canada comes out after it has studied this phenomenon and says very bluntly the reason for sudden acceleration is pedal misapplication.

This captures exactly how carmakers for many years had used NHTSA's 1989 report against anyone who accused them of negligence. But we were now well prepared to deal with government reports.

The second trial lasted about four weeks, during which Dr. Anderson demystified EMI by using a portable radio as a receiver to demonstrate how electromagnetic interference from various pieces of equipment in the courtroom caused interference in the radio.

The turning point came when I confronted a former Ford employee named William Koeppel, who took over Edward L.

Richardson's job in the Automotive Safety Office after Richardson retired in mid-1988. Koeppel's role was to blunt the impact of the Updegrove investigation by connecting the rising level of reports during the 1980s with media publicity. Koeppel was vulnerable, however, because he was well aware that prior to Richardson's retirement, the Safety Office had extensively studied reports submitted by field engineers that implicated the cruise control electronics. But so far we had only uncovered a handful of these reports that, as described earlier, I had used in cross-examining Richardson. Nevertheless, since federal law mandated that safety-related records be retained for five years, if we could prove that Ford had violated that requirement it would be devastating to Ford. Therefore, I began by establishing that SIRs were safety-related records.

**Q:** Back in that period, 1980-1986, did Ford look upon sudden acceleration reports as safety records?

**A:** Yes, I think that is fair to say.

**Q:** [W]ould that be the kind of report that a dealer might ask to have investigated by a district service engineer?

**A:** That's conceivable, yes.

**Q:** It wasn't conceivable, that's what happened, isn't it?

**A:** Well, you know, each dealer is going to make that judgment differently. Clearly, some dealers did ask district service engineers to do that, but whether all of them did it, I don't know.

**Q:** And these district service engineers, as Mr. Updegrove told us, received regular, special training in trying to diagnose what may have caused a reported occurrence, true?

**A:** My knowledge is that district service engineers would regularly come to Dearborn for training. I do not know the extent to which or whether or not that training includes the specifics of sudden acceleration.

**Q:** Have you read Mr. Updegrove's testimony?

**A:** Not recently.

**Q:** Have you ever read it?

**A:** Yes.

**Q:** When did you last read it?

**A:** Probably at least a year ago.

**Q:** You don't question, do you, that these district service engineers were specifically trained to investigate, determine the likely cause, and recommend a repair on a standard form known as a service investigation report?

**A:** My knowledge is that district service engineers regularly came to Dearborn for training . . . .

***

We've seen that while the Safety Office was reviewing service investigation reports, Richardson had kept a "book of data" with information relating to sudden accelerations. But when we formally requested a copy of the data book, what we were given contained mostly newspaper and magazine articles, but not a single SIR. Therefore, when Koeppel claimed not to remember whether Richardson kept SIRs in his data book, I saw an opening:

**Q:** Did you see his book of data?

**A:** Yes.

**Q:** If the issue was whether Ford had a safety problem, can you tell us whether newspaper reports or service investigation reports would be considered a more reliable source of information?

**A:** The newspaper reports are going to contain different information. Clearly a newspaper reporter is not going to be as technically qualified as a service engineer. At the same time, a newspaper reporter is going to have access to different information and possibly more information than a service engineer is. So I can't say one is going to be more important than the other. You have to look at both of them along with all the other kinds of inputs to develop some time of conclusion or some type of hypothesis . . . .

***

Since I could not have scripted a better evasion, I gave Koeppel plenty of rope to expand on his answer.

**Q:** Who at Ford would be better prepared to do a first-rate investigation, find a cause, and recommend a repair than district service engineers?

**A:** The design engineer that designed the parts in question, I think, would be more qualified, because the field engineer has to be a generalist who has to know a little bit about every part of the automobile, where the design engineer as a specialist knows a whole lot about one specific part of the automobile.

**Q:** What do you call these people?

**A:** Design engineers, the person that designs and releases the component.

**Q:** Do you know if Ford ever had a design engineer investigate a sudden acceleration?

**A:** I don't know.

**Q:** Did you ever try to find out?

**A:** No. To my knowledge, this is the first time you have asked me that question.

**Q:** Prior to 1987, who, other than district service engineers, were doing investigations following a sudden acceleration?

**A:** To my knowledge, district service engineers had that responsibility.

***

Koeppel, like Richardson, struck me as a decent and loyal former employee who knew just enough to use generalities in court. When I turned to Ford's retention policy for sudden acceleration-related SIRs, therefore, my target was senior management, and not Koeppel.

**Q:** Do you know what Ford's document retention policy for service investigation reports was in 1986?

**A:** I knew it at the time. I'm not sure I remember it well enough. It would have depended on a number of things, whether or not the subject involved a safety issue, whether it didn't involve a safety issue, it could be a different document retention period.

**Q:** If it involved a safety issue?

**A:** It was a longer documentation period.

**Q:** How long?

**A:** At that time it was probably either five or eight years.

**Q:** Your best recollection is that Ford's document retention policy for reports dealing with safety issues was five or eight years, did I understand that correctly?

**A:** That's my recollection, but I also qualified that by saying it's been a long time since I looked at that. And those policies change periodically, so I would want to refer back to the actual records of that time, and I'd be happy to stand corrected.

**Q:** Mr. Koeppel, think back. Was there a change in the document retention policy for service investigation reports concerning sudden accelerations in the year 1987?

**A:** Not to my knowledge.

**Q:** Well, if I represent to you that Ford has answered an interrogatory indicating a change, would you have any reason to disagree?

**Mr. Coleman:** I object to the form of this question, your Honor, if he has an interrogatory, he ought to read it to him.

**Mr. Murray:** I assure you we have it.

**The Court:** All right, then it's overruled.

***

I welcomed Coleman's objection because it underscored the importance of the interrogatory response I was about to introduce:

**Q:** Are you aware of that interrogatory?

**A:** I'm not aware of the interrogatory, and I have no personal knowledge beyond what I've told you . . . .

**Q:** Are you telling us you can't recall any change in Ford's document retention policy in 1987?

**A:** My earlier testimony was that the period five or eight years was a period I remember, that I would like to refer to what the actual policy was because the policies changed from time to time. That is the extent of my memory . . . .

**Q:** Do you remember in 1987, Ford changing its document retention policy for service investigation reports relative to sudden acceleration from a period of five or eight years to one year, with the requirement that the document was to be destroyed in the year it was generated?

**A:** Mr. Murray, I can only repeat what I've told you two times before . . . the extent of my memory is that in that period, reports from the field, service investigation reports, customer reports, that were perceived as safety related, had a five or eight year retention period. But retention periods changed, and I would refer to the actual documents from that time to refresh my recollection . . . .

***

The stage was now set to confront Koeppel with what must rank among the most damaging evidence against a car company to emerge in court:

**Q:** Mr. Koeppel, I'll show you an interrogatory response given us by Ford, and ask you, please, to read both the interrogatory question and the answer to yourself. For the record, sir, what interrogatory number are you reading?

**A:** Fifteen. I'm sorry. I'm not finished reading it. All right.

**Q:** Mr. Koeppel, would you please read the interrogatory to the jury?

**A:** The question is: "With respect to the following internal Ford reports known as . . . [SIRs], [do they] state whether any such documents reflecting instances of alleged sudden acceleration in Ford or Lincoln Mercury vehicles were destroyed, erased, deleted, lost or otherwise rendered unavailable from 1980 to the present. If so, then if any were destroyed pursuant to Ford's records destruction or retention policy or program, describe said policy or program with particularity and provide a writing that explains the policy."

**Q:** Now, sir, read Ford's answer.

**A:** "Without waiving the objection stated below, as Alan Updegrove set forth in his deposition, . . . in early 1987, field engineers were asked not to use the . . . service investigation form when investigating alleged sudden acceleration incidents . . . . Further, service investigation reports . . . relating to sudden acceleration claims have a retention period of one year . . . . "

**Q:** Let's break that down. Ford says that in 1987 the district service engineers who had been doing these investigations in the field were told not to use that form any longer?

**A:** Yes. They were using the longer, more complete, what we called the Updegrove inspection form.

***

Since Koeppel had come close to acknowledging that sudden acceleration-related SIRs had been reclassified to facilitate concealment from NHTSA, I decided to pin him down farther.

**Q:** Now, it says that as of 1987 service investigation reports had a one-year retention?

**A:** Yes.

**Q:** When, sir, did Ford institute a one-year retention period for service investigation reports regarding sudden accelerations?

**A:** As far as I know, the one-year retention period for service investigation reports had always been there, there was nothing changed for sudden acceleration reports . . . .

**Q:** How do you know that?

**A:** That's my recollection of retention practices.

**Q:** Have you read Ford's document retention policy as of 1987?

**A:** At the time I had read it. What I remember of it is what I remember now.

**Q:** Which is?

**A:** Records like general service investigation reports and customer complaints were retained for one year; safety records had a longer record retention period, as I testified yesterday, of five years or eight years . . . .

***

Several years would pass before we grasped the full implications of Koeppel's responses. At that moment, however, I decided to nail down the critical significance of Ford's interrogatory response:

**Q:** Did Ford as of 1987 consider service investigation reports prepared by district service engineers to be safety reports?

**A:** If they were complying with the one-year record retention, apparently not.

**Q:** Are you telling this jury that, as best you know, in 1987 Ford did not consider service investigation reports of sudden acceleration to be safety-related documents?

**A:** Mr. Murray, based on this interrogatory and my knowledge, I can tell you if there was a one-year retention period applied, that would be the case.

***

After Koeppel left the witness stand, Fred Weisman asked, with wide-eyed disbelief, "Did I miss something, or did this guy admit that Ford committed a felony by assigning a one-year retention period to safety reports so they could be trashed?"

"So it would seem," I replied.

At this point, Judge Cirigliano asked if the parties were interested in trying to settle the case. Ford's response was a tribute to John Coleman, who in the Tennessee case had shown considerable skill in assessing the risk of taking a verdict. In any event, with Judge Cirigliano's help, the parties reached a confidential settlement moments before final arguments were to begin.

Although more than a decade had elapsed since the Manigault's Crown Victoria smashed into a neighbor's house and destroyed their lives, they had finally obtained a measure of justice. But that was only because during the intervening years we had uncovered enough evidence to counteract the otherwise devastating effect of NHTSA's 1989 study and other government reports that had relied on it. The fact that such countervailing evidence has not been available to countless people who have been denied compensation because of these government reports doesn't answer the question we now turn to, namely, whether there is credible empirical or scientific evidence to support these government reports? Unless it can be shown that such proof exists, it means that untold numbers of people and their families have been cheated of justice by the combined and oppressive power of the car industry and the federal government.

PART 3

# THE COLOR OF CORRUPTION

# INTRODUCTION

**ON OCTOBER 16, 1987, THE U.S. DEPARTMENT OF TRANSPORTATION** announced that NHTSA had "ordered an independent study of the 'sudden acceleration' phenomenon which for many years has been a leading consumer automotive safety complaint." This was a gross understatement because there were thousands of reports in the agency's files of cars suddenly accelerating, overpowering the brakes and crashing. Indeed, by 1987 runaway cars had caused thousands of serious injuries and hundreds of fatalities; and what had NHTSA done in response to this carnage? According to the agency's administrator, Diane Steed, it had been a paragon of regulatory efficiency:

> Although we are not aware of any stone that has been left unturned, we believe a comprehensive, independent review of the facts could be helpful. We want to know if additional information exists, or could be developed, that bears on this problem.

As we will learn in Part Three, however, NHTSA had carefully refrained from looking under any stone that might have made a safety recall unavoidable. Although that's a serious charge, I intend to prove every word of it.

CHAPTER 46

# THE ORIGINS OF A REGULATORY DEBACLE

## AUDI: SHIFTING THE BLAME

In January 1984, Alice Weinstein prepared to back out of her driveway by shifting her Audi 5000 transmission from park into reverse. When she did, the car sped into a snow bank. When she took the car to her New York dealer, the dealer told her that nothing was wrong with the car and that she must have unwittingly stepped on the gas. Despite some misgivings, Weinstein accepted the explanation and kept driving the car. Almost a year later Weinstein got into her car with her teen-aged daughter. She shifted the car from park to drive, and the car suddenly accelerated again. This time the car shot forward across the lawn and hit a tree, sending Alice Weinstein and her daughter into the windshield.

*The Multinational Monitor*, May 1987, Vol. 8., No. 5

**WHEN CBS'S *60 MINUTES* BROADCAST A STORY IN 1986 ABOUT** Volkswagen of America's Audi 5000, pundits were already calling sudden acceleration the "AIDS" of the car industry.

"Do you recall," Molly prodded me in the spring of 2010, "what the sudden acceleration accident rate was for the Audi 5000 when *60 Minutes* ran that story?"

"In a word, no."

"According to the chronology of events Richardson prepared, it was one for every 155 vehicles, by far the highest of any model at that time."

"Do we know when NHTSA began investigating the Audi 5000?"

"In early November, 1981."

"What was Audi's response?"

"Volkswagen of America, Audi's parent company, claimed that loose floor mats were the problem, so it voluntarily recalled floor mats to attach guards on 1978-1982 Audi 5000s."

"I recall that, but didn't VWoA have another trick up its sleeve?"

"Yes; VWoA agreed to a voluntary recall in September of 1982 to prevent the right side of a driver's foot from applying the accelerator when the brakes were applied and the company agreed to modify the position of the brake pedal."

"Any other hot news?"

"Do you remember how Ford's public relations director, Jim Cain, attacked Steve Eckert following NBC *Dateline*'s story about the *Manigault* case?"

"Of course I do, but what does that have to do with the Audi 5000?"

"Would you believe that VWoA attacked the producer of the *60 Minutes* story, Alan Maraynes, whose assistant was none other than Steve Eckert?"

Intrigued, I sat back in my chair and waited for Molly to continue.

"We think this assault on Alan Maraynes shows that Volkswagen already had a strategy in place that the entire industry eventually copied to take advantage of poor, defenseless NHTSA." Molly's tone was sarcastic.

"That's strong medicine, Molly."

"Maybe. But let me read to you how this nasty little letter to the CBS producer began."

> . . . I can't figure out why any absolutely bright and articulate individual . . . is clinging so tenaciously to a completely untenable and illogical conclusion, i.e., that the Audi 5000 is afflicted with some sort of *non-repeatable, intermittent, multiple system* failure mode that *defies diagnosis and correction* by the auto industry's engineering talent pool. [Emphasis added.]

"Good grief, Charlie Brown," I blurted, "that bit about 'some sort of non-repeatable, intermittent, multiple system failure mode' is almost verbatim what ended up in NHTSA's 1989 report."

"Exactly," rejoined Molly. "Furthermore, following this letter, the entire industry began telling NHTSA the same thing."

"Read what came next in this letter," I asked, now completely in the moment. Molly read:

> You and other proponents of this bizarre theory cannot offer a single piece of hard evidence to support your position. On the contrary, literally all the actual evidence is completely to the contrary.
>
> Of your so-called "experts," Rosenbluth has been totally discredited and is now little more than a laughingstock . . . . [He] simply doesn't know what he's talking about . . . .

Molly looked up from the letter. "Does that remind you of Ford's blasts against Sero after Judge Calabrese found that it had committed a fraud?"

"That's exactly what I was thinking," I replied, as Molly returned to the letter:

> We know, *for an absolute fact,* that unintended acceleration claimants were not stepping on the brake pedal. Had they been, their cars would not have moved, or had they been in motion, they would have been brought to a stop. If they were not stepping on the brake pedal, just what do you suppose they *were* stepping on?
>
> Let's see, now. The car was accelerating, as though someone were stepping on the accelerator. An inspection of the foot well area of an Audi 5000 shows that there is literally no room for a human foot anywhere but on the brake or accelerator . . . . [Emphasis original.]
>
> Your repeated statement to me that all the claimants are saying the same thing indicates a couple of things. One, they're all doing the same thing and two, there's a fair amount of active and passive coaching of claimants going on, as you know. It's mighty peculiar that the incidences of unintended accelerations have [sic] gone up dramatically since all the publicity began about eight months ago.

"Where do they find people to write insulting stuff like this?" I mused, when Molly paused. "This guy was insinuating that Audi's problems were due to publicity, and that people were being prodded to make up fairy tales about cars taking off on their own."

"And who do you suppose was behind these fairy tales?"

Before I could respond, Molly continued. "This nasty little company man was thinking about trial lawyers, who everybody knows compulsively chase ambulances to make life difficult for defenseless car companies."

I couldn't help laughing. "Isn't that a touch paranoid?"

"Perhaps. But that doesn't mean they aren't out to get trial lawyers." Molly handed me a copy of the letter. "Read the last two paragraphs and tell me this guy didn't see a trial lawyer lurking behind every bush."

> While I realize that the workings of an automobile are a mystery to most Americans, the simple fact of the matter is that a passenger car is a pretty technologically primitive device . . . . [T]here is literally nothing in any modern car that can't be doped out by any properly trained and competent technician, given a reasonable time period to test and diagnose. We're not talking about a Boeing 757, with its EFIS and fly-by-wire flight control system, or the space shuttle. We're talking about a bloody car.
>
> The suggestion that an electrical or mechanical malfunction in a car would baffle all the Audi dealership technicians in the United States as well as the combined engineering staffs of Ford, GM, Audi, and NHTSA is patently absurd.

"I don't know if this guy was spooked by trial lawyers, Molly, but he sure knew how to be a supercilious jerk."

Before I left the office that evening, Molly handed me a lengthy letter written by Clarence Ditlow, who we met earlier, to Diane Steed, NHTSA's administrator during the heat of the Audi 5000 debacle. "I wish we had found this earlier, because it proves that NHTSA is not only stupid, it's in bed with the car industry."

"I can't wait to read it; give me a quick summary."

"In 1987, NHTSA announced that VWoA had agreed to recall Audi 5000 models to install shift-lock devices that required light pressure on the brake pedal to shift out of park. This was touted, of course, as a way to prevent drivers from mistakenly stomping on the gas pedal. Ditlow saw through that farce and told the press he was shocked that NHTSA would allow VWoA to palm off the shift lock as a remedy for sudden accelerations. That ticked Steed off enough that she told the press Ditlow's criticism was 'irresponsible.' He basically rammed that remark down her throat. It's great happy hour reading."

CHAPTER 47

# A TONGUE LASHING FROM CLARENCE DITLOW

## A ROUTINE ROAD TEST TURNS INTO TERROR RIDE

In New Jersey, a road inspector got into an Audi 5000, put his foot on the brake, and turned on the ignition. Seconds later, the Audi had sped out of the garage and smashed into a tree, injuring the inspector. The inspector stated that as soon as he put the vehicle into gear, it accelerated suddenly and that he did not take his foot off of the brake during the entire incident. Further, other inspectors and employees at the scene said that the vehicle's brake lights were on the entire time the vehicle traveled forward. When local TV stations aired the story, sales of Audis plummeted in the area and the State of New Jersey refused to perform any driven inspection tests in Audi vehicles.

*Detroit News*, December 13, 1987

**CLARENCE DITLOW'S JANUARY 30, 1987 REPLY TO DIANE STEED'S** accusation that it was "irresponsible" to criticize the shift lock, was even more scorching than Molly had indicated. It began by debunking the "automatic shift lock" as a cure for sudden accelerations:

> You not only knew in advance that the shift lock was not working, you had good reason to know [it] could never work because it flies in the face of the facts of *virtually every runaway Audi accident* ever reported to you. In those cases, drivers consistently reported that their foot was not on the accelerator when they shifted from park to drive or reverse—yet the car still accelerated uncontrollably.
>
> If anyone is being irresponsible, it is you—by helping Audi cover up a deadly defect through a phony fix; you are encouraging owners to develop a false sense of security that their Audis are now going to be "free" of sudden acceleration problems. [Emphasis original.]

That Ditlow smelled a cover-up is clear from his rebuke that "there was a time when NHTSA would have been the first to expose a voluntary recall that was nothing more than a charade .... How things have changed for the worse under your tenure as NHTSA Deputy Administrator and Administrator!"

Ditlow struck even closer to the bone when he accused NHTSA of having "established a pattern of dropping or shelving investigations after the manufacturer agreed to a remedy the agency knew to be either unproven or unrelated to the defect NHTSA had been investigating."

> After Audi agreed to its first recall for sudden acceleration in 1982 ..., NHTSA closed its first low-level Audi sudden acceleration investigation. In 1983, after continuing

> reports of runaway Audi accidents, NHTSA asked Audi to conduct a second recall, and VWoA again agreed to recall its 5000 models for "a problem that was *not what owners* were reporting . . . . Now once again, continuing reports of Audi sudden acceleration accidents have prompted NHTSA to ask Audi for a *third recall*."
>
> For the *third time*, NHTSA is allowing Audi to employ a fix which assumes that drivers are hitting the wrong pedal. Audi will install shift-lock devices . . . [which] merely require Audi owners to do what they have been doing all along—press the brake lightly before shifting into gear. [Emphasis original.]

Clarence Ditlow was proven right when VWoA was forced to acknowledge having received 396 reports involving Audi 5000s *with shift lock;* and since it wasn't necessary to turn over a stone to find this evidence, we are left to wonder what kind of stones Steed was referring to in her self-congratulatory statement on October 16, 1987.

CHAPTER 48

# A CONGRESSIONAL PLEA

It has now been nearly two months since the Center for Auto Safety, New York Attorney General Robert Abrams, the New York Public Interest Research Group and Audi accident victim Alice Weinstein petitioned the U.S. Department of Transportation and NHTSA to investigate and recall 200,000 1978-86 Audi 5000S cars which suddenly accelerate after shifts out of "Park." On April 21, 1986, having heard not a word from your office concerning this defect since our petition, and having received over 100 new accident reports detailing 39 injuries and 1 death since March 19, we wrote you again, urging your agency to respond to this pressing problem and to warn Audi owners and the public of the dangers they face from Audi sudden acceleration. So far all the public has heard from NHTSA and DOT about the Audi sudden acceleration problem is

> deadly silence. Meanwhile, runaway Audis are continuing to injure and kill people.
>
> *Letter to Diane Steed from Center for Auto Safety,* May 8, 1986

**DURING THE AUDI 5000 DEBACLE IN THE MID-1980S, A GROUP CALLING** itself the "Audi Victims Network" urged George Hochbrueckner, a member of the House of Representatives with a background in electronics from his work in the aerospace industry, to get Congress involved. Hochbrueckner enlisted fourteen prominent Congressional colleagues to sign a letter dated July 28, 1987, to then-Transportation Secretary, Elizabeth Dole, calling her attention "to a serious safety defect in Audi 5000 cars." The letter said that the recent "voluntary recall" to install shift interlocks had failed to eliminate the safety threat, as shown by hundreds of incidents, accidents, injuries or deaths associated with runaway Audi 5000s in 1986 alone—"an astonishing accident rate of one out of every 155 cars sold, the highest accident rate associated with an auto safety defect investigation in NHTSA's history."

That these members of Congress suspected NHTSA of being more interested in protecting carmakers than people seems clear:

> Since NHTSA's first investigation of Audi 5000s in 1981, . . . the agency has consistently shown a disturbing readiness to *disregard owner reports* and other evidence that vehicles were self-accelerating, and has accepted Volkswagen of America's claims that accidents are due to driver error . . . . [Emphasis original.]

Hochbrueckner also pointed out to Dole that the driver error theory was "implausible, based on the phenomenal accident rate;" and that "unless NHTSA has proof of driver error, the available information dictates that there is a clearly documented *performance problem affecting the safety of Audi 5000s.* A recall can be issued on this basis." As our story unfolds, this reference to "vehicle performance-based" safety recall will take on increasing importance.

The letter, whose signers included the late Senator Daniel Patrick Moynihan, expressed the "strong belief . . . that NHTSA will not act to obtain a meaningful remedy unless you intervene personally," an exhortation that fell on deaf ears with terrible consequences for countless people worldwide.

Finally, Audi's problems had the entire industry on tenterhooks. Early in 1987, the Detroit-based Motor Vehicle Manufacturers Association met in closed session to take a public stand before, according to an unnamed attendee, "Audi's dilemma begins to wash over the entire industry." In the words of an executive with the Auto Importers of America, "[I]f Audi can be hit, any of us could, too, and . . . maybe we need a way to handle this in [the] event it steamrolls." (*Multinational Monitor,* May 1987.) In fact, the steamrolling had already begun.

CHAPTER 49

# A SHOCKING DEPARTURE

**CRASH KILLS MD. WOMAN, GRANDSON, 6, GRANDDAUGHTER, 8 INJURED IN VA.**

A grandmother from Baltimore was picking up her two grandchildren after a church service in Fairfax County, Va. People in the neighborhood observed the car, driven by the grandmother, pull forward, drive across two lanes of traffic, and crash into the home of one of their neighbors. The police report showed that as the car attempted to enter back onto the road, it accelerated very rapidly and sped across the street and into the yard where it ultimately smashed into the porch of the house. Tragically, the grandmother and her 6-year-old grandson died in the hospital of injuries from the accident, and the granddaughter was severely injured.

*Washington Post,* April 25, 1988

**CONGRESSMAN HOCHBRUECKNER BEGAN A LETTER ON MARCH** 1, 1988 to NHTSA Administrator, Diane Steed, by calling her attention to VWoA's refusal to turn over numerous reports relating to sudden accelerations in Audi 5000s. Hochbrueckner said it was a violation of federal law "to keep from public knowledge" that VWoA's shift lock recall had not reversed the tide of sudden accelerations in Audi 5000s. Citing a memorandum prepared by NHTSA's Wolfgang Reinhardt, Hochbrueckner accused NHTSA of having "willingly acquiesced in VWoA's refusal to turn over the incident reports":

> [The Reinhardt memorandum] actually describes an unprecedented arrangement in which a manufacturer is *permitted to withhold* its consumer complaints from the public and gives NHTSA the opportunity to review the incident reports only in the *privacy of the manufacturer's offices.* [Italics added.]

This collusion was too much for Hochbrueckner: "As a result of NHTSA's apparent cooperation with VWoA, the public has been denied the opportunity to study significant evidence which might highlight the ineffectiveness of a shift-lock device in the Audi 5000 to curtail sudden acceleration incidents." "This," he charged, "was *a shocking departure from the established practices* in these matters." Hochbrueckner's accusation was an understatement. Federal law mandates that a carmaker must report to NHTSA "within a reasonable time" a "defect that relates to motor vehicle safety." Thereafter, it must notify all owners of the defect and offer to repair the vehicle in question, or at the manufacturer's option, to repurchase it; and since a vehicle that suddenly accelerates on its own obviously has a defect that must be reported to NHTSA, the "unprecedented arrangement" Hochbrueckner had uncovered amounted to outright complicity by NHTSA in a brazen violation of federal law. If that doesn't prove—as Ronald Reagan claimed—that government is the problem and not the solution, it is hard to imagine what would. In any event, while all this was going on, Diane Steed, like Nero fiddling while Rome burned, waited passively for the German automaker to decide what it would deign to turn over to the federal government.

In another understatement that would prove prescient, Hochbrueckner told Steed he had gotten "the firm impression that . . . . NHTSA believed sudden acceleration was due to driver error and, drawing on his background in electronics, he pointed out to Steed where NHTSA needed to focus its attention":

> Logic dictates that the shift-lock device is not the cure to the sudden acceleration problem. I hope NHTSA will . . . begin to investigate the possibilities of intermittent computer operation as well as the role electromagnetic interference (EMI), radio frequency interference (RFI), alternator power spikes, and other related factors may play in the sudden acceleration problem.

Hochbrueckner's sage "hope" that NHTSA would investigate "the role of electromagnetic interference . . . in the sudden acceleration problem" should have ended this automotive disaster, seriously investigating the "role of electromagnetic interference" was one stone this invincibly inept agency didn't dare turn over.

CHAPTER 50

# DITLOW'S FIRST FORD PETITION

The danger posed by the conditions described in these bulletins is evident from the reports received by the Center for Auto Safety and NHTSA. The sudden acceleration problem usually occurs without prior warning and with frightening consequences. As numerous complaints indicate, the accelerated condition causes loss of control; the increase in speed occurs so rapidly that drivers simply cannot react in time. Even when they do, the acceleration is so great that applying the brakes is ineffective.

*Letter to Diane Steed from Center for Auto Safety,*
August 30, 1985

**IN RESPONSE TO A CENTER FOR AUTO SAFETY PETITION, NHTSA** opened its initial Ford investigation on September 30, 1985. Ten months later, the agency issued this one-page closing résumé:

> In response to ODI's request for information on the alleged defect, Ford provided a total of 62 sudden acceleration complaints. Ford defined "surging" as a term "commonly used within he [sic] automotive industry to describe a momentary irregularity in engine output, either at steady vehicle speeds of [sic] during acceleration" which " . . . does not threaten the driver with loss of vehicle control."
>
> ANALYSIS: Reports involving only "surge" and reports not mentioning loss of control due to acceleration were not considered in this analysis. Initially, 24 complaints of "uncontrollable" acceleration were received for the 1984-85 model year vehicles . . . .
>
> Accelerations of the magnitude described require that the throttle be wide open. However, tests at ODI's Engineering Test Facility have verified the ability of the brakes to hold a similar vehicle. Driver error as a factor can neither be proved nor disproved. No common component has been identified as the causal factor for the alleged sudden accelerations.
>
> PROPOSED ACTION: Close this Preliminary Evaluation.

Molly was beside herself. "Can you believe these morons actually invited Ford to grossly understate the number of reports."

"After you explain it," I replied, "I'm sure I will."

"Ford gave the government 62 reports, which we know from our records was only a small fraction of the actual number. But those bureaucratic functionaries wanted to whittle that number down even further, so unless the driver specifically used the term 'loss of vehicle control,' they tossed the report. That left only 24 reports that could easily be brushed aside."

"So you think NHTSA was deliberately letting Ford off the hook?"

"At first I didn't, but after thinking about this puny closing résumé, I changed my mind."

"Why?"

"Take the ODI's brake testing. All they did was have someone press on the brake pedal hard with one foot, and push the accelerator pedal to the floor with the other one. That was like testing whether someone who knows ahead of time his car is going to suddenly accelerate at gear engagement can prevent it by hard braking *before* it happens. That tells me these people were already angling to blame drivers."

"I agree the government's testing was stupid, but I don't think it necessarily proves NHTSA was looking to blame drivers."

"I might agree," retorted Molly, "if these bumblers had not also said that 'driver error as a factor can neither be proved nor disproved.' That was like saying that drunk driving can neither be proved nor disproved. Did it ever occur to these idiots that they were not being paid to investigate drivers, but cars that were wiping people out faster than any other problem in automotive history up to that point?"

Before I could respond, Molly continued her tirade. "If you think that's excessive, explain the comment in the closing résumé that 'no common component has been identified as the causal factor for the alleged sudden accelerations.'"

"That showed an abysmal ignorance about electronics, but how do you get from there to blaming drivers?"

"Simple; NHTSA couldn't blame drivers without first exonerating the industry. That meant swallowing the notion that if you couldn't find the problem by inspecting electronic components, there was no problem. That, of course, left drivers, even if it also meant ignoring overwhelming evidence that they were not the problem. It was outrageous, but that's how those political hacks managed to stick it to the people who were paying their salaries."

Molly wasn't the only one outraged by NHTSA's cursory dismissal of the CFAS petition.

CHAPTER 51

# DITLOW'S SECOND PETITION

> NHTSA's [first] inquiry was little more than a sham. Despite repeated requests from the Center, NHTSA refused to examine vehicles for the very engine and computer malfunctions described in Ford's own service bulletins. NHTSA even refused to investigate a fatal accident in St. Petersburg on March 3, 1986, which left one man dead and a woman comatose. NHTSA's inaction makes a mockery of the notion that NHTSA has seriously investigated Ford sudden acceleration.
>
> *Letter to Secretary of Transportation Elizabeth Dole from Clarence Ditlow, Executive Director, Center for Auto Safety,* November 20, 1986

**IN RESPONSE TO NHTSA'S PERFUNCTORY CLOSING RÉSUMÉ,** Clarence Ditlow began collecting data for a second Ford petition. Meanwhile, the Florida Public Interest Research Group (FPIRG) was being inundated with reports in that state. The two groups collaborated on a second petition filed on November 20, 1986, that began:

> "Over a year ago, the Center for Auto Safety asked the National Highway Traffic Safety Administration (NHTSA) to investigate sudden acceleration in 1984-1985 Ford full- and mid-size fuel injected cars. Despite receiving nearly 200 reports of sudden acceleration, . . . NHTSA quietly closed an eleven-month 'preliminary evaluation.' Yet, since NHTSA closed its investigation in August 1986, there have been more accidents . . . . "

The petitioners scolded NHTSA for ignoring a tragic crash in Florida that:

> . . . would have allowed the agency "the rare opportunity to analyze an unaltered vehicle which appears to have exhibited the classic sudden acceleration failure mode." The agency did not even respond to this request of the Center's April 30, 1986, follow-up. [Emphasis original.]

The petitioners next took NHTSA to task for downplaying reports of ineffective braking because it contradicted "the firsthand experience of scores of accident victims who state that *braking did not stop their vehicles.*" The agency's earlier inquiry "showed only that NHTSA *could not find a defect it did not look for* . . . . Across the country, Ford's sudden acceleration continues to demonstrate its frightening consequences." [Emphasis original.]

That NHTSA was "downplaying reports of ineffective braking" was clear from the evidence. Drivers from the beginning had insisted that braking did not stop the car. Moreover, neither the car industry nor NHTSA to this day *has produced a shred of empirical or scientific evidence contradicting the credibility of these reports.*

Echoing Congressman Hochbrueckner's adjurations, the petitioners reminded NHTSA that *it could order a performance-based recall:*

> As NHTSA well knows, the courts have firmly held that NHTSA can establish a safety defect and order a recall "by showing a significant number of failures without making any showing of cause." The fact that NHTSA says it cannot isolate the precise failed component is no excuse not to order a recall under the law of the land. But . . . NHTSA could satisfy even its higher standard if only it would conduct a thorough investigation.

With lives increasingly being destroyed by runaway cars, why didn't NHTSA initiate a recall? While that question will haunt the remainder of this tale, it was at this point in our story that a CBS *60 Minutes* story about the Audi 5000 made the American public aware for the first time of this often deadly automotive behavior.

CHAPTER 52

# SIGNIFICANT MODIFICATIONS?

During the course of its preliminary evaluation, NHTSA even refused to investigate a March 3, 1986, sudden acceleration accident in St. Petersburg, Florida which killed the driver and seriously injured a 19-year-old woman. In the accident, Lewis E. Connor was driving a brand new 1986 Mercury Grand Marquis off the dealer's lot when the vehicle accelerated over 150 feet, across six lanes of traffic and crashed into the vehicle driven by Charlene Meehan. On March 28, 1986 the Center urged NHTSA to investigate the accident because it would have allowed the agency '*the rare opportunity to analyze an unaltered vehicle which appears to have exhibited the classic sudden acceleration failure mode*.' The agency did not even respond to this request of the Center's April 30, 1986 follow-up, choosing instead to address other issues raised in the Center's correspondence.

*Center for Auto Safety petition*, November 20, 1986

**1987 BEGAN ON A SOUR NOTE FOR FORD. IN THE MAIL AFTER THE** holidays was a notification that NHTSA had identified "439 sudden acceleration reports, resulting in 191 accidents, 101 injuries, and five fatalities" that could result in a recall. While the mere mention of a possible recall was unnerving, it was the following information requests that threatened to expose the truth behind the snowballing devastation runaway cars were inflicting:

> Identify and describe all significant modifications or changes that could relate to the alleged defect in the manufacture, design, or operating strategy of the ignition, fuel, or throttle control system used in the subject vehicles.
>
> Furnish the number and copies of all owner complaints, field reports, service and technical bulletins, studies, surveys, or investigations from all sources, either received or authorized by Ford, or of which Ford is aware, pertaining to the alleged defect.
>
> Identify and describe all accidents, subrogation claims, or lawsuits known to Ford pertaining to the alleged defect . . . [and] provide Ford's analysis of each . . . .

Let's start with the 439 reports cited by NHTSA. When the Senate held hearings in 2000 in the wake of the Firestone tire recall, Senator John McCain asked the Department of Transportation's Office of Inspector General (OIG) to review the record of NHTSA's Office of Defects Investigation (ODI), in identifying safety defects. Two years later, the OIG issued a blistering critique of the agency's defect investigation process. The report said the agency's data was flawed and limited, that it had no real process for investigating problems, and that its database "contained less than 10% of the complaints" registered with carmakers.

If the 439 reports cited by NHTSA were about 10% of those known to Ford, the company would have known about roughly

4,000 reports; and if the ratio of injuries and fatalities was about the same, they would have caused about 1,000 injuries and 50 fatalities.

Keeping in mind that it was still early in the history of this automotive tragedy, let's examine how Ford responded to NHTSA's request regarding "significant modifications or changes . . . in the throttle control system." In fact, there had been three "significant modifications" in the "operating strategy . . . of the throttle control system," any one of which might have ended this serial manslaughter decades ago. The most obvious change, perhaps, was the transition from carbureted to electronic engine controls, particularly in 1983 models. Although Ford had sold one million 1983 models with manual transmissions and carbureted engines, none had reportedly spontaneously accelerated out of control. Ford's Achilles heel was the half a million models equipped with electronic cruise controls that accounted for every report involving a 1983 model. This was not just a clue that might have ended the growing automotive slaughter that ensued: it was indisputable evidence that linked sudden accelerations with electronic cruise control.

Had Ford turned over every report involving a 1983 model, the connection between electronic cruise control and sudden acceleration would have been clear on the public record. Ford knew, of course, that if a consumer advocate like Clarence Ditlow discovered this connection, it would only be a matter of time until media pressure impelled NHTSA to initiate a recall, which brings us to a critical moment in this unfolding tragedy when Ford, by coming clean, might have led the industry out of the moral squalor it had created for itself. Unfortunately, NHTSA's behavior had signaled its reluctance to dig too deeply into what was causing thousands of cars every year to suddenly race out of control. This was a temptation that Ford, despite the life-and-death consequences, couldn't resist. The strategy it chose was elegantly simple. Ford asked NHTSA if it could limit its responses to "fuel-injected engines only;" and since this was tantamount to acknowledging *that there were no reports involving cars with a carbureted engine system,* had NHTSA rebuffed this request, the cat would have been out of the bag and the automotive catastrophe that eventually spread throughout the world would not have happened. As we will learn in the remainder of this sad tale, this abject failure of NHTSA to protect the lives and safety of people was a harbinger of things to come. In any event, it hardly matters whether acceding to Ford's request was the result of stupidity or complicity in a cover-up, it concealed from the public unambiguous evidence that runaway car disasters across the industry were being caused by dangerously designed throttle control electronics.

Molly was convinced that NHTSA knew there were new reports involving cars with carbureted engines. "Letting Ford limit its responses to cars with fuel-injected engines," she fumed, "was like looking for a connection between smoking and lung cancer by studying only the records of smokers with lung cancer."

"Molly," I said forlornly, "I only wish someone had turned you loose before a Congressional committee back in the 1980s."

***

Ford's second "significant modification" was its advanced electronic engine control system, the EEC-IV, it first introduced in 1984 models. We've seen that the EEC-IV sent reports through the roof, and since there had been no change in the cruise control electronics, it was obvious that the spike in reports was directly related to the increased complexity of the engine electronics. Figure 52-1, which was prepared by an engineer in Ford's Automotive Safety Office, illustrates how this pattern was consistent across the industry as automotive electronics became more complex after 1983. The graph also shows that after NHTSA's 1989 report was published, complaints to the agency declined precipitously, indicating that many people now believed it was pointless to report a sudden acceleration to NHTSA.

***

The final "significant modification" calls for some background. Because the EEC-IV required additional space in the engine compartment, Ford had merged the cruise control electronics in the EEC-IV microprocessor, thereby eliminating the need for a separate cruise control module. The term "integrated vehicle speed control," or IVSC, was coined to describe the integrated electronics. While this modification reduced the cost of a cruise control unit by about $8, it also caused reports to soar in models with the IVSC. Two senior electrical engineers who understood

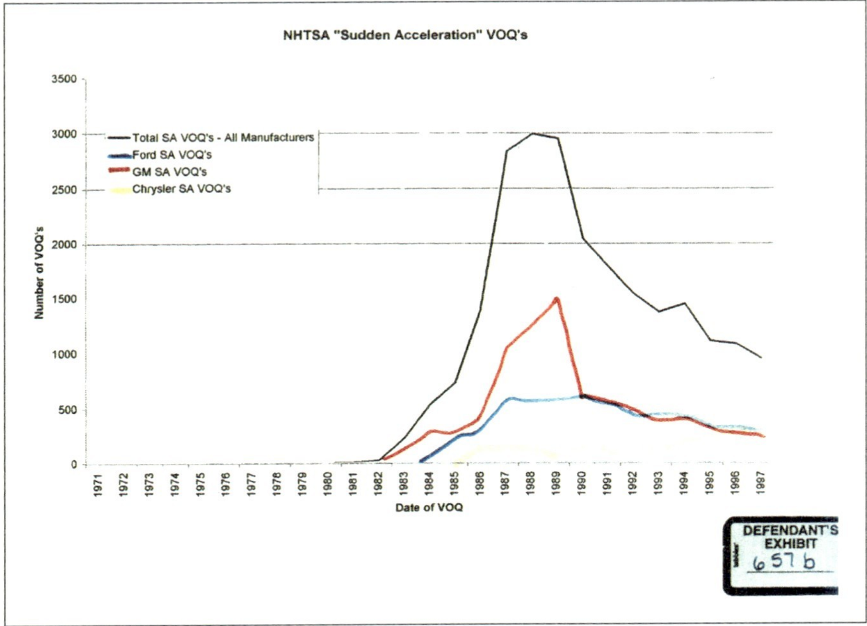


*Figure 52-1*

the implications of this modification, James Auiler and Stephen Hahn, were also members of the sudden acceleration task force that was studying how interactions between the throttle and cruise control electronics were contributing to this automotive behavior. On March 11, 1987, Auiler and Hahn received this memorandum from a subordinate of Max Jurosek, the company officer in charge of the sudden acceleration task force:

> Attached is the corporate response to the NHTSA. Please review, comment and/or concur by close of business Thursday, March 12, 1987. Thanks.—Tom Queneville

The corporate response Auiler and Hahn were being asked to view stated:

> Engine engineering, electrical and electronics division, and chassis engineering have informed us *that no significant modifications have been made* to the ignition, fuel, or throttle control systems on the subject vehicles that could have any causal or corrective connection to the alleged defect. [Italics added.]

Beneath Queneville's signature was a notation: "The Safety Office has asked us to give special attention to the response to Request No. 4"—regarding significant modifications—next to which Auiler scribbled a note to Hahn: "Let's discuss item 4 change."

Molly was sure Auiler and Hahn had been manipulated. "The big shots were shaking in their boots that outsiders like us might find out about the task force, and they wanted Auiler and Hahn to know they were claiming that the IVSC was not a 'significant modification.'"

I was skeptical. "Since they were asked for their comments, isn't that a stretch?"

"No," Molly shot back. "The company's response was sent unchanged to NHTSA two days later. If management wanted their input about the IVSC, these guys would have seen the company's response much earlier."

With that, let us turn to how Ford responded to the second request mentioned earlier, namely, for sudden acceleration-related "field reports."

CHAPTER 53

# NEEDLES IN A HAYSTACK

Across the country, Ford sudden acceleration continues to demonstrate its frightening consequences. In addition to the St. Petersburg fatality, a June 21 accident in Chattanooga, TN caused the death of a husband and wife. William and Ethelyn Chambers backed their 1986 Grand Marquis out of the driveway and shifted into drive. The vehicle suddenly accelerated, sideswiped a tree and traveled over 500 feet on a downward incline before striking a brick house at an estimated speed of 70–75 mph. A police investigator concluded that the entire event took about 4–5 seconds and that the accident was not caused by a medical condition. Although the couple was wearing seat belts, Mr. Chambers died instantly. Mrs. Chambers died a few days later.

Other recent accidents have caused serious injury. On May 12, Patricia Detore, of Rutherford, NJ entered her

1984 Ford Thunderbird and was about to leave her office parking lot. According to an account of the accident:

> As she was leaving Lot #1, she shifted into reverse and the car suddenly accelerated at great speed striking a fire hydrant. She then put the vehicle into drive, with her foot on the brake, the car again accelerated and shot across the aisle and a row of parking spaces (approximately 50 feet), it became airborne, before landing on top of two parked cars in Lot #2. Lot #2 is approximately five feet below the elevation of Lot #1. Mrs. Detore suffered injuries involving her head, neck and back.
>
> *Center for Auto Safety petition,* November 20, 1986

**WE LEARNED EARLIER THAT, ON OCTOBER 21, 1986, FORD'S** Electrical and Electronics Division submitted a report to senior management showing that the company's advanced engine electronics—the EEC-V—had caused a 400% increase in cruise control malfunctions. Ford had responded with a multidisciplinary task force to study how interactions between the engine and cruise control electronics were contributing to sudden accelerations. Meanwhile, field engineers were turning in service investigation reports—SIRs—confirming the connection between the complexity of the engine electronics and the company's sudden acceleration rate. These events presented Ford with a Hobson's choice: disclose the truth or remain in lockstep with the industry's insistence that there was no evidence of a defect that could explain this automotive behavior.

Following Edward L. Richardson's initial deposition, Molly announced that she and Jo Ellen had discovered that "Ford never mentioned field reports in its responses to NHTSA just two months after it created a sudden acceleration task force."

This came as a jolt. "Are you sure of that? Field reports are one of the first things NHTSA always asks for; failing to even mention them would be like a fire alarm."

"We've read every piece of paper Ford gave the government, and there's no mention of field reports."

"What about field reports that Ford refers to as SIRs?"

"There's no mention of SIRs either. But that shouldn't surprise you after the way Richardson danced around your questions about SIRs during the trial in Tennessee. Anyway, let me walk you through what we've found so far, beginning with how Ford handled the specific request for field reports."

Molly handed me a copy of what she was referring to. "Look at how Ford began its response regarding SIRs":

> Searches of those Ford central office files in which the materials of the kind requested . . . would ordinarily be expected to be found were conducted to locate reports alleging that a subject vehicle accelerated unexpectedly and rapidly (without operator input or beyond input perceived by the operator) such that the vehicle controllability would have been compromised.

When I finished reading, Molly became sardonic: "What would you say if during an appendicitis attack, the doctor said he would operate where your appendix would ordinarily be expected to be found?"

"Let me see your medical degree, Doc."

Molly wasn't amused. "I'd say, 'You idiot, where else would you expect to find my appendix?' This response was so obviously phony NHTSA had to be brain dead not to see what was going on, particularly since it knew from past experience that field engineers investigated problems like this one. The next part of this response was only more baloney":

> Obviously, reviewers of potentially responsive documents were confronted with the subjective nature of the individual complainants' description of the vehicle performance, e.g., did the vehicle accelerate, how rapid was the acceleration, was vehicle control affected?

Molly was still seething. "Imagine that! The whole damned industry was drowning in sudden acceleration reports, and Ford was struggling with questions like 'did the vehicle accelerate; how rapid was the acceleration; was vehicle control affected?'" Molly's ire was thick enough to photograph. "This is so sophomoric, it shows Ford knew it could treat NHTSA like a bunch of morons."

"So this wordplay was meant to conceal that Ford was hiding SIRs?"

"It's more devious than that, because even with NHTSA guarding the hen house, Ford couldn't risk concealing every field report."

"Hold on," I interrupted, "does that mean it gave the government some field reports?" I was struggling to grasp what I was hearing.

"Yes, but it was how Ford pulled it off that shows it was an 'inside job.'"

"Meaning?"

"Meaning that NHTSA was like a bank manager who disables a burglar alarm because he's conspiring with people planning to rob the vault."

"I usually like your analogies, Molly, but that one limps so badly it needs a wheelchair."

"All analogies limp, but this one less than most. First, concealing safety-related records from the government is a felony. Second, intentionally letting a car company commit such a dangerous felony is worse than colluding with bank robbers because destroying lives is worse than letting crooks get away with money in a bank vault. Anyway, the issue is not whether my analogy is perfect, but how NHTSA let Ford successfully conceal hundreds of incriminating reports with crude little tricks."

"OK, so don't keep me in suspense."

"Although Ford gave NHTSA a handful of field reports, they were concealed like needles in a haystack among about 1,000 unrelated documents, such as police reports, customer letters, insurance claims and so forth. But I'll let Jo Ellen tell you what she discovered when she began picking through the haystack one piece at a time."

"After we went over about 50 pages, we started finding SIRs blaming the cruise control. Maybe we should have looked for more reports right then, but we were extremely busy that day, and we decided to stick to our plan of carefully going through this stack of paperwork a page at a time. It really was like looking for needles in a haystack, but eventually we found seventeen reports scattered here and there that identified the cruise control as the cause of a sudden acceleration."

"So these SIRs were mixed in with completely unrelated paperwork?"

"Yes," Molly replied, "but I'll let Jo Ellen tell you what else we discovered when we took a close look at these 17 SIRs."

Jo Ellen posed a question that caught me off guard. "Do you know how many district offices scattered throughout the country employ field engineers?"

"Honestly, I've never given it a thought."

"We didn't know either until Molly remembered that the electronic summaries with Updegrove's final report listed Ford's district offices. Can you guess how many were identified on the electronic summaries?"

"Ten or fifteen?"

"Try thirty-three, which means there were twice as many district offices as there were SIRs in Ford's responses."

I was still catching my breath when Molly asked, "Do you remember Alan Updegrove's testimony about how many engineers were employed in these district offices back in 1987?"

"No."

"He testified that 200 field engineers were told on March 3, 1987 to discontinue using the SIR format."

My mind was racing. I knew that Ford had more than 5,000 dealerships that relied on field engineers when they were stumped about the cause of a customer's complaint. Because runaway cars were the most serious problem facing the industry at that time, field engineers would have been called upon to investigate occurrences reported to dealers; and yet Ford had not only failed to mention SIRs, it had apparently assumed that even if NHTSA happened to notice them in this paper haystack, it wouldn't do anything about it.

Molly interrupted my reverie. "Have you thought about how many SIRs Richardson's people must have reviewed prior to Ford's responses on March 13, 1987?"

"Are you trying to embarrass an old lawyer?"

"No," chortled Molly, "because we hadn't given it thought until Jo Ellen began coming across these SIRs."

"So let's have it."

"If the three people Richardson had reviewing these reports read only two SIRs a week over just 18 months, there should have been about 450 SIRs with Ford's responses on March 13, 1987, which would mean that Ford illegally withheld hundreds of incriminating SIRs. But that's not all."

I waited for Molly to continue.

"We know from Richardson that not a single field engineer found that a driver had caused a sudden acceleration. These

NHTSA dimwits didn't have to turn over stones to know that, it was staring them in the face."

I couldn't help laughing. "As Yogi Berra might have said, 'If you don't see it, you can't turn it over.'"

***

In fact, it hardly mattered how many SIRs Ford concealed. It had unquestionably concealed evidence it was required by federal law to disclose, and which should have ended one of the most destructive safety problems in automotive history. Molly again broke into my thoughts.

"Are you convinced yet that NHTSA has been in bed with the car industry all along?"

"I'm teetering on the brink."

"In that case, we'll push you over the edge. When Jo Ellen took a close look at these seventeen SIRs, she noticed two things that blew us away."

"May I join you?"

Without missing a beat, Molly explained that *eight of the seventeen reports were prepared by the same engineer in the Louisville district office, and that two others also came from that office.*

I was incredulous. "Are you sure Ford never turned over even one SIR from 25 district offices, and only one from seven others, because that's incredible."

"Of course it is; but it's also consistent with Updegrove's testimony that 200 field engineers were told on March 3, 1987 to stop using the SIR format when they investigated a sudden acceleration."

"Frankly, Molly, I'd forgotten about that."

"So did we, until we went back over Updegrove's testimony, which also reminded us of an interrogatory response you read to the jury when you questioned Koeppel during the second

*Manigault* trial. Let me read the key words: 'In early 1987 field engineers were asked not to use the service investigation report form when investigating alleged sudden acceleration incidents.' That was a reference, of course, to the meeting on March 3, 1987 in Dearborn when Ford pulled the plug on the SIR format, *but only for sudden accelerations.*"

My mind was reeling. "Don't let this go to your heads, but you guys have done a remarkable job of piecing all this together."

"We'd prefer a raise," rejoined Molly. "But there is more we still haven't mentioned. Until we re-read Updegrove's testimony, we had forgotten that he was so concerned about the inflammatory nature of SIRs that he wanted the company to develop a new way of investigating sudden accelerations."

"Did he actually use the word 'inflammatory'?"

"We knew you'd ask us that, so we brought you a copy of Updegrove's testimony. What matters is that Ford approved Updegrove's recommendation, and he was told to assemble a team of people to develop a new format."

"Do we know who was part of that team?" I wanted to know.

"According to Updegrove's final report, it included people from Powertrain Electronics, the Customer Service Division, the legal department and the Automotive Safety Office."

I was struggling to keep up with the pieces of a mind-numbing picture that were now falling into place. "Are you sure this new format was implemented at that meeting in Dearborn on March 3, 1987?"

"Yes," replied Molly, "because Updegrove's final report specifically says it was implemented early in 1987."

A light went on in my head. "Therefore, the elimination of the SIR format for sudden accelerations, the OGC's purge order, and the new format were all part of the same strategy."

"You're in the bull's eye, boss. Ford knew it couldn't discontinue investigating these reports, but it still needed an approach that did not allow investigators to identify a cause. In fact, Updegrove's final report shows that these SIRs convinced Ford to come up with a new way of investigating."

Molly wasn't finished. "Updegrove's testimony also made us remember something else about the interrogatory response you read to the jury in *Manigault*. Following the trial in Tennessee, I wrote a letter demanding that Ford turn over SIRs dating back to 1982."

"Why did you pick that year?"

"Because federal law requires that safety-related records must be retained for five years, and we knew at the time that NHTSA had asked Ford in early 1987 for these SIRs. Now let me quote again from this interrogatory response: 'Service investigation reports relating to sudden acceleration claims have a retention period of one year, not five years as indicated by plaintiff's counsel in their letter dated August 1, 2002.'"

"Hold on, Molly; didn't Koeppel grudgingly admit in *Manigault* that these SIRs were safety-related records?"

"Yes, but he didn't have a choice because any other answer would have made him look foolish."

"Didn't he also admit that federal law requires companies to retain safety-related records for five years?"

"Sure he did, but what else could he say?"

"I agree he was trapped, but the crucial question in my mind is, when were these SIRs assigned a one-year retention period? If I recall correctly, Koeppel became a cat on a hot tin roof when I tried to pin him down on that point."

"You remember correctly, but that was back in 2004, before we re-read Updegrove's testimony."

"Did Updegrove say when SIRs were assigned a one-year retention period?"

"In spades. He was quite clear, in fact, that in early 1987 the OGC issued an order that SIRs relating to sudden accelerations were to be purged in the year they were prepared. In other words, they were retroactively assigned a one-year retention period."

Dumbstruck, I formed a "T" with my hands that I needed a time out to collect my thoughts. Although NHTSA's request for SIRs was dated December 31, 1986, Ford would not have received it until early in the New Year; and since the Safety Office had probably reviewed several hundred incriminating SIRs by that point, NHTSA's request must have caused panic in the upper echelons of the company. One result was the OGC's purge order. Then, ten days before Ford answered NHTSA's request for SIRs, 200 field engineers were instructed not to use the SIR format when investigating sudden accelerations. This time it was Jo Ellen that broke into my reverie.

"Take a close look at these," she enjoined, handing me several SIRs. "Can you tell why Ford hid these reports in this paper haystack?"

I saw immediately what Jo Ellen was driving at. The first report I looked at had the words "retain record copy through 1991" stamped next to the words "cruise control" in the space for a "description of the causal part." Other SIRs had similar stamps. When I finished my perusal, Molly observed "if Clarence Ditlow had discovered these SIRs stamped with a five-year retention period, he would have seen immediately these SIRs were scattered throughout this stack of papers to hide a cover-up."

Molly's comment was sobering. Despite his proven success in forcing NHTSA to comply with federal safety regulations, Clarence Ditlow was not only overwhelmed with work, but had to devote much of his time to fundraising to support the work of the Center for Auto Safety. This realization is one reason I decided to write this book.

While I could tell my dream teamers had more to say, I told them I had to leave for a deposition and suggested that we resume our discussion the following morning.

"Get a good night's sleep," Molly chided, "because as the saying goes, 'You ain't seen nothing yet.'"

When I told Ann that evening about these discussions, she replied simply, "I know you like big challenges, Tom, but taking on the car industry and the federal government is about as big as it gets. Make sure you get your facts straight."

CHAPTER 54

# MORE EVIDENCE OF GOVERNMENT COLLUSION

*Sharply contradicting the NHTSA/Ford theory that driver error is the problem,* even highly skilled police officers have had sudden acceleration accidents with these Fords. On June 23, a Warwick RI police officer, Thomas Carmody, had a sudden acceleration accident while operating a 1986 Crown Victoria police car. According to Officer Thomas:

> I had stopped at the drive-up window of a Dunkin Donuts coffee shop and had placed the car in park. When I received my purchase, I shifted from park into drive, the car rapidly accelerated and I went over a parking area, across four lanes of a highway and drove through the front wall of an office building. The vehicle traveled a distance of 109 feet. The sensation was the most rapid acceleration I have ever experienced. I

> believe that it was possibly a defect in the electronic fuel injection on the computer that operates it. I did about $10,000 damage to the building and was not able to work for one month due to arm, head and lower back injuries.
>
> *Center for Auto Safety petition*, November 20, 1986

**MOLLY AND JO ELLEN EXPLAINED THE NEXT MORNING HOW FORD** had given the government carefully crafted summaries of "94 owner reports" that were so incriminating they should have led to a recall. When I asked for more, they said it wasn't just the summaries, which were incriminating enough, but "all the other stuff Ford tossed in pertaining to the 94 owner reports" that, as they put it, "blew us away."

"What other stuff are you referring to?" I asked.

Jo Ellen said there were "police reports, lawsuits, insurance company claims, letters from customers describing in detail a sudden acceleration, etc. We didn't count them, but I'm sure there must be 1,000 pages there."

"Does all this material support the conclusion of the field engineers regarding the cruise control electronics?"

"In spades," interjected Molly. "In fact, I defy anybody to read through this stuff and come up with any other conclusion."

"Do these summaries indicate whether drivers said they applied the brakes?"

"Good question," replied Molly. "One of the first things that struck us was that none of these 94 summaries even mentions braking. But the other stuff is loaded with statements and evidence that the brakes were applied. Only a nitwit wouldn't realize how suspicious it was that the summaries make no mention of braking."

I couldn't help laughing. "I take it that's your way of damning NHTSA with faint praise."

Molly ignored the quip. "There's something else about these summaries that sticks out like a sore thumb. About half of them indicate that a Ford representative inspected the car without finding anything wrong."

"Was this a reference to a field engineer or someone from a dealership?"

"If the car was inspected by a dealer representative, the summary says so. That indicates that about half of the reported occurrences were investigated by a field engineer who would have submitted a written report to company headquarters."

"If you're right, Molly, it means that a field engineer investigated about 47 of these reports. Do we know how many of the seventeen SIRs Ford sprinkled in with its responses pertained to a case included in these summaries?"

"Would it shock you if there were none, zero, zip?"

"Frankly, I'm beyond shock at this point."

"Then maybe our opinion that runaway cars have probably caused at least $5 billion just in economic loss won't come as a surprise."

"Sounds high. But try me."

"Do you recall that study published in 2002 showing there were more than 25,000 sudden acceleration reports on file at NHTSA by May of 2001?"

"Yes."

"Well, we did a rough estimate of the average property damage caused by the crashes described in these 94 summaries, and came up with about $10,000. About half the events in the Updegrove study ended in a crash. We figure that was probably also true of the 25,000 occurrences in that 2001 study. At $10,000 a crash, that would come to $125 million in property damage. Now assume the Inspector General was right that NHTSA's database contains only 10% of reports made to car companies. If so, there may have been as many as 250,000 reports known to the industry by 2001. If half of those ended in a crash, that would add up to 1.25 billion in property damage."

"That's a long way from $5 billion."

"I haven't finished," interrupted Molly. "That estimate doesn't include medical or hospital expenses incurred by injured people or their loss of income. When that's factored in, the total economic loss by 2001, we think, would have been at least $2.5 billion. Furthermore, there have been thousands of sudden acceleration accidents since 2001. When you factor for inflation, economic loss since 2001 could be equal to or greater than before 2001. That's how we got the $5 billion."

"That's an impressive piece of work," I remarked. "Now that I think about it, your estimate might be on the low side."

"What really grates on me," growled Molly, "is that most of the bill was paid by insurance premiums, Medicare, Social Security, etc. Poor John Q. Public, thanks to NHTSA, has no idea the car industry is secretly making him pay through the nose for its mistakes. What a rip-off!"

"Speaking of a cover-up, how many of these summaries reflect the gimmick of having someone test drive the car to see if it would take off again?"

"There are beaucoup summaries indicating the car was inspected and road tested without finding anything wrong. That little charade, of course, was like betting on the same six numbers that won last week's Super Lotto. It was also a way of keeping dealerships clueless, who then returned unrepaired cars to the owners, as happened to the Manigaults."

It was Jo Ellen's turn. "About 25% of the cars in the Updegrove investigation had at least one prior sudden acceleration. Therefore, returning unrepaired cars meant exposing people to a much greater risk of being killed or injured."

Molly weighed in. "Those NHTSA hacks knew that many people were reporting multiple sudden accelerations in the same car. If there's better evidence of government complicity in a cover-up, I haven't been able to think of it. Anyway, tell us what you think about this next summary."

Molly pointed to a description of how a Mercury Grand Marquis suddenly accelerated in a parking lot and crashed into five other vehicles. After inspecting the car and finding it to be operating properly, a Ford representative had "stall tested" the engine with the emergency brakes applied and discovered that:

> The brakes would not hold the vehicle in place, the rear wheels would turn and the vehicle would move forward. A dealer body shop mechanic started the engine by reaching in through the door and turning the key. He stated that the engine started and went to a "wide-open throttle condition." Further attempts by the dealership personnel to duplicate this condition were unsuccessful. The central office file contains no information on any repairs other than those associated with the body damage.

"This report," Molly interjected, "exposes the nonsense about failure to replicate these malfunctions meant there was no defect."

We turned next to a summary describing how the driver and a passenger were injured when a Ford Crown Victoria suddenly raced out of control on a driveway, crashed into the driver's garage, and when he shifted to reverse, the car "sped" back down the driveway, across the street, onto a lawn, before crashing into the central air conditioning unit of a neighbor's home. According to the summary, a Ford representative noted that the floor mat on the driver's side was "inverted and on the gas pedal."

Molly was irate. "Sam Sero has tried everything he can think of to find out if it is possible for a mat to floor the accelerator pedal."

Surprised, I asked "When did you learn that?"

"When I read that Toyota is claiming that floor mats are responsible for many of the sudden accelerations it is experiencing, I called Sam, who told me he had been retained in several Toyota cases and decided to test whether it was possible for a floor mat to depress the accelerator pedal to the floor, much less keep it there."

"And?"

"He struck out completely. He asked me a question we would like you to take a crack at."

"Fire away."

"Why do you suppose no car company has videotaped a demonstration proving that a floor mat can cause a car to suddenly take off at wide-open throttle?"

"I honestly hadn't thought about it."

"Sam stressed that he wasn't saying that a loose floor mat can't interfere with the driver's foot on the accelerator, which could certainly pose a safety problem. But he is convinced a loose floor mat, by itself, can't possibly cause a car to rapidly accelerate."

"I take it then that Sam believes the only way a floor mat can be involved is if it is on the accelerator pedal to begin with, and the driver for some reason pushes on it hard enough to open the throttle. But doesn't that assume that drivers, with or without floor mat interference, sometimes actually floor the gas pedal accidentally?"

"Yes; and that's why he says that until somebody proves drivers do something that amazingly spastic, even rarely, floor mats will remain a concoction to divert attention from bad electronics."

The two hours I had set aside for our discussion were now gone, and since we had a busy day ahead I suggested that we meet again the next day.

CHAPTER 55

# STILL MORE EVIDENCE OF GOVERNMENT COLLUSION

> The vehicle owner alleges that on 8-25-84, the day she purchased the vehicle, upon starting the engine, she " . . . shifted into 'Drive', whereupon the vehicle immediately lurched forward at full throttle, jumped over a curb, became airborne, and crashed at the bottom of a hill with great force . . . . " Extensive damage was reported to the vehicle and the passenger, Ralph West, was hospitalized with serious personal injuries, including fractures of the cervical spine and damage to the spinal cord, which have resulted in quadriplegia.
>
> *Ford's submission to NHTSA*, March 13, 1987

**AS IT HAPPENED, IT WASN'T UNTIL TWO WEEKS LATER THAT WE** finally took up NHTSA's request for a "description" of all sudden acceleration-related "accidents, subrogation claims or lawsuits," including an “analysis of each case.” Once again, Ford had given NHTSA carefully crafted summaries like the one cited in the headnote that upset Molly.

“Can you imagine the horror and pain this woman must have experienced being suddenly left with a paralyzed husband because her new car suddenly took off and crashed at the bottom of a hill?”

“Are there other cases like this in these summaries?” I asked.

“Many; it’s outrageous that the government would turn its back on people like the Wests. Talk about bureaucratic negligence, NHTSA specifically asked for ‘an analysis’ of these particular cases, and what did they get: one word - ‘settled’. The only thing settled,” Molly fumed, “was NHTSA’s willingness to leave people like the Wests at the mercy of these indifferent companies.”

The next summary only fueled Molly’s ire. A Mercury Grand Marquis had suddenly accelerated from the driveway, crossed the street, and “crashed into a neighbor’s brick home, killing the driver and passenger.” Ford again had ignored the government’s request for “an analysis” of the event.

At this point, Jo Ellen exhorted me to “read this next summary carefully because there’s something that goes with it.”

A 1985 Thunderbird had rapidly accelerated in reverse from a driveway, “made two complete circles on the street,” before crashing into a large pecan tree on the opposite side of the street. According to a lawsuit mentioned in the summary, the owner suffered “intensive physical pain and extreme mental anguish.” His stepson, a passenger, was fatally injured.

Handing me a copy of a police report, Jo Ellen asked me to read the statement of a witness to this event:

> I heard a loud noise and looked around; the dark blue car from across the road was traveling in reverse at a high rate of speed. The car came across the road with the young

> boy, Jacob, hanging out of the car because the door of the car was open. I heard the young boy call out "George! George! George!" The car then entered my driveway . . . . I heard the impact of the car hitting the pecan tree. I ran to the car. Jacob was not moving. George was lying in the car stretched out on the console between the driver's and rider's seats. His head and shoulder were lying on the back seat of the rider's side of the car. His feet were about one foot from the gas pedal. His body was stiff as a board. His hands were clenched. His whole body was jerking.

When I put the police report down, Jo Ellen's voice was quivering with emotion. "A Hollywood stuntman couldn't make a car do what this one did. Sam Sero said it would have cost about a dollar to prevent something this terrible. If enough people marched on Washington and demanded Congressional action, something might finally get done."

I could see that my "dream teamers" needed some words of encouragement: "The way you have organized and explained this material has opened my eyes to some critically important things I might otherwise have overlooked. I know these awful cases are painful to read about, and I don't blame you for being upset. You probably know that psychologists recommend dealing with anger by redirecting it to something positive."

Molly lightened the mood. "To hell with psychology! My motto is: Don't get mad, get even. We appreciate the compliment, but we think you should also read what we think is some of the most damaging evidence against NHTSA."

Jo Ellen handed me a stack of letters to Ford from customers, their lawyers and insurance companies. What follows is just one among dozens of similar letters:

Mr. Thomas J. Wagner
Vice President Lincoln-Mercury Division
Ford Motor Company
American Road
Dearborn, Michigan

Dear Mr. Wagner:

On February 19, 1986, my father had pulled to a stop in his 1984 Grand Marquis Mercury. When he attempted to start up and enter the highway, the Mercury mysteriously accelerated out of human control. By using every bit of his body strength, father managed to avoid hitting an oncoming car and finally got the Mercury stopped on a steel pole!!!

My father was hospitalized. Though subsequently released he has spent the past five weeks in misery from his injuries. He is still on a walker and terribly weak.

The malfunction in this automobile was not the first one! I had complained to the Jacksonville, Florida Ford Center about its poor performance, but was told to go back to the dealer. (I had already been there.) Again, I approached Carlisle Mercury in Clearwater, Florida where the car was purchased and received another temporary fix.

This wrecked Grand Marquis has been under repair for several weeks at Walker Ford in Clearwater, Florida. I am afraid to ever get behind the wheel of this car again, even to drive it home!

My father was a firefighter accustomed to driving emergency fire vehicles and was always considered an excellent driver. This Mercury had malfunctioned when I was driving and it was he who advised me how to operate the car until we get help.

My father has been a 'Ford man' fifty-plus years. Now he has lost confidence in your automobiles!

Sincerely,
Irene L. Dillon

cc: Donald Peterson
Chairman & Chief Executive Officer

Many letters were accompanied by a police diagram, like the one in Figure 55-1, showing that a runaway car traveled several hundred feet before crashing into something. There were so many occurrences like the one depicted in Figure 55-1 that it seemed

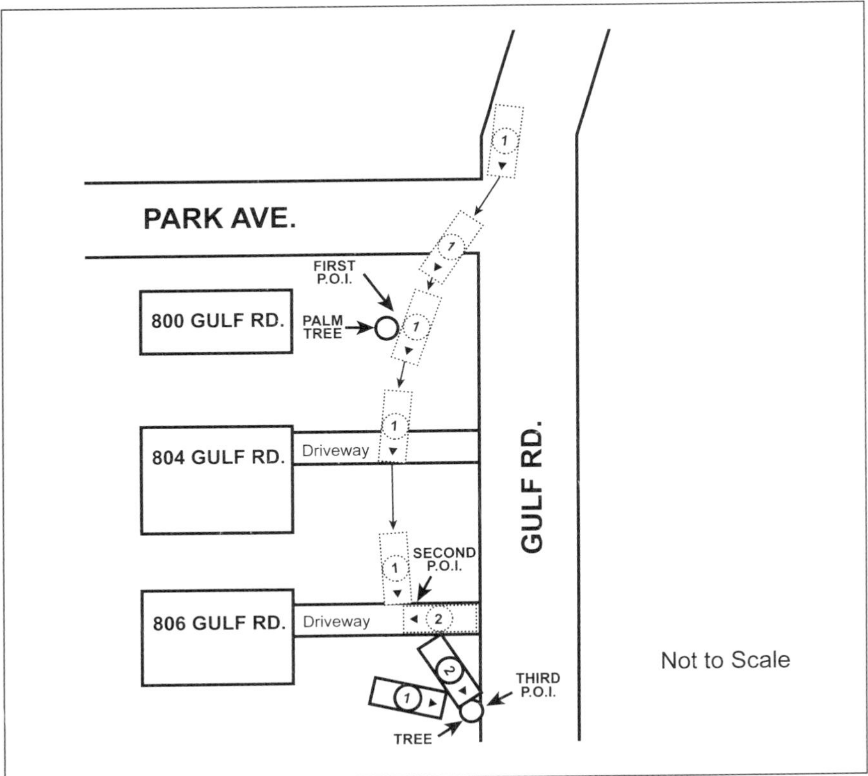


*Figure 55-1*

impossible that anyone could believe they were caused by driver error; and yet that is precisely what the federal government was soon to conclude following an industry-wide study. Before we go there, however, let us consider the second prong of the industry's standard defense, namely, that "the brakes will always win" and safely stop a runaway car.

CHAPTER 56

# WHY THE BRAKES DON'T ALWAYS WIN

## ACCELERATION PUBLICITY WORRIES ALL AUTOMAKERS

"I moved the shift lever . . . and all hell broke loose." Henry Givens was in a Southgate parking lot on Sept. 23 when his 1986 Ford Crown Victoria suddenly accelerated and smashed into a van. The 68-year-old Clinton Township man said damages totaled $8,000. "With my foot on the brake, I moved the shift lever from park to reverse, and within a split second all hell broke loose. The engine roared immediately to full throttle and the car surged backward. Amidst a roaring motor, screeching tires, and screaming brakes, I had moved backward two or three car lengths before I realized that my brakes were not going to stop me from colliding with parked cars behind me, and possibly

> pedestrians . . . . With the motor still roaring full-throttle, tires still screeching and brakes still screaming, I finally managed to stop by turning off the ignition."
>
> *Detroit News*, December 16, 1987

**LIKE THE FALLACY THAT "ABSENCE OF PROOF, IS PROOF OF** absence," the claim that "the brakes will always win" is equally spurious. It was the Ford Motor Company, ironically, that gave the agency the evidence that exposed this falsehood.

On January 29, 1988, NHTSA asked Ford for previously undisclosed studies to assist its soon to begin industry-wide study. This prompted a meeting in the company's Safety Office on February 12, 1988 attended by Stephen Hahn, the team leader of the Task Force created a year earlier to study how interactions between the engine and cruise control electronics were inducing these failures. On February 24, 1988, Hahn circulated a memorandum to task force members that began:

> In the February 12, 1988, meeting with ASO it was confirmed that NHTSA was requesting information relative to "WOT or full throttle" unexpected acceleration . . . .
>
> Relative to the high acceleration rate level of the sudden acceleration phenomenon, an analysis of the EEC-IV engine control shows that only when the vehicle speed control function is integrated into the EEC-IV system does the EEC system have the potential to produce close to wide open throttle acceleration.

Hahn was pointing out here that only by interacting with the cruise control electronics could the EEC-IV contribute to a "wide open throttle acceleration." Moreover, such interactions were different in kind from simultaneous and detectable hardwire faults the industry claimed were prerequisites for a sudden, uncommanded, and sustained acceleration. Hahn's memo, therefore, suggests that he had apparently forgotten Jurosek's admonition a year earlier about avoiding a paper trail that "could be used in court."

Further complicating things for Ford, models with the engine and cruise control electronics merged in the same microprocessor—the IVSC—had a sudden acceleration rate several times greater than models without this modification. This striking disparity in failure rates, in fact, may help to explain what came next in Hahn's memorandum:

> This system [IVSC] has the same *redundant disabling backup features* of other Ford Vehicle Speed Control Systems (i.e. brake electrical disconnect and mechanical venting system) to ensure the ability to disable the system even with speed control component malfunctions or failures.
>
> [T]ests were performed to ensure that even in the event of multiple redundant failures the vehicle could be brought to a stop. Attachment 1 shows the resulting acceleration and stopping ability of a Mercury Sable with integral EEC-IV vehicle speed control failing in the 'accel' mode and with all backup systems disabled . . . .

The tests Hahn referred to are crucial to our story. First, however, let's scrutinize the claim that "with all backup systems disabled, the vehicle could be brought to a stop." In fact, there were only two "backup systems." One was the "brake electrical disconnect"—the brake on/off switch or BOO. But it couldn't help the driver because the BOO switch was being bypassed by some fault that was also bypassing the throttle control logic. That left only what Hahn called the "mechanical venting system." Before examining why this mechanical redundancy has failed to prevent thousands of destructive outcomes, we need to understand how this "mechanical venting system" worked.

To begin with, the mere existence of a mechanical redundancy tacitly acknowledged that something was needed that didn't depend on the electronics. What Ford and its competitors came up with was a small plastic device with a plunger—a so-called "dump valve" attached to the brake pedal arm. When the brakes were applied, the plunger would expose a hole allowing air to enter the cruise control servo through a hose and "dump" the vacuum, thereby closing the throttle. Although carmakers hoped this would allow the brakes to control the car, there were many slips between cup and lip in this concept . . . .

For one thing, there are many variables that influenced the time required to "dump" vacuum in the servo. Sam Sero's testing, for example, showed that it typically took two to four seconds to clear the vacuum and close the throttle. Add the time required for the terrified driver to receive and react to what was happening, and the rpm level might be too much for the brakes to overcome. Moreover, drivers have never been told about the possibility of the throttle seizing control of the car or warned that pumping the brake pedal rapidly depletes vacuum assist in the brake booster. As to the latter point, Kathy Jarvis's response of pumping the brake pedal with both feet shows that it is entirely foreseeable that some terrified drivers will instinctively react this way when the car doesn't respond as expected to their initial brake application.

A particularly baffling aspect of this automotive behavior has been the huge number of people who have insisted their foot was on the brake pedal when their car took off. Although most cars had a shift lock, drivers were adamant that the car had accelerated *before shifting was completed*. At first blush, it is easy to see why this might arouse skepticism, even by members of the driver's own family. But, as Sam Sero demonstrated, a failure can occur *either before or after shifting is completed,* prompting me to ask "how, if a driver's foot was already on the brake pedal, a car could possibly get enough of a head start that it couldn't be quickly stopped?"

Sero pointed out that "simply placing your foot lightly on the brake pedal will activate the shift lock, but not the dump valve, which requires that the pedal must be depressed about three quarters of an inch."

"OK, Sam. If my foot is lightly on the brake pedal to begin with, why can't I push on the pedal and stop the car before the rpm level overpowers the brakes?"

"I'm sure many people have done exactly that, and prevented an accident. But I think you're forgetting something important. Try to imagine how shocking and totally unexpected it is to have your car take off while your foot is on the brake pedal. Do you remember what happened during the first test run in *Manigault* when we simulated a sudden acceleration in a Crown Victoria with Bill Berg as the test driver?"

"I'll never forget it. He panicked and aborted the test by switching off the servo."

"Do you remember how far the car traveled before he got it stopped?"

"As I recall, it was about three or four car lengths."

"And he knew the servo would pull the throttle open as soon as he activated it, and that he could instantly deactivate the servo by flipping a switch."

"Your point then is that before the driver realizes what is happening and pushes on the brake pedal, the engine might have reached an rpm level at which braking won't stop the car."

"That's exactly the point," replied Sero. "In fact, whether the driver's foot is on or off the brake pedal may not matter. The critical factor is how quickly the driver recognizes what is happening and applies enough brake pedal force to overcome the engine. These events are so unexpected and shocking that having one's foot on the brake pedal could actually add to the time lapse before hard braking begins. What disgusts me is that carmakers have known all along that split seconds can make a life or death difference once the throttle takes over. Do you remember the warning Ford gives its technicians in that shop manual I found?"

He was referring to the following instruction to technicians while road testing the cruise control:

> WARNING: IF AT ANYTIME DURING THE FOLLOWING STEPS THE SYSTEM SHOULD APPEAR TO GO OUT OF CONTROL AND OVERSPEED, BE PREPARED TO TURN THE SYSTEM OFF AT ONCE WITH THE OFF SWITCH OR THE IGNITION SWITCH.

"That warning, Sam, assumed that the cruise control was engaged when the throttle went out of control and, therefore, could be disengaged electrically. How is that relevant?"

"It is indirectly relevant because there would be no need for this instruction if the brakes will 'always win,' as these companies never tire of claiming. Also, the fact that shop technicians were never warned about sudden acceleration *when the cruise control is not engaged* shows a determination to conceal the truth even from the company's tech people. Ford, of course, isn't alone. The entire industry left terrified drivers to figure out for themselves, in split seconds, how to respond to these hellish emergencies."

When I told Molly about our conversation, she showed me an email Jo Ellen had recently found in our repository sent by a Ford engineer who, after experiencing a sudden acceleration, told colleagues that "if you . . . have a wide open throttle (WOT), the engine no longer produces vacuum. If you lose vacuum, or the engine goes to WOT, you will have only one press of the brakes with assist. The next time you hit the brake, you will have SUBSTANTIALLY less braking power, since the brakes are power-assist . . . . In this scenario, if a customer pumps the brakes once or twice, he's in BIG trouble." [Emphasis original.]

One shudders at the thought of how many terrified people have found themselves in "BIG TROUBLE" during the final moments before their lives were destroyed. That thousands of people have been subjected to such a terrible experience is indefensible enough; the abject failure to warn people about the possibility of a sudden acceleration and what must be done immediately in such an emergency represents a conscious indifference to the lives and safety of human beings that will continue unless, and until, juries begin bringing these companies to their senses by assessing punitive damages large enough to make it unprofitable to play automobile roulette with our lives.

We turn now to the most revealing part of Stephen Hahn's February 24, 1988 memorandum to members of Ford's sudden acceleration task force.

CHAPTER 57

# WHY THE BRAKES DON'T ALWAYS WIN: PART 2

> Mrs. Horn reports that after she moved the transmission selector lever from Neutral to Drive to release the parking brake, the vehicle "suddenly accelerated and leaped through the back of the garage." The vehicle went into the backyard, turned in a complete circle, and dug "little ditches" in the grass before it could be turned off. She also states that "she rode the brake through the garage and across the lawn with the engine still accelerating."
>
> *Ford's submission to NHTSA*, March 13, 1987

**HAHN'S FEBRUARY 24, 1988 MEMORANDUM INCLUDED THIS** description of brake testing Ford had performed to convince NHTSA that "the brakes will always win."

> [T]ests were performed to ensure that even in the event of multiple, redundant, failures the vehicle could be brought to a stop. *Attachment I shows the resulting acceleration and stopping ability of a Mercury Sable with integral systems disabled. The vehicle could still be stopped.* [Italics added.]

"Attachment I" included a pair of graphs containing a wealth of data recorded during two brake test runs. The graph shown in Figure 57-1, which was included with Ford's responses to NHTSA on March 7, 1988, bears careful scrutiny.

The scale on the left indicates the speed at each moment during two test runs; the scale on the right shows the engine rpms; and the scales at the top and bottom record the elapsed time during the tests. The words "forced servo" at the upper left indicate that an electrical device, like the one Sam Sero has used during similar testing, was used to suddenly open the throttle in the test car, a Mercury Sable. Before the tests runs began, both the BOO switch and dump valve were disabled. When the Sable reached 60 mph, the driver applied the brakes and brought the car to a stop in about

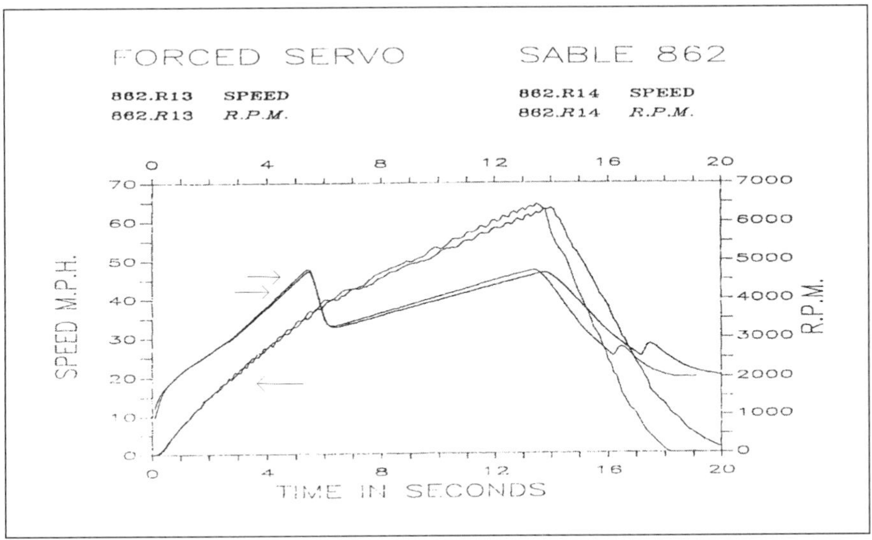


*Figure 57-1*

six seconds: an impressive demonstration, you may be thinking, of the brakes' ability to control a sudden acceleration with no help from an electrical or mechanical redundancy. But see if you can tell what's missing on this graph. If you guessed it is the amount of force exerted by the test driver on the brake pedal, you were right.

Now look at the right-hand scale on Figure 57-2 *that NHTSA never saw indicating force on the brake pedal*—the graph uses the term "pressure." Notice that initially the driver applied nearly 160 pounds of force for nearly three seconds, and not less than 90 pounds until the car came to a stop after about six seconds. In other words, the driver applied roughly ten times more pedal force than normal during the first three seconds, and never less than five times greater than normal force until the car stopped. But why was so much force required? Here it is worth considering how all braking systems work.

When the brakes are applied, force is transmitted hydraulically to bring the brake shoes into frictional contact with the brake discs or drums. The force supplied by the driver is amplified about

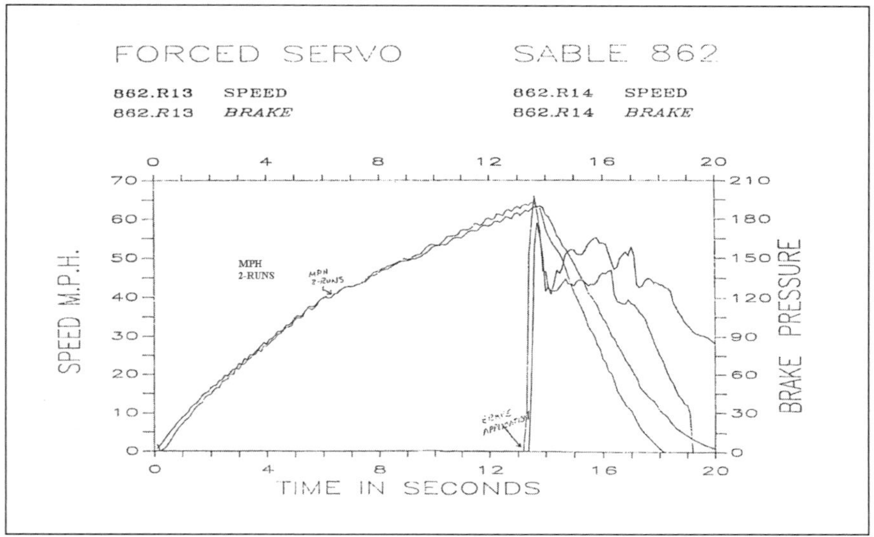


*Figure 57-2*

500% by vacuum in a brake booster, thus enabling the brakes to halt a car quickly under most conditions. The brake booster is comprised of a canister with a flexible diaphragm dividing it into two vacuum chambers. The center of the diaphragm is attached to a rod that connects the brake pedal and the hydraulically operated master braking cylinder. Ordinarily, the engine acts as a suction pump drawing air out of the two chambers and creating a vacuum in each. Because the reduction in pressure on each side of the diaphragm is the same, there is no force exerted on the diaphragm and the connection rod. With braking, however, a valve opens, allowing air to enter one chamber creating a pressure differential between one side of the diaphragm and the other that produces a force on the diaphragm that augments the brake force applied by the driver. When the driver releases the brakes, the air valve closes and the vacuum is re-established by engine suction. Obviously, if vacuum is not maintained, there will be no boost, and the driver must brake many times harder to get the same braking effect.

Moreover, when the throttle is wide open, there is no constriction of the airflow into the engine and, consequently, no vacuum is generated. Therefore, if the brakes are pumped—as American drivers were taught to do before the advent of anti-lock brakes—the vacuum is depleted even faster, and brake boost will rapidly disappear. When that happens, up to 250 pounds of brake pedal force may be required to lock up the wheels and stop the car. *These factors are as applicable today as during the eighties and nineties.*

Let's return for a moment to the graph NHTSA never saw. Notice that it took less than three seconds for the engine rpms to reach 2500, a level at which, as noted earlier, Ford's Powertrain engineers found that a car is "very difficult to stop by braking." Consequently, unless the shocked driver rapidly applied many times the pedal force usually needed to stop a car, the chances of braking to a stop were slim, a terrible truth that explains why the brakes have failed to prevent countless catastrophic outcomes.

Now for a final look at the graph NHTSA did see. Like the undisclosed graph, it also shows that within three seconds the rpms were at 2500, the level at which a car is "very difficult to stop by braking." But only the undisclosed data revealed that *five times more than normal pedal force—90 pounds—was needed to hold the car in place after it came to a stop*; and that the test car traveled about 30 feet in two seconds, 40 feet in three, and almost 50 feet in about four seconds, which is why so many cars have run someone down or crashed into something at locations where there was little time or space for maneuver—remember the catastrophe at the Rockford Baptist Church in Maryville, Tennessee. But no matter where a sudden acceleration happens, the difference between successful braking and devastation often depends on such razor thin factors as how quickly the driver gets on the brake pedal, with what force, and whether or not he/she in a panic pumps the brake pedal. Should NHTSA have suspected that Ford had withheld crucial brake testing data? My guess is that NHTSA knew many things were hidden under stones it couldn't afford to overturn, unless it was also prepared to honestly respond to what it found.

CHAPTER 58

# SCIENCE FROM A RABBIT HOLE

### NEW STUDY MAY UNRAVEL THE MYSTERY

The people who make the cars prefer not to talk about it. The people who drive the cars don't know what to do about it. That leaves it up to the people at the National Highway Traffic Safety Administration to solve the mystery of sudden acceleration. But they have no answers. "This is really one of the most baffling things we've ever looked at," said NHTSA Administrator Diane Steed, explaining why NHTSA has ordered an unprecedented worldwide study of the phenomenon to begin this month.

*Detroit News*, December 17, 1987

**WE HAVE ARRIVED AT ANOTHER TURNING POINT IN THE HISTORY** of runaway cars. In January 1989, NHTSA released its much-anticipated report, intended to "resolve the controversy" over sudden acceleration. The announcement summarized its conclusion:

> [A]n exhaustive, independent study of the sudden acceleration phenomenon in cars concluded that pedal misapplications that may be aggravated by vehicle design are the most probable explanation for most reports of sudden acceleration.

This statement, with its strangely indefinite conditional "may be" and tentative "probable explanation" was to have disastrous consequences for countless people in their struggles to obtain compensation for devastating losses. Not only was the car industry completely vindicated, NHTSA could now wash its hands of the problem and concentrate on easy-to-find mechanical defects that carmakers were usually willing to fix without a fight. But as cars every year became less mechanical and more electronic, this meant that NHTSA in thought and action would remain a Model T agency. Consequently, as runaway cars after 1989 continued to destroy hundreds of lives every year, NHTSA increasingly became dysfunctional with results described in Part Four.

But that doesn't answer how, after opening and closing dozens of investigations during the 1980s, NHTSA decided, in effect, there is no such thing as sudden acceleration, only driver error?

Let us begin with the ballyhooed "independence" of this study, whose provenance was the report-for-hire Transportation Systems Center and its incestuous relationship with NHTSA. The preface begins: "This report was prepared by the U.S. Department of Transportation, Transportation Systems Center (TSC), for the National Highway Traffic Safety Administration, Office of Defects Investigation." This characterization of the TSC—now the John A. Volpe National Transportation Systems Center—as a "government organization independent of

NHTSA" was deliberately misleading. The TSC operates under the Department of Transportation, as does NHTSA, whose relationship with TSC is so close some commentators have been led to believe that TSC is actually staffed by NHTSA. TSC boasts on its website that it "differs from most federal organizations in that it receives no direct appropriation from Congress." Instead, it is funded 100% through a for-service structure in which costs are covered by whoever is footing the bill for the project. Under this funding arrangement, according to one prominent electrical engineer, "the chances of TSC expressing independent views are pretty well near zero."

TSC describes its role as assisting—not conducting investigations—for "federal, state, and local governments, industry, and academia in a number of areas, foremost among which is 'human factors' research." "Human factors" is a soft science that studies the interactions between people and machines with an eye, for example, to how humans respond when something goes wrong. This is significant because we know from Congressman Hochbrueckner's experience that NHTSA was angling from the beginning to blame drivers; and, in fact, the preface to the 1989 report specifies that "the work was performed by TSC's Operator Performance and Safety Analysis Division." In other words, this project was assigned to people whose expertise included drivers and their driving habits, rather than what can go wrong in an automobile. Hence, if there was evidence to be found that pedal misapplications were behind this phenomenon, these were the dudes who would have found it.

Although NHTSA had promised an "investigation," *there was no actual investigation*. In fact, the 1989 report's title describes it as "An Examination of Sudden Acceleration", accurately indicating that the authors did little more than review existing information relating to the problem.

The 1989 report defines "sudden acceleration incidents" (SAI) as "unintended, unexpected, high powered accelerations from a stationary position or very slow initial speed accompanied by an apparent loss of braking effectiveness." This definition is far from value neutral. Since only people can have "intent", the sly inclusion of the word "unintended" points inconvertibly to the driver. So, too, the term "unexpected", because sudden accelerations by definition are "unexpected" or they would be something else; and since the vehicle does not have either intent or expectation, this term, too, subtly implicates the driver. Unfortunately, without realizing it, people who use such terms help to perpetuate the subliminal message that drivers actually cause this dreadful automotive behavior.

It is the definition's inclusion of the phrase "apparent loss of braking power", however, that is especially tendentious. Before it retained the TSC, NHTSA was faced with thousands of credible reports from people of many backgrounds, including police officers and professional drivers, describing how braking had failed to stop a runaway car. To blame drivers, therefore, this study had to accept the industry's mantra that "the brakes will always win." While that meant turning a blind eye to the evidence, this apparently didn't trouble the TSC any more than the proposition that "absence of proof by inspection proved the absence of a defect."

With that in mind, let's see how these definitional elements worked their way into the 1989 report. A good starting point is a series of "logical assumptions" on which the authors based their conclusions. While the report lists nine "assumptions", four are essentially variations of those that will now be examined.

1. If the cause of a sudden acceleration is an electro-mechanical or mechanical failure, it should produce evidence of failure.

    Although Ford's Updegrove investigation proved conclusively that sudden accelerations often "produce evidence of failure"—illuminated brake lights and evidence of braking on the road surface are two examples—this assumption implicitly narrows the inquiry to evidence detectible by inspecting components in the automobile. This is similar to a physician ignoring signs and symptoms of a patient's illness unless they can be found by a clinical examination of the patient or by a diagnostic test such as an x-ray. As the Updegrove investigation proved, however, this automotive illness must be *diagnosed by matching the observations of the driver and other witnesses with the physical facts and circumstances surrounding the event.*

2. If the cause is an intermittent electronic failure, physical evidence may be very difficult to find, but the failure mode should be reproducible either through in-vehicle or laboratory bench tests.

   Any capable electrical engineer or standard work on electronics could have told NHTSA that if the cause is electromagnetic interference, it is unlikely that the "failure mode would be reproducible either by in-vehicle or laboratory bench tests." Indeed, if the truth were otherwise, carmakers could easily have corrected the problem long ago. Nevertheless, NHTSA still clings to this spurious notion like a drowning man to a life preserver.

3. Sudden acceleration could be the result of a single primary causal factor or could result from the action of a number of factors which contribute to or increase the likelihood of a sudden acceleration.

   Because electronics are highly interactive, complex, technical, and require specialized expertise to understand, let alone test, this assumption is transparently aimed at drivers, who alone qualify as a "single primary causal factor". That conclusion is also consistent with the fact that the report's authors are mostly human factors, not automotive experts.

4. If a sudden acceleration is initiated by a pedal misapplication of which the driver is unaware, loss of control can occur.

   This statement is so insipid it leaves one almost tongue-tied. Driver error technology, as it happens, is remarkably elementary. There is a foot; there is a pedal; and there is evidence left by thousands of virtually identical sudden accelerations. As NHTSA would have it, however, people began committing a particular kind of pedal error concurrently with the advent of automatic transmissions and electronic cruise control. Drivers, of course, do occasionally make pedal errors. But the five star question is whether *they make this particular kind of pedal error*. Unless there is scientific or empirical verification that drivers, however rarely, sometimes accidentally floor the gas pedal and keep it there while their car speeds out of control, the NHTSA/TSC Report is nothing short of a fraud on the taxpayers who funded it.

5. If the sudden acceleration begins with a vehicle-system malfunction, loss of control could occur through braking system failure or the driver's failure to press the brake with sufficient force.

   This is doubly insulting to drivers who reported a sudden acceleration. It insinuates that without evidence of "braking system failure," their reports were not credible; and it gratuitously expands "pedal error" to include not only stepping on the wrong pedal, but not applying sufficient force on the right one—in other words, some drivers don't know enough to push hard on the brake pedal during an emergency stop. In any event, given the sheer number of credible reports of drivers literally standing on the brake pedal without being able to stop the car, only a study "fixed" to blame drivers would resort to such shabby manipulations of the evidence.

CHAPTER 59

# MORE SCIENCE FROM A RABBIT HOLE

> The plaintiffs' complaint alleges that on 3-3-86 a defective electronic engine control system caused a vehicle operated by Mr. Conner to exit a parking lot, cross a street, enter another parking lot, strike a parked vehicle, enter another street, and strike a second vehicle being driven by the plaintiff, Charleen M. Meehan. Allegedly, Mr. Conner died as a result of injuries sustained in the accident and Charleen Meehan received unspecified injuries. Damage to the vehicles involved was not specified.
>
> *Ford's submission to NHTSA*, March 13, 1987

**NHTSA'S 1989 REPORT IS SO PREGNANT WITH INDICATIONS THAT ITS** conclusions were preordained that it would take several chapters to examine them all. What follows, therefore, is a representative sampling, beginning with this demonstrably fallacious proposition:

> If component malfunctions were the primary cause of sudden acceleration incidents, the incidence of problems should be about the same regardless of transmission type, since most of the other powertrain components are common or very similar . . . .

In other words, if there was a safety defect, the rate of component malfunctions and sudden accelerations should be about equal. This, however, was only a thinly disguised variation of the spurious notion that "absence of proof, is proof of absence" that was resoundingly contradicted by overwhelming evidence in NHTSA's files. Nevertheless, it was only a short step from this spurious assumption to the conclusion that drivers were the problem.

As we are about to learn, the 1989 report's most striking feature *is the complete absence of empirical or scientific support for shifting the blame to drivers.* Indeed, if such evidence existed, the authors had every reason to cite it. Consequently, the absence of such evidence in the report shows that the authors were confronted with either acknowledging this lack of empirical or scientific evidence, or inventing reasons for pretending that such support existed. As a result, the 1989 report often reads like a tract of the Flat Earth Society, which would be laughable were it not for the imprimatur of the United States government that carmakers have used to inflict terrible injustices on catastrophically injured people.

My next selection is an example of how this report uses insinuation as a substitute for actual proof:

> The true number of events . . . may be substantially larger than the number of sudden acceleration reports, because many drivers, *who made pedal misapplications* perceive them as such and do not register complaints . . . . When the media . . . suggest . . . unknown mechanical or electronic

causes, the perceptions of *some . . . drivers may . . .* cause them to *conclude that their vehicles must be at fault.* [Italics added.]

This implies that because people occasionally make "pedal misapplications"—a truism—they must also occasionally send a car hurtling out of control by stomping on the gas pedal. However, unless there is proof that people actually do this, insinuating that they do is like asking a witness "when did you stop beating your wife?" This is only one of many examples of how this report plucks support for its conclusions from thin air, which calls to mind the dictum of the late U.S. Senator, Daniel Patrick Moynihan, that "everyone is entitled to his own opinion, but not to his own facts;" everyone, apparently, except organizations hired by a government agency to help protect powerful corporations from their recklessness.

The problem with inventing "facts" is that it usually requires further inventions, like the insinuation here that there was actually proof that "many drivers perceive" what they did and "do not register complaints." If that were true, one would expect the 1989 report to include at least a few case histories recounting how an honest soul admitted having made such a dangerous mistake. But lacking such evidence, these human behaviorists needed something, anything, that might explain why for several years sudden acceleration reports had been relentlessly on the rise. Happily, a favorite whipping boy of powerful interests who know how to shoot the messenger was readily at hand; and, alas, the fanciful notion that "*when the media suggests* unknown mechanical or electronic causes, the perceptions of some drivers may cause them to conclude that their vehicles must be at fault." Thus, with the stroke of an insinuation, roughly 10,000 credible runaway car reports in NHTSA's files were put to naught.

My next selection shows that shooting the messenger wasn't always as easy as blaming the media:

> If the accelerator moves down, *seemingly of its own accord,* in a sudden acceleration, a cruise control problem is a likely explanation. [Emphasis added.]

I have witnessed numerous simulations of a wide-open throttle acceleration in cars with a vacuum-operated servo, and there is nothing "seemingly" about what happens to the accelerator pedal, which is visibly pulled to the floor as the throttle goes open. Furthermore, a cruise control malfunction isn't the "likely explanation," *it is the only possible explanation.* Although hundreds of drivers and passengers have reported observing the gas pedal move to the floor during a sudden acceleration, this comment slyly implies that they only "seemed" to see what they reported. But instead of exploring what could cause this to occur, the 1989 report resorted to yet another insinuation:

> Every cruise control examined was designed so that it could not engage below some specific value, typically 25–30 mph . . . .

If anyone at NHTSA/TSC had bothered to obtain publicly available information about vacuum-operated cruise control servos, they would have discovered—as Sam Sero did several years later when he obtained a copy of Ford's troubleshooting guide—that power was supplied at ignition to the cruise control servo, a design feature that made a sudden acceleration possible whether or not the cruise control was engaged. Furthermore, it was blindingly obvious from thousands of credible reports that sudden accelerations were usually happening *when the cruise control was not engaged.* My next selection demonstrates NHTSA's tragic fall in allowing Ford—and perhaps other carmakers as well—to limit its responses to models with fuel injected engine systems.

> Examination of the sudden acceleration incident database shows that almost none of the incidents have occurred in vehicles with manual transmissions.

This was an understatement. In fact, there was *not a single report* in NHTSA's database of a car with a manual transmission and carbureted engine having sped out of control without driver input, a fact that left unchallenged *the unambiguous historical connection* between sudden acceleration and the advent of electronic cruise control. This connection had always been so obvious that only willful blindness can explain why the DOT and NHTSA allowed this destructive automotive behavior to become a national disaster; and because those who allowed it now found themselves trapped by what had become an automotive epidemic, taxpayers were made to pay for nonsense like my next selection:

> With [manual] transmissions, the driver's feet must be properly aligned with the pedals in order to carry out the relatively complex set of coordinated movements necessary to put the car in motion, thereby greatly reducing the probability of a pedal misapplication.

How about that? Although people who learned to drive cars with manual transmissions had to master a "complex" ballet of pedal applications, automatic transmissions had created a population of drivers who couldn't get their feet properly aligned with the pedals, tell which pedal was which, detect whether their foot was on a low, soft pedal or a high, hard one, and, worst of all, were prone to accidentally pushing the gas pedal to the floor oblivious to why their car was speeding out of control. Already a bad science fiction story about a mysterious force that disconnects people's brains from the operation of their feet, there was more.

Another inconvenient fact confronting NHTSA/TSC was the strikingly disproportionate sudden acceleration rate for certain high-end models, like Ford's Lincoln Town Cars and Thunderbirds/Cougars whose failure rates were many times greater than the same models sold earlier. This striking disparity challenged the creativity of the report's authors who, like Jack of nursery rhyme fame, rose nimbly to the occasion:

> Wealthier, better-educated drivers may have a higher propensity to make their sudden acceleration accidents known to the government and the media, which could lead to a higher complaint rate for expensive cars.

Molly saw this as further proof of "NHTSA's complicity in a cover-up."

Surprised, I asked for an explanation.

"We know that reports involving high-end models like Lincoln Town Cars and Thunderbirds/Cougars shot up dramatically after Ford equipped them with the IVSC."

"Meaning?"

"Meaning that drivers of certain models couldn't possibly have begun making ten times more grotesque pedal errors than drivers of the same earlier models. Rule out that absurd possibility, and the only thing left was a change in the throttle control electronics."

"That makes good sense, Molly, but do you think the TSC spotted this pattern?"

Molly found the question amusing. "This was so obvious, it wouldn't surprise me if the TSC ran to NHTSA and asked what it should do."

"How do you think NHTSA responded?"

"They probably reminded the TSC who was buttering its bread, and that it was being paid to figure out ways around such thorny problems."

My next selection shows that the TSC knew who was buttering its bread:

> Survey research has shown that a consumer who believes a manufacturer has intentionally covered up a product defect is twice as likely to complain as one who does not hold that belief. In other areas, there are *usually obvious malfunctions,* which are more easily verified by investigators, so the changes in consumer perception are less likely to be a problem. [Italics added.]

This implies that because the cause of a sudden acceleration was not "obvious," owners were more likely to believe that the "manufacturer" was intentionally covering up a product defect. This turned the obvious on its head. Because owners were repeatedly being told there was nothing wrong with their cars, *they had good reason to believe* the "manufacturer was intentionally covering up a product defect."

Also, it is only common sense that car owners are more likely to accept what they are told about a verified malfunction, than if they are told there is nothing wrong with the car, particularly following a sudden acceleration. Hence, this is another example of how an insinuation was used to imply that because there was no evidence of an "obvious malfunction," reports pouring in to NHTSA were not trustworthy. As the Mad Hatter in Alice's Wonderland might have put it, "sudden acceleration reports mean what I say they mean."

Speaking of seeing things through a LOOKING-GLASS, consider this gem from the 1989 report:

> When the driver becomes heavily over-loaded with information to process and motor responses to initiate actions, as in an out-of-control situation, it is possible that verification by neurofeedback to the effect that the intended event has really occurred, may become a low-priority activity for the brain. That is, when the brain is too busy, it simply assumes the muscles are performing as desired and ignores or misinterprets the feedback provided by the vehicle's movement. For example, if neuromuscular feedback indicates that a pedal is depressed, the brain assumes it is the intended pedal even when the opposite may be the case. [The more subtle the difference in "feel" between the pedals, the more likely this kind of error.] In other words, the brain occasionally remembers the neuromuscular commands it gave rather than the responses made to those commands. [Brackets original.]

This shows how creative "experts" can be when they are forced to substitute pipedreams for verifiable facts. Later in our story we will meet a character who has been paid good money to help car companies defend sudden acceleration cases by serving up such nonsense to help car companies blame drivers. For the moment, however, some final thoughts about the 1989 report.

Even putting aside its illogical assumptions, fatuous inventions, circular reasoning, and unabashed slant toward predetermined conclusions, the 1989 report is still a sham. With this study, NHTSA/TSC included the Audi 5000 study on the same topic, by a team that included the two named authors of the 1989 report, John Pollard and E. Donald Sussman. Released in September 1988 and entitled the "Study of mechanical and driver-related systems of the Audi 5000 capable of producing uncontrolled sudden acceleration incidents", the study was repeated almost verbatim in the 1989 report, and reached the same conclusion. All NHTSA/TSC had to do, in other words, was repackage the Audi report and plug in the same conclusions. (The Audi report is included *in toto* in the 1989 report as Appendix H.)

The narrowness of references in this report deviates from accepted practice by taking no account of the wealth of material available on such subjects as EMI and intermittent faults in electronic control systems, not to mention the general state of understanding in the late eighties of sudden acceleration. The report barely mentions other credible research into the cause of the phenomenon. For example, in 1988—concurrently with the preparation of the NHTSA/TSC report—a Swedish researcher, Mats Gunnerhed, an expert on the reliability of technical systems with the Swedish Defense Research Establishment, published a report requested by the Swedish Road Safety Office, his country's counterpart to NHTSA. In "A Risk Assessment of Cruise Control", Gunnerhed described how by manipulating just one of the connections on the printed circuit board for the cruise control, he was able to induce a wide-open throttle activation. This made two things crystal clear: it was not necessary for a sudden acceleration that the cruise control be engaged, and a single fault could induce an open throttle acceleration. The latter point, in particular, directly contradicted the industry's claim that multiple and detectable hardwire faults were required before a sudden acceleration was even theoretically possible.

Finally, the TSC was awarded this contract near the end of Diane Steed's tenure as NHTSA Administrator; and since the agency had fruitlessly opened and closed dozens of investigations on her watch, a report implicating the industry's electronics would have embarrassed her and DOT Secretary, Elizabeth Dole. Indeed, it may even have rained on their ambitions to cash in on their government service by serving the interests of the car industry.

This tragically fallacious report has never been disavowed by NHTSA, which has continued to throw good taxpayer money after bad in increasingly pathetic attempts to justify the 1989 report, a subject we will return to later. Making matters worse, the 1989 report has been cited by government agencies around the world as the last word regarding this lethal automotive behavior—a sobering example of the dangers that follow when a government organization with life and death responsibilities is allowed to invent "its own facts."

CHAPTER 60

# THE "MOTHER OF ALL DECEPTIONS"

### BOY, 6, SUCCUMBS TO CRASH INJURIES

Bruce Ferguson, 6, one of three children seriously injured Saturday in a car accident in a supermarket parking lot in the city's Wynnefield Heights section, died yesterday afternoon from head trauma . . . after he and two siblings were struck by an out-of-control 1986 Mercury Marquis . . . . All three children were waiting at a bus stop with their father when they were hit . . . . Police said Holtzin was leaving the Pathmark parking lot about 9 a.m. Saturday when his car suddenly accelerated, raced over a concrete riser, struck a tree, then flew into the air. It landed on the sidewalk, where it hit the children. The

> Mercury went on to collide with a 1988 Toyota before smashing into a fence outside a home on Ford Road . . . .
>
> *Philadelphia Inquirer*, July 19, 1993

**THE 1989 REPORT DEALT A CRUSHING BLOW TO PEOPLE HARMED** by a runaway car. Faced with a report that could not be cross-examined and an industry determined to exploit it, few lawyers would risk the resources these cases required. Worst of all, it gave carmakers a reason not to invest in making throttle control electronics failsafe. Meanwhile, Ford was presented with another chance to lead the industry away from the path of concealment and deception. In the fall of 1988, 30 Ford engineers completed an engineering evaluation that might have mooted the 1989 report. Known as an Ishikawa diagram, the study laid out how EMI from interactions between the engine and cruise control electronics were capable of inducing a sudden acceleration. That was particularly important because, rather than looking for defects in individual components, this approach started with a precise definition of the problem, and then worked backward to identify factors or conditions that might cause or contribute to the unwanted behavior, which the engineers defined as a "sustained, unintended, wide-open throttle torque condition or vehicle acceleration."

This definition underscores why a sudden acceleration is always dangerous: The term "vehicle acceleration," in conjunction with "open throttle . . . torque condition," implicitly recognizes that loss of both throttle and braking control are intrinsic to this vehicular behavior. It was, however, the various factors and conditions the engineers identified as potential causes of this vehicle behavior that might have—dare I say, should have—prevented thousands of runaway car disasters over the ensuing years.

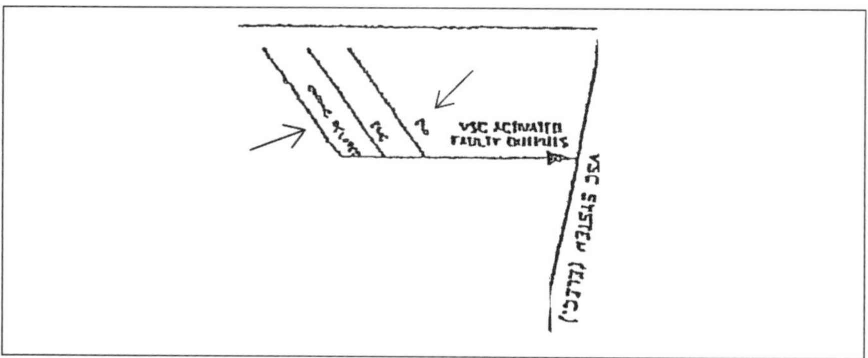


*Figure 60-1*

The Ishikawa diagram was divided into two sections: one identified anything in the engine control electronics that could contribute to the defined behavior, while a separate section identified mechanical, electrical, or driver-related factors that by interacting with engine controls could cause or contribute to the defined automotive behavior. When Jo Ellen came across a copy of the diagram in our repository, she showed it to Molly, who immediately suspected that the entries she indicated with arrows on Figure 60-1 had been doctored to conceal EMI as the cause of Ford's runaway car problems. I was incredulous.

"This isn't a Grisham potboiler, Molly, about criminality in a corporate boardroom; you'll have to convince me beyond a reasonable doubt that Ford would do something that cynical. Start by telling me how you came up with this shocking idea."

Molly stood her ground. "Let's start with the fact that this diagram was completed in the fall of 1988 while a request was pending from NHTSA for anything relevant to the industry-wide study."

"Did Ford give NHTSA a copy?"

"Yes, but it waited until a year after the 1989 report was published, which is one reason I'm convinced this diagram was doctored to conceal something that would have shot down the nonsense about multiple hardwire faults being the only thing that could possibly cause a sudden acceleration."

"Fine, but how do you get from there to entries altered to conceal something as crucial as EMI?"

"What do you make of the words 'vehicle speed control activated faulty outputs' just to the right of my arrows?"

"Why don't you tell me?"

"They obviously refer to signals that controlled the operation of the servo. But take a close look at the three illegible entries between my arrows."

"They're obviously unreadable, but so what?"

"Two of those entries are clearly abbreviations for something the diagram shows could directly trigger a sustained, open throttle malfunction."

Molly could see from my expression that I was struggling to catch on, so she continued with her analysis.

"I wracked my brain to figure out what should logically appear where these abbreviations are, and EMI was the only thing I could come up with."

"Why?"

"Because, according to the layout of the diagram, EMI is the only thing that logically fits where those illegible entries are. The clincher for me is that one of the engineers who worked on this diagram was James Auiler, who, you may recall, began studying interactions between the engine and cruise control electronics in early 1987 as part of Ford's sudden acceleration task force."

It suddenly struck me what Molly was driving at.

"So the layout of this diagram shows that these engineers were specifically focused on interactions between the engine and speed control electronics."

Molly laughed. “I would say you’re a quick study, except that it took Jo Ellen and me about five minutes to figure that out. Anyway, if one of these entries turns out to be EMI, it means that these engineers concluded that interactions between these two electronic systems were causing the vehicle behavior they were studying.”

I was still pondering the implications of what Molly was suggesting when she asked, “Do you remember what happened less than three months before Ford created a task force to study false electronic interactions?”

“Wasn’t that about when the Technical Affairs Committee learned what had caused undiagnosed malfunctions in electronic components under warranty to go through the roof? As I recall, that report was prepared by the company’s Electrical and Electronics Division.”

“That’s exactly right,” Molly replied, “and the important point is that the report specifically *identified EMI as the explanation for a 400% increase in undiagnosed cruise control servo malfunctions*. If I’m right about these illegible entries, this diagram could have blown the entire industry’s cover-up out of the water.”

I was still catching my breath when Molly asked me to take a look at another part of the diagram shown in Figure 60-2. “Can you think of any reason entries relating to the driver are so easy to read, except that Ford wanted the attention on drivers rather than on its electronics?”

“Your point is well taken, but why didn’t Ford just purge the diagram?”

“If one or two engineers had worked on it, that’s probably what they would have done. But they couldn’t risk trying to cover up the work of 30 engineers.”

“OK, but why wait until *after* the 1989 study was published to give a doctored copy to NHTSA?”

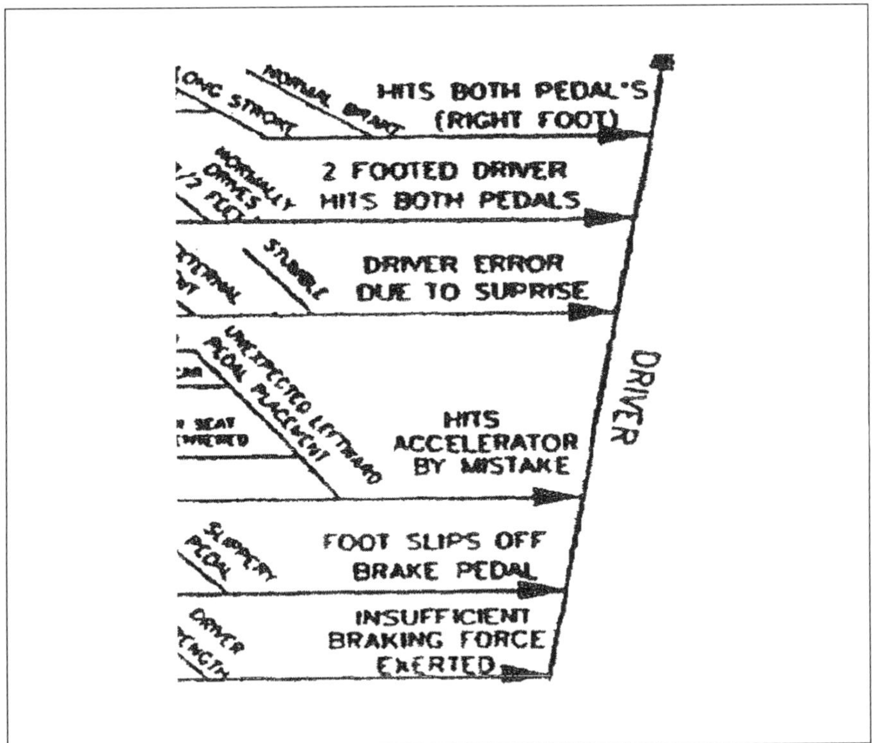


*Figure 60-2*

"My guess is that the big wigs wrestled with that question, and decided that if someone like Clarence Ditlow noticed these illegible entries and demanded that the DOT or NHTSA obtain a readable diagram, there would be no way to escape a recall. They probably figured that because NHTSA had staked its reputation on the 1989 report, it would be easier to slip these illegible entries past the agency after all the commotion surrounding the 1989 report died down."

"Do we know for sure, Molly, that Ford gave the government a copy on which these same entries were illegible?"

"All we know is that this is the copy in our repository."

"But that doesn't prove Ford gave NHTSA an unreadable copy."

Molly's response was pointed. "If I'm right about these entries, and Ford turned over a legible copy, why didn't the whole world learn the truth in 1989?"

My doubts were crumbling under Molly's tenacity. "You win," I sighed. "Do whatever it takes to make Ford cough up a readable copy of this diagram."

CHAPTER 61

# THE "MOTHER OF ALL DECEPTIONS": PART 2

**FORD CITED FOR WITHHOLDING KEY EVIDENCE**

It was far from an isolated incident when a Texas judge fined Ford Motor Co. $44,000 in February for failing to produce internal documents about substandard pickup truck door handles. In recent years, Ford has drawn fines and sanctions from courts in product liability lawsuits across the country. Judges have accused the automaker of withholding key documents and—in a few cases—concealing evidence.

*The Detroit News Auto Insider,* May 26, 2004

**MOLLY BEGAN HER QUEST FOR A READABLE DIAGRAM WITH A** letter politely asking for a legible copy. Ford politely replied that none existed. When she was rebuffed again, she filed a formal discovery request for a legible copy in a case pending in Philadelphia, but Ford said that we had "an exact copy of the analysis in Ford's possession," prompting Molly to remind me that I had doubted Ford would doctor an engineering study submitted to the government. She next asked Ford to identify each engineer who worked on the diagram, but was told there was "no reasonable or practical means" by which to "identify the participants in the development of the program," which made her livid.

"We can't let these paper-pushing prevaricators get away with this."

I couldn't suppress a laugh. "Whence this nifty bit of alliteration?"

"The credit belongs to Ford's OGC. If it was ordered to tell the truth, the shock might wipe out the legal department."

Molly's persistence finally paid off when a judge in Dade County, Florida ordered Ford to produce a legible copy of the Ishikawa diagram shown in Figure 61-1. Voila! There was the

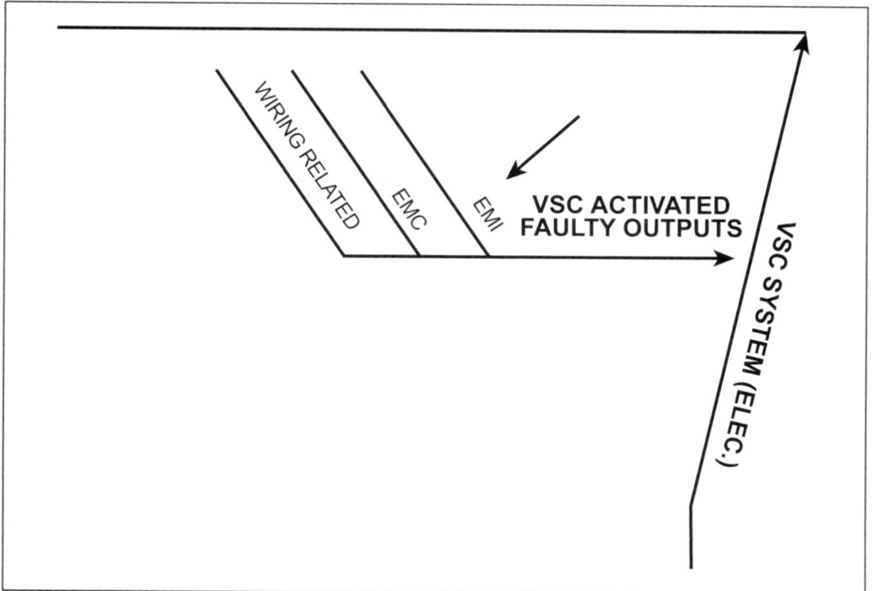


*Figure 61-1*

indisputable proof that 30 engineers had pinpointed EMI as a potential cause of a sustained, wide open throttle acceleration. The companion abbreviation—EMC—refers to electromagnetic compatibility, a term often used interchangeably with EMI; and since the previously illegible third entry identified "wiring-related faults"—conditions that can contribute to EMI—Molly's tenacity had produced a trifecta, the importance of which will become apparent in the pages ahead.

Not long after Ford finally coughed up a readable Ishikawa diagram, Molly gave me a memorandum that summarized testimony she had recently obtained from James Auiler, one of the engineers who developed the diagram:

> We worked with the Al Updegrove database. We had this task force, and in my mind they're linked . . . . [T]he Al Updegrove database was a special study to get premium factual information so that we could do engineering analysis [the Ishikawa diagram] and due diligence and understand what was really going on.

It was clear that this testimony connected the Ishikawa diagram with the Updegrove investigation which was critical because, except for a fraction of the 2,877 occurrences, this massive investigation had eliminated all causes except EMI. When I finished reading her memorandum, Molly asked what I thought might have happened "if Ford had given NHTSA a legible copy of the Ishikawa diagram?"

I said NHTSA "would probably have ignored it, but anyone who understood how science works would have immediately grasped the significance of these entries."

"Explain that," she insisted.

"Think of Isaac Newton famously sitting under a tree in the English countryside waiting to discover gravity when a falling apple bounces off his brainy noggin. Would Sir Isaac have learned anything by looking inside the apple?"

"Whether it had worms."

"I'll ignore that. This diagram illustrates why looking for the cause of an EMI-induced sudden acceleration inside cars was as futile as looking for gravity inside an apple. Can you guess who made that point crystal clear?"

"It certainly wasn't Sir Isaac."

"No, but he would have been the first to see that the Updegrove investigation proved the futility of inspecting and testing components."

I reminded Molly at this point that Ford's field investigators had looked for such things as whether a passenger had observed braking, whether the driver or passenger saw the accelerator pedal move by itself to the floor, whether witnesses outside the automobile observed brake lights, and so on—in other words, the kind of data typically collected to test a theory or hypothesis. I also pointed out that developing a useful hypothesis in these cases was relatively simple because there were only three possibilities—a mechanical defect, an electronic malfunction, or driver error—and the evidence for each possibility would usually be easily distinguishable.

"So Ford's methodology was to collect data and evidence bearing on these three possibilities, and then to deduce in each case what had actually caused that specific event?"

"That's well put; and that's the reason Ford was so spooked by the results that it falsely claimed in *Jarvis* that Updegrove's final report was privileged; it knew that if those results became known, it would only be a matter of time until this mess blew up in its face."

Molly moved to a window in my office overlooking Lake Erie. It was a cloudless day and in the distance we could make out the monument to Commodore Oliver Hazard Perry, who defeated the British in the Battle of Lake Erie during the war of 1812. I waited, sensing she needed to vent frustration that had been building for some time. When she finally spoke, there was weary resignation in her voice. "It's sickening that a trillion-dollar industry would hide the truth to cheat people it harmed of justice."

There was a long pause before Molly continued.

"Damn it, Tom, Ford pulled this trick on NHTSA 20 years ago. If those witless bureaucrats had just demanded a legible copy, think how much suffering could have been prevented. I suppose it isn't surprising that people with a bottom-line mentality who run these companies won't own up to their mistakes. The people who infuriate me are the political appointees who fall all over themselves to feather their nests for future jobs supporting car companies. That doctored Ishikawa diagram was so blatantly suspicious that only servile government functionaries would let Ford get away with something that brazen."

"While you're beating up on NHTSA, Molly, what's your take on whether it should have smelled a rat because Ford waited a whole year after the 1989 report was published to turn over this doctored copy of the diagram?"

"That's a good question, because it ties in nicely with what I consider the 'mother of all Ford's deceptions.'"

Molly was referring to events described in the chapters that follow.

CHAPTER 62

# THE "MOTHER OF ALL DECEPTIONS": PART 3

**FAMILY SAYS VICTIM HAD COMPLAINED OF CAR**

The family of a man who drowned after his Mercury Grand Marquis sped 150 feet across a street, crashed through a fence, and plunged into a river are alleging that the accident was caused by sudden acceleration. They say that the man had purchased the vehicle from a Ford dealership and that he had complained many times of a malfunction in the engine that caused the vehicle to accelerate suddenly. Despite the man's incessant complaints, he was not taken seriously by Ford.

*The Boston Globe*, Tuesday, March 15, 1994

**IN OCTOBER OF 1989, NHTSA NOTIFIED FORD THAT IT HAD "RECEIVED** four reports of alleged throttle malfunctions in Cougar models," and asked for all "studies, surveys, or investigations" bearing on the reports. This was a perilous request because the 1989 Cougars were equipped with the engine and cruise control electronics integrated in the same microprocessor—the so-called IVSC—and had a sudden acceleration rate several times greater than Cougars without this modification. Further complicating matters, Ford had acknowledged in March of 1988 that certain models were equipped with the IVSC, but without identifying them.

As if that wasn't worrisome enough, NHTSA had a new administrator, a retired general named Jerry Curry, and it was anybody's guess whether he would be as friendly to the industry as his predecessor, Diane Steed, had been, particularly since sudden acceleration reports were still piling up at NHTSA. Under these circumstances, it would be too risky to simply ignore the glaring disparity in reports for models with and without the IVSC.

That was the backdrop for what Molly called the "mother of all deceptions," that began with Ford's response to NHTSA's request for "studies, surveys or investigations" regarding "throttle malfunctions in Cougar models." Although the ongoing Updegrove investigation showed there was scant, if any, credible evidence that drivers were causing sudden accelerations, here is how Ford began its response:

> Ford has received and investigated reports alleging SAI-type incidents, both with and without explicit allegations of brake failure, on virtually all vehicles it produces . . . . Ford's investigations, like those of NHTSA and others, encompass numerous components, systems, complex interrelationships, and human factors. The typical scope of such analysis is manifested by the diverse studies documented within the Transportation Systems Center report.

While this never mentioned the Updegrove investigation, the suggestion that "the typical scope" of Ford's investigations was similar to "the diverse studies documented" in the 1989 report was like comparing a trip to the moon with pole vaulting. But NHTSA was simply being reeled in for the catch:

> Similar efforts continue at Ford, as exemplified by a schematic diagram [the Ishikawa diagram], . . . which was formulated by Ford engineering personnel to structure sudden acceleration incident-type analysis. *Ford's investigation of these SAI-type incidents leads to the same conclusion as the TSC report; i.e., pedal misapplication is the most plausible cause.* [Italics added.]

Had it given NHTSA a legible Ishikawa diagram, Ford could have made this claim, a deception it compounded by claiming that investigations based on the Ishikawa diagram confirmed that driver error was the "most plausible cause." It isn't just that the very opposite was true that makes this so breathtakingly brazen. It is also the spectacle of a government agency swallowing this response while overwhelming evidence to the contrary was staring it in the face. If NHTSA was actually deceived by this tactic—rather than deliberately turning a blind eye to the obvious—it is because it had proven itself to be "the mother of all country bumpkins" inside Washington, D.C.'s beltway.

The calculated nature of Ford's deceitfulness is captured in a memorandum prepared shortly after it made these assertions. Prepared in 1990 by someone familiar with the Updegrove results, it contained the following recommendation:

> Advise dealers, based on [the Updegrove investigation], that owners of pre-1990 vehicles alleging unintended acceleration events are usually traceable to a vehicle

> concern. Their efforts should be to find these incidents and make necessary repairs.

Updegrove initially said he authored the memorandum, but later changed his mind, although he acknowledged it was prepared by someone thoroughly familiar with the results of the investigation. Regardless, this recommendation was a morally courageous attempt to prevent the kind of catastrophes that were befalling people after a dealer, as happened to the Manigaults, returned an unrepaired car following a sudden acceleration. It will come as no surprise that Ford rejected the recommendation.

All this begs the obvious question how NHTSA could possibly have failed to notice that a crucial part of the Ishikawa diagram had been doctored, particularly since Molly recognized almost immediately that the illegible entries were where EMI logically belonged. There would seem to be only two possibilities: either NHTSA is so invincibly incompetent that its suspicions were not aroused, or it recognized the deception but understood that pursuing a legible diagram might expose the 1989 report for what it is. In any event, if there is a line that separates dim-witted incompetence from corrupt complicity, we will see in Part Four how NHTSA continues to operate on both sides of the line.

Let us turn now to the man who was at NHTSA's helm when Ford succeeded in passing a doctored Ishikawa diagram under the agency's nose.

CHAPTER 63

# THE MAN WHO WOULD BE PRESIDENT

### SEN. BOXER INTRODUCES BILL TO CLOSE A 'REVOLVING DOOR' BETWEEN CARMAKERS AND NHTSA

Sen. Barbara Boxer (D-Calif.) introduced legislation Wednesday to close the "revolving door" between government service and automobile companies, which she said allows the automakers to have "undue influence" on actions by the agency that regulates them.

Boxer's bill would require that National Highway Traffic Safety Administration employees who leave the agency wait three years before they can work for automakers in any capacity that requires written or oral communication with NHTSA.

*Washington Post,* April 29, 2010

**NHTSA'S ADMINISTRATOR WHEN FORD TURNED OVER A DOCTORED** Ishikawa diagram was retired General, Jerry Curry, who I deposed in 2002. Before I began this chapter, I asked Molly to look into what the General had been up to in the meantime. Looking like the cat that swallowed the canary, she announced her findings a few days later.

"Guess what General Curry did fifteen years after leaving NHTSA?"

"Take up skydiving?"

"Very funny; in fact, he took a shot at the presidency."

"The presidency of what, the Association of Retired Generals?" It was a wisecrack to let me catch my breath, and Molly ignored it.

"Read this," she insisted, handing me a press release dated December 17, 2007 with the bold caption:

"General Jerry Ralph Curry, New Presidential Candidate."

Flabbergasted, I asked her to sit down while I read the press release to be sure it wasn't a practical joke. The first sentence only increased my amazement:

> General Curry is a breath of fresh air and a proven leader—a much better choice than all the political types out there—Michael Huckabee, Rudy Giuliani, Mitt Romney, and John McCain on the Republican side, and Hillary Clinton, Barack Obama, Dennis Kucinich, and various others on the Democratic side.

A breath of fresh air in presidential politics seemed like a good idea, so I read on:

> *The news from Baghdad is good*, in the sense that 27 million people who lived under Saddam Hussein's tyranny for many decades, most of their lives, are now free and have

> self-determination and economic opportunity they never knew under the prior tyranny. [Italics added.]

Because Sunnis and Shiites were busy blowing up each other and Americans at the time, I welcomed "good news from Baghdad." But, alas, the "good news" was about the General's qualifications to put things right in that war-torn, fratricidal country:

> General Jerry Curry, *better than all other political wannabes out there, understands the world dynamics that face our country* and the leadership responsibilities needed to protect our liberty and advance economic productivity all our people and country want and need. This is not a time to select a leader *without a chest.* [Italics added.]

Was this, perchance, the reason NHTSA had failed to notice a doctored diagram that might have ended this calamitous automotive fiasco? Had the General been so preoccupied with "world dynamics" that he had missed the diagram's glaringly suspicious appearance? And who were these anatomical wonders without a chest? John McCain? Rudy Giuliani? Mitt Romney? Michael Huckabee? Barack Obama? Dennis Kucinich? Obama and Kucinich I could understand, but the others were barrel-chested guys who, sans pin-striped suits, could pass for bouncers at a local pub. Happily, the General cleared things up:

> *Men or women without chests* in political office are a scourge, as we found with former British Prime Minister Neville Chamberlain, who blinked at Adolph Hitler and almost lost a country and empire because of pure pacifist naïveté and political cowardice. No leadership until Winston Churchill came along and bailed everyone out. *Curry, like Churchill, is a man with a chest* . . . . [Italics added.]

Curry, "like Churchill, a man with a chest"? Suddenly I was eight years old again watching newsreels of the war time British Prime Minister—all 300 pounds of him, shuffling along behind a big cigar—and being quite unable to tell where the great man's chest ended and his stomach began. Older readers who watched the same newsreels will understand this. As for younger readers, I can only say there is no way to make up stuff like this. Anyway, I couldn't write this chapter without at least trying to learn why this aspiring leader of the free world was so proud of his chest, so I asked Jo Ellen to find a picture of him, but she struck out. This left me no choice; I had to read the deposition:

> **Q:** So you began your present consulting business shortly after leaving the [George H. W.] Bush administration [in 1992]?
>
> **A:** About a year and a half later.
>
> **Q:** Have you been continuously doing the same kind of consulting work since you began in 1994?
>
> **A:** Yes . . . .
>
> **Q:** What percentage of your work today is for automotive manufacturers?
>
> **A:** About 90%.
>
> **Q:** That would include all of the U.S. automakers?
>
> **A:** From time to time.
>
> **Q:** Does it include foreign automakers?
>
> **A:** Yes. I have recently been doing work for Hyundai and Mazda.
>
> **Q:** What is your hourly charge for your work?
>
> **A:** $370 an hour.

***

Curry's hourly rate in today's dollars being about $500 raises the question why a car company would cough up such a princely sum to a former NHTSA administrator? Here was Curry's answer:

**Q:** And you've been called upon as a consultant for automotive companies, including Ford Motor Company, in cases involving sudden acceleration since you ended your tour of duty with NHTSA, have you not?

**A:** Since 1994.

**Q:** And in those cases, I take it you were asked to do basically the same thing you're doing here: to discuss NHTSA, its function, its organization, and this 1989 study that we'll be talking about . . . .

**A:** Yes.

***

This last response led me to believe that Curry must have discussed the 1989 report with his predecessor, Diane Steed. I was wrong.

**Q:** In serving as a consultant for automotive companies in sudden acceleration cases, have you ever met with or talked with Ms. Diane Steed about the 1989 report?

**A:** I don't think I have ever discussed that report with her.

I naturally assumed that an agency confronted with one of history's most dangerous automotive problems would have investigated when this phenomenon began. But, again, I was wrong:

**Q:** Do you know whether the agency ever inquired as to when Ford introduced electronic cruise control in any make or model for the first time?

**A:** That's a strange question. The agency doesn't usually inquire into that sort of thing . . . .

***

When this dangerous automotive behavior began, "a strange question"? That was like suggesting there was something strange about an epidemiologist being interested in when the signs of a dangerous disease first surfaced. This response also showed that Curry was apparently not aware of the unambiguous historical link between sudden acceleration and the advent of electronic cruise control. My surprise increased when the General pleaded ignorance regarding NHTSA's 1989 report, and then admitted having taken the time to read NHTSA's denial of a petition by an Arkansas lawyer named Sandy McMath asking the agency to reopen its earlier investigation. Because McMath, who we will meet later, had cited the Updegrove investigation as a compelling reason for revisiting the 1989 study, this seemed like promising grist for cross-examination:

**Q:** I'd like to know what you've done to learn the specifics of the Updegrove investigation.

**A:** The answer is that I really haven't done anything as concerns the Updegrove investigation until the name came up in the NHTSA Office of Defects Investigation's response to Mr. Sandy McMath.

**Q:** Now, at that point, what did you do?

**A:** I read the NHTSA response to the defect.

**Q:** So you read some references to Mr. Updegrove in that response; is that correct?

**A:** That's right.

**Q:** Have you done anything else?

**A:** I have not.

**Q:** I assume that you intend to testify in this case in a way that is helpful to the Court and jury in learning about any studies that have been done of sudden acceleration; isn't that a truism?

**A:** No. It's not. I don't intend to attempt to educate the Court on all the studies on sudden acceleration.

***

Although these responses already made Curry a sitting duck for cross-examination at trial, I sensed there was more:

**Q:** While you visited NHTSA, did you ask anybody if they would show you exactly what they considered from the Updegrove investigation when they prepared [the McMath denial]? In other words, what did they get from Ford regarding the results of the Updegrove investigation?

**A:** I do not know. I did not ask the question, if that's your question.

**Q:** Yes, that's my question. Do you know whether or not the agency obtained from Ford any of the specific findings made during the Updegrove investigation?

**A:** I'm sure they did. If they had not . . . they would not have it in their report.

**Q:** What did they receive?

**A:** I can't give you the page numbers and the titles of each page. I know how NHTSA operates. I know what the requirements are. I know how they do their business. I know when it comes to something like these studies, they have a vacuum cleaner . . . .

**Q:** Do you intend before giving testimony in this case . . . to find out what NHTSA obtained from Ford regarding the Updegrove study prior to publishing the McMath denial?

**A:** I do not.

***

Curry's lack of curiosity about the Updegrove investigation and NHTSA's 1989 report meant he was damned if he knew the results, and damned if he didn't. It was no surprise, therefore, that Curry was never called as a witness.

Molly had also located a PBS *Frontline* interview with Curry in October, 2001. Keeping in mind, that she had forced Ford to disgorge a legible copy of its Ishikawa diagram, the reader should find Curry's view of trial lawyers interesting:

> **Moderator:** What is the role of the safety advocates and plaintiffs' attorneys? Have they become in some way *de facto* regulators in our system?
>
> **Curry:** Plaintiff lawyers and the safety advocates attempt to become the *de facto* regulators. If they had their way, they would in fact be regulators. And they would regulate it in a way that they can litigate it in court and make an awful lot of money out of it. That's what drives them—*the greed, the money* that's involved in the process . . . .
>
> So I think if you were to ask me: what should the role be of plaintiffs' lawyers? The answer is they *should not have a role.* They *do not have a role* in safety. They have a role in the legal system. They have a role in trying to redress grievances. They have a role there. But in terms of the safety system, they don't have a role, and they should not be playing a role. [Emphasis added.]

***

Curry's barbs about trial lawyers came straight from the playbook of big business tort reformers, but his interviewer wasn't buying:

> **Moderator:** Even NHTSA has said that they often rely on plaintiffs' lawyers and safety advocates, that those people should bring them notice of a problem when they see it . . . . But is that the way it should work?
>
> **Curry:** It should not work that way. Lawyers cannot be

> trusted to bring safety problems to NHTSA. And the reason is they're trying to make money, and they want to hide these safety problems so they can spring them in court in the litigation process. So these folks aren't interested in saving lives; these folks are interested in making money through winning court cases. And they will tell NHTSA as little or as much as they want them to know. And you can be sure they will safe-side the information and not give them what they need to know.
>
> I've seen many cases where lawyers have sat on what they claimed—some great safety problem. And they never told NHTSA about it at all, because they didn't want NHTSA to do anything about it. [Emphasis added.]

***

Curry's vitriolic outburst is an example of how tort reformers use sweeping generalities to sow seeds of doubt about the one institution they fear the most: trial by jury. Despite tort reform propaganda that amounts to a crude form of jury tampering, trial by jury remains an indispensable bastion against attempts by big business to corrupt our legal system. With Curry's dark view of trial lawyers in mind, let us examine what happened when one trial lawyer valiantly tried to convince NHTSA to re-examine the conclusions in its 1989 report.

CHAPTER 64

# THE McMATH PETITION

### DRIVER MAY FACE CHARGES AFTER MAN DIES. POLICE WILL TURN CASE OVER TO STATE'S ATTORNEY'S OFFICE

Elgin police today will ask the Kane County State's Attorney's Office if it wants to file criminal charges against the driver of a car that ran down an 83-year-old man late last month as he walked in Sherman Hospital's parking lot. Gerald E. Tripp, 83, of East Dundee died Sunday at the hospital as a result of the multiple injuries and trauma he suffered in the Aug. 30 crash. According to police report, Tripp was walking in the parking lot outside Sherman Hospital around 7:30 a.m. when a Ford Taurus, which was driving slowly near the hospital's entrance, suddenly accelerated and crashed into him. He was thrown into the air, landing on a sidewalk about 15 feet away. Tripp suffered multiple bone fractures, head trauma and internal injuries. Ultimately, Tripp died as a result of kidney failure

> and pneumonia, both of which were complications of the injuries he suffered in the crash.
>
> *Chicago Daily Herald,* September 21, 2000

**SANDY McMATH IS THE SON OF FORMER ARKANSAS GOVERNOR,** the late Sidney McMath, one of the few politicians who stood up to the race-baiting Orval Faubus, the Arkansas governor who forced President Eisenhower to send paratroopers to Little Rock to enforce the Supreme Court's decision in *Brown v. Board of Education.* Sandy is his father's son, a lawyer willing to take on tough cases despite financial risk to himself. *Chapman v. Ford* was such a case.

In the early evening of June 7, 1995, a Lincoln Town Car operated by Marlene Fett suddenly accelerated out of control in the parking lot of a Walmart store in Mountain Home, Arkansas. As Fett struggled to regain control, her granddaughter watched helplessly as she pushed on the brake pedal to no avail. As the car hurtled toward the store's main entrance, Fett desperately steered away from the building, but was unable to negotiate the turn. The car ran down two children in a play area before the horrified eyes of their parents. Eight-month-old Nathaniel Chapman was crushed to death. The right leg of his two-year-old brother, Jonathan, was severed. Witnesses described how the car, for no apparent reason, had suddenly sped out of control toward the storefront before veering toward the play area.

The Chapmans retained Mountain Home lawyer, Rick Spencer, who asked Sandy McMath to join the case. When he immersed himself in the history of runaway automobiles, McMath was shocked to discover that *hundreds of children had been run down by cars suddenly gone wildly out of control,* and he was outraged that Ford had routinely used NHTSA's 1989 report to blame innocent people like Mrs. Fett. When he saw the *Dateline* story about the *Manigault* case, McMath asked if he could review our files; and, not long after his visit to Sandusky, he called to say he was about to petition NHTSA to reopen its industry-wide investigation. I was skeptical. "Do you really think this industry-friendly agency will reopen something that's been closed for ten years?"

"I don't know," replied Sandy. "But the thought of Ford waving the 1989 NHTSA report in front of a jury turns my stomach. I won't be able to live with myself if I don't try to prevent that."

McMath's petition on July 19, 1999, described the *Chapman* case and spelled out how NHTSA's 1989 report overlooked crucial evidence showing that electronic failures, not drivers, were the problem. After describing Sero's discovery that "voltage is supplied to the cruise control servo at ignition," the petition described how Ford concealed that the cruise control servo was powered at ignition.

> [I]n no uncertain terms, Ford expressly represented to the government that cruise control malfunctions capable of opening the throttle without driver input simply do not occur in stationary vehicles because the cruise control system must first be activated, and since the cruise control system cannot be activated below 26 mph, no such malfunction is possible. A close review of the 1989 report reveals that NHTSA accepted this representation as accurate. Witness, for example, the following passage from the report's Technical Discussion and Conclusion:
>
>> The Panel considered the conditions under which a cruise control could malfunction. For most of the tested vehicles, *the cruise control cannot function unless it receives electrical power through the cruise control master switch* and through the gear selector

> inter-lock . . . . [I]f these conditions are not present . . . cruise-control failure is not a plausible explanation for an SAI. [Emphasis original.]

McMath concluded with a succinct recapitulation of the reasons for a new investigation:

> In summary, petitioner offers the following reasons this agency should institute a new investigation into the cause or causes of sudden acceleration: (1) to date, NHTSA has neglected to consider the mechanisms that can cause sudden acceleration by bypassing the control logic of the cruise control system and thus can induce sudden acceleration in a stationary vehicle; (2) NHTSA has apparently failed to consider the data collected by Ford Motor Company in its investigation of 2,800 incidents of sudden acceleration during 1989-1992; and (3) NHTSA has not addressed the fact that there is no true failsafe mechanism to overcome sudden acceleration.

This petition presented NHTSA with a stark choice: re-examine the 1989 report or invent reasons for rejecting it, a choice we will come to presently.

When I called Sandy several months later to learn if there was any news from Washington, he told me "All I know is, they sent some guy named Robert Young to inspect the Lincoln Town Car and to interview the current owner, who lives in Salem, Arkansas, a small town near the Chapmans."

"Did he talk to the Chapmans, Mrs. Fett, or her granddaughter?" I asked.

"Not yet, at least."

"What about Sam Sero?"

"Sam says nobody has contacted him."

"Has anybody from NHTSA contacted you?"

"Nope," said Sandy. "You warned me not to expect much, but I thought they would at least talk to me."

"What the hell is going on, Sandy!" I exclaimed. "I assumed Marlene Fett, Sam Sero, and you would be the first people they'd talk to."

"I agree it doesn't have a good feel to it," Sandy replied, sounding disconsolate.

"What do you know about this Dr. Riccardo Martinez, Clinton's man who is now running NHTSA?" I asked.

"I found an article in *Automotive News* where he dumped on safety advocates like Ralph Nader, Joan Claybrook, and Clarence Ditlow because they believe that the best way to reduce traffic deaths and injuries is to regulate cars."

"What kind of nonsense is that? Joan Claybrook has made it absolutely clear that regulating car safety is just one of the functions Congress gave NHTSA."

"You're preaching to the choir, Tom."

"I thought your former governor, Bill Clinton, had enough concern for ordinary people not to appoint hacks who kiss up to big business."

"Good luck. Clinton sold the idea to Democrats who voted for Ronald Reagan that he could be as friendly to big business as the Republicans. In my opinion, he would welcome a business party with two branches. The only difference is that Democrats, as we like to say around here, are more 'down home' than Republicans."

"Maybe you should have thought of that before you filed your petition," I said, half jokingly.

"I hope you're wrong, Tom, but my gut tells me you're right."

It is not known whether Clinton's administrator, Riccardo Martinez, ever saw Sandy McMath's petition. Regardless, as head of the agency, he bore direct responsibility for the denial in April

2000 that was hardly less unscientific and flagrantly dishonest than the 1989 NHTSA/TSC report.

CHAPTER 65

# THE McMATH DENIAL

> The plaintiff, Judith C. Ware, alleges that on 6-21-86 her parents, Mr. and Mrs. W. Arnold Chambers, started their new 1986 Mercury Grand Marquis and when placed in forward gear, " . . . the car accelerated" down their driveway and their street, leaving the roadway and crashing into a neighbor's brick home. The car and home were severely damaged. Reportedly, Mr. Chambers died shortly after the crash, and Mrs. Chambers died four days following the accident. Damage to the vehicle and the house were not specified.
>
> *Ford's submission to NHTSA,* March 13, 1987

**TEN YEARS PRIOR TO THE McMATH PETITION, FORD HAD PLAYED** NHTSA for the fool with a doctored diagram and outlandishly false claims regarding the results of the Updegrove investigation. But thanks to Sandy McMath's persistence, the agency had obtained a copy of Updegrove's final report with the attached electronic summaries indicating the *causal category assigned to each case.* These were included with a letter from J. P. King, the manager of the office that had employed Updegrove until his retirement in the mid-90s. Although the electronic summaries showed that only a miniscule number of cases were classified as a "pedal misapplication," here is how King described the results of Ford's massive investigation:

> Sixty percent of the incidents reviewed by Updegrove involved sudden acceleration as previously defined in Section 2.1. The team focused on determining whether the alleged unintended engine power increase could be verified by physical evidence. In December 1992, the project was discontinued *without identifying a root cause,* although there were indications that drivers were mistakenly *pressing the gas pedal* instead of the brake pedal, e.g., "pedal misapplication." [Emphasis added.]

It's hard to imagine stronger proof than this that Ford saw NHTSA as a harmless nuisance. Since Updegrove's final report clearly stated that each case had been given a causal category that was included in the electronic summaries, it would have taken the agency about 15 minutes to learn that only a tiny fraction of 2,877 occurrences had been classified as a "pedal misapplication." That assumes, of course, that NHTSA was interested in the truth. King's letter shows, however, that Ford was sure NHTSA wouldn't do anything that might expose its 1989 report as a sellout to the industry. In fact, Ford had good reason to be confident. From the McMath denial:

> Mr. Sero's theory is based on his observation that "voltage is supplied to the servo the moment the ignition is turned on" and "under this condition, all that is necessary to induce a

> wide open throttle is a completion of a circuit to the servo." However, a failure consistent with the petitioner's multiple servo solenoid ground fault theory could not have contributed to the June 7, 1995, sudden acceleration incident in Mountain Home, Arkansas, because the 1988 Town Car was equipped with an *"integrated" cruise control system.*
>
> In some cases, certain identical models were initially equipped with stand-alone cruise controls; then were built with integrated systems; then returned to the stand-alone system; and finally were built without vacuum service at all. These changes provide an excellent opportunity to assess Mr. Sero's theory. *If the rate of sudden accelerations for vehicles equipped with the stand-alone system was significantly greater than those without it, it would support the theory.* [Emphasis added.]

The mind boggles at such statements on behalf of the federal government. Ford's electronic summaries showed that models with the engine and cruise control electronics integrated on the same microprocessor—the IVSC—had a sudden acceleration rate several times greater than models without it. With the electronic summaries staring it in the face, NHTSA needed only count the sudden acceleration rate for models with and without the IVSC to discover a crucial modification in the electronics that sent sudden acceleration skyrocketing. Moreover, Figure 65-1—taken from the McMath denial—removes any doubt that NHTSA knew exactly which models were equipped with the IVSC and which had the stand-alone system. Therefore, it only needed to count to learn that there were *just ten reports* involving the 1985-1987 Lincolns with the stand-alone cruise control, compared to *126 reports for the 1988-1990 Town Cars with the IVSC;* and that Thunderbirds/Cougars with the integrated electronics had a

| 1985 | 1986 | 1987 | 1988 | 1989 | 1990 | 1991 | 1992 | 1993 | 1994 | 1995 | 1996 |
|---|---|---|---|---|---|---|---|---|---|---|---|
| VacSA | VacSA | VacSA | VacEC | VacEC | VacEC | VacSA | NGSC | NGSC | NGSC | NGSC | NGSC |

VacSA = Vacuum system with stand alone amplifier
VacEC = Vacuum system with amplifier function in EEC
NGSC = Electronic speed control - no vacuum

*Figure 65-1*

sudden acceleration rate 15 times greater than the same models with the stand-alone system.

Because Sandy McMath had given NHTSA compelling reasons for a new investigation, we must ask ourselves whether its denial was just an honest mistake, or something more sinister to cover the agency's tracks? Let's consider that question in light of references to Mr. Sero's work like the following in the denial:

> If Sero's theory were valid, the sudden acceleration incident rate for Town Cars built with the integrated system should be significantly *lower* than for those with a "stand-alone" system. This is because there is insufficient power to activate the servo's solenoids in this system even if ground faults occur while the vehicle is stationary. However, the rate is about the same for both the stand-alone and integrated systems .... [T]he relatively constant sudden acceleration incident rate when comparing both Ford cruise control systems is a strong indicator that cruise control ground circuit faults are not contributing to sudden acceleration incidents. [Emphasis original.]

NHTSA either couldn't count, or it had no qualms about falsifying things rather than admit Sero was right. The statement that the incident rate was "about the same for both stand alone and integrated systems . . . " is incomprehensible in view of the electronic summaries. But having thus manipulated the facts,

NHTSA concluded that "the relatively constant sudden acceleration incident rate when comparing both Ford cruise control systems is a strong indicator that cruise control ground circuit faults are not contributing to sudden acceleration incidents"—proof of what bureaucrats can accomplish by inventing their own facts.

Hardly less damning to NHTSA is its version of the *Daubert* hearing before Naomi Buchwald in the *Jarvis* case:

> During the hearing . . . Sero was questioned by Judge Naomi Reice Buchwald:
>
> **Q:** I'm just asking whether it's possible, if you had a mindset to learn this information, to find physical evidence of the conditions that you are talking about.
>
> **Mr. Sero:** The only thing I can tell you, your Honor, is that you may. In reality, you probably won't. You'll find loose grounds, they're easy to find. But the other conditions, I doubt that you will ever find them. Will they exist? They may, . . . but, if they're happening from contamination or moisture or gas, they would go away.
>
> To date, no one known to NHTSA, including the petitioner and Mr. Sero, has found any credible evidence that sudden acceleration incidents are occurring as a result of simultaneous, undetectable, electrical and mechanical failures in any vehicle (including Fords).

First, Sero made it crystal clear during the *Daubert* hearings in *Jarvis* that EMI, rather than hardwire faults, was the likely cause of most sudden accelerations; and, second, McMath's petition was unequivocal that Sero's opinions were not based on the occurrence of "simultaneous, undetectable, electrical and mechanical failures."

Perhaps the best evidence of NHTSA's deviousness is this from the McMath denial:

> Thus, the petitioner [McMath] and his consultant [Sero] take the position that drivers are not responsible for the safe operation of their vehicle. This concept is contrary to the motor vehicle laws in each of the fifty states which hold the driver ultimately responsible for safe vehicle operation.

In fact, neither McMath nor Sero has ever suggested that *drivers are not responsible for the safe operation of their cars,* which makes this statement particularly invidious. On the other hand, deliberately concealing a potentially fatal automotive defect is not only contrary to the law of every state, it is the kind of corporate misconduct that many states punish with punitive damages.

In the final analysis, the McMath denial is so slipshod and dishonest that it raises again how a government agency could exhibit such callous indifference to human life and safety. Was there, perhaps, something in the temper of the times that fostered this attitude? The final chapter of Part Three may help to answer that question.

CHAPTER 66

# NHTSA AND TORT REFORM

### 'NO FAULT' IN CRUISE-CONTROL TERROR CAR

A police investigation into Melbourne's runaway cruise-control vehicle has failed to find a fault to explain the terror ride but driver Chase Weir says he "couldn't care less" what conclusions people draw from the results . . . "On that day, the car was in its own world." In a near-hysterical emergency call, Mr. Weir told how his cruise control had become locked at 100km/h as he drove on the EastLink tollway. Slamming on the brakes only slowed it to 80km/h. The gears were locked in drive and the ignition key wouldn't turn either, he said. "Oh my God. Oh my God, I'm gonna die!" he screamed over the phone as he swerved into on-coming traffic.

*The Age*, January 7, 2010

**IT IS NO ACCIDENT THAT THE SO-CALLED TORT REFORM MOVEMENT** began early in the first term of Ronald Reagan, a dedicated deregulator, who liked to say that "government is the problem, not the solution." It will be recalled that during Reagan's second term, in what Congressman Hochbrueckner called a "shocking departure from customary practice," NHTSA had allowed Volkswagen of America to decide for itself what the government would be allowed to see regarding hundreds of runaway car reports involving the Audi 5000. We've also seen how Reagan's DOT secretary, Elizabeth Dole, and his NHTSA administrator, Diane Steed, simply ignored Hochbrueckner's pleas on behalf of people harmed by a runaway Audi 5000.

Although "tort reform" is an oxymoron—once committed, a tort cannot be reformed—the people behind this movement are only interested in using measures like caps on economic and punitive damages to limit what injured people can recover because of corporate negligence. In that regard, car companies benefit from both deregulation as practiced by the DOT/NHTSA, and from tort reform laws limiting people's damages.

During the 1992 Presidential race, Vice President Dan Quayle made tort reform a national issue by claiming that jury verdicts, lawyers' fees, rising insurances rates, and the cost of defending lawsuits were costing 300 billion dollars per year, an argument he padded with the contention that, as the only major country that allows juries to determine liability and set damages in civil cases, this country is at a disadvantage internationally.

But tort reformers are good at manipulating the facts. Legal scholars responded to Quayle by pointing out that the actual cost of litigation was less than half what the Vice President claimed, and that when plaintiffs do win damage awards, they are usually much lower than tort reform proponents claimed. For example, between 1981 and 1985, the midpoint of all verdicts in Chicago, including those against corporations was just $19,382. A similar study of 27 state courts set the figure at under $30,000.

Because Quayle and other tort reformers were too savvy to attack the people on juries who made these awards, they needed a scapegoat which they discovered in the form of "greedy trial lawyers" bent on winning a pot of gold at the end of the litigation rainbow, a theme that was picked up by authors of books with catchy titles like "The Litigation Society," "The Lawsuit Lottery," and "The Case Against Lawyers." Here is just one example of how these authors portrayed the work of lawyers, like the author, who dare to sue a car company simply because it destroyed someone's life by secretly subjecting him/her to a game of automobile roulette:

> We are permitting the plaintiffs to determine state and national policy. Its motives are no purer than those of corporate special interest groups, and its tactics are the same. These legal groups contribute millions of dollars to those officials who can assist in their schemes, and billions are returned back to them as contingency fees.

These attacks against trial lawyers call to mind the comments to *PBS Frontline* in October, 2001 by the first President Bush's NHTSA Administrator, Jerry Curry. (See Chapter Sixty-Three.) We've seen that Curry is among those who took advantage of their time at NHTSA to later serve the car industry in one capacity or another; and it was on Curry's watch, of course, that Ford gave NHTSA an engineering analysis doctored to conceal what might have ended this deadly automotive fiasco two decades ago. What grates on tort reformers like Curry, however, is that trial lawyers are often the last line of defense ordinary citizens have against the power of big business to trample on their rights by manipulating legislation and the legal system. Just how far tort reformers are willing to go is illustrated by the campaign they mounted after a jury in New Mexico awarded more than two million dollars in punitive damages against McDonald's to a woman who spilled hot coffee on her lap.

Although "frivolous lawsuits" were already a rallying cry for tort reformers, the verdict in New Mexico was like raw meat to a pride of hungry lions. The Great Coffee Spill soon became the banner for expressions like "jackpot justice" and "litigation lottery," insinuating that trial lawyers were lining their pockets by gaming the legal system with frivolous lawsuits. The drum beat of propaganda generated by the spilled coffee case was so effective, in fact, that trial lawyers around the country soon discovered that virtually every prospective juror had heard about it; and that many believed or at least suspected that awarding a large sum of money to a clumsy woman for spilling coffee on herself showed that the legal system was awash in silly lawsuits. That, of course, begged whether the spilled coffee case was actually "frivolous."

In 2011, *HBO* aired a documentary entitled "Hot Coffee" that finally burned the tort reformers. It revealed that the burn victim was a passenger, not the driver; there was no coffee holder in the car; the coffee was heated to 180 degrees, enough to cause extensive third degree burns that required several skin grafts; and that several hundred other people had reported to McDonalds being burned by scalding hot coffee.

And that multi-million dollar punitive damage award? Jurors interviewed by *HBO* said the damages were equal to two days of coffee sales by the company. Nevertheless, the punitive award was eventually reduced to less than $500,000, about equal to coffee sales by 10 a.m. on a typical day.

The Great Coffee Spill became a political football during the George W. Bush Administration when, according to *HBO*, tort reform strategy was often orchestrated from the White House by the President's political advisor, Karl Rove. The "hot coffee" debacle, therefore, was part of a well-financed, highly sophisticated effort by big business interests to save money at the expense of people harmed by corporate disregard for their safety. But as we will learn in the final section of our story, even rich and powerful corporations cannot cover up their deadly mistakes forever.

PART 4

# TOYOTA AND THE UNRAVELING OF A COVER-UP

# INTRODUCTION

**WE'VE SEEN HOW NHTSA BRUSHED ASIDE SANDY McMATH'S** attempt to convince the agency its 1989 report was tragically wrong. But that was late in the Clinton administration when cars were about to undergo a fundamental change in design as dramatic as the shift two decades earlier from carbureted to electronically-controlled engine systems. "The first car in the world to use 'by-wire' technology for throttle, brakes, and gear shift simultaneously" is how Toyota described this revolutionary design change for its 2003 Prius Hybrid. While a brochure touted "shorter activation times, faster communications between electronic systems, and weight reduction" as benefits of this new technology, it elided over the fact that a computer, *not the driver's foot on the accelerator pedal,* would now control the throttle. In other words, Toyota was gambling that the most safety-critical systems could be entrusted to a computer.

As other companies took the same gamble early in the new millennium, sudden acceleration reports rose rapidly. We've seen that the same thing happened in the 1980s as throttle control electronics became more complex, a pattern that NHTSA pretended not to notice. The question at the dawn of the new millennium, therefore, was whether NHTSA would respond differently this time around to unmistakable evidence that a fundamental change in throttle control electronics was behind this new surge in runaway car disasters. Part Four answers that question.

CHAPTER 67

# TOYOTA'S TROUBLES BEGIN

### TOYOTA SAYS STUCK ACCELERATOR PROBLEM ENTIRELY DUE TO FLOOR-MAT JAMS

> Toyota said today that its cars don't have a rampant sudden acceleration problem for any reason other than driver's side floor mats that can become lodged under the gas pedal. "The question of unintended acceleration involving Toyota and Lexus vehicles has been repeatedly and thoroughly investigated by NHTSA, without any finding of defect other than the risk from an unsecured or incompatible driver's floor mat," said Bob Daly, senior vice-president for Toyota Motor Sales USA, in a statement.
>
> *USA Today*, November 2, 2009

**SUDDEN ACCELERATIONS INVOLVING TOYOTA MODELS WITH "BY-WIRE"** electronics surfaced almost immediately. In March 2004, NHTSA opened a preliminary investigation of 2002-2003 Toyota Camrys,

Solaras, and Lexus ES300s. *The San Diego Union-Tribune* provided this historical background, including a reference to Sonia Sotomayor's ruling in the *Jarvis* case:

> The specter of sudden acceleration has surfaced before.
>
> In the 1980s, Audi of America was nearly driven out of the United States by claims that its Audi 5000 sedan was prone to accelerate suddenly and uncontrollably.
>
> Claims dropped after Audi installed shift-lock mechanisms, which require a motorist to step on the brake before shifting into drive or reverse. All vehicles with automatic transmissions, including those with electronic throttles, now have shift locks.
>
> NHTSA has concluded in many previous cases that most incidents of sudden acceleration are caused not by vehicles' defects but by drivers' errors. Drivers mistakenly stomp on gas pedals instead of the brakes, the agency says.
>
> Nearly every automaker has faced such claims from time to time.
>
> Most of the cases allege faults in cruise-control systems.
>
> The 2nd U.S. Circuit Court of Appeals in 2002 reinstated a $1.1 million judgment against Ford in response to the crash of a 1991 Ford Aerostar. Jurors had found that the crash was caused partly by a negligently designed cruise-control system. (*The San Diego Union-Tribune*, March 27, 2004).

In fact, storm clouds had formed over Toyota's throttle electronics before 2004. As a trial run for by-wire cars, it had introduced a limited version in selected 1998-1999 Lexus models. An early sign of trouble was a petition to NHTSA by Peter Boddaert of Braintree, Massachusetts, who described how his 1999 Lexus suddenly accelerated "even when no pressure was applied to the accelerator pedal." Boddaert said he had found 271 complaints about the Lexus on the agency's web site, 36 involving a sudden acceleration, several of which ended in a crash.

Boddaert wasn't alone. On January 15, 2004, Carol J. Mathews asked NHTSA to investigate 2002 and 2003 Lexus ES300s because her "throttle control system malfunctioned on several occasions, one of which resulted in a crash." NHTSA assigned the case to Scott Yon, who eventually sent an email to Toyota's Christopher Santucci, who until recently had been a colleague of Yon's in the agency's Office of Defects Investigation. Yon told Santucci that seven Toyota models with by-wire throttle control had experienced the following increases in sudden acceleration reports:

1. Camry–400%
2. Tacoma–1,400%
3. The Four R Runner–600%
4. Lexus ES–500%
5. Highlander–280%
6. Avalon–200%
7. Lexus RX–180%

Nevertheless, a Toyota Vice President said that "unsecured or incompatible drivers' side floor mats" were behind these reports. As the headnote to this chapter shows, Toyota was still making this claim five years after it received Yon's email.

CHAPTER 68

# IGNORING THE OBVIOUS

**OWNERS OF TOYOTA CARS IN REBELLION OVER SERIES OF ACCIDENTS CAUSED BY SUDDEN ACCELERATION**

ABC News Investigation Uncovers Reports of 16 Deaths, Over 200 Accidents; Toyota Owners Demand Answers. Refusing to accept the explanation of Toyota and the federal government, hundreds of Toyota owners are in rebellion after a series of accidents caused by what they call "runaway cars." Safety analysts found an estimated 2000 cases in which owners of Toyota cars including Camry, Prius and Lexus, reported that their cars surged without warning up to speeds of 100 miles per hour.

*ABC News*, November 3, 2009

**NHTSA ASKED TOYOTA IN MARCH OF 2004 TO TURN OVER "OWNER** complaints, field reports, etc., . . . that might relate to . . . engine speed increase without the driver pressing on the accelerator pedal." Had Toyota given NHTSA what it asked for, the true scope of Toyota's runaway car problems would have been on the record for all to see. This was another pivotal moment in the history of this automotive disaster when thousands of terrible injuries might have been prevented had NHTSA simply applied the law. But NHTSA still wasn't interested in anything that might expose the truth about the 1989 NHTSA/TSC report. That Toyota knew this is apparent from its response to the agency's information requests:

> *. . . Toyota did not include consumer complaints alleging one of the following that clearly do not relate to the alleged defect:* (1) an incident alleging uncontrollable acceleration that *occurred for a long duration*; (2) an incident in which the customer alleged that they could not control a vehicle *by applying the brake*; (3) an incident alleging unintended acceleration when moving the shift lever to reverse or the drive position; (4) incidents involving dissatisfaction with drivability, such as shift lock or engine response; and (5) no explanation of the circumstances (customer complained about unintended acceleration, but did not actually experience a subject defect, or just stated their concern). [Italics added.]

Let's consider the five categories of "consumer complaints" Toyota said were unrelated "to an increase in engine speed without the driver pressing on the accelerator pedal.":

1. An incident alleging uncontrollable acceleration that occurred for a long duration.

    Since long duration sudden accelerations were particularly deadly, this exclusion was like a pharmaceutical company telling the Federal Drug Administration that the most dangerous side effects of a particular drug were unimportant.

2. An incident in which the customer alleged that they could not control a vehicle by applying the brake.

   Taking the dangerous medicine analogy a step further, this is like a drug company telling the FDA it could ignore reported life-threatening side effects that the user was unable to remedy him/herself.

3. An incident alleging unintended acceleration when moving the shift lever to the reverse or drive position.

   Because the 1989 study had focused primarily on events that began at gear engagement, Toyota knew that it was unlikely that NHTSA would do anything that might resurrect reports it had whitewashed 15 years earlier.

4. Incidents involving dissatisfaction with driveability, such as shift lock or engine response.

   Since an uncommanded acceleration by definition compromises driveability, this exclusion was like a doctor refusing to treat someone dissatisfied with having been injured in a car accident. But that virtually eliminated every occurrence reported either to Toyota or NHTSA.

5. No explanation of the circumstances (customer complained about unintended acceleration, but did not actually experience a subject defect, or just stated their concern).

   In other words, NHTSA need not trouble itself over how many people were expressing their fear that the throttle might suddenly seize control of their car. But these people had good reason to fear for the safety of their loved ones and themselves.

CHAPTER 69

# SANTUCCI

### FAMILY BELIEVES TOYOTA IS AT FAULT FOR ACCIDENT AFTER CAR ACCELERATES ON ITS OWN

A family slams into a building after their vehicle begins to accelerate on its own, and they believe it's the manufacturer's fault. A seven-year-old was injured when a Toyota Camry accelerated on its own, sending the car into the side of an apartment building. The car's owner says this is not the first time the car has revved up without hitting the gas pedal. Toyota says it's still investigating what really happened but initially blamed "pedal confusion." The owner, Clarence Jackson says the car is a death trap and Toyota needs to replace it. "I was hitting the brakes, hitting the brakes wouldn't do any good. Only thing that stopped it was hitting that brick wall."

*KMOV.com,* May 1, 2013

**AFTER WORKING FOR AN AUTOMOTIVE PARTS MAKER, CHRISTOPHER** Santucci was hired in 2001 by NHTSA's ODI, where he met Scott Yon, who two years later told him about an opening in Toyota's Washington, D.C. office. Santucci was hired by Toyota in September 2003 to help with responses to NHTSA's information requests; and because he had not worked on sudden acceleration issues at NHTSA, he could be questioned about what he had learned about NHTSA's responses to Toyota's problems, which is what Hike Heiskell did on December 8, 2009 with amazing results.

Hike was particularly interested in how NHTSA could have accepted Toyota's exclusion of "long duration" occurrences, and he asked for my thoughts before he deposed Santucci. I said it was "like a doctor refusing to treat patients with the most serious symptoms of a dangerous disease."

"I like that analogy," laughed Hike, whose late father was a physician. "Toyota knew that poor old Doc NHTSA would welcome any excuse for keeping its head buried in the sand. Do you have any suggestions?"

"I'm sure you've seen the memorandum written by the ODI's Scott Yon that was part of NHTSA's opening resume on March 20, 2004?"

"Yes, in fact, that memorandum is one of the most incriminating pieces of evidence against NHTSA that I've seen." Here's what Hike was referring to:

> ODI has opened this investigation based on owner reports alleging that: (a) an engine speed increase occurred without pressing on the accelerator pedal or (b) the engine speed failed to decrease when the accelerator pedal was no longer depressed. In either event, ODI's position is that if such a failure were

> to occur, the driver would be able to control or stop vehicle movement by pressing on the brake pedal. However, in certain close-quarters driving situations (such as parking), should the subject vehicle throttle control system open the throttle valve without driver intent, the resultant vehicle surge could result in a momentary loss of vehicle control. In some instances, a crash may then result when the driver is unable to react in time to apply the brakes effectively. *Longer duration incidents involving uncontrollable acceleration where brake pedal application allegedly had no effect are not within the scope of this investigation.* Accordingly, based on the information gathered from complainant interviews, ODI is revising the number of *pertinent VOQs* to 11, of which five reports involve a vehicle crash. No injuries have been identified. A list of the pertinent VOQ numbers is included as an attachment to this memo. [Emphasis added.]

By eliminating "longer duration incidents," etc., NHTSA had quite literally managed to reduce thousands of credible reports to just 11 VOQs, each describing events lasting no more than a second or two and which caused no injuries. This was so astounding that I recommended to Hike that he zero in immediately on how NHTSA defined "longer duration incidents," which he did:

**Q:** You were working for Toyota when this information request came down, correct?

**A:** Correct.

**Q:** And your role was to help respond to it, correct?

**A:** Correct.

**Q:** Can you recall any limiting language from NHTSA prior to this information response?

**A:** Again, the letter itself is a public document. I don't recall exactly what it says, but it would certainly have a definition of the alleged defect in it.

**Q:** When this process was occurring inside Toyota, . . . who decided that you could exclude incidents alleging uncontrollable acceleration that occurred for a long duration?

**A:** I believe it was NHTSA.

**Q:** NHTSA decided that before you made your information request responses?

**A:** I believe so.

**Q:** Do you have any specific recollection of a document by which NHTSA did that, or in which NHTSA did that?

**A:** I believe it's this [Yon's] memorandum.

***

While I was stunned to learn that NHTSA had actually invited Toyota to exclude "longer duration incidents," what came next made my jaw drop:

**Q:** Who helped Mr. Yon come to this conclusion expressed in his memorandum . . . .

**A:** I don't know, I can't speak on behalf of Mr. Yon.

**Q:** Who negotiated with him?

**A:** It could have been his direct supervisor, the Division Chief, Mr. Quandt.

**Q:** Did you talk with Mr. Quandt about eliminating this universe of customer events or complaints?

**A:** They may have talked to us about it, if I recall.

**Q:** And what do you recall about those conversations?

**A:** I recall them saying to us, Toyota, myself, that they were not interested in reports alleging uncontrolled acceleration that occurred for a long duration [one second or longer]. I do recall them saying that.

**Q:** Who told you that?
**A:** Either Mr. Quandt or Mr. Yon.

***

The "Division Chief" of NHTSA's ODI, except for its administrator, may be the agency's most important person which makes this from Santucci particularly mind-numbing:

**Q:** What is it in that language that would logically permit the exclusion of surges or sudden unwanted accelerations lasting one second or longer?
**A:** It was in there, because . . . there was a portion about where the brakes could stop the vehicle. Long duration events imply that the brakes would not be able to stop the vehicle.

***

This testimony removes any doubt that despite many thousands of credible reports describing how the brakes failed to stop a runaway car, NHTSA perversely refuses to accept any claim that the brakes failed to stop or control a runaway car. Before I read Santucci's testimony, I had suspected there was an unspoken bargain between NHTSA and the car industry. The agency would pretend to investigate runaway car reports, and carmakers would pretend to cooperate. But the "one second" test showed that NHTSA wouldn't even pretend to investigate.

CHAPTER 70

# THE ZIPRIN PETITION

### RAISED TOYOTA CONCERNS IN 2004

> In the latest development in the recall crisis facing Toyota Motor Corp., U.S. insurer State Farm Insurance says it has reviewed its records and found it had contacted safety regulators in 2004. It was initially thought State Farm had contacted the National Highway Traffic Safety Administration in late 2007, but the insurer went back to its records in light of the widespread interest provoked by Toyota's decision to recall millions of vehicles.
>
> *The Daily Telegraph*, February 22, 2010

**JORDAN ZIPRIN'S PETITION ON JULY 8, 2005 DESCRIBED HOW** his stationary Camry took off and crashed after he shifted into "reverse." Ziprin cited 1,122 complaints to NHTSA describing an "abnormal throttle control event" involving the 2002-2005 Camry, Solara and Lexus models. If Ziprin expected to stir the agency to action, the opening resume of the ODI's Scott Yon shows he was sadly mistaken:

> There is no factor or trend indicating *that a vehicle or component defect exists.* Toyota believes this defect petition to be similar to other prior petitions and investigations into mechanical throttle controls. *Toyota has found no evidence* . . . that vehicles equipped with electronic throttle controls can suddenly accelerate when compared to those equipped with mechanical throttle controls. Toyota has not found any evidence in the subject vehicles *of brake failure, let alone brake failure concurrent with electronic throttle control failure.* [Italics added.]

One unfamiliar with the context here might think this was written by someone in Toyota's public relations office. Actually, it was plucked almost verbatim from the 1989 NHTSA/TSC report, which suggests a defensive attitude regarding the agency's sudden acceleration history.

When NHTSA summarily dismissed Jordan Ziprin's petition, he responded with an angry letter:

> Frankly, I anticipated that decision from the very first time I was in contact with Mr. Scott Yon, the assigned investigator. He made statements during our telephone conversation . . . that the purpose of this inquiry was to establish a basis to dismiss the petition based *upon NHTSA's policy rather than dealing with and examining all of the facts and circumstances involved* . . . . [Italics added.]

Is it conceivable that a government agency being paid to protect people funding its existence from unsafe cars was deliberately refusing to "examine . . . the facts and circumstances" surrounding runaway car calamities, so it could dismiss a petition like Jordan Ziprin's? When NHTSA opened an investigation into the cause of "engine surging" in 2002-2006 Camrys, here's how Toyota's Christopher Santucci responded to a colleague by email:

> Hopefully, this is just an exercise that NHTSA needs to go through to meet its obligation to the petitioner. Hopefully, they will not grant the petition and open another investigation.

Jordan Ziprin couldn't have said it better.

CHAPTER 71

# $100M FLOOR MATS

### TOYOTA SAID IT SAVED MORE THAN $100M IN '07 RECALL

Washington—Toyota Motor Corp. officials bragged in July about avoiding a costly wholesale recall related to sudden acceleration complaints, a document turned over to congressional investigators shows. A limited recall saved the Japanese automaker, whose executives will be grilled by congressional committees starting Tuesday, more than $100 million, according to the presentation obtained by *The Detroit News* on Sunday. The document, an internal presentation from the company's Washington office, raises new questions about the company's handling of safety issues. It was among the papers and records turned over to Congress as part of its demand for information on recent recalls and safety actions.

*The Detroit News*, February 21, 2010

**WHEN NHTSA BEGAN INVESTIGATING THE 2007 LEXUS ES350, IT** asked about "accessory floor mats interfering with the throttle pedal." Ecstatic at a chance to get the monkey off the back of its electronics, Toyota promptly notified ES350 owners "not to install all-weather floor mats on top of existing floor mats." NHTSA responded by timidly pointing out to the company that there were "too many complaints in this one vehicle to drop the issue."

Molly was convinced that Toyota's floor mat advisory would satisfy NHTSA, which proved correct when the agency meekly acquiesced in Toyota's decision to notify owners that driver side floor mats could be returned to dealers, and then stopped the sale of all-weather floor mats. Toyota's executives were so pleased they crowed in an email about their cleverness:

> Of note, NHTSA was beginning to look at vehicle design parameters as being a culprit, focusing on the accelerator pedal geometry coupled with the push button 'off' switch. We estimate that had the agency instead pushed hard for a recall of the throttle assembly, for instance, we would be looking at upwards of 100 million plus in unnecessary cost.

Why did these executives think that Toyota would have been "looking at upwards of $100 million plus in unnecessary costs" had NHTSA "pushed hard for a recall of the throttle assembly?" Jot that question down in your memory for when we take a close look at why by-wire electronics in most late model cars are vulnerable to a sudden loss of throttle control. But for the moment, let's find out how Toyota tried to capitalize on NHTSA's $100 million gift to the company's bottom line.

CHAPTER 72

# OBFUSCATION WITH A VENGEANCE

## AP NEWSBREAK: TOYOTA TO REPLACE 3.8M GAS PEDALS

Washington—Toyota Motor Corp. will replace gas pedals on 3.8 million recalled vehicles in the United States to address problems with sudden acceleration or the pedal becoming stuck in the floor mat, *The Associated Press* has learned. As a temporary step, Toyota will have dealers shorten the length of the gas pedals beginning in January while the company develops replacement pedals for their vehicles, the Transportation Department said in a statement provided to the AP. New pedals will be available beginning in April, and some vehicles will have brake override systems installed as a precaution.

*The Associated Press*, November 25, 2009

**HERE IS HOW NHTSA DEFINED THE "ALLEGED DEFECT" WHEN IT OPENED** an investigation involving 2006–2007 Tacoma pick-up trucks:

> [A]llegations or complaints that the accelerator and or cruise control system operated improperly, malfunctioned, failed, or operated in an unsafe manner, including but not limited to, allegations that the engine speed (power output) increased without driver application of the accelerator pedal (including allegations that may be related to cycling of the air conditioning compressor clutch or other so called 'normal' idle speed/engine control functions), or allegations that the engine speed (power output) failed to return to an idle state after the operator released the accelerator pedal (including allegations that may be related to engine speeds experienced between gear shifts on manual transmission vehicles at road speeds) or allegations that the cruise control system caused the engine speed (power output) to change in an unsafe manner.

This 133-word monstrosity was so indecipherable that Toyota side-stepped the issue by telling the agency there was no evidence of a safety defect; that complaints in the agency's database "in and of themselves do not justify an investigation;" and that Toyota "had been the subject of extensive media coverage that tended to generate consumer interest and complaints to the government." For an agency increasingly beleaguered by events, this was a way out and NHTSA summarily closed the inquiry on August 27, 2008 with a trademark evasion:

> For those vehicles where the throttle control system did not perform as the owner believes it should have, the information suggesting a possible defect related to motor vehicle safety is quite limited. Additional investigation is

unlikely to result in a finding that a defect related to motor vehicle safety exists . . . .

Since every sudden acceleration reported to NHTSA came from someone who believed "the throttle control system did not perform as it should", claiming that "information suggesting a possible defect related to motor vehicle safety was quite limited," was a disguised way of ignoring occurrences lasting longer than a second. But with the national media now scrutinizing Toyota's claims regarding its electronics, the company needed something more plausible than floor mats to draw attention away from its throttle control electronics. In the fall of 2008, Toyota found what it needed.

On October 15, 2008, Toyota made a confidential PowerPoint presentation to the ODI purporting to demonstrate how an accelerator pedal trim panel *could interfere with the accelerator if the pedal was fully depressed.* It claimed that a preliminary field survey had found *one Sienna model with a defect that "could interfere with the accelerator if the pedal was fully depressed."* Because there were many similar reports in models sold in Europe, Toyota knew it was only a matter of time until sticky pedals became an issue in the United States. It decided, therefore, to voluntarily recall certain Sienna models to "correct the alleged trim panel interference problem . . . should the trim panel retaining clips go missing because of improper servicing or other reasons."

In January of 2009, Jeffrey Pepski asked NHTSA to investigate after his 2007 Lexus suddenly accelerated to 80 mph. When the ODI opened an investigation, we wondered if it was a sign that NHTSA might take Pepski's petition seriously. When Toyota claimed that an inspection of Pepski's Lexus found evidence of floor mat interference, however, Santucci indicated in an internal email that he knew from discussions with former NHTSA colleagues the agency *wanted Toyota to blame the Pepski occurrence on a loose floor mat because, otherwise, the agency would have to ask "for non-floor mat reports":*

> So they should ask us for non-floor mat related reports, right? But they are concerned that if they ask for these other reports, *they will have many reports that just cannot be explained.* And since they do not think that they can explain them, they don't really want them. Does that make sense? I think it is good news for Toyota. [Italics added.]

If this were a fictional story about a government willing to investigate only what it could explain and, therefore, needed no investigation, it would be in the running for the worst novel of the year. But there was nothing fictional about the horrendous event that was about to make Toyota sudden acceleration's poster child in the new millennium.

CHAPTER 73

# HOLD ON! PRAY!!

## FINAL WORDS BEFORE FATAL CAR CRASH ON 9-1-1 TAPE

Accelerator was stuck, caller said. A harrowing 9-1-1 call made by a passenger in a fated Lexus that crashed seconds later and killed four people Aug. 28 was released yesterday by the California Highway Patrol. In the 50-second tape, crash victim Chris Lastrella begins by telling the dispatcher: "We're in a Lexus . . . we're going north [State Route 125] and our accelerator is stuck." . . . "We're going 120 [mph]! Mission Gorge! We're in trouble—we can't—there's no brakes." The last words heard on the tape are: "hold on" and "pray," . . . . Killed in the crash were CHP officer Mark Saylor and his wife, Cleofe, who were both 45; their 13-year-old daughter, Mahala; and Lastrella, 38, who was Cleofe Saylor's brother.

*SignOnSanDiego.com*, September 11, 2009

**"THE ACCELERATOR IS STUCK; WE'RE GOING 100 MILES AN HOUR;** there are no brakes!!" Moments later the Lexus ES350 driven by an off-duty California Highway Patrolman, Mark Saylor, careened through an intersection, collided with a Ford Explorer, jumped a curb, plowed through a fence, hit an embankment, and went airborne into the bed of the San Diego River, where it rolled over several times before bursting into flames. The last words from the doomed automobile were: "Hold on! Pray!!" Saylor, his wife, daughter, and brother-in-law perished in the flaming crash.

The Saylor catastrophe captured headlines around the world, making runaway car crashes headline news again. It also presented Toyota with a stark choice of either denying its electronics were faulty or taking a page from Johnson & Johnson's response in 1982 when it learned that several people had died after ingesting Tylenol tablets. The company immediately removed the painkiller from store shelves, an action often cited in business schools as a shining example of how to protect a company's reputation with prompt and forthright crisis management. Despite the looming peril to its reputation, Toyota issued a "safety advisory" saying it had "taken a closer look" *at the potential for the accelerator to get "stuck in the full open position" due to interfering floor mats.* Owners were told that if their car "*continues to accelerate rapidly* after releasing the accelerator," they should: (1) dislodge the floor mat; (2) if that didn't work, step on the brake with both feet but not pump; (3) shift to neutral; (4) if they couldn't shift to neutral, turn the engine to OFF; and (5) in a car with an engine stop/start button, keep it depressed for three seconds. [Italics added.]

This so-called "safety advisory" as we will learn in due course, was a disguised way of telling owners how to respond to a sudden, electronically-induced vehicle acceleration. As such, it was both dangerous and deceptive. Dangerous because it didn't warn that turning off the engine would disable the power assist for steering and brakes, said nothing about steering to a safe location off the roadway, and does not recommend that the car should be towed to a dealer and not driven again until the problem was fixed. It was deceptive because it implied that floor mat interference was the only way the accelerator could get "stuck in the full open position," thereby leading owners with models without floor mats to believe that their cars were immune to a sudden loss of throttle control.

While there's much more to say about warnings, that subject will be taken up after we consider some of the events that occurred in the wake of the Saylor tragedy.

CHAPTER 74

# TRAPPED

**REGULATORS SLAM TOYOTA OVER 'NO DEFECT' CLAIM**

**U.S. AUTO SAFETY AGENCY REBUKES AN ASSERTION THAT IT FOUND NOTHING WRONG IN VEHICLES INVOLVED IN A MASSIVE RECALL OVER INCIDENTS OF UNINTENDED ACCELERATION.**

Federal safety regulators have sharply rebuked Toyota Motor Corp. for issuing "inaccurate and misleading" statements asserting that no defect exists in the 3.8 million vehicles it recalled after a Lexus sedan accelerated out of control in San Diego County, killing four people. The National Highway Traffic Safety Administration issued a statement Wednesday that the recalled Toyota and Lexus vehicles do have an "underlying defect" that involves the design of the accelerator pedal and the driver's foot well.

*LATimes.com*, November 5, 2009

**TOYOTA'S RESPONSE TO THE SPECTACULARLY PUBLIC DEATH OF A** California Highway Patrolman and his family reveals a company trapped by evasions made possible by NHTSA's mindless approach to runaway car reports. During the 1980s, it had ignored evidence pointing inexorably to a dangerous problem. Now, twenty years later, the agency was doing a passable imitation of the Bourbons of whom it was famously said "they forgot nothing, and learned nothing." NHTSA had not forgotten how easy it had been to make drivers the culprit; and since then it had learned nothing about the power of this country's legal system to expose both corporate and governmental malfeasance. But then, quite unexpectedly, Toyota made a misstep from which not even NHTSA could rescue it. Less than three months after the Saylor tragedy, it issued the following press release:

> Toyota Motor Sales . . . today announced that it has begun mailing letters to owners of certain Toyota and Lexus models regarding the potential for an unsecured or incompatible driver's floor mat to interfere with the accelerator pedal and cause it to get stuck in the wide-open position. The letter, in compliance with the National Traffic and Motor Vehicle Safety Act and reviewed by the National Highway Traffic Safety Administration . . . *also confirms that no defect exists in vehicles in which the driver's floor mat is compatible with the vehicle and properly secured.*

This was too much to stomach, even for NHTSA, which promptly announced that it had informed Toyota that the floor mat recall was *an interim measure that did not correct the underlying defect.* An email by a senior manager, Katsuhiko Koganei, shows that Toyota knew it had stepped in something. Koganei admonished a subordinate that "we should not mention about mechanical failures of the accelerator pedal because we have not *clarified the real cause of the sticking accelerator pedal formally, and the remedy for the matter has not yet been confirmed.*" [Italics added.] Three days after Koganei's email, a meeting took place between NHTSA and two senior Toyota executives, James Lentz, and Yoshimi Inaba, prior to which a company Vice President, Irv Miller, emailed Koganei:

> I hate to break this to you but WE HAVE A tendency for MECHANICAL failure in accelerator pedals of a certain manufacturer on certain models. We are not protecting our customers by keeping this quiet. *The time to hide on this one is over. We need to come clean* and I believe that Jim Lentz and Yoshi are on the way to DC for meetings with NHTSA to discuss options.
>
> We better just hope that they can get NHTSA to work with us in coming up with a workable solution that does not put us out of business. [Emphasis original.]

Was Miller referring only to mechanically stuck accelerator pedals? Since Toyota had 40 billion dollars in cash reserves and sticky accelerator pedals could be corrected at a relatively modest cost, it is hard to imagine that Miller was thinking of sticky pedals when he expressed the hope that NHTSA would "work with us in coming up with a workable solution that does not put us out of business." Miller's "hope" that NHTSA would "work with us in coming up with a workable solution that does not put us out of business," suggests that he was concerned about how to steer NHTSA away from the company's throttle control electronics. In fact, since Toyota was sitting on a cash reserve of 40 billion dollars, that is the only interpretation consistent with Miller's allusion to Toyota being "put out of business." If that's what Miller intended, it was a gross exaggeration of what might have happened had Toyota decided to "come clean" about its electronics. Since by-wire electronics across the industry were experiencing sudden accelerations, Toyota had an opportunity to single itself out as the one company willing to let the lives and safety of people trump bottom line considerations. Had it done so, its competitors would have had no choice but to follow suit, and the entire industry would have shared the cost of making its throttle control electronics "failsafe."

Unfortunately, Toyota had a much different strategy in mind. As we are about the see, however, events were now working against NHTSA's ability to continue letting Toyota off the hook.

CHAPTER 75

# AN AGENCY IN CRISIS

### RUNAWAY TOYOTA CASES IGNORED

### SAFETY INVESTIGATORS DISMISSED NUMEROUS REPORTS OF SUDDEN ACCELERATION, THEN SAID DATA WERE LACKING

More than 1,000 Toyota and Lexus owners have reported since 2001 that their vehicles suddenly accelerated on their own, in many cases slamming into trees, parked cars and brick walls, among other obstacles, a *Times* review of federal records has found. The crashes resulted in at least 19 deaths and scores of injuries over the last decade, records show. Federal regulators say that is far more than any other automaker has experienced. Owner complaints helped trigger at least eight investigations into sudden acceleration in Toyota and Lexus vehicles by the National Highway Traffic Safety Administration in the last seven years. Toyota Motor Corp. recalled fewer than 85,000 vehicles in response

> to two of those probes, and the federal agency closed six other cases without finding a defect. But those investigations systematically excluded or dismissed the majority of complaints by owners that their Toyota and Lexus vehicles had suddenly accelerated, which sharply narrowed the scope of the probe, the *Times* investigation revealed.
>
> *LATimes.com*, November 8, 2009

**THE CALLER IN EARLY JANUARY 2010 IDENTIFIED HIMSELF AS** Jeffrey Quandt, NHTSA's ODI director. "I understand you may have located some experts who could help us."

"I assume you're referring to Toyota's problems."

"Yes."

"In fact, Mr. Quandt, I'm preparing for a trial in which one of our witnesses is a recognized expert in the field of functional electronic safety, which is exactly what you're looking for." I was referring to Keith Armstrong, who was also helping me with the technical aspects of this book and who we will meet again in an upcoming chapter. I told Quandt that I needed "to consult with my colleagues."

"When can you let me know?"

"Why don't you call me back in a week; I should have an answer by then."

While I was dubious about having Keith Armstrong talk with Quandt, Hike had a different slant.

"I don't trust NHTSA any more than you do, Tom, but if we can save lives by waking these people up, I think as responsible citizens we should at least try to do it."

When Quandt called back, I told him that Keith Armstrong needed to return to England immediately after testifying, and suggested an interview by telephone. After they talked, I asked Keith how it went.

"I explained why Toyota was having so many problems with its electronics."

"What was the response?"

"Mr. Quandt was polite, but kept bringing up floor mat interference."

This infuriated Hike. "Quandt's the guy who came up with that absurd one-second test, and now he's in a panic because Congress is about to investigate what NHTSA's been doing while runaway cars have been wiping people out. This floor mat nonsense shows that the ODI is grasping at straws to protect its reputation."

"It seems to me, Hike, that Quandt and his sidekick, Yon, are only minor functionaries who have been indoctrinated by the people upstairs itching to trade time at NHTSA for a big money job promoting the interests of the car industry."

"I couldn't agree more, and that's why it's so scary that people like Quandt and Yon are free to concoct something as dangerous as a one-second test."

"Didn't the ODI come up with that farce during George W.'s second term, and wasn't that followed by a long stretch during which President Obama left the position of NHTSA Administrator unfilled?"

"That may be true, but it doesn't change the fact that the ODI was operating within a bureaucratic culture rooted in the notion promoted by big business that government regulation should be kept at an absolute minimum, regardless of the consequences to ordinary people. I'm a Republican, but so are many of the people whose lives are being destroyed because DOT Secretaries and NHTSA Administrators under both Republican and Democratic administrations have bought into this idea that these companies shouldn't be bothered by safety regulations. They seem to forget there's a crucial difference between regulations that protect people's lives, and those that are simply intrusive. One reason I became a lawyer was to help the government enforce regulations to help protect people from corporations that have trouble making that distinction."

"All I can say, Hike, is 'Amen brother!' I know that keeping the pressure on NHTSA won't be easy, but . . . "

"If we greedy trial lawyers don't do it," Hike chortled, finishing the thought, "who will?"

CHAPTER 76

# A SECRET RECALL?

### TOYOTA HAS PATTERN OF SLOW RESPONSE ON SAFETY ISSUES

> Toyota's recalls and disclosures in recent months are part of a lengthy pattern in which the automaker has often reacted slowly to safety concerns, in some instances making design changes without telling customers about problems with vehicles already on the road, an examination of its record shows.
>
> *The New York Times*, February 7, 2010

**SHORTLY BEFORE CONGRESSIONAL HEARINGS ON TOYOTA'S RUNAWAY** car problems were scheduled to begin, the company informed NHTSA that a certain brand of accelerator pedal could have a "sticking" defect. When NHTSA prodded Toyota to correct the problem, it voluntarily recalled 2.3 million vehicles ostensibly to fix sticking pedals; and then, a short time later, Toyota suspended sales of eight models involved in the sticky pedal recall, an action it said was "necessary until a remedy is finalized." Toyota later expanded the recall to cover an additional 1.1 million vehicles.

Molly smelled a conspiracy. "Sticking pedals were a godsend to NHTSA, because the last thing it wanted was to have Congress start asking tough questions about why it wasn't investigating Toyota's electronics."

"It takes two to tango, Molly. So what was in it for Toyota?"

"First of all, it desperately needed something it could use before Congress to deflect attention from its electronics. The floor mat and sticky pedal recalls may have been phony, but they were better than nothing."

"How does that jive with your theory that these recalls gave Toyota a chance to secretly get rid of 'bugs' in its computer programs?"

"Hand in glove. Recalling millions of cars to dealers to check for sticky pedals was a perfect opportunity for reprogramming computers, which took about five minutes. Do you remember what happened when NHTSA imposed about $50 million in civil penalties because Toyota knew about sticky pedals for a long time, but didn't report them?"

"Didn't it fork over the money without a whimper?"

Molly laughed. "In fact, it couldn't fork over the money fast enough; and isn't it strange how, after that, reports involving the recalled models suddenly declined."

Surprised, I asked, "Are you sure about that?"

"Absolutely sure; in fact that was mentioned in several newspaper articles about the recall. So what does that tell you?"

"That these models had one hell of a lot of sticky pedals, or something else was going on."

"I agree, but how could a sticky accelerator pedal possibly cause a car to rapidly accelerate, as opposed to not decelerating when the driver wanted the car to slow down?"

"It can't, so you think the recalls were a strategy to get rid of 'bugs' that were contributing to sudden accelerations?"

"Can you think of any other reason for this sudden decline in reports?"

"No! In fact, your logic is so impeccable, Molly, I'm sure events will prove that your instincts are correct."

Not long after this conversation, we discovered that a car company with by-wire electronics virtually identical to Toyota's had responded to sudden acceleration reports by reflashing—i.e., reprogramming—computers that controlled the throttle.

CHAPTER 77

# CONGRESS ACTS

### CONGRESSMEN QUESTION TOYOTA'S DEFECTS TESTING

WASHINGTON—U.S. Reps. Bart Stupak and Henry Waxman told Toyota today that it had failed to produce any evidence it has tested its electronic engine controls as a possible source of sudden acceleration defects. In a letter to the Japanese automaker, the lawmakers said Toyota did not appear to have any basis for claiming it was "confident" of no defects in its electronic throttle controls or other systems.

*Freep.com*, March 5, 2010

**SHORTLY AFTER CONGRESSIONAL HEARINGS BEGAN, THE CO-**Chairmen of the House Subcommittee on Oversight and Investigations, Henry Waxman and Bart Stupak, sent an open letter on February 22, 2010 to Toyota's James Lentz that began by mentioning three "significant concerns" the Committee had regarding the company's responses to its information requests:

- "[T]he documents appear to show that Toyota consistently dismissed the possibility that electronic failures could be responsible for incidents of sudden unintended acceleration."

For a quarter of a century, NHTSA had passively accepted the industry's claims regarding its electronics, and yet it had taken this Congressional Committee only weeks to recognize that the *only logical explanation for sudden accelerations was "electronic failures."*

- "Since 2001 when it first began installing electronic throttle controls in vehicles, Toyota has received thousands of consumer complaints of sudden unintended acceleration."

To which the committee might have added that NHTSA had responded by refusing to consider spontaneous, uncontrolled accelerations lasting longer than a second.

- "Toyota appears to have conducted no systematic investigation into whether electronic defects could lead to sudden unintended acceleration."

This shows the extent to which the car industry viewed NHTSA as a paper tiger. But as what comes next shows, this Committee was marching to a different drummer than NHTSA:

- [T]he *one report that Toyota has produced that purports to test* and analyze potential electronic causes of sudden unintended acceleration was initiated just two months ago and appears to have serious flaws. This report *was prepared for Toyota by the consulting firm Exponent, Inc.* at the request of Toyota's defense counsel, Bowman & Brooke, LLP. *Michael Pecht,* a professor of mechanical engineering at the University of Maryland, and director of the University's Center for Advanced Life Cycle Engineering (CALCE), *told the Committee that Exponent "did not conduct a fault tree analysis, a failure modes and effects analysis* . . . or provide any other scientific or rigorous study to describe all the various potential ways in which a sudden acceleration event could be triggered"; "only to have focused on some simple and obvious failure cases"; used "extremely small sample sizes"; and as a result produced a report that "I would not consider . . . of value . . . in getting to the root causes of sudden acceleration in Toyota vehicles." [Italics added.]

The one report Toyota has produced . . . was prepared by the consulting firm Exponent, Inc., at the request of Toyota's defense counsel.

While NHTSA may not have blinked an eye at a report from a science-for-hire company like Exponent, Inc., this Committee had done its homework and realized how suspicious it was that Toyota had not relied on the engineers who designed, developed, and tested its electronics to defend their safety:

- Dr. Michael Pecht . . . told the Committee that Exponent "did not conduct a fault tree analysis, a failure modes and effects analysis . . . or provide any other scientific or rigorous study to describe all the various potential ways in which a sudden acceleration event could be triggered."

Dr. Pecht had not only exposed the slipshod nature of the Exponent report, he had also unmasked Toyota's strategy of treating sudden acceleration as a public relations problem:

> Toyota's public statements about the adequacy of its recent recalls appear to be misleading. In a February 1, 2010, appearance on the *Today Show*, you stated that Toyota has "studied the events of unintended acceleration, and [it] is quite clear that it has come down to two different issues," entrapment of accelerator pedals in floor mats and *sticky accelerator pedals*. In an appearance the same day on CNBC you repeated this claim and reported that Toyota is "very confident that the fix in place is going to stop what's going on."

The following reveals how risky it was for Toyota to treat plaintiffs' sudden acceleration crisis as a public relations problem:

> The documents provided to the Committee appear to undermine these public claims. We wrote to you on February 2, 2010, to request any analyses by Toyota that show sticky pedals can cause sudden unintended acceleration. *Toyota did not produce any such analyses.* To the contrary, Toyota's counsel informed the Committee on February 5 that a sticky pedal *"[t]ypically . . . does not translate into a sudden, high-speed acceleration event."* Moreover, our review of the consumer complaints produced by Toyota shows that in cases reported to the company's telephone complaint lines, *Toyota personnel identified pedals or floor mats as [a potential] cause of only 16% of the sudden unintended acceleration incident reports.* Approximately 70% of the sudden unintended acceleration events in Toyota's own customer call database involved vehicles that are not subject to the 2009 and 2010 floor mat and "sticky pedal" recalls. [Italics added.]

- Toyota did not produce any analyses . . . that sticky pedals can cause sudden unintended acceleration. Toyota's counsel informed the Committee that a sticky pedal "[t]ypically . . . does not translate into a sudden, high-speed acceleration event."

By acknowledging that a sticky pedal could not possibly cause a sudden, high-speed acceleration, Toyota's counsel had pointed out something that should've been obvious to NHTSA. Furthermore, with sticky pedals eliminated, the only possibilities left were floor mats and "electronic defects." But since a floor mat by itself could also not cause a sudden, high-speed acceleration, the only remaining explanation for events that met that definition was dangerously designed throttle control electronics.

We turn now to some of the most stunning revelations about Toyota's runaway car problems that emerge from these congressional hearings.

CHAPTER 78

# INCRIMINATING NUMBERS

## COVER STORY

**COULD ELECTRONICS BE WHAT'S CAUSING RUNAWAY CARS? NHTSA STEPS IN TO INVESTIGATE EMI: ELECTROMAGNETIC INTERFERENCE**

Allegations of unintended acceleration by Toyota models that are not part of the recall and by cars from other automakers have revived debate over whether electromagnetic interference is the cause of such incidents.

The theory is that electrical signals—from sources as diverse as cellphones, airport radar and even a car's own systems—briefly and unpredictably wreak havoc with sensitive electronic controls in vehicles. It's an argument trial lawyers and consumer advocates have made for years . . . .

"If these congressional hearings probe deeply enough, they'll discover that the car industry has known from the beginning that the most likely cause of sudden acceleration is internal electromagnetic interference," charges Tom Murray, a Sandusky, Ohio, attorney who brought dozens of acceleration lawsuits and is writing a book on sudden acceleration.

Toyota, however, says floor mat interference and sticky gas pedals are the causes of unintended acceleration in the more than eight million vehicles it has recalled in the USA for either problem.

*USA Today*, February 23, 2010

**THE WAXMAN/STUPAK COMMITTEE'S OPEN LETTER TO TOYOTA THE** day before the foregoing *USA Today* story, suggests the scope of Toyota's crisis:

> In response to the Committee's January 28, 2010, request for internal Toyota documents, the company provided a representative sample of reports describing calls received through the company's telephone complaint line. To produce this sample, *Toyota started with 37,900 customer contact reports* from the company's database that Toyota identified (via the company's complaint coding system) as potentially related to sudden unintended acceleration. [Italics added.]

- Toyota started with 37,900 customer contact reports . . . [that were] . . . potentially related to sudden unintended acceleration.

This raises more questions than it answers. What code words did Toyota use to identify reports "potentially related to sudden, unintended acceleration"? Our research shows, for example, that drivers frequently use words other than "sudden acceleration" when reporting this vehicle behavior. Was Toyota's search limited to reports that used these words, or did it also encompass such terms as "engine surge," "throttle stuck," "cruise control malfunction," "car was out of control," "car wouldn't stop," or another of the many descriptions we have found in car company records or in reports to NHTSA? How many reports did Toyota receive other than through its telephone complaint line? At this writing, in fact, discovery in our Toyota cases indicates that it may have received as many as *60,000 customer contact reports involving Camrys alone*. But Toyota had no intention of turning over thousands of reports to Congress:

> Toyota randomly selected 3,430 of these complaints for review, ultimately determining that 1,008 of these records directly related to consumer concerns about sudden unintended acceleration, engine surge, or similar problems. Toyota provided these 1,008 reports to the Committee.

How did Toyota "randomly" determine which reports Congress would be allowed to see? What did it mean by the ambiguous reference to occurrences "directly related" to consumer concerns about sudden unintended acceleration? Did this mean that only reports that used the term "sudden acceleration" were selected? How many of the 1,008 reports resulted in injuries or fatalities? We are left to speculate about answers to such questions.

If this Committee was suspicious of Toyota's tactics, the company's reliance on a report from a science-for-hire company like Exponent, Inc., didn't help its cause:

> In response to your public statements, we wrote to Toyota on February 2, 2010, to request "all analyses or documents that substantiate" your claim that electronic malfunctions were not causing sudden unintended acceleration. In response, Toyota provided two types of documents to the Committee: (1) reports of internal testing of various

> components and features of Toyota's electronic throttle control system, and (2) *a single evaluation of the potential for sudden unintended acceleration in Toyota and Lexus vehicles by the consulting firm Exponent, Inc.* Neither category of documents appears to justify your public comments. [Italics added.]

Was Toyota's senior management in Tokyo so out of touch with reality that it didn't realize that relying on a report from Exponent, Inc. would be seen as a tacit admission that it couldn't call upon its own engineers to defend the safety of its electronics? Indeed, Toyota's tactics couldn't help but arouse the Committee's suspicions:

> The electronics testing documents Toyota provided include thousands of pages of engineering standards; test methods; pre-production vehicle and component evaluations; email correspondence between Toyota engineers about field testing of new features of the company's Electronic Throttle Control System; engineering change instructions; reports on field testing of competitor vehicles; and sketches, diagrams, test engineering reports, photographs, emails, and PowerPoint presentations by Toyota and part manufacturers related to proposed fixes for "sticky pedals." *Except for one recent report, the documents did not include any analyses that purported comprehensively to test and analyze possible electronic causes of sudden unintended acceleration.* [Italics added.]

- Except for one recent report [from Exponent], the documents did not include any analyses that purported comprehensively to test and analyze possible electronic causes of sudden unintended acceleration.

In fact, Toyota had responded to the Committee's information requests by turning over reams of technical data that only added to the Committee's displeasure over its tactics:

> The only document Toyota produced that claims to address the phenomenon of sudden unintended acceleration in a systematic way is a February 2010 report on testing conducted by Exponent, a scientific and engineering consulting firm located in Menlo Park, California. This report was commissioned in December 2009 by Toyota defense counsel Bowman & Brooke, LLP. Exponent representatives told the Committee staff that Bowman & Brooke requested the report *just days before its publication date of February 4, 2010, at approximately the same time that we sought substantiation of your claims about electronics testing.* According to Exponent, at the time the report was written, testing was still on-going and an interim report like this one is not customary for the company. [Italics added.]

- The Exponent report was commissioned in December, 2009 by Toyota defense counsel, . . . just days before its publication date of February 4, 2010, at approximately the same time we sought substantiation of your claims about electronics testing.

Here is how David Michael's 2008 book *Doubt is Their Product* described Exponent's *modus operandi*:

> Exponent's scientists are prolific writers of scientific reports and papers. While some may exist, I have yet to see an Exponent study that does not support the conclusion needed by the corporation or trade association that is paying the bill.

Although this Committee was probably unaware of David Michael's book, it certainly knew that law firms defending companies in product liability cases hire experts to help prove there is nothing wrong with the company's products. Hence, Toyota's strategy suggests that it saw Congress *not as a representative of the American people* trying to improve automotive safety through legislation, but as an adversary. Making matters worse for the Japanese automaker, the Committee had interviewed a primary author of the Exponent report:

> On February 19, 2010, the Committee staff interviewed one of the primary authors of the Exponent report, Dr. Paul Taylor. He stated that the report did not examine any vehicles or components that consumers reported to have had unintended acceleration events. He also said that *the study did not analyze the vehicles' computer systems, seek to identify potential chip failures, examine software and programming of the vehicles' electronic control modules, conduct any testing under differing environmental conditions, or assess the effects of electromagnetic or radio frequency interference on the electronic throttle control system.* According to Dr. Taylor, these are not among his or his co-authors' "areas of expertise." Dr. Taylor said that Toyota's counsel has hired other researchers at Exponent to conduct such tests of Toyota and Lexus vehicles, but Toyota did not request that Exponent provide interim reports on these additional studies. [Italics added.]

- Exponent did not analyze the vehicles' computer systems, seek to identify potential chip failures, examine software and programming of the vehicles' electronic control modules, conduct any testing under differing environmental conditions, or assess the effects of electromagnetic or radio frequency interference on the electronic throttle control system.

These Committee comments reflect a keen awareness that electronics in modern cars involve complex interactions between software programs and hardware systems that control safety-critical functions like throttle control, braking, steering, stability and airbag deployment, a matter crucial to our story that we will return to in due course.

That the Waxman/Stupak Committee also suspected that floor mats and sticky pedals were red herrings seems clear from its open letter, the remainder of which is the subject of our next chapter.

CHAPTER 79

# HOW NOT TO WIN FRIENDS IN THE U.S. CONGRESS

**TOYOTA HALTS SALES OF EIGHT MODELS IN U.S. FOR PEDAL FLAW**

> Toyota Motor, still struggling to resolve a problem with accelerator pedals, said Tuesday that it would temporarily stop building and selling eight models, including the popular Camry and Corolla sedans, in the North American market. The unusual move follows two recalls of millions of vehicles in the last two months for a problem that the company has described as a "rare" condition in which the gas pedal can stick and cause a vehicle to speed up unintentionally.
>
> *The New York Times,* January 27, 2010

**THE WAXMAN/STUPAK COMMITTEE ALSO INTERVIEWED TWO** independent experts, Neil Hannemann, an engineer with over thirty years of experience in automotive product design and development, and Dr. Michael Pecht, a professor of engineering at the University of Maryland:

> According to Mr. Hannemann, *"this report does not follow a scientific method* . . . . [I]t is not clear if the testing is appropriate to the issue, since the extent of the problem was not defined . . . . To even have a conclusion with such a poorly stated problem is inappropriate." Dr. Pecht reached a similar conclusion:
>
> > Exponent did not provide a methodology which showed that they identified the potential causes of unintended acceleration in Toyota vehicles. *Exponent did not conduct a fault tree analysis, a failure modes and effects analysis (FMEA) . . . or provide any other scientific and rigorous study to describe all the various potential ways in which a sudden acceleration event could be triggered.* This would be necessary to plan and ensure that the testing and analysis was complete, thorough and of value. Exponent appeared to have only focused on some simple and obvious failure causes and did not provide any rationale to rule out other potential causes (e.g., software). [Italics added.]

- The Exponent report "does not follow a scientific method . . . ."

From the very beginning, in fact, the federal government has failed "to follow a scientific method" in its approach to automotive electronics. The 1989 NHTSA/TSC report, for example, could not cite a shred of empirical or scientific evidence for shifting the blame to drivers. The agency's McMath denial in 1999 is a shameful example of intellectual dishonesty masquerading as a legitimate investigation; and NHTSA's embrace of floor mats and sticky pedals, and its abominable one-second test reflect an outright contempt for the "scientific method."

That Exponent had not employed even rudimentary engineering techniques in analyzing Toyota's electronics speaks volumes about the company's attitude toward the U.S. Congress. But as what came next shows, Toyota had badly underestimated the lengths to which this Committee would go to learn the truth:

> Toyota's public statements about the adequacy of its recent recalls appear to be misleading. In a February 1, 2010, appearance on the *Today Show*, you stated that Toyota has "studied the events of unintended acceleration, and [it] is quite clear that it has come down to two different issues," entrapment of accelerator pedals in floor mats and *sticky accelerator pedals.* In an appearance the same day on CNBC you repeated this claim and reported that Toyota is "very confident that *the fix in place is going to stop what's going on.*"
>
> The documents provided to the Committee appear to undermine these public claims. We wrote to you on February 2, 2010, to request any analyses by Toyota that show sticky pedals can cause sudden unintended acceleration. Toyota did not produce any such analyses. To the contrary, Toyota's counsel informed the Committee on February 5 that a sticky pedal *"[t]ypically . . . does not translate into a sudden, high-speed acceleration event."* Moreover, our review of the consumer complaints produced by Toyota shows that in cases reported to the company's telephone complaint lines, *Toyota personnel identified pedals or floor mats as [a potential] cause of only 16% of the sudden unintended acceleration incident reports.* Approximately 70% of the sudden unintended

> acceleration events in Toyota's own customer call database involved vehicles that are not subject to the 2009 and 2010 floor mat and "sticky pedal" recalls. [Italics added.]

- Toyota did not produce any analyses . . . that sticky pedals can cause sudden unintended acceleration. To the contrary, Toyota's counsel informed the Committee that a sticky pedal "[t]ypically . . . does not translate into a sudden, high speed acceleration event."

Although the Committee suspected the sticky pedal recall was as phony as a three dollar bill, why had Toyota voluntarily recalled several million cars and eventually ponied up 50 million dollars for not reporting sticky pedals earlier? In fact, 50 million dollars was a pin prick for a company with a 40 billion dollar cash reserve that it didn't wish to spend on compensating people for the company's mistakes, much less on correcting a problem in electronics it had touted as a revolutionary advance in automotive design.

Although Toyota's own legal counsel had candidly acknowledged that a sticky pedal could not cause a "sudden, high-speed acceleration," Toyota had continued to insist that a sticky pedal or floor mat interference could explain virtually every report. The Waxman/Stupak Committee was incredulous:

> [W]hy would you tell the public on February 1, 2010, that the recall of 2.3 million vehicles to replace "sticky pedals" would "fix . . . what's going on" if Toyota had no studies linking sticky pedals to sudden unintended acceleration?

In fact, the committee may have suspected that the "sticky pedal" recall was a cover-up for something else:

> Toyota's own data also appear to conflict with the assurances that you gave on February 1, 2010. As noted above, the data from Toyota's consumer complaint telephone line show

> that floor mats or pedal problems have been identified as the cause of only 16% of the sudden unintended acceleration reports received through the complaint line. Over 80% of the complaints do not identify either of these factors as causes of the reported problems. Furthermore, almost 70% of the sudden unintended acceleration events in Toyota's customer call database involved vehicles that are not subject to the 2009 and 2010 floor mat and "sticky pedal" recalls.

Did Toyota really think that a Congressional committee wouldn't notice that 80% of the reports it gave Congress contained no indication of either floor mat interference or a sticky pedal, and that nearly 70% of the reports in its customer complaint database involved vehicles not included in either the floor mat or sticky pedal recalls? Further evidence of how its evasions had placed Toyota in a trap, is the testimony on March 2, 2010 of a company Vice President, Takeshi Uchiyamada to the Senate Committee on Commerce, Science and Transportation. Uchiyamada claimed that the company's electronic throttle control system was tested "extensively both in the design phase and after it was developed to ensure that there is no possibility of 'sudden unintended acceleration.'" However, because Toyota relies on suppliers to perform electronic testing, this put a foot firmly in the company's mouth; and when its engineers later told Congress that the company *does not impose controls on manufacturers of sensors and circuit boards for its electronic throttle control system,* the company's foot-in-mouth ailment worsened.

Toyota engineers also told Congress that "there is no particular or special testing that would directly *prove there is no unintended acceleration.*" But this was only another way of saying that proving a negative can be difficult, a banality that was left dangling by thousands of detailed, credible, and often substantiated descriptions of runaway car occurrences. Moreover, the suggestion that "special testing" could not "directly prove that there is no unintended acceleration" was like a doctor telling a patient suffering debilitating headaches that because tests were negative, there was no way to know whether he/she was actually experiencing headaches.

***

A follow-up letter on March 5, 2010 from the Waxman/Stupak Committee to a Toyota Vice President, James Lentz, left no doubt that it was rapidly losing patience with the company's foot-dragging:

> *We do not understand the basis for Toyota's repeated assertions that it is 'confident' there are no electronic defects contributing to incidents of sudden acceleration.* We wrote you on February 2, 2010 to request 'all analyses or documents that substantiate' Toyota's claim that electronic malfunctions are not causing sudden unintended acceleration. The documents that Toyota provided in response to this request did not provide convincing substantiation. We explained our concerns about the failure of Toyota to substantiate its assertions in our letter to you on February 22, 2010.
>
> After we sent our letter on February 22, Toyota provided a few additional documents to the committee early in the morning on the day of the hearing. Several of these documents were written in Japanese. While some of these documents appear to contain preliminary fault analyses that *could be used in planning a rigorous study of potential cause of sudden unintended acceleration, not one of them suggested that such a rigorous study had taken place.* As we explained in our February 22

> letter, the only document Toyota has provided to the committee that claims to study the phenomenon of sudden unintended acceleration in a comprehensive way, is an interim report from the consulting firm Exponent, Inc. This report has serious deficiencies, as we explained in our February 22 letter. [Italics added.]

- We do not understand the basis for Toyota's repeated assertions that it is 'confident' there are no electronic defects contributing to incidents of sudden acceleration.

While this was a polite way of telling Toyota that the committee wasn't buying the company's claims, it also suggests a committee stymied by stonewalling tactics of a foreign corporation regarding a problem that was continuing to destroy American lives.

- While some documents appear to contain preliminary fault analyses that could be used in planning a rigorous study of the potential cause of sudden unintended acceleration, not one of them suggested that such a rigorous study had taken place.

The committee's reference to a "preliminary fault analyses that could be used in planning a rigorous study of the potential cause of sudden acceleration" will become important when we take a closer look at some fundamental problems with throttle-by-wire electronics. But that is to again get ahead of our story.

The Waxman/Stupak letter ended with a polite but pointed criticism of Toyota's tactics.

> Sudden unintended acceleration in vehicles is a serious and highly dangerous event. Our preliminary assessment is that Toyota resisted the possibility that electronic defects could cause safety concerns, relied on a flawed engineering report, and made misleading public statements concerning the adequacy of recent recalls to address the risk of sudden

unintended acceleration. We hope that tomorrow's hearing provides the Committee with additional information about Toyota's response to incidents of sudden unintended acceleration over the past decade.

Sincerely,
Henry A. Waxman
Chairman

Bart Stupak
Chairman Subcommittee on Oversight and Investigations

While the Waxman/Stupak Committee focused on Toyota's evasive tactics, a U.S. Senate committee was gearing up to find out exactly what the DOT and NHTSA were doing to protect the public from runaway cars.

CHAPTER 80

# SENATORIAL JABS

### TOYOTA TECHNICIANS INVESTIGATE CAR IN RESTAURANT CRASH

SEATTLE—Technicians are investigating a runaway Lexus that rammed into a restaurant last week.

Both the runaway car and the damaged restaurant belong to the Lee family, who are angry at Toyota. They are convinced the carmaker is hiding critical information about the crash.

Hyekeong Lee was pulling into the parking lot of the Kalbi Grill Express last week when her Lexus RX350 reportedly accelerated out of control and crashed into the building.

"My daughter said, 'Mom, what are you doing?' So I said, 'Oh, brake doesn't work,'" she said, adding she was certain she hit the brakes. "Yes, so many times."

On Thursday Toyota technicians allowed KOMO News to watch their initial physical inspection.

But when they started downloading crash information from the vehicle's event data recorder, Toyota officials didn't let anyone—not even the Lees—take photos or video.

And the Lees don't trust Toyota to tell the truth.

"COULD BE YOUR FAMILY," said Tony Lee. "COULD BE YOU."

*KOMO News*, July 13, 2012

**ON MARCH 2, 2010, SENATOR JAY ROCKEFELLER OF WEST VIRGINIA** opened hearings into Toyota's floor mat and sticky pedal recalls that offer unsettling evidence of the limitations on Congressional power to learn whether regulatory agencies created and funded by Congress, like NHTSA, are actually fulfilling their public duties. The political tension that permeated the hearings is captured in Senator Rockefeller's opening remarks:

> At its core, today's hearing is about millions of Americans who drive to work, drive to a grocery store or car-pool their kids to school and other activities every day. It's about their safety and their security, and nothing is more important than that. We are all here today because we know that something has gone terribly wrong. *The system meant to safeguard against faulty vehicles has failed and needs to be fixed, and it needs to be fixed right away.*

How tragic that it took thirty years for Congress to finally recognize that the DOT/NHTSA have allowed every man, woman and child that gets near an automobile to remain at the mercy of the car industry regarding throttle control electronics. But Senator Rockefeller was only getting warmed up:

*This is an important hearing,* one to which we have dedicated an entire day. We've never done that before that I can remember, to one subject, so that we can examine the problems and get to the solutions. It is most immediately about the Toyota recalls, but, more broadly, and just as urgently, *it's about the safety oversight system and how to fix it.*

It's not just for some future problem, but right now, in order to get to the *bottom of the dangers of sudden acceleration, which are not addressed in the recalls.* I believe the way we respond to this serious situation will and must have a lasting impact on the carmaker and its employees, on the *federal agency overseeing safety,* and the confidence of the public for years to come. This morning's hearing will focus on the government's role and this afternoon we will focus on the company's role in this very serious situation.

Rockefeller now became pointed:

It's clear that somewhere along the way, public safety took a back seat and corporate profits drove the company's decisions. If Toyota wants to remain successful and regain consumer confidence and trust, it needs to find this balance once again . . . .

It is also apparent that the government's NHTSA did not fulfill its responsibility in the past, and has more to do in the present, and needs greater resources and authority in the future. NHTSA's actions and inactions in the years leading up to today are deeply troubling. The American people count on NHTSA to protect them and to provide them with clear and reliable safety information, and even today that picture is not clear. And what's more, the American people do not yet clearly understand how this happened and how it will be solved—which defects have been addressed and what

> dangers remain, and what recalls are fixing and what they are not fixing. So we need to look back and focus forward . . . .
>
> We will hear from NHTSA and DOT officials why they did not adequately connect the dots about the safety situation and why they did not move aggressively to investigate. But I also want to know NHTSA's plan to get to the bottom of sudden acceleration, industry-wide, and to make sure that it has the resources and authority to fulfill that mission . . . .

Which defects have been addressed? What dangers remain? What recalls are fixing and what they are not fixing? While these insightful questions undoubtedly made the DOT/NHTSA squirm, no Congressional Committee, unfortunately, has the resources required to pry loose secrets a major multinational corporation is determined to conceal. Indeed, this book represents the first attempt by anyone to systematically dig deeply into an automotive problem that has probably caused at least 100,000 serious injuries just in the United States. How sobering, moreover, that this book is the work of a handful of people in a small Midwestern town, a fact that illustrates how vulnerable we are when the federal government decides to leave us to the tender mercies of a powerful industry. If this book proves anything, it is that dangerously designed automotive electronics will continue to threaten our safety until the existing regulatory apparatus is overhauled from top to bottom. Is that a realistic possibility? Until recently, I might have said "no." But, on the very day this chapter was written, events were unfolding that may herald the beginning of the end of this automotive carnage. But for now, let us find out what happened when DOT Secretary, Ray LaHood, appeared before this Senate Committee.

CHAPTER 81

# BLUSTER BEFORE THE SENATE

### TOYOTA RECALL: REPORTS OF RUNAWAY CARS

### FOUR DEAD IN DALLAS CRASH WHERE PROBLEM FLOOR MATS FOUND IN TRUNK

Toyota, which launched the largest auto recall in U.S. history last fall after incidents of random acceleration resulting in fatalities, has just announced an additional recall of 2.3 million vehicles to correct sticking accelerator pedals.

. . . In the most tragic incident, on the day after Christmas, four people died in Southlake, Texas, a suburb of Dallas, where a 2008 Toyota sped off the road, through a fence and landed upside down in a pond. The car's floor mats were found in the trunk of the car, where owners had been advised to put them as part of the recall. "There's one thing that didn't cause the accident," said Southlake police spokesman Lt. Ben Brown.

*ABC News,* Jan 21, 2010

**TRANSPORTATION SECRETARY RAY LAHOOD BEGAN HIS APPEARANCE** before the Senate on a self-congratulatory note:

> **LaHood:** One of the hallmarks of my time as Transportation Secretary has been our work on distracted driving. For all of you with cell phones and Blackberries and other electronic devices, I'm on a rampage about people talking and texting while driving a car, bus, train or plane. It's a menace to society and we certainly have exercised our authority to ban truck drivers from texting while driving.

LaHood's political posturing continued:

> [T]he Toyota recall situation is very serious and we are treating it seriously. Three recalls involving Toyota are among the largest in automobile history, affecting more than six million people in this country. And I would like to say a word directly to consumers: first, if you notice that your gas pedal or your brake is not responding as it normally would, contact your Toyota dealer right away.

Although this played into Toyota's hands by implying to the world that the company's voluntary recalls had corrected the problem, LaHood was soon skating on thin ice:

> The recent recalls involve first, accelerator pedal entrapment by floor mats which can lead to uncontrolled acceleration at very high speeds. It's important to take your floor mats out of the driver's side of your vehicle until your car has been repaired for this problem by a Toyota dealer; and second, accelerator pedal sticking or returning slowly after being depressed. If the pedal is harder to depress or slow to return after releasing, this could be the precursor to what is known as sticky pedal. If your pedal has

> these symptoms, contact your Toyota dealer immediately. If your gas pedal becomes stuck for any reason, steadily apply the brake, put the car in neutral, bring it to a stop in a safe place and call your dealer.

LaHood was apparently unaware that two weeks earlier the Waxman/Stupak Committee had found that the overwhelming majority of occurrences reported to Toyota could not possibly be explained by either floor mats or sticky pedals. That is consistent at least with this next bit of bluster from the DOT secretary:

> I want everyone to know that the National Highway Traffic Safety Administration has the most active defect investigation program in the world. Known as NHTSA, its job is to investigate complaints and to look for defects. It receives more than 30,000 complaints from consumers every year and reviews every one of those complaints quickly. We don't ignore any of them. We examine them all. We look up all of them very carefully.

This unsolicited, self-serving commercial for the DOT and NHTSA suggests that the agency had actually been studying the flood of reports that followed Toyota's introduction of by-wire electronics ten years earlier. We know, however, that NHTSA at this point was systematically disregarding *any occurrence that lasted longer than a second.* While LaHood cannot be faulted for not knowing the details of how the ODI was being run, it is clear that he had done little or nothing to learn for himself why NHTSA found itself in the Congressional crosshairs. That's what made remarks like this next one particularly embarrassing:

> In January, our new Administrator, David Strickland, who's with me today, and Ron Medford, now our Deputy Administrator, told the President of Toyota North America

> in no uncertain terms that we expect prompt action following the disclosure of the sticky pedal problem. Toyota publicly announced that recall two days later. I personally talked to Mr. Toyoda prior to him coming to the United States and emphasized this is very serious.

This shows that LaHood was apparently unaware that (a) reports turned over to the Waxman/Stupak Committee showed there was no evidence of a sticky pedal in the overwhelming majority of these reports; and that, in any event, (b) Toyota's legal counsel had acknowledged that a sticky pedal *could not possibly cause a sudden acceleration.* As if mentioning that NHTSA had scolded Toyota's North American President wasn't embarrassing enough, LaHood's next claim was enough to make a gorilla blush:

> Regarding potentially fatal defects on the road, NHTSA has pressed hard to expedite these safety fixes. If NHTSA had opened a formal investigation and Toyota had resisted a recall, this would have consumed an enormous amount of time and resources in effect extending the period in which owners of affected vehicles were at risk. By engaging Toyota directly and persuading the company to take action, the agency avoided a lengthy investigation that would have delayed fixes for a year or more.

There is something surreal about the claim that NHTSA had persuaded Toyota to "fix" something that Toyota's legal counsel had acknowledged could not cause a "sudden, high-speed acceleration." Although LaHood would have been wise to quit while he was behind, he chose instead to continue making the hole he was in even deeper:

> Some people believe that electromagnetic interference has a dangerous effect on these vehicles, and although we are

> not aware of any incidents proved to be caused by such interference, NHTSA is now doing a thorough review of that subject to insure safety because *we've heard from enough members of Congress that they think that this is a problem.* So we're going to look into and review the electronics on these cars. If NHTSA finds a problem, we'll make sure that it's resolved.

At this point, there were literally thousands of highly credible runaway car reports on file at NHTSA for which, as the Waxman/Stupak Committee had pointed out, the only logical explanation was "electronic defects." Indeed, that is what makes LaHood's comments about electromagnetic interference an unwitting indictment of the federal government's abject failure to protect the public from one of the most dangerous problems in automotive history:

- *Some people believe that electromagnetic interference has a dangerous effect on these vehicles . . . .*

It is a good bet that this assertion came directly from the ODI through Strickland to LaHood. If so, it reveals how dangerous minor functionaries in a government bureaucracy can be if they have the power to promote an ingrained institutional bias at the public's expense.

- *We are not aware of any incidents proved to be caused by such interference.*

This simply repeated the insipidly false claim that "if it can't be found by inspecting components, it can't be EMI." Again, it seems likely that this bit of industry-sponsored propaganda came from people determined to keep NHTSA from being exposed as the car industry's "lap poodle."

- *NHTSA is now doing a thorough review of that subject [EMI] to ensure safety because we've heard from enough members of Congress that they think that this is a problem.*

Was this an indication that the rumblings of Congress might finally convince the DOT/NHTSA to stop coddling car companies and start protecting the lives and safety of people? Stay tuned.

CHAPTER 82

# A NEAR DEATH EXPERIENCE

### ANALYSIS FINDS UNEASY MIX IN AUTO INDUSTRY AND REGULATION

A *Washington Post* analysis shows that as many as 33 former National Highway Traffic Safety Administration employees and Transportation Department appointees left those jobs in recent years and now work for automakers as lawyers, consultants, and lobbyists and in other jobs that deal with government safety probes, recalls and regulations . . . . But critics of the revolving-door-practice say that it has contributed to flaws in federal oversight and enforcement.

*The Washington Post*, March 9, 2010

**"[C]RITICS OF THE REVOLVING-DOOR-PRACTICE SAY THAT IT HAS** contributed to flaws in federal oversight and enforcement." Talk about understatements. NHTSA's Administrator from 1983 to

1989, Diane Steed, became a consultant for auto industry front groups; Jerry Curry, "the man who would be President," became an expert witness for automobile manufacturers after serving from 1989 to 1993 as Administrator; another administrator, Marion Blakely, became the owner of a public relations firm representing auto industry interests; and the beat went on. In the meantime, a secret and deadly game of automobile roulette spread like a disease around the world, and all because the best-funded car safety agency on the planet betrayed the trust of the American public.

One person lucky enough to survive the consequences of this betrayal was Rhonda Smith, who told her story to the Congressional Committee on Oversight and Government reform:

> I am writing these words to try and convey some of *my feelings of a near death experience,* which occurred on October 12, 2006 between approximately 10:50 and 11 a.m.
>
> On this Thursday, I had planned on visiting my 85-year-old father in Doxville. I was driving my 2007 Lexus ES350 from my home in Sevierville down Highway 66 to I-40 East. Upon entering I-40 I accelerated with everyone else, into the flow of traffic. At this point, I merged over into the second lane, not going into passing gear.
>
> It is at this time I lost all control of the acceleration of the vehicle. The car went into passing gear and the cruise light came on. At this time, I'm thinking that maybe the cruise is what has caused the car to accelerate, as my foot is not on the gas pedal. I take off the cruise control. The car continues to accelerate, and is now up to 80 mph. The brakes do not slow the car at all. Now I am at 85-90 mph. I push the car into neutral and it makes a revving noise. I push the emergency brake on, but nothing helps. I continue hitting and slamming the brakes. Now I'm at 85-

> 90 mph. I look at the traffic ahead to see if I can maneuver in and out of the upcoming cars and trucks, or if I'm going to need to put the car into the guardrail and into the trees.
>
> The last time I looked at the speedometer it read 100 mph. At this time, I had the emergency brake on while frantically shifting between all the gears besides park, but I mainly had it in reverse with the emergency brake on. I finally figured the car was going to go to its maximum speed and was praying to God to please help me. After about three miles had passed, I thought it was my time to die, and I called my husband on Bluetooth. I knew he couldn't help me in this particular situation, but I just needed to hear his voice. What an awful 9-1-1 call he received at work.
>
> I had not tried anything different than I had frantically tried before to slow the vehicle, yet the car began to slow down ever so slowly. It slowed enough for me to pull to the left median, with the motor still revving up and down. At 35 mph it would not shut off.
>
> Finally, at 33 mph I was able to turn the engine off. However, the radio remained and I was not about to touch any button in that car ever again.

Rhonda Smith was extraordinarily lucky because after three desperate miles her car for some reason slowed to 33 mph, and she was able to "turn the engine off." The reaction of her dealer to this near death experience illustrates a particularly iniquitous aspect of the industry's behavior:

> The dealership was told this story and they advised they would thoroughly check it out. After several weeks we were advised they could find nothing wrong with the car. We refused to accept this answer and attempted to let

> Toyota know by phone that we felt they had an electronics issue that could lead to serious injury and death. Toyota advised they would check on our situation and contact us. After a week to ten days we had not received a call back. We called again and got the same story of "we will check and contact you as soon as possible." This happened the same way several times over the next few weeks and we finally forced a written reply from them that stated, and I quote, "*when properly maintained, the brakes will always override the accelerator.*"

While telling the Smiths that "properly maintained brakes will always override the accelerator" was an insult, it was also the result governmental indifference that the Smiths had experienced "up close and personal" when they turned for help to NHTSA.

> During this time we contacted NHTSA and after some prodding, we were contacted by Mr. Steve Chan and Mr. D. Scott Yon, safety defects engineers. This was about the middle of March, 2007.
>
> Mr. Yon took over our claim and seemed to be very receptive to our concerns for this sudden unintended acceleration causing serious injury and possibly death. We furnished pictures of the car and documentation of what had transpired since October 2006. On April 11, 2007, Mr. Yon flew to Knoxville, and drove to Sevierville to inspect our vehicle. It had been towed to the local car dealer's lot and secured for Mr. Yon's inspection. He seemed to arrive with the pre-conceived idea to sell to us that it was a floor mat problem. We continually insisted that it was not the mats, but instead somewhere in the electronics. Mr. Yon took the vehicle on a short drive with my husband. He performed several tests at the speed of 50 mph or less. These tests

> included placing the car in neutral while accelerating, and trying to stop the vehicle with the accelerator engaged and the foot brake fully applied. The transmission did disengage when put in neutral, but the car would not come to a complete stop with the foot brake engaged. Upon returning it to the car lot, Mr. Yon and my husband placed the vehicle on a hydraulic lift and removed the wheels and tires. All of the *brake pads were totally burnt up and the rotors and drums were ruined. Eventually this was something we had to pay to repair ourselves.*
>
> After insisting it was "probably" floor mats, Mr. Yon issued his final report and put the blame on the floor mats. These floor mats were a heavy gauge rubber mat placed on top of the summer mats by the dealer. It would have taken a magic trick for this mat to turn up enough or slide forward enough to cause this sudden unintended acceleration. The report was issued on May 2, 2007. In it Mr. Yon claimed to have performed a test with the floor mat in our presence that would show cause for the floor mat to be blamed. *This was never demonstrated to us or shown to us that it could ever happen accidentally. Once again we advised NHTSA and Mr. Yon that this sudden unintended acceleration problem was going to eventually cause the loss of life and serious injury.*

The spectacle of a bureaucratic lightweight ignoring burned out brake pads while insisting to people who were helping to pay his salary that the problem was floor mat interference, should be enough to cool the ardor of even the most rabid deregulator.

Rhonda Smith ended her testimony on a poignant note:

> In summary, we would like to inform this Committee and the American public that we feel we put forth our best

> effort in 2006 and 2007 to inform Toyota Motor Company and NHTSA of the potential for sudden unintended acceleration to become a deadly issue . . . .

We will end this chapter with the testimony of Kevin Haggerty before the Committee on Oversight and Government Reform regarding his experience in a 2007 Toyota Avalon:

> On December 28, 2009 I was driving to work on Route 78 in New Jersey. The car began to accelerate without my foot on the gas pedal. As I pushed on the brake, the car continued to accelerate. At that time I was not able to stop my vehicle by pressing on the brake pedal. The only way I was able to slow the car down was to put the car into neutral. I got off at the next exit which was the exit for the dealership. Determined to get the car to the dealership and show them firsthand that this was happening, I drove approximately five miles by alternating from neutral to drive and pressing very firmly on the brakes. On my way there I called them and asked for the service manager to meet me outside. As I pulled into the front of the dealership, I put the car into neutral and exited the car. With the brakes smoking from the excessive braking and the car's rpms racing, the manager entered my car. He confirmed that the gas pedal was not obstructed, the mats were properly in place and that the rpms were very high. They contacted a Toyota technician to come to the dealership and look at my car. He arrived within a few hours.
>
> The dealership had my car for one and one half weeks. When I was told the car was ready to be picked up, I asked what problem they had found. I was told by the service manager that "per Toyota" they replaced the throttle body and accelerator assembly including one or two of the

> sensors. Since they could not tell me exactly what problem they found with these parts and why they were replaced, I started doing some research about Toyotas online. I came across Sean Kane's name in multiple articles I read and decided to contact him. When I reached him, I explained my situation and expressed my fear of driving this car in light of what just happened. I no longer felt safe in it since nobody could explain why the acceleration problem occurred in the first place. Sean did not have an answer for the cause and was surprised that the dealership replaced parts and witnessed it firsthand.
>
> I was then contacted by *ABC News* and they were interested in doing a follow-up story on accelerator problems. ABC also confirmed with Toyota that the parts taken out of my car were sent to Toyota's corporate offices to be evaluated. I agreed to an interview mainly because I wanted to help people understand how to safely stop a car by putting it into neutral. I continued driving my car out of necessity but refused to put my children in it . . . .

That Kevin Haggerty finally turned to *ABC News* for help in making people aware of how to safely stop a runaway car, is an indictment of every DOT Secretary and NHTSA Administrator who has pocketed taxpayer money without lifting a finger to prepare people for such a dangerous emergency. Perhaps this book will remind people appointed to run regulatory agencies that they risk disgrace if they put their own careers ahead of their public duties.

Finally, Haggerty's reference to Sean Kane will become important after we examine events that occurred shortly after the Congressional hearings.

CHAPTER 83

# A PRESS CONFERENCE

**APPLE FOUNDER WOZNIAK SAYS TOYOTA TROUBLE IS ELECTRONIC**

Toyota says it has received dozens of complaints about brake problems with its popular Prius hybrid—which has not been recalled—from customers in the U.S. and Japan, a company spokeswoman said Wednesday. The announcement comes after comments from Apple co-founder Steve Wozniak on Tuesday that his Prius regularly sped up while in cruise-control. Wozniak suggested in media interviews that Toyota's troubles with a defective accelerator pedal may have to do with software, after his Prius sped up while in cruise-control. The automaker was investigating the complaints, which involve the new Prius model rolled out last year, a Toyota spokeswoman said on Wednesday. "As of the end of last year, we had dozens of complaints from dealers in Japan and North America," said Toyota spokeswoman Mieko Iwasaki.

*Foxnews.com*, February 03, 2010

**TOYOTA'S DISSEMBLING WITH CONGRESS CONVINCED ME TO RETAIN** a public relations firm in Washington, D.C. to manage a press conference at which Keith Armstrong, Dr. Antony Anderson, and a colleague of theirs, Dr. Brian Kirk, a computer expert, could enlighten the media about the problems with Toyota's electronics. When we arrived for the event on March 23, 2010 at the National Press Club, television cameras from around the world were crowded into the back of the room, while about 300 news outlets were waiting for our presentation on the internet. The live audience included the National Press, car magazines, car company representatives, automotive safety experts, lawyers, and engineers. About ten minutes before we began, I asked Hike for suggestions.

"Everybody's heard about greedy trial lawyers like us who pick deep corporate pockets with frivolous lawsuits, so I recommend that you let the experts do the talking."

"Not to worry, Hike," I laughed, "our distinguished moderator, Joan Claybrook, has enjoined me not to open my well-traveled mouth."

Several minutes later, Ms. Claybrook took the podium and introduced the program:

> Good morning. My name is Joan Claybrook. I'm the former Administrator of the National Highway Traffic Safety Administration and I'm President Emeritus of Public Citizen. We're here today to hear from three electronics experts who will demystify some of the electronics issues concerning Toyota sudden acceleration. They will

> challenge Toyota's claim of redundancy in the electronic systems and explain why testing for the electronic problem does not work.
>
> This contentious issue is at the heart of the Department of Transportation's investigation of sudden acceleration of over five million Toyota vehicles that Toyota claims experienced this problem because of floor mats. Toyota has sworn under oath to Congress that their vehicles do not have an electronics problem, they have told the Department of Transportation this on numerous occasions in response to requests in writing for specific answers and they have made this claim publicly in press conferences and with elaborate demonstrations. *If Toyota is misleading the government, the investigators and the Congress, it is liable for criminal penalties under 18 U.S.C. 1001. Thus, we can count on Toyota to continue to deny that any electronics problem is causing sudden acceleration and so we must turn to experts who can dissect these issues for us.*

As Claybrook spoke, I sensed that interest in our program was building:

> Today we have three electronics experts from the United Kingdom who do consulting all over the world in transportation and other areas. Mr. Keith Armstrong, an expert in electronics and electromagnetic compatibility, will make the initial presentation. We will also hear from Dr. Antony Anderson, an electrical engineering expert, and Brian Kirk, an electronics system expert. Also speaking will be Clarence Ditlow, Director of the Center for Auto Safety. And to tell his story about his runaway Toyota Tacoma that rolled over several times, went airborne and rolled over again is a sudden acceleration survivor, Frank

Visconi. He is a retired Chief Operations Officer of the National Insurance Crime Bureau, who will be available for interviews after the press conference.

I want to thank Tom Murray of Sandusky, Ohio who introduced us to these experts. Mr. Murray is a philanthropist, an author, and a lawyer turned activist who in his practice has specialized in uncovering problems causing sudden acceleration in Ford Motor vehicles and also recently became counsel in several Toyota cases. We will begin with Mr. Armstrong.

The three British experts had prepared a crisp PowerPoint presentation analyzing safety-related flaws in Toyota's electronics. Keith Armstrong, who spoke for the group, stressed these salient points:

- "By-wire" electronics removed direct control of the throttle from the driver. No longer was there a direct mechanical link between the accelerator pedal and the throttle. Instead, sensors on the gas pedal sent signals to the electronic throttle and engine control, making the engine control computer the intermediary between the driver and the throttle. This change created a host of dangerous new failure possibilities against which there was no "failsafe" protection in Toyota's "by-wire" electronics.
- These electronics are susceptible to computer glitches that disappear after the fact.
- Computer programmers cannot make automotive software "bug" free.
- Conventional automotive testing cannot identify many kinds of EMI-induced faults.
- There are well-established design and testing techniques used in other industries that car companies could employ at a

reasonable cost to make their electronics safe. Congress should mandate that NHTSA promulgate rules, in consultation with the Institute of Electrical and Electronic Engineers in New York, requiring automakers to comply with standards for electronic safety established by other industries.

- Rather than pursuing its disastrous present course, it was critical that NHTSA obtain from Toyota the safety specifications, software source codes, hardware design schematics, and test specifications that electronics experts could use to identify all potential failure mechanisms and conditions with the potential to cause or contribute to a potentially catastrophic malfunction. This was essentially the failure analysis approach of other industries that manufacture electronic equipment with the potential to fail catastrophically if they are not designed with failsafe protection against that possibility.

Following Keith's presentation, Clarence Ditlow made a stunning announcement:

> Today we posted documents on our website showing that in 1986-87, . . . . NHTSA found a Toyota Cressida which would occasionally suddenly accelerate, so they knew it was a bad vehicle. They took the Cressida to their Vehicle Research Test Center in Ohio, where they determined it had something to do with the cruise control computer, although they could never find what the failure mode was in the computer. All they knew was that if they took the cruise control computer from a bad Cressida and put it into a good Cressida, the two vehicles would switch their roles.
>
> Toyota demanded that the agency give it the computer to take to Japan to analyze. Once it was there, Toyota

determined that in fact there was a flaw in the computer which NHTSA could not find. NHTSA asked Toyota to do a recall because they had found Toyota had installed a failsafe circuit in the computer in later models that would prevent the acceleration. Toyota's response to NHTSA was just because we do a design change that improves the performance of the vehicle doesn't mean there's a safety defect. *Toyota told NHTSA the demand for a recall was absurd. Just as Toyota is saying to NHTSA today; if we can't find it, the request for a recall is absurd.*

I was still grappling with Ditlow's revelation when he added to my astonishment:

> The agency also explored the very problems that Mr. Armstrong was looking at today and they required Toyota to produce information on their EMI testing, their electromagnetic comparability procedures in the vehicles, and they forewarned that with the increasing complexity in electronic controls in vehicles, we're going to see more and more failures in those systems leading to safety consequences such as unintended acceleration. Unfortunately, Toyota turned over some information to the government and, just as they are doing now, they claimed that it was proprietary. The public has never seen what Toyota submitted to the agency in the 1980s or in the 2000s in terms of electromagnetic compatibility and EMI and, indeed, the computer programming in the vehicles themselves.

This put to rest any lingering doubts I may have had about whether NHTSA during the 1980s knew that EMI posed a serious sudden acceleration risk, but chose to protect carmakers rather than people. What else could explain allowing Volkswagen of America to unilaterally decide what records pertaining to sudden accelerations in the Audi 5000 the agency would be allowed to see? (See Chapter Forty-Nine.)

But I digress because Ditlow had another zinger:

> We did an analysis of recent recalls; and the trend is to reprogram the computer in the vehicle and on our website we have a listing of nine exemplary recalls, three of which involved an electronic transmission in which a cell phone can trigger the transmission to shift gears. So in other words, yes indeed, there are recalls to show that interference will cause electronic malfunctions. And the correction for that was to reprogram the computer in those vehicles. In addition, there are seven other recalls that we have cited including two of which, one by General Motors, one by Volkswagen in which computer malfunctioning can cause the throttle to open and the correction once again was to reprogram the computer. There are other examples of failures in other critical systems that resulted in recalls and the answer was to reprogram the computer. And so for any company to say that it can't happen, well it happened in the 80s, it's happening now and we need to get to the bottom of this and do the type of electronic investigation that Mr. Armstrong and the other experts have suggested needs to be done to pinpoint the problem . . . .

That GM and Volkswagen had reprogrammed computers confirmed for Molly that the real purpose of Toyota's sticky pedal and floor mat recalls was to get rid of "bugs" it had discovered in its software.

A high point occurred during the question and answer period when Antony Anderson held up an accelerator pedal from a

Toyota model. The effect was electric, as everyone in the room edged forward in their seats to get a better look, as Dr. Anderson displayed his teaching skills:

> I'll just take you through this. Here is a typical electronic pedal mechanism. The pedal looks exactly the same as a manual system, except you have here a sensor which measures throttle position. If you want to examine this afterwards, you will notice that there are places where moisture could get in and, more significantly, there are places underneath where moisture can also get in because this is not a hermetically sealed package.
>
> If we take a close look at this accelerator pedal, we can see one little rectangular, black chip with 14 pins, or connectors, on it. Now the two sensors are controlled by that chip. Although they are not electrically connected, they are on the same chip. The important thing is that the leads that come out through the end I'm pointing to go back to the engine control computer, which means that these leads are connected all the way by magnetic coupling. In other words, you have transient impulses or, if you prefer, electromagnetic interference, coming into these leads from somewhere else in the engine, that can affect both sensors equally.
>
> *As Dr. Gilbert pointed out [to Congress], the problem is that the failure software might detect a single fault if one of the sensors goes wrong, but if both sensors go wrong from a common cause such as EMI, the difference between them remains the same.* By way of an example, if you put a magnet close to these leads, you'll get voltage changing equally on both and the fault detection code won't pick it up because it will look just as if you moved the pedal with the same voltage potential. Unfortunately, the strategy for

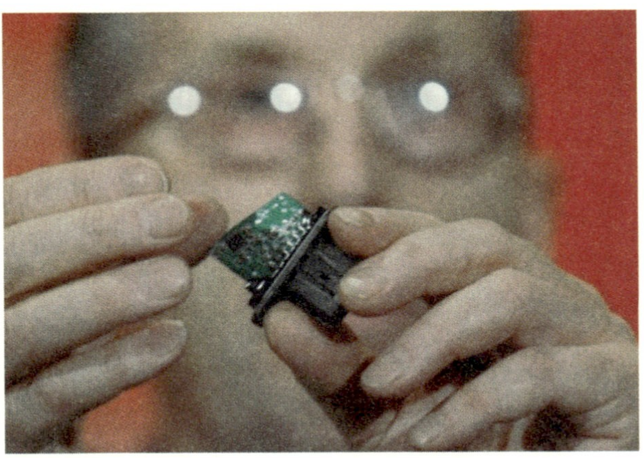

*http://cosmiclog.nbcnews.com/_news/2010/04/02/4351196-cars-vs-cosmic-rays?lite*

> detecting faults in this design doesn't cover all possible failure potentials, and that's the reason it should have failsafe protection for all potential failure modes built into the design. (Dr. David Gilbert's testimony is discussed in an upcoming chapter.)

We'll come back to Dr. Gilbert's testimony to Congress when it comes time to take a close look at the problems with drive-by-wire electronics.

We were cautioned that a press conference longer than 30 minutes would turn off the media. But people were still asking questions and passing the little pedal sensor from hand to hand around the room, turning it over, examining it, and repeatedly photographing it, long after the press conference ended. It became quite a celebrity and appeared in newspapers around the world.

Following the conference, the three Brits and I visited the staffs of three Congressional Committees investigating Toyota's problems, each of which showed a keen interest in what we had to say. We were also pleased to learn that the Library of Congress had asked for a DVD of our press conference.

Joan Claybrook called later to say she had arranged a meeting for us with NHTSA representatives the following day. When I invited Hike to join us, he recoiled: "No way! In my opinion, NHTSA is doing everything possible to hide the truth. Why else would they keep bringing up floor mats after Keith Armstrong told them basically what your panel said? I don't trust myself to be in the same room with those people, and I'll be surprised if they don't make your blood pressure go through the roof."

"I suspect you're right, Hike, but Joan Claybrook is trying to do what she can to help us expose what's going on."

Hike was skeptical. "Good luck, and don't forget to take your blood pressure medicine."

It turned out to be good advice.

CHAPTER 84

# IN "RIP VAN WINKLE'S DEN"

### A TOUGHER CAR SAFETY AGENCY

> The recall of millions of Toyota cars and trucks because of persistent problems of uncontrolled acceleration has exposed unacceptable weaknesses in the regulatory system. These weaknesses are allowing potentially fatal flaws to remain undetected. Democrats in Congress are pushing legislation to improve regulation and oversight of auto safety. It should be passed into law without delay.
>
> *The New York Times,* July 30, 2010

**NHTSA'S SPRAWLING HEADQUARTERS REMINDED ME OF A BALL** bearing factory, an image well suited to an agency that has remained sound asleep, like Rip Van Winkle, during the revolutionary transition from mechanically-controlled cars to an era in which every safety-critical system is electronic. After we passed through the cumbersome security procedures at the entrance, we were taken to a small conference room where our group seated itself on one side of a rectangular table. Presently, several people led by John Maddox, an associate administrator, took their places on the other side of the table, leaving Maddox and me at opposite ends. Glancing ostentatiously at his watch and looking at me, Maddox announced that he had "another appointment in thirty minutes, so let's hear what your visitors have to say." I almost stood up and announced that if this disgraceful agency couldn't find more than thirty minutes for three distinguished experts who had come all the way from England to offer their help, we were wasting our time. But I bit my tongue and sank back in my seat, as the three Brits began their presentations. About ten minutes later, a man with a palpably sullen demeanor, who Maddox introduced as Jeffrey Quandt, entered the room and seated himself on NHTSA's side of the table immediately to my right. Quandt never spoke a word and maintained the pose of someone awaiting a root canal.

As the three experts took turns describing why Toyota's by-wire electronics were dangerously defective, there was a stony-faced silence on NHTSA's side of the table until Maddox interjected that NHTSA had not identified a fact pattern indicating a safety defect. I was dumbstruck. Thirty unbroken years of cars suddenly racing out of control, overpowering the brakes, crashing and leaving in their wake a trail of carnage on a scale with our losses in Afghanistan and Iraq combined, and this invincibly mindless agency couldn't detect a fact pattern showing a safety defect. It was more than I could stomach. I stood up, announced that I was writing a book about runaway cars, and if NHTSA didn't stop coddling the car industry and start protecting people from unsafe electronics, I would paint it "as the most incompetent regulatory agency in U. S. history." With that, I headed for the door. Before I got there, however, Maddox remarked, "Mr. Murray, that sounded like a threat."

Pausing at the end of the table, I looked the associate administrator in the eye and replied, "It was a threat, Mr. Maddox, but I intended it as a constructive threat"; and with that, I turned on my heel and, to punctuate my "constructive threat," slammed the door behind me.

"You can't say I didn't warn you," Hike reminded me, when I told him what happened.

The three Brits told me later they had never before experienced the kind of resistance to the truth they had sensed during that meeting. On the other hand, these highly credentialed experts felt vindicated when Congress a short time later announced that it had directed the Department of Transportation to commission research by a team of NASA engineers into the cause of Toyota's problems. Had our press conference and meetings with three Congressional Committees helped to convince Congress that a serious investigation of this automotive behavior was long overdue? Perhaps; but as we will learn soon enough, there was no way that the DOT and NHTSA were prepared to let anyone expose their betrayals of the American public.

CHAPTER 85

# CITIZEN KANE: AN INDUSTRY'S NEMESIS

## U.S. WOMAN SURVIVES RUNAWAY VEHICLE SCARE

An Iowa woman has been caught up in a police chase in Missouri as local state troopers tried to help the woman stop her 2011 Kia Sorento that allegedly had had its accelerator become stuck while travelling at more than 160km/h . . . . Two troopers from the Missouri State Highway Patrol arrived just in time to see—and record—the action unfold on Interstate 35, with one trooper following the stray Kia Sorento while the other focused on clearing a path in front of the vehicle . . . . According to police, the Sorento's brakes were burnt out, the gearbox had failed and Ubelstad was unable to remove the car's key as the vehicle employs a push button start ignition system.

*Car Advice,* August 7, 2012

**I FIRST HEARD THE NAME SEAN KANE FROM HIKE HEISKELL, WHO** described him as a "major advocate" for automotive safety. Kane cut an unusual figure in the small world of automotive defect analysis. He is not a lawyer, forensic investigator, or engineer—just a bright young man who turned his love for well-designed cars and social justice into a business that drew on the public record and other sources to analyze automotive defects. His company, Safety Research & Strategies, located in rural Rehoboth, Mass., became well known among automobile manufacturers, lawyers, the National Highway Traffic Safety Administration officials and journalists for its success in ferreting out the truth and raising the public profile of safety hazards that were causing injuries and deaths.

Kane found his niche somewhat circuitously. After graduating from Stonehill College in Easton, Massachusetts, with a political science degree, he dreamed of finding a job at Saab, a company that produced cars he admired. Instead, Kane landed his first job at a tire company in Boston, where one of his responsibilities was evaluating warranty claims. He was fascinated by the way defects came to light through warranty claims, but his training emphasized finding ways to deny claims—even if they were legitimate. He soon began looking elsewhere for a career in the automotive field that would help consumers, instead of trying to evade their problems.

Kane found it at the Center for Auto Safety (CAS), started by safety crusader Ralph Nader in 1970. He took a big pay cut to take the $18,000-a-year job as a staffer for Executive Director Clarence Ditlow. It proved to be a life-changing experience. At the Center, Kane enjoyed his first success as an auto safety advocate, forcing Volkswagen and Chrysler to recall hundreds of thousands of vehicles for heater core explosions that were causing second- and third-degree burns and crashes when drivers, startled by a gush of super-heated steam onto their feet, lost control of their vehicles. He also learned at CAS about unintended acceleration through Miriam Grant, a public relations expert in Washington, D.C., who had been injured when her Toyota Corolla suddenly accelerated from a car wash and crashed. Grant wanted to establish a network of people injured in a runaway car crash, and Kane approached Ditlow about the possibility. But the CAS didn't have the resources necessary to investigate a technically complicated defect while also supporting a victims' network. It would be another two decades before Kane would be in a position to tackle uncontrolled accelerations involving Toyota—and battle the world's number one automaker and the National Highway Traffic Safety Administration over its root causes.

Kane received a valuable education at CAS in defect trend spotting and in harnessing media pressure to make automakers correct safety problems. But, he saw few opportunities for advancement or to earn a living wage there. After 18 months, he went to work for Ralph Hoar, a former airbag lobbyist who had also done a stint at the Insurance Institute for Highway Safety. He accepted the position on the condition that he could continue his advocacy work. Ralph Hoar & Associates gained notoriety when Kane focused attention on a dangerous defect behind Nissan van fires that eventually made the company buy back the entire model line after four failed recall attempts.

In 2004, Kane with new partners started Safety Research & Strategies, Inc., with a staff possessing research skills in a range of disciplines, from library and information science to engineering, law, and journalism that allowed his small company to gain widespread recognition for its first-rate journalism covering automotive and product safety issues. SRS's newsletter and blog, *The Safety Record,* became a must-read for Washington, D.C. policymakers, the auto industry, lawyers and other journalists.

I visited Kane in June of 2012 to discuss his continuing work on Toyota unintended acceleration that has earned him respect among consumers and mainstream journalists who have tapped his depth of knowledge, and his willingness to challenge Toyota and NHTSA that the only causes are mechanical or driver error.

In July 2009, *The Safety Record* began publishing a series of stories about runaway Toyotas. The issue by then had garnered some media attention. Although NHTSA had opened several investigations, we've seen how keen the agency was to close them without finding a cause. But because these brief investigations occurred over several years and involved multiple models, nobody had yet pieced together the growing public record of unexplained incidents and fruitless government probes. Therefore, SRS was soon being asked by lawyers with Toyota cases for its assistance. Kane told me his team of people at SRS was struck by the fact that Toyota never claimed *that any of the 37,900 events reported through its telephone complaint line that it disclosed to Congress had triggered a DTC and automatically reduced engine speed to a controllable level.*

"That clinched it for us," Kane said. "We realized that NHTSA had no intention of seriously investigating Toyota's electronics. That's why it knuckled under to Toyota's claims and embraced floor mat entrapment, sticky pedals and driver error—simplistic explanations that didn't require a serious investigation."

According to Kane, "it became obvious that NHTSA's ODI was ill-motivated and poorly equipped to address complex electronic issues, and that the agency was grasping at whatever explanation Toyota served up. Adding to the problem, the agency had failed to set standards for functional safety of vehicle electronics—much the same way it had failed to regulate vehicle stability during the SUV boom in the 1980s and 1990s that led to thousands of catastrophic rollover accidents each year."

When I asked Kane to elaborate, he pointed out that throttle control systems are subject to the 1972 version of Federal Motor Vehicle Safety Standard (FMVSS) 124, which mandates that the throttle must return to neutral within one second after the driver releases pressure on the accelerator pedal. Faced with thousands of reports describing how cars rapidly accelerated after the accelerator was released, often in response to braking, the agency proposed to upgrade the standard and sought the industry's comments. The result was summarized in the *Federal Register:*

> "In general, the comments of vehicle and engine manufacturers did not address the specific questions in the notice. Instead, they voiced a preference for rescinding the standard altogether, suggesting that market forces *and litigation pressure are sufficient to assure fail-safe performance* without a Federal Motor Vehicle Safety Standard." [Italics added.]

Ironically, about the same time the industry was claiming that "litigation pressure" was "sufficient to assure fail-safe performance without a Federal Motor Vehicle Safety Standard." General Jerry Curry, "the man who would be President" (See Chapter Sixty-Three) was telling PBS *Frontline* that "because lawyers are driven by greed, they should not have a role in safety."

In any event, when NHTSA several years later again proposed changes to FMVSS 124, the industry, led by Toyota and the Alliance of Automotive Manufacturers, opposed it and, in 2004, the agency withdrew the proposed rule changes, saying it would do further research. Eight years later, spurred by Toyota's sudden acceleration crisis, the agency proposed another revision. The 2012 proposal, however, *did not address malfunctions of electronic throttle control systems,* only mechanical causes, such as floor mat entrapment of the accelerator pedal. In other words, as far as electronic malfunctions are concerned, the industry has succeeded in making this rule change all but meaningless.

In February 2010, SRS released the first in a series of reports documenting the history of Toyota sudden accelerations, as told through NHTSA investigation documents, Congressional hearings, publicly released Toyota communications and interviews with consumers who had experienced an uncontrollable acceleration in a Toyota or Lexus model.

"We wanted to alert the public that we had studied hundreds of reports that couldn't possibly be explained by anything mechanical. Up to this point, we didn't have the resources to do much more than try to help people who we felt were underdogs with compelling stories, and who were being victimized in two ways: by a car company who sold them a defective car, and by a society, whether it was law enforcement or family members who wouldn't believe them because of the myth of driver error perpetrated by the industry and NHTSA was so pervasive that no one would believe their stories, no matter how much physical evidence there was to support them. I found that repugnant; I couldn't stand it."

CHAPTER 86

# CITIZEN KANE: PART 2

### TOYOTA ACCELERATIONS REVISITED—HANGING BY A (TIN) WHISKER

A NASA paper delivered at the International Tin Whisker Symposium last year reported on tin whisker growth in Toyota accelerator pedal position sensors that, depending on pedal rate of movement, could lead to unintended acceleration.

*eetimes.com*, January 10, 2012

**DR. DAVID GILBERT WAS AN UNLIKELY WHISTLEBLOWER IN THE** Toyota runaway car controversy. An automotive electronics expert from Southern Illinois University Carbondale, with more than 30 years experience teaching automotive electronics to generations of auto techs, he had been invited by Honda to examine its Electronic Throttle Control diagnostics, and Toyota had donated vehicles to assist his university research. One of the first things Gilbert told Sean Kane when they met by phone in January 2009 was that he is a Toyota fan and owner.

"He is one of the smartest guys I've met," Kane told me, "and one of the most understated people you can imagine, especially in the world he works in. He is so careful and scientific and plodding in his work, that when he gives you something, you can go to the bank with it. He is always right, absolutely right, because he dots every 'i' and crosses every 't' before he will open his mouth."

Dr. Gilbert, who drives a Tundra, had done some informal testing out of professional and personal curiosity. What he learned greatly disturbed him: The accelerator pedal position sensors—the vehicle's major throttle input—didn't always fail safely. Because the signals in the sensors were located too close together, it didn't take much to bridge them and send a wide-open-throttle signal that the electronic control module would regard as correct. Because he felt this should never be possible, Gilbert phoned someone he knew at Toyota and reported his results, but the company's response was silence.

Out of a sense of moral obligation to report a life-threatening safety defect, Gilbert next turned to NHTSA, but the agency never responded. "That's when he turned to me," Kane explained, "hoping SRS could help him. When I asked him what we could do, he said he needed some tools to construct a demonstration. We paid him a whopping $1800 for what he needed to perform tests that turned out to be a major breakthrough in identifying what Toyota said could never happen."

Gilbert used "standard electronic testing techniques." With vehicle service information as a guide, "he back-probed the Accelerator Pedal Position (APP) connectors to tap into the supply signal and ground circuits of the sensor. He took voltmeter readings to verify the circuit integrity of the test connections. He then used an oscilloscope to visually monitor voltage changes in the APP circuits, after which he began to explore potential types of circuit abnormalities. He also painstakingly examined Diagnostic Trouble Code (DTC) detection capabilities that were supposed to recognize abnormal conditions affecting the Accelerator Pedal Position sensor, the Electronic Control Module (ECM), or short circuits between the VPA and VPA2 circuits, which are Accelerator Pedal Position signal circuits.

Kane said Gilbert had "monitored the APP signal voltages with the ignition 'Key ON-Engine OFF,' while introducing different resistances between the two APP signal circuits," and quickly found that "certain short circuit resistances between VPA and VPA2 were undetectable by the Electronic Throttle Control Module, the main by-wire computer."

Kane hired Gilbert to put together a preliminary report on the electronic weaknesses in the accelerator pedal position sensors. Gilbert, and his associate, Omar Trinidad, performed an initial analysis, producing a short technical paper summarizing their limited, but important findings, based on the standard automotive diagnostic technique they had used. They demonstrated that Toyota's diagnostics do not always pick up potentially deadly faults affecting these safety critical pedal sensors. "That cut to the core of Toyota's claim that its central control module will always detect a fault, set a Diagnostic Trouble Code and immediately reduce engine speed to a safely controllable level."

On February 2, 2010, Sean Kane and David Gilbert appeared before the House Subcommittee on Oversight and Investigations. Kane described how Gilbert's "plainspoken, Midwestern demeanor" had impressed the Committee "with the significance of his finding that a sudden acceleration in Toyota models would not always set a trouble code."

"That was so threatening to Toyota," Kane explained, "that it retained the science-for-hire firm, Exponent, to produce a report that accused Dave of demonstrating something that could not happen in the real world: But Dave never claimed that he was demonstrating a failure mechanism that was likely to happen in a car. In fact, he was quite clear that his testing was designed to find out why so many Toyota accelerations were not triggering a Diagnostic Trouble Code or immediately reducing speed to a controllable level—the so-called 'limp-home mode.' That was crucial because Toyota claimed an electronic failure would always set a fault code, and, therefore, its problems had to be due to mechanical things or driver error. Because Dave showed that wasn't true, he was a huge threat to Toyota. That's why it arranged a press conference at which Exponent's experts accused him of rigging his testing because it didn't represent something that could happen in the real world."

"Didn't the thousands of Toyota reports showing that a trouble code failed to trigger the 'limp-home mode' prove that Gilbert was right?" I asked.

"That was exactly Dave's point; but what the public heard from the media was Toyota's spin that what he did was akin to rigging tests to show something that could never occur in the real world. It took courage to do what he did, and now he's paid a heavy price. This has had a chilling effect on other scientists and academics who have critical expertise and findings to share on public safety matters."

This brings us to Sean Kane's most important contributions to this book.

CHAPTER 87

# CITIZEN KANE: PART 3

**TOYOTA PROBES TAKE A NEW TURN. INVESTIGATIONS ARE FOCUSING ON ELECTRONIC THROTTLE SYSTEMS.**

The potential for electronic defects in Toyota vehicles to cause sudden acceleration came under intensifying scrutiny Tuesday as both federal safety regulators and congressional leaders said they had begun new probes of the issue. Toyota has blamed more than 2,000 reported cases of sudden acceleration in its vehicles over the last decade on floor mats and sticky gas pedals, triggering massive recalls worldwide. The automaker has insisted that it knows of no electronic defect that could cause drivers to lose control of its vehicles. But federal safety regulators disclosed Tuesday that they had begun a "fresh review" of the electronic throttle system in Toyota and Lexus vehicles, which connect a driver's foot to the engine through sensors, computers and wires, rather

> than a mechanical link. Regulators are also considering civil fines against the automaker for its handling of the recall, an official said.
>
> *LAtimes.com*, February 2, 2010

**IN THE SPRING OF 2011, AT THE REQUEST OF CONGRESS, NHTSA** enlisted NASA engineers to conduct new research into whether electronic system malfunctions or electromagnetic interference played a role in sudden accelerations involving Toyota models. When the NHTSA/NASA report was released a year later, Secretary of Transportation Ray LaHood with much fanfare announced: "The verdict is in; there is no electronic-based cause for unintended, high-speed acceleration in Toyotas."

This bombastic proclamation was untrue. What NASA scientists actually said was:

> "Today's vehicles are sufficiently complex that no reasonable amount of analysis or testing can prove electronics and software have no errors . . . [and] . . . therefore, absence of proof that the electronic control system has caused a sudden acceleration does not vindicate the system."

I have it from reliable sources that one of the NASA scientists watching LaHood's announcement on television threw a shoe at the screen in disgust; and no wonder. These scientists had less than two months on a shoe-string budget to do their work, although that was enough to convince them that "absence of proof" from inspecting or testing components could not possibly justify LaHood's claim that "there is no electronic-based cause for unintended high-speed acceleration in Toyotas." Furthermore, these scientists were probably unaware that NHTSA's files are crammed with evidence confirming the accuracy of their conclusion that "absence of proof . . . did not vindicate . . . the safety" of Toyota's throttle control electronics. What makes one's blood boil, however, is that this evidence has been staring NHTSA in the face for three decades while it squandered millions of tax dollars looking for answers *exactly where any qualified electrical engineer could have told the agency the problem could not be found.*

One person who wasn't taken in by LaHood's embarrassing bombast was Sean Kane whose discoveries, one hopes, will help to convince Congress that unless there is a top to bottom shakeup in how NHTSA currently operates, the car industry is unlikely to invest sufficiently in electronic safety. In fact, when Kane studied NASA's report with the help of experts, it became clear that, rather than exonerating Toyota's electronics, the NASA scientists *had actually identified serious vulnerabilities to failure in its electronics.* "Unfortunately," Kane explained, "the NASA engineers were not allowed to complete their work."

"With NHTSA's reputation at stake, is there any evidence that it tried to influence the outcome?" I asked.

"Yes; in fact, Toyota made sure that the science-for-hire firm, Exponent, was available to give the ODI all the 'help' it needed to make sure NASA wouldn't do anything that might sink the ship."

"How do you know that?"

"We obtained an email via the Freedom of Information Act showing that a critical warranty data analysis was sent by an Exponent scientist Subbaiah Malladi to Jeffrey Quandt at NHTSA's ODI. This is crucial *because the warranty analysis was used in the NHTSA/NASA report to discredit the physical findings of NASA's scientists.* The email from Malladi to Quandt addresses the warranty data and how it was examined—it's very clear that *this was done by Exponent for NHTSA*, yet there is no acknowledgement in the report that Exponent was involved."

I was incredulous. "Are you sure Quandt allowed Exponent to do an evaluation of warranty data that was used to discredit these scientists?"

"You can read the email for yourself."

"But how was the warranty data used to accomplish this?"

"It's a bit convoluted, but here's a summary. Exponent postulated that an electronic malfunction that could cause a sudden acceleration not detected by a diagnostic trouble code would most likely be the result of two simultaneous or double faults, sometimes referred to as common cause failures."

"Didn't Dr. Michael Pecht tell Congress about the risk posed by double faults?"

"Yes, which is why Exponent's meddling was so pernicious."

"In what respect?"

"The NHTSA/NASA report—not the NASA scientists—accepted Exponent's assumption that most single faults would be detected and set a Diagnostic Trouble Code. Exponent also postulated that single faults should be more common than double faults which was the lynch pin Exponent needed to get Toyota off the hook."

"You'll have to explain that, Sean."

"They looked at two pools of data—customer reports and brake failure claims lodged with NHTSA in Vehicle Owner Questionnaires. Since there was no indication in that database that the reported events triggered a Diagnostic Trouble Code, they classified that data as a double-fault event. The second data pool was composed of warranty claims that represented the single-fault failures that triggered a DTC and immediately reduced speed to a level controllable by the driver."

"Where did that get them?"

Kane laughed. "You mean how did Exponent come up with a way to manipulate this data to get both Toyota and NHTSA off the hook?"

"How did it?"

"Exponent sold the idea that if the number of warranty claims was greater than the number of VOQs, that would point to the electronics. But *if there were more sudden acceleration related VOQs, that would prove the electronics were not the cause.*"

I was flabbergasted. "Are you telling me that because there were more VOQs than warranty complaints for an accelerator pedal-related problem, that exonerated Toyota's electronics?"

"Yes, and that was exactly what Exponent needed to help Toyota out of a jam, and what NHTSA needed to avoid disgrace."

"I assume you mean that with the electronics out of way, both Toyota and NHTSA were delighted to have the entire problem reduced to sticky pedals, floor mat interference or driver error."

"Exactly; and what makes that so absurd is Toyota's admission that sticky pedals and floor mat interference were possibilities in less than 20% of the reports they received, and there's little evidence to support even that figure."

"Were the NASA people aware that Toyota admitted to Congress having received thousands of sudden acceleration reports, and that it never claimed to Congress that these occurrences had tripped a trouble code that put the car in the limp-home mode?"

"I doubt it; these scientists were already extremely busy and they were given just a little more than six weeks to delve into Toyota's problems. They might have been aware of the Congressional hearings, but it's unlikely, for example, that they knew about David Gilbert's findings regarding Toyota's diagnostic trouble code, or that Toyota admitted receiving 37,900 reports through its telephone complaint line."

"What did the experts you consulted say about the NHTSA/NASA report?"

"I asked several Ph.D. scientists for their impressions of the report. They said that on first read they could understand only about 20% of it. It is an incredibly opaque report written in a way to obfuscate what was really going on. These NASA scientists have too much integrity to write a report like that, so in my opinion NHTSA's fingerprints are all over a report that might look impressive superficially, but in fact it's missing numerous crucial pieces."

"Sean, I find all this amazing."

"What's really amazing is that we heard from several sources that NHTSA referred to Toyota as a 'regulatory partner.' How's that for regulatory capture with a capital C."

"Wasn't there also a National Academy of Sciences report?"

"Yes, in 2011, DOT Secretary LaHood asked the National Academy of Sciences to appoint an independent committee to identify possible causes of unintended acceleration and make recommendations to NHTSA to 'assure the future safety of electronic throttle control and other vehicle control functions.'"

"What did they find?"

"First, to be clear, the NAS did not present a scientific report. They never did any science. Instead, they simply reviewed the record. The important thing is their conclusion that NHTSA is ill-equipped to detect problems with high tech electronics commonplace in today's cars. They called this 'troubling'—quite an understatement. They also said NHTSA needed an advisory panel to help it handle potentially serious electronic risks, and they recognized that NHTSA's credibility has been seriously damaged by its handling of Toyota's sudden acceleration crisis."

"It seems to me, Sean, that it took guts to speak out like that."

"I agree. As I see it, the challenge now is to get Congress to respond to the panel's recommendations regarding what needs to be done to finally bring NHTSA into the electronic age."

It turns out that the National Academy of Sciences was not the only entity to skewer NHTSA for its handling of runaway car disasters.

CHAPTER 88

# STATISTICS THAT WAG THE TALE

## TOYOTAS' SUDDEN ACCELERATIONS BLAMED FOR MORE DEATHS

More than 100 deaths have now been blamed on sudden acceleration of Toyota Motor Corp. vehicles, nearly twice the number that had been reported two months ago, according to a *Times* review of public records. With a recent surge of complaints to the National Highway Traffic Safety Administration factored in, sudden acceleration has been raised as a possible cause of crashes involving Toyota vehicles that led to 102 deaths, according to NHTSA records, lawsuits and police reports. Toyota has recalled millions of vehicles to repair defects it said could in rare instances cause gas pedals to stick. The company insists the electronic throttle control system in its newer vehicles is

> not to blame. "It is normal to see an increase in complaints following the kind of publicity that this issue has taken on," Toyota spokesman John Hanson said Thursday. "We are diligently going to investigate all of these claims. We are doing it with more people and we are doing it as quickly as we can. We have found no evidence at all of any electronic problems that could have led to unintended acceleration."
>
> *L.A. Times,* March 26, 2010

**FOLLOWING THE 2010 CONGRESSIONAL HEARINGS, THE DOT'S** Office of Inspector General issued a report that included the chart shown in Figure 88-1 identifying five companies that accounted for 73% of sudden acceleration reports submitted to NHTSA between 2002 and 2009. Shortly after the report was published, an *L.A. Times* story—see headnote—related finding evidence of 102 sudden acceleration-related deaths involving Toyota models in "NHTSA records, lawsuits and police reports." This was all the more remarkable because research published in 2003 showed that up to May of 2001 *only seven sudden acceleration-related deaths attributed to Toyota had been reported to NHTSA* prior to May of 2001. By comparison, the same data showed that runaway car fatalities for General Motors up to that point were 17 times greater, for Ford, ten times greater, and for Daimler-Chrysler, six times greater than Toyota's fatality rate. Even factoring in the comparatively larger market shares of the Big 3 American companies at that time, this quantum leap in Toyota's fatality rate *after May 2001 is astounding.*

Figure 88-1 also helps to put in perspective the scope of the disaster drive-by-wire electronics has caused. We've seen that the DOT's Inspector General found in a report published in January 2002 that NHTSA's database contained less than 10% of defect-related reports owners made to manufacturers. If we

| Manufacturer | Number of Complaints | Percentage of Complaints |
|---|---|---|
| General Motors | 1,966 | 14% |
| Ford | 3,018 | 22% |
| Chrysler | 1,587 | 12% |
| Toyota | 2,407 | 17% |
| Honda | 1,093 | 8% |
| Other | 3,707 | 27% |
| TOTAL: | 13,778 | 100% |

*Figure 88-1*

multiply the 2407 Toyota-related complaints in Figure 88-1 by ten, we come up with about 24,000 occurrences known to Toyota between 2002 and 2009. But that appalling number is still far short of the 39,700 reports Toyota acknowledged to Congress having received just through its telephone complaint line. But for the sake of argument, let us assume that 24,000 runaway car reports were registered with Toyota between 2002 and 2009. According to the research published in 2003, by May of 2001 NHTSA had *received 25,181 sudden acceleration reports that accounted for 5,412 injuries and 303 deaths.* If we apply this same injury and death rate to 24,000 assumed occurrences known to Toyota between 2002 and 2009, those occurrences may well have caused about 5,000 injuries and 300 deaths.

With that, let's take a final stab at getting our minds around the magnitude of the harm caused by this dreadful automotive behavior. If we multiply the 25,000 sudden accelerations reported to NHTSA by 2001 by ten, we come up with about 250,000 reports known to carmakers by May of 2001 which may have caused about 54,000 injuries and 3,000 deaths. If we also multiply by ten the 13,778 total reports to NHTSA between 2002 and 2009, carmakers would have received about 140,000 reports resulting in some 35,000 injuries and 2,000 deaths; and if we make these same extrapolations for the period from 2009 down to the present, it is possible that there have been at least 500,000 sudden accelerations reported to car companies that have caused about 100,000 injuries and more than 5,000 fatalities. While these are rough estimates, it is worth noting that Toyota's 17% share of the figures shown in Figure 88-1 multiplied by ten is quite consistent with 102 Toyota-related fatalities the *L.A. Times* found by *examining NHTSA data,* lawsuits and police reports.

Readers are entitled to ask whether these estimates take into account that many occurrences reported to NHTSA would also have been reported to a manufacturer. There are two reasons I believe a multiplier of ten is nevertheless reasonable. First, the research published in 2003 only covered reports to NHTSA that specifically used the words "sudden acceleration." Since drivers frequently describe this vehicle behavior with words like "engine surge," "engine revving," "accelerator stuck," and so on, it is clear that many more sudden accelerations were reported to NHTSA than indicated by this research published. By the same token, it is equally certain that many sudden accelerations have never been reported either to the government or a carmaker because, among other reasons, no one survived to describe what happened or because no one recognized the actual nature of the occurrence. Therefore, until someone demonstrates that multiplying reports to NHTSA by a factor of ten exaggerates the problem, I believe it can be defended as a reasonable rule of thumb.

Finally, the Inspector General's scathing critique of NHTSA found that the agency:

- Needs improvement in its defect processes.
- Has not adequately tracked, retained, or documented pre-investigation actions.

- Lacks a systematic process or criteria for identifying the need for third-party or Vehicle Research and Test Center (VRTC) assistance.
- Has not met timeliness goals for completing investigations.
- Has not properly documented investigations.
- Has not conducted a work force assessment.
- Has not developed a formal training program to keep safety skill sets current.

Any privately run company with a scorecard like this would soon be out of business. Unfortunately, with political gridlock now gripping Washington, it seems unlikely that this searing assessment of NHTSA will bring about critically needed changes anytime soon. That's unfortunate because the families of Democrats, Republicans, and Independents alike are secretly being subjected every day to a potentially lethal game of automobile roulette.

The horrendous carnage reflected in these calculations begs for an answer to why throttle-by-wire electronics are exacting such a terrible toll in the United States and around the world.

CHAPTER 89

# FATAL MISTAKES REPEATED

## FRESH TOYOTA SUIT FEATURES PANICKED CALL FOR HELP

The family of a 59-year-old woman who drowned when her 2009 Camry sped out of control and plummeted into a river near Sacramento, Calif., has sued Toyota Motor Corp., which already faces hundreds of lawsuits over deaths and injuries caused by accidents attributed to sudden acceleration . . . . She called her daughter, Sadaf Chaudhary, complaining that her vehicle's brakes weren't working. She then called 9-1-1, hysterical and speaking at times in Punjabi. "My car—river!" she told a California Highway Patrol 9-1-1 operator, who responded, "Your car is in the river?" She replied: "River, river." . . . Minutes later, the connection was lost.

*The National Law Journal*, 04-19-13

**HOW COULD AN INDUSTRY THAT EMPLOYS THOUSANDS OF ENGINEERS** and computer experts have failed so miserably to make throttle-by-wire electronics failsafe against something as dangerous as a sudden loss of throttle control? I posed that question to several experts familiar with this latest concept in automotive design, including some who appear in these pages. Up to this point in our story I have listened to the whisperings of my better angels not to forget that many readers, as is true in my case as well, do not have a technical background. Nevertheless, because it will help readers better understand how the throttle operates in today's cars and underscores the importance of the climactic chapters to follow, I will summarize what I have learned about this still-evolving technology:

*A. How throttle-by-wire electronics function when everything is working as it should*

The basic components of most throttle-by-wire electronic systems are shown in Figure 89-1 prepared by Keith Armstrong, one of the experts who has assisted me with this book. A master Electronic Control Module (ECM) directs the system, which in theory should work as follows: When the accelerator pedal is depressed, two independent sensors in the accelerator pedal detect the angle of the pedal. Each pedal sensor then sends a proportional signal to an independent computer processing unit, or CPU, that separately computes the opening angle for the throttle valve to that requested by the driver's input on the accelerator pedal.

Like the accelerator pedal, the throttle valve is fitted with two independent angle sensors that send electrical signals back to separate CPUs that continually compare their results with each other to detect mismatches with safety implications. For example, if one pedal sensor signals that the accelerator pedal is being fully

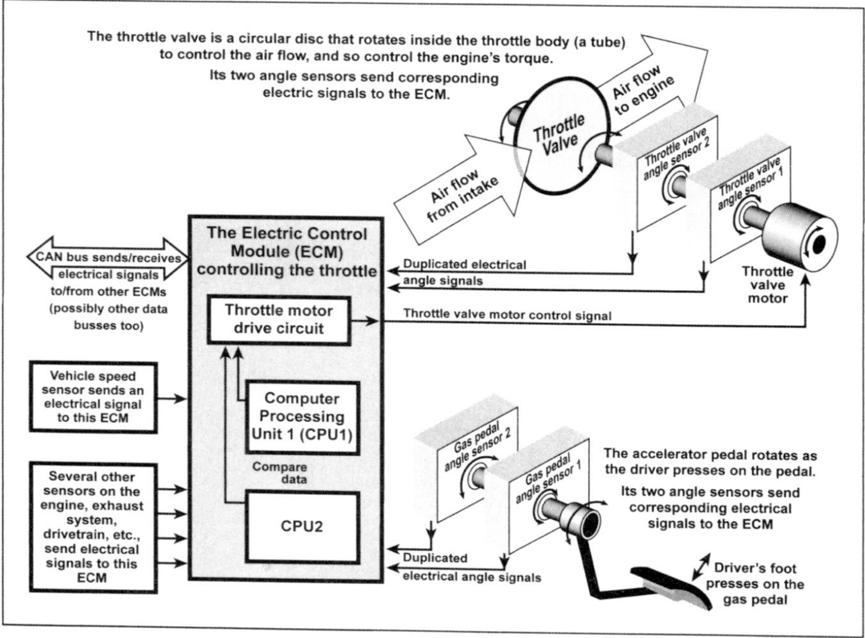

*Figure 89-1 Keith Armstrong's Diagram of ECM unit*

depressed, while the other signals that it is only partially depressed, the discrepancy tells the master ECM to immediately limit vehicle speed to about 20 mph—a so-called limp-home mode—making it possible for the driver to maneuver the car to safety. But, as with so many well-intentioned human endeavors, there can be many a slip between cup and lip in this resourceful concept.

### *B. Why throttle-by-wire can fail with catastrophic consequences*

Throttle-by-wire electronics confronted design engineers with three daunting challenges: 1) writing software capable of instantly detecting potentially dangerous faults; 2) designing hardware able to safely transmit signals between 50 and 100 interactive control modules monitored by the master ECM; and 3) safely managing hugely complex interactions between software and hardware components. In discussing these issues with Keith Armstrong and other experts, they impressed on me the following points:

1. The basic functions of hardware and software

What we call hardware encompasses a wide variety of physical components, such as resistors, capacitors, transistors and integrated circuits or "microchips." These devices are generally soldered onto printed circuit boards (PCBs) that use electrical connectors and wires to connect different PCBs to other electronic units, and to the source of their electrical power—the car's battery, and the alternator that charges it up.

The same component that has given us personal computers and smartphones—the microprocessor—has made throttle-by-wire possible in automobiles. Microprocessors, and their siblings called microcontrollers, can be programmed to process electrical signals governing a great variety of different hardware operations; and because a small range of microprocessors can be produced in large volumes—making them low-cost components—software programs can make them perform an almost infinite variety of functions.

A typical microprocessor contains hundreds of thousands of almost impossibly miniaturized transistors on a silicon chip, and is so complex that it can never be thoroughly tested. Microprocessors are controlled by a number of instruction codes, which are like a list of shopping instructions about what to buy at a grocery store. For example, the instruction "multiply input signal one by two, add it to input signal two, send the result to output signal one", would require providing the microprocessor with the codes for the three different instructions, and in a specific sequence. Providing the microprocessor with the right codes in a different order, of course, would produce a different result, as would sending different codes (e.g. subtracting signal two instead of adding it).

Software is often called "code" because it is essentially a list of codes for processing sequences performed by a microprocessor. The software for a given microprocessor is saved in a dedicated "memory IC"—a type of microchip that can store long lists of instruction codes for decades, much like we might use a piece of paper to store a list of people we've met over the years.

The great advantage of being able to store data is the flexibility it provides for modifying software. For example, if programmers discover a way to improve gas mileage by modifying the software code for the engine system, dealers can reprogram the engine control software in the vehicle to deliver better gas mileage from then on. The same principle applies to discovering safety-critical errors. If a safety-critical programming error in the software is discovered, it can be eliminated either by the manufacturer in future models or by a dealer during routine maintenance. Unfortunately, however, the software in modern automobiles is so complex that it cannot be fully tested for "bugs" in any reasonable period of time. A testing time of 20 years, for instance, would not be unusual even for a simple software program; but no carmaker can wait that long to be sure that the software code in its master Electronic Control Unit will be able to detect every potentially dangerous glitch in the system. Consequently, there is a high probability that at least some potentially dangerous "bugs" will not be discovered until it is too late, which is undoubtedly the explanation for many runaway car calamities.

2. Why do these systems require so many lines of software code?

Cars have long since ceased being simply a battery, an alternator, a few lamps and a radio. In addition to "throttle-by-wire" there are also electronic control modules for braking, steering, stability, air bag deployment, and other safety-related systems; and there are also modules for non-safety critical components such as the radio, entertainment systems, navigational displays, power windows and so on. But the problem isn't so much the number of control modules *per se*, but the immense number of electrical signals they must process instantly for the master ECM to be able to instantly detect rogue signals with failure potential.

3. Interacting control modules

The master ECM might interact with anywhere from 50 to 100 control modules located in the car body, roof, dash and just about anywhere else designers decide to put them. These modules communicate between themselves through electrical cables that are generically called "data buses". There are many different types of data buses designed for different purposes, but the type that is used to communicate safety-critical data with priority over less important signals (e.g. for changing the A/C settings) is known as the Controller Area Network bus, or CANbus.

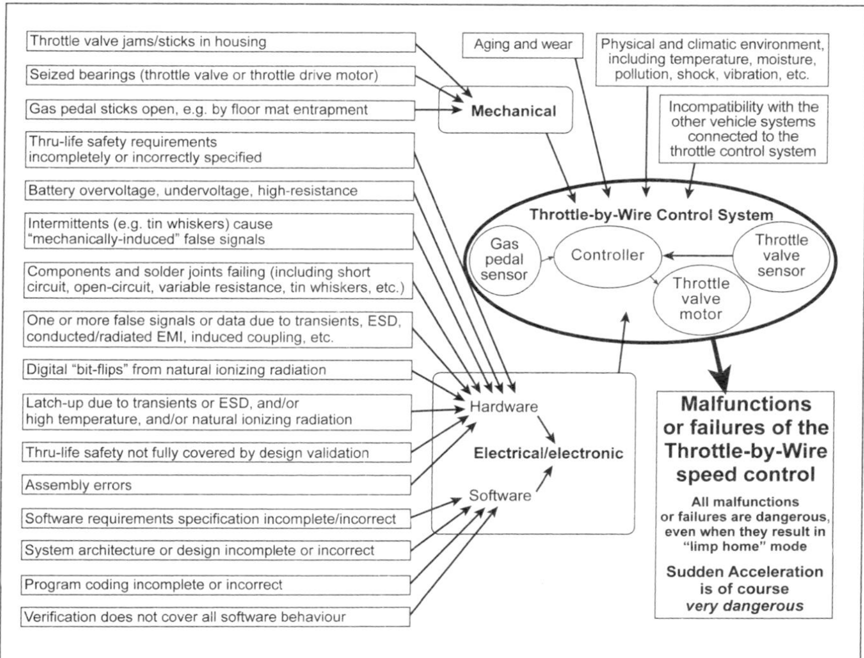


*Figure 89-2 Summary of potential failure modes for Throttle-by-Wire prepared by Keith Armstrong*

4. So, what's the basic problem with the software?

It may come as a surprise that the software in today's cars requires about 15 times more lines of code than in a modern jetliner. While Boeing's new 797 Dreamliner, for instance, requires about 6.5 million lines of software code to operate its avionics and onboard support systems, the multiple electronic control and entertainment systems in a top-of-the-line car *may contain up to 100 million lines of software code.*

The sheer complexity of instantly processing so much data means, as a practical matter, that bug-free software isn't realistically achievable, no matter what design and development process is used to create it; and if there are software bugs that haven't yet been fixed, they can dangerously influence the driver's control of engine torque.

5. How does hardware factor into this equation?

While data bus cables eliminated the highly complex wiring systems in older cars, Figure 89-2, also prepared by Keith Armstrong,

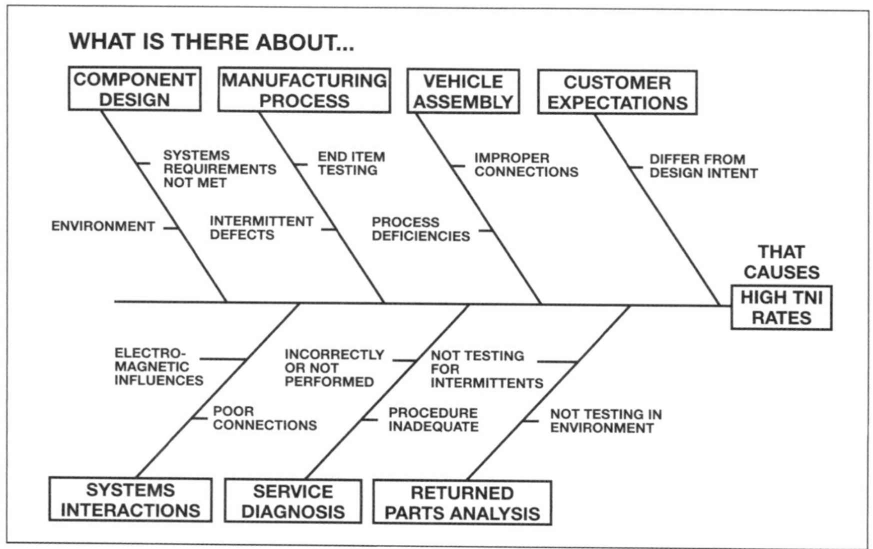


*Figure 89-3*

depicts just some of the ways electrical signals can nevertheless be disrupted or altered by a wide variety of possible conditions.

Figure 89-2 describes many of the conditions and occurrences that can cause or contribute to a dangerous electronic malfunction. For example, picture a car in stop-and-go traffic on a hot summer day with the air conditioning on and the radio playing. In such conditions, there can be the equivalent of an electrical signal traffic jam that can alter or interfere with the software's ability to control the behavior of electronic systems—including electronic throttle controls. The experts I talked to stressed that *such accidental signal alterations are never good news.*

There are many other conditions endemic to electronics with the potential to disrupt or alter electrical signals, some of which are indicated on Figure 89-3 that I promised earlier would become particularly important to our story. (See Chapter Forty.)

6. What does Figure 89-3 tell us?

It will be recalled that this diagram is part of a report to Ford's senior management in 1986 that explained the reasons behind a dramatic spike in undiagnosed malfunctions in electronic components that met "all the requirements of engineering tests that were established to reflect design intent." According to the report, "this higher trouble-not-identified rate was coincident with the increasing complexity of electrical systems in the company's vehicles." The report stressed that this complexity increased the potential for "electromagnetic influences in the vehicle environment" to induce electronic malfunctions.

Although the electronics in modern cars are different from models sold in the 1980s and '90s, Figure 89-3 nevertheless reflects conditions in today's cars that can disrupt or alter the electrical signals that control safety-critical systems. For example, the branch identified as "systems interactions" denotes how something as basic in the hardware as a "poor connection" can disrupt current flow and induce a failure that can't be diagnosed by conventional "engineering tests that were established to reflect design intent." But a bad connection is just one of countless conditions with the potential to alter electrical signals. In fact, the horizontal line in the center of the graph running to the causes of unidentified component failures indicates the almost limitless interactive conditions in a car that can disrupt or alter electrical signals with potentially disastrous consequences.

Because these conditions are endemic to electronics, it is tragic that carmakers have not been willing to adequately invest in protections against software errors, hardware conditions, and their interactions.

7. Why thousands of sudden accelerations have not triggered a diagnostic trouble code and put the car into a limp-home mode.

There is indisputable proof that throttle-by-wire electronics are vulnerable to two particular failure modes: single point faults and double faults, also known as common mode or common cause failures. The first, as the name implies, is a single fault that the ECM software fails to detect and instantly set a "trouble code" reducing speed to a safely controllable level. There are many reasons this can occur, ranging from incomplete analysis of possible failure modes, to intentional neglect of some faults to keep a software program small enough for a microprocessor to cope with it.

Double faults, as Dr. Gilbert demonstrated for Congress, are those that affect independent throttle monitoring systems at the same time in the same way; and because they see the same error, they can't tell that an error even exists. Examples of events that can give rise to common cause failures include temperatures that exceed the range the electronics are designed for (whether too high, or too low), various kinds of conducted and radiated EMI, etc.

As noted earlier, Toyota's failure to claim that any of the 37,900 occurrences disclosed to Congress had set a trouble code, strongly suggests that a significant percentage of these events were triggered by double faults.

The possibility of a double fault failure is increased if throttle control processing units are identical. For example, if an automaker—whether from ignorance or a desire to keep costs low—uses the same type of angle sensor for both accelerator pedal sensors, and for both throttle valve sensors, or uses the same type of hardware and software for the independent CPUs in the master ECM, the potential for a double fault failure is significantly increased. Under such conditions, there are many different types of doubt fault failures that can initiate *a dangerous throttle malfunction that will not set a trouble code.*

8. How could software and hardware designers have made many of the same mistakes that led to this automotive tragedy in the first place?

We saw earlier how the car industry badly underestimated the risk posed by EMI and by the time they realized their mistake, they faced a Hobson's choice of either correcting the problem at great cost or covering up their life-endangering mistakes. When NHTSA buried its head in the sand, carmakers correctly surmised that they could redesign their throttle electronics at a pace and cost to their liking, while also fending off legal liability with government reports that supported a driver error defense. That is briefly where matters stood at the beginning of the new millennium when throttle-by-wire came along.

But that doesn't answer how this huge industry could have rushed untested by-wire electronics to market, the same mistake that produced this catastrophe in the first place. Did car companies again gamble with the lives and safety of people with inadequately tested electronics? Consider this from a 2005 Society of Automotive Engineers publication:

> Automakers and vendors know that a reliable, fault tolerant bus is needed for such applications. Controller Area Network (CAN) buses, which are commonly used for powertrain and other automotive controls, are not considered reliable enough for drive-by-wire. The problem with CAN is that it is only event-based, so there's always a possibility the message won't get through.

In other words, carmakers and their suppliers knew that drive-by-wire controls were not "reliable enough," but decided to put people's lives at risk anyway. That decision would be reprehensible enough had they at least warned people who bought their products about the possibility of a sudden acceleration and how to respond during such an emergency. In that vein, let us consider the remarkable story of a man that demonstrates how cynically disregardful of human life it has been for this industry over thirty long years to leave people unprepared to survive a sudden loss of throttle control.

CHAPTER 90

# McCLELLAND

### TOYOTA'S MURKY DATA

Though most drivers don't realize it, two-thirds of new U.S. automobiles have black boxes, too. They're called "event data recorders." . . . In theory these black boxes could help explain what's causing the sudden acceleration problems that led Toyota to recall millions of vehicles. There's just one catch: Toyota keeps its data secret. Ford, GM, and Chrysler's black boxes use an open platform that allows law-enforcement officials to download data. But only Toyota is able to download the proprietary data off its devices. In fact, there's just one laptop in the entire country capable of reading a Toyota data recorder, and Toyota will download one only under court order, or at the request of law enforcement or NHTSA.

*Newsweek*, February 12, 2012

**EARLY ON THE MORNING OF MAY 5, 2011, JOSEPH McCLELLAND** left his home in Waynesboro, Pennsylvania and began the 75-minute drive in his 2004 Prius to the Federal Energy Regulatory Commission in Washington, D.C., where he is the Director of the Office of Electric Reliability, with responsibilities for cyber security in our nation's power grid. When he purchased it in 2004, the Prius registered about 8,000 miles. Since then McClelland had performed regular maintenance on the car, such as relining the brakes, replacing the rear wheel bearings, replacing the oxygen sensor in the engine, etc. Although McClelland had never experienced a sudden acceleration, he had followed reports about Toyota models and, fortunately, had thought through what he would do if his Prius suddenly sped out of control.

About 20 minutes into the trip, as the Prius was going up a severe incline with the accelerator pedal depressed, it suddenly accelerated with the engine racing. Because he had read about Toyota's floor mat recall, McClelland's first reaction, described in a sworn statement, was to "check the position of the floor mat," which "wasn't up against the accelerator pedal," and then put his foot behind the accelerator pedal to make sure it was in the fully returned position, which it was. Reacting as he had imagined, he quickly shifted to neutral, applied hard steady force on the brake pedal, and guided the car safely to a stop off the roadway.

McClelland said that he "would have returned home and changed vehicles, but I was to appear before the Senate that day, so to make my appearance on the Hill I needed to continue." When he restarted the car, "it seemed to act normally. I was now aware that the vehicle could accelerate, and as I was traveling on Route 16 and the Blue Ridge Summit, and was slightly accelerating to maintain speed when the engine again started to rev, almost roaring, and the car started to rapidly pick up speed." Once again he shifted into neutral, applied the brakes and guided the car off the road where he "put it in park, reset it, and got the vehicle moving again."

Although he made it to the Senate hearings, his Prius suddenly accelerated again near the CIA headquarters, "so I put the vehicle in neutral again, pressed the brake pedal, guided the vehicle off the road, put it in park, shut it off, reset it, and drove the rest of the way into my headquarters."

Notice that during these sudden accelerations the Prius never went into the limp-home mode. Had it done so, in fact, there would have been no need for his corrective responses, although he may have "limped" into D.C. late for his Senate appearance.

When he finally got the car home, McClelland checked NHTSA's website "to determine whether this case was still open, what the recommendations were, and what the problems associated with it were." But the only references were either to floor mats, stuck pedals, or operator error, none of which applied to what he had experienced. When he contacted NHTSA, "they asked me if I had driven the vehicle since the incidents, and I said no. They told me to leave it in the garage, and they would come out and talk with me about what happened, take a look at the vehicle, and see what might be happening with it."

A short time later, two engineers from the ODI appeared at McClelland's home where he carefully described each incident. They said NHTSA's investigations showed that such occurrences were caused by a misplaced floor mat, a sticky accelerator pedal, or operator error. "I told them that none of those three was the case with my vehicle. At that point they asked if I thought the vehicle would repeat the behavior. I said I didn't know, but we could start it and try. So they asked if I would take them on a test drive to see if the vehicle would demonstrate the same behavior."

McClelland suggested that they "retrace the same route I took to work on May 5, and see if it happens at the same point on the

Metzger Gap Road because it's a severe incline." When they got there with one ODI engineer in the right front passenger seat and the other behind McClelland recording what happened on a smart phone, "we drove to the same exact spot at the top of the Metzger Gap Road where the car, as before, suddenly accelerated. The engine was racing and they asked whether the floor mat was in place or if the accelerator was stuck, and I said 'Check for yourself.' So the engineer in the front seat leaned over and saw the floor mat in place and the accelerator was all the way up to a position where it wasn't depressed and he confirmed, 'you're right. This vehicle is doing it on its own.' They also asked what I would do to stop it, so I shifted to neutral, applied the brakes and brought the car safely to a stop on the shoulder."

They did two more runs and each time the Prius suddenly accelerated at the same location. "I don't recall which time it was, but I glanced over my shoulder," McClelland recalled, "and the engineer in the back seat with the smart phone was taping the event."

McClelland recounted how the ODI engineers acknowledged that there was no floor mat interference and that the accelerator pedal was in the full return position. "They said they had never been in a vehicle that accelerated while they were in it. They also confirmed to each other that they were taping the event, and agreed that there was a safety issue. I remember these specific comments; the overall theme was that they had now been in a vehicle that did exhibit sudden acceleration."

After the Prius was safely back in McClelland's garage, the engineers "plugged a PC into the controls to pull codes from the diagnostic port on the car, but they couldn't pull any codes off the vehicle." They then called a contact at NHTSA to learn how they could "reconfigure the laptop to capture any data or codes that might be generated from the vehicle." About an hour later they asked McClelland to start the car. "They plugged in the PC and said 'Bingo! It's working;' and they were extracting voluminous data from the vehicle. They explained that they were capturing information in real time and putting it in a PDF spreadsheet format so they could go back to NHTSA and evaluate it."

At this point, one of the engineers showed McClelland "a particular field where the voltage from the accelerator showed zero volts, which means it wasn't engaged and wasn't depressed. So even in the parked mode, it went into sudden acceleration, and they were pulling that information in real time and that was just one data field. It looked like they had a lot of other data fields that they were capturing and keeping for further analysis, so I expected that software versions and a printed copy would be available."

McClelland remembered how the two NHTSA engineers "seemed excited. They said they hadn't seen a vehicle display this type of behavior before, or been able to capture information in real time; they said this could be an important vehicle for sudden accelerations and it might help put some of the pieces together." When the discussion turned to whether NHTSA might acquire the Prius for further analysis, McClelland was told "they didn't have the authorization to make that decision, but that occasionally NHTSA will decide to buy vehicles back for safety research; and they said that, from their perspective, it was a vehicle NHTSA would be interested in buying. They said not to drive the car, to keep it secure, and that they would be back in contact with me about NHTSA purchasing it."

Let us pause to consider the ramifications of McClelland's experience. Imagine the suffering and loss that might have been prevented had either the car industry or NHTSA instructed drivers to respond exactly as McClelland did. "The first point," he noted, "is to get out of drive by putting it in neutral so the engine is no longer engaged. When it gets into neutral, depress the brake and guide the vehicle to a stop."

Although NHTSA hasn't lifted a finger to help people survive a sudden acceleration, it happens that "Consumer Reports" has published an advisory entitled "How to Cope With Sudden Unintended Acceleration, Five Steps that Could Save Your Life:"

1. *Brake firmly.* Do not pump the brakes. Do not turn off the engine yet—because doing so would disable the power assist for your steering and brakes.
2. *Shift the transmission into Neutral.* Don't worry if the engine revs up alarmingly; most cars have rev-limiters to protect against damage.
3. *Steer to a safe location and come to a full stop.*
4. *Shut off the engine with the transmission still in Neutral.*
5. *Finally, shift the transmission into Park* or, with a manual transmission, set the emergency brake. Then breathe deep and call for help. Do not drive the car.

> Memorize these steps to prepare for the rare chance that you might experience unintended acceleration. Better yet, practice them in a safe location at low speeds until you feel comfortable with them. They could save your life. (www.consumerreports.org 012910)

NHTSA might have prevented countless tragedies had it required carmakers to provide owners with a similar advisory. But it couldn't take that step without publicly acknowledging that the 1989 NHTSA/TSC report shifting the blame to drivers is tragically erroneous. The deafening silence of DOT/NHTSA on this point is both shameful and a stain on this nation's honor, particularly since the 1989 report has been embraced by numerous governments around the world as a scientifically valid study of this automotive phenomenon. Sadly, the history of this automotive behavior shows that unless DOT/NHTSA are compelled to repudiate the 1989 report, this blemish on our nation's honor will remain.

CHAPTER 91

# McCLELLAND: PART 2

## PLAINTIFFS VIE FOR A LOOK AT TOYOTA'S "CROWN JEWELS"

In the sudden acceleration cases against Toyota, there are confidential documents and highly confidential documents. And then there is what the judge overseeing most of the cases called the company's "crown jewels"—the source software code behind the electronics of its vehicles, which almost no one has seen.

Toyota, facing hundreds of cases alleging defects that caused its vehicles to suddenly accelerate, has kept a tight lid on discovery during three years of litigation, primarily through protective orders requiring that certain documents be redacts, sealed or approved by its Japan headquarters before anyone can get access to them.

From Toyota's perspective, the code represents a trade secret that it must keep out of the hands of its competitors. Plaintiffs' lawyers insist it will provide evidence that defects in the electronic throttle control system caused sudden acceleration in Toyota vehicles.

*The National Law Journal, www.nlj.com,* May 6, 2013

**NHTSA DIDN'T MAKE A DECISION ABOUT McCLELLAND'S PRIUS** until August 2011, when an agency representative called to advise him that NHTSA was "not going to purchase the Prius because they determined it was an end-of-life issue. In other words, it had so many miles on it that it wasn't pertinent to their interest in the sudden acceleration cases with Toyota. They decided on that basis not to buy the vehicle."

When McClelland asked what had caused the sudden accelerations, he was told that "one of the hybrid cells had failed in the battery, and that had caused a low voltage condition; and because of the low voltage condition, the on-board computer was asking the car engine to accelerate to charge the low voltage cell, which was what had caused the unintended accelerations."

Unconvinced, McClelland asked "if that could happen at the beginning of a vehicle's life. It seemed to me like a hybrid cell could fail earlier on, and that could be an issue regardless of the life cycle of the vehicle. They said they really hadn't examined that aspect, but they were not going to purchase the vehicle."

As an experienced electrical engineer who has worked with electrical engineers for many years, McClelland's conscience told him he could not let matters rest there. He was particularly troubled that each time the Prius had spontaneously accelerated, "braking had no effect on the rpm level. The engine continued to race. The vehicle still wanted to accelerate. Braking did not slow the vehicle or have any effect on the drivetrain or the racing of the vehicle." He was also perplexed that the ODI engineers "seemed at first to be enthusiastic about finding a vehicle that was exhibiting this behavior and being able to capture that information, and at having a videotape of those occurrences that could be seen first hand."

McClelland recalled reading about Sean Kane's testimony before Congress, and a short time later Kane met with McClelland at his home. After hearing his story, Kane asked McClelland if he would give a sworn statement, and he agreed to do so.

When I asked several electronics engineers familiar with Toyota sudden acceleration history, whether NHTSA was justified in not purchasing McClelland's Prius, they explained there were countless conditions other than a defective fuel cell in the battery that can cause a low voltage condition with failure potential. Consequently they were convinced that the Prius offered NHTSA an excellent opportunity to learn why Toyota's fault code was not detecting failures caused by these conditions.

In the final analysis, McClelland's experience demonstrates again NHTSA's determination to protect its own reputation at the expense of people's safety. With that, let us turn to one of the many surprises that will begin to bring this sad tale of corporate cowardice and government corruption to an end.

CHAPTER 92

# BETSY BENJAMINSON'S "BOMB"

## IS TOYOTA TELLING THE TRUTH ABOUT SUDDEN ACCELERATION?

On the day he died, Mark Saylor was doing what he did for a living: driving on a California highway. Only he wasn't driving his state-issued highway patrol car that day in late August 2009. Nor was he driving his own Lexus 250, which was at the dealer for servicing. He was driving a loaner with his wife, daughter, and brother-in-law on a leisurely family outing northeast of San Diego—until suddenly the car inexplicably took off. And no amount of braking could slow it down. As Saylor frantically tried to gain control, his brother-in-law called 9-1-1. "Our accelerator is stuck!" he told the dispatcher. "We're going 120!"

It wasn't just the speed that made this so dangerous. He read the sign they were passing: "End freeway one-half mile." The car was barreling toward a T-shaped

> intersection. When it got there, it hit another car, flew through a fence, rolled into a field, and burst into flames. The last word before the screams was, "Pray!"
>
> This wasn't the first time that someone driving a Toyota had experienced sudden unintended acceleration. And it's not a problem that's unique to Toyota. But this was the event that Toyota cites as the beginning of its ongoing crisis.
>
> How has it responded? The company has moved aggressively to contain the damage. Shifting floor mats were identified as a primary cause of many of these episodes. The company found that the loaner that the 45-year-old Mark Saylor was driving was equipped with mats that had never been intended for that car. Later, the company fingered accelerator pedals manufactured by a third party as prone to sticking. And Toyota says that many accidents are caused by drivers who inadvertently step on the gas instead of the brake . . . .
>
> *Corporate Counsel,* March 14, 2013

**IN EARLY MARCH OF 2013 I RECEIVED A SURPRISE CALL FROM** David Hechler, the editor of *Corporate Counsel,* a magazine for in-house company lawyers. "I'm writing a story about Toyota's sudden acceleration problems, and I've heard that you are writing a book about the history of this automotive problem; I would like to obtain a copy."

Intrigued, I asked, "What is the thrust of your story?"

"Do you remember reading about some whistleblowers convincing Senator Grassley to demand some straight answers from NHTSA regarding Toyota's problems?"

"Yes."

"Well, one of those whistleblowers is a lady named Betsy Benjaminson who was hired to translate documents written in Japanese into English. She's given us copies with some information we think will interest our readers. Your book should add to the story."

"Actually, Mr. Hechler, I haven't quite finished my manuscript, so my book won't be out for several months."

"Any chance I can get a copy of your manuscript?"

"I'm afraid not. I've already turned down similar requests from the media. But I will be happy to send you a copy as soon as the book is published."

"Fine; I'll send you a copy of our next edition of our magazine as soon as it's available."

On the cover of that April edition was a larger than life picture of Toyota's president, Akio Toyoda, surrounded by media microphones, along with the caption:

> LOST IN TRANSLATION. TOYOTA HOPED ITS SUDDEN ACCELERATION MESS WAS OVER. BUT INTERNAL DOCUMENTS RAISE QUESTIONS.
> By David Hechler (See Figure 92-1)

I am grateful to Mr. Hechler for his permission to quote liberally from his excellent article.

I've entitled this chapter "Betsy Benjaminson's Bomb" because the Toyota documents she gave Hechler resoundingly expose the kind of deceitful corporate behavior NHTSA's willful blindness has fostered. What follows are excerpts from his eight-page article with some brief comments.

- *Corporate Counsel* obtained scores of internal documents written by employees [of Toyota] who were struggling to understand why cars were suddenly accelerating, and where the company could have gone wrong. Among the writers were executives, managers, lawyers, public relations specialists and engineers.

*Figure 92-1*

*Author's comment:*

Although I have not read the "scores of internal documents" referred to in the article, those mentioned vindicate the work my "dream team" and I have put into this book.

- Many of the documents are marked "secret" and "confidential". They were provided by Betsy Benjaminson, a translator who has worked for several agencies that translate Toyota documents from the Japanese (and who translated several of those quoted in this article) . . . . Benjaminson provided these and many more documents last year to Senator Charles Grassley (R-Iowa), the ranking member of the Judiciary Committee, who then wrote a letter to NHTSA expressing his concern that questions about electronics have not been resolved . . . . Benjaminson is revealing her identity for the first time here. She decided to go public because lives are at stake, she says, adding, "Up to now the Corporate PR megaphone has completely drowned out the victims."

*Author's comment:*

Because it has taken us years to laboriously accumulate the evidence examined in this book, I felt a twinge of envy at David Hechler's opportunity at a stroke of his PC to shed new light on a dreadfully intransigent public safety problem. After noting that the CEO of Toyota Motor Sales USA, Inc., Jim Lentz, had told a Congressional Committee that "we have done extensive testing on this system, and we have never found a malfunction that caused unintended acceleration," Hechler zeroed in on this dubious claim.

- The documents seemed to tell a different story. An email written by Hiroshi Hagiwara, a Toyota Vice-President in Washington, D.C., and sent to executives in Japan a month before the hearings hints at the turmoil beneath the surface. Hagiwara and Chris Tinto, a VP for technical and regulatory affairs and safety, had been talking about the U.S. investigation and an earlier one in Europe that also involved unintended acceleration (UA).

  "Tinto is extremely pessimistic," Hagiwara wrote, "and is saying . . . someone will go to jail, I can't completely take care of the pedal problem, etc. ." . . . Still speaking of Tinto, who worked for NHTSA in the 1990s before he was hired away by Toyota, Hagiwara continued: "He appears to question how Toyota has grasped and handled the overall UA problem (mat, accelerator pedal, ECU [electronic control unit], and electronic throttle systems, etc.)."

Hagiwara reminded the executives to be careful what they put in writing. He asked them to fax any investigative reports related to Europe. "It is OK to write various things to me in emails written in Japanese," he advised, "but as much as possible only send materials that would not be controversial if disclosed (namely, things that have been reviewed), and it is best, I think, to discuss things orally."

*Author's comment:*

Hagiwara's concern about corporate executives putting things in writing is reminiscent of the paranoia of a Ford Vice-President, Max L. Jurosek, about a paper trail that "could be used in court." (See Chapter Forty-Two.) What makes this corporate culture of secrecy so disturbing is the way DOT/NHTSA have encouraged it by perversely refusing to enforce regulations intended to prevent deadly cover-ups.

- Some documents require translation by specialists. An undated spreadsheet showed test results of an engine's electronic throttle control system, including numerous faults that the document said cause sudden acceleration . . . . Several documents illustrated what the experts describe as a propensity of Toyota employees to define problems as they wish them to be, regardless of the facts. One is Toyota's analysis —performed three days after Saylor's death—of car owners' complaints received by NHTSA. Some drivers described their own harrowing experiences. Several were adamant that theirs had nothing to do with floor mats, yet that didn't always matter to Toyota's reviewer.

*Author's comment:*

This see-no-evil attitude of Toyota's "reviewers" is also evident in the following story in Hechler's article:

- One woman riding in a 2006 Toyota Tacoma said that it was the third such experience she'd had with the car. "Two times previously Toyota had replaced the cruise control," she reported. "This is not a cruise control problem. This is a gas pedal issue. I was told previously the mat was under the gas pedal. This is hardly the problem." In the column provided for the cause, the reviewer wrote: "The mat catches (specifics unknown)." It was the most common cause listed on the chart, regardless of what the drivers had to say. Antony Anderson, an independent electrical consultant who specializes in electrical machine and control system failure investigations (and has provided independent expert testimony for plaintiffs who sued Toyota), says the document shows how Toyota's "poor analysis" makes it appear that the incidence of stuck floor mats "is very much higher than it really is."

Hechler's report also contains this troubling summary of how Toyota responded to Dr. David Gilbert's testimony to Congress:

- The biggest challenge during the [Congressional] hearings came from a surprising source. David Gilbert is an automotive technology professor at the University of Southern Illinois in Carbondale, which, it so happens, receives resources and funding from Toyota. But he came to the hearing to talk about an experiment he cooked up that challenged claims Toyota made about its electronics. Toyota insisted that any electrical fault in its cars would trip an error code, which would immediately reduce power and send the car into "limp-home mode." Gilbert decided to test this assertion by rewiring Toyota's throttle in a way that would mimic a short circuit and send the rpms surging. Then he'd check for an error code.

At the hearing he revealed what he'd found (previewed the night before on the *NBC News*). The cars he tested hadn't produced the code, suggesting a vulnerability in the system. Politicians seemed deeply impressed, and Toyota was caught off guard.

Toyota arranged a multi-pronged "rebuttal." It had hired Exponent, a scientific and engineering consultancy, to work on technical issues in connection with the inquiry. It was now tapped to respond to Gilbert . . . . Behind the scenes, Toyota played hardball with critics. A public relations manager named Masami Doi had spelled out the approach in a December email. "There are at most around ten people who are the sources of negative tone communications. If they can be suppressed, I think we will be able to manage it somehow. Like you said, let's go with an intention of destroying each individual person's ability to oppose us, one by one. (To do or not to do is a separate question.)".

*Author's comment:*

Although I don't know the identity of the "ten people" whose "ability to oppose" Toyota needed to be destroyed "one by one," I only hope this book causes the list to swell until Toyota is convinced that, given this country's respect for the rule of law, the better part of valor is to stop making enemy lists and start telling the truth about its electronics.

We will return to Hechler's story after we examine a surprising turn of events that occurred shortly before its publication.

CHAPTER 93

# SETTLEMENT

### TOYOTA IN $1.1 BILLION GAS-PEDAL SETTLEMENT

> Toyota Motor Corp. agreed to pay about $1.1 billion to settle a class-action lawsuit stemming from complaints of unintended acceleration in its vehicles that soured its reputation for quality and undermined its sales globally.
>
> *The Wall Street Journal*, December 27, 2012

**ON DECEMBER 18, 2012, HIKE REPORTED THAT "RUMORS ARE** floating around that a settlement with Toyota is imminent." He was referring to class actions consolidated in the Federal District Court in Los Angeles that we are part of.

"Assuming that's true, any ideas what the terms may be?" I asked.

"No clue," Hike replied, "which isn't surprising. A leak before terms are finalized could scuttle a deal."

"Any chance Toyota might admit that the root cause of the problem is in the design of its electronic throttle control system?"

It was a crucial issue, and there was a pause as Hike pondered the question.

"I think that's unlikely. If Toyota made such an admission, it would be wonderful for the families we are representing, and it would mean that Toyota and other companies with similar by-wire electronics couldn't pin the blame on innocent drivers. Unfortunately," Hike continued, "these companies have been claiming there's nothing wrong with their electronics for so long that changing their position would be a public relations nightmare. It's too bad your book isn't finished because it might be enough to convince Toyota that coming clean is better business than being pecked away at in these individual cases."

When a settlement was announced on December 26, 2012, we learned the terms from media reports like the extensive coverage given the agreement by *The Wall Street Journal* on December

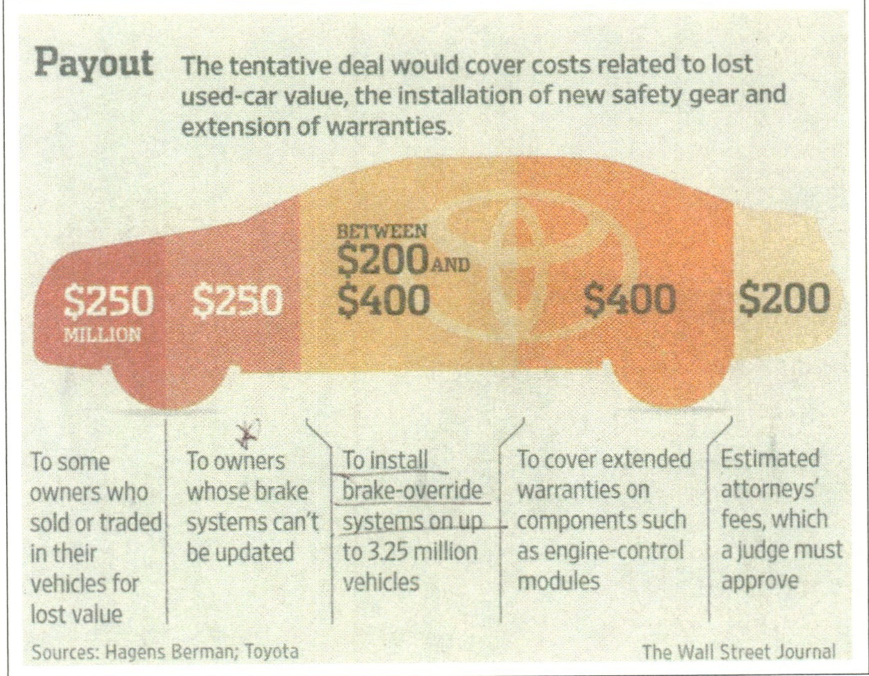


*Figure 93-1*

27, 2012, which included a graphic snapshot of the settlement depicted in Figure 93-1.

Did the documents Betsy Benjaminson was soon to give David Hechler play a part in convincing Toyota to settle? That certainly seems possible; and while the settlement did not include an admission of fault by Toyota, we were nevertheless hopeful that Toyota would recognize the futility of continuing to defend the indefensible. Hike described Toyota's predicament:

"It can't say its electronics are safe without risking being hit with huge punitive damage awards in states where tort reformers haven't convinced legislators to do away with them."

"Maybe my book can help the cause after all."

Hike laughed. "Then get back to work and finish it!"

CHAPTER 94

# "BIG IDEAS"

**LEXUS INVESTIGATES ACCELERATION COMPLAINT FROM GWINNETT WOMAN**

GWINNETT COUNTY, GA—Less than two hours after reporting on Toyota's $1 billion settlement over sudden acceleration, Channel 2 consumer investigator Jim Strickland got a tip about a new case out of Gwinnett County.

"It was probably the most devastating and terrifying thing that's ever happened to me," said cardiology nurse Kim Walker.

She arrived for her interview with Strickland in a rented Chrysler. Her Lexus IS 250 had a crushed front end. Walker's lawyer told her to leave it in the garage, where it crashed last Saturday.

"That car had a mind of its own, and it was going to do its thing. I mean I was standing practically on that brake," said Walker, who crashed into the stairs leading from the garage into the kitchen.

"I knew she was hitting the brakes as hard as she could and it just kept going faster and faster. I thought we were going to be in the kitchen," said Katharine Bryant, Walker's daughter and a passenger in the car.

David Walker showed Strickland records that the 2009 recall to prevent sudden acceleration was already done on the car. He also showed Strickland the electronic module that controls the throttle.

*Walker, the driver's husband, is an ASE certified master mechanic with 30-years experience. He works at a Chevrolet dealership.*

*"It could have been electronic interference from somewhere that fooled the module into thinking the driver wanted that throttle open," he explained.*

"No evidence of electronic defect has been found in Toyota and Lexus throttle control systems," said spokesman Mike Michel via email.

*www.wsbtv.com,* December 28, 2012

**THE FOREGOING MEDIA REPORT PROVOKED THIS RESPONSE FROM** Hike: "Despite warnings about the danger posed by electromagnetic interference, car companies rushed untested electronics to market in the late seventies and early eighties. When they finally woke up to what they'd done, they decided it would be cheaper to hide their mistakes than spend the money to correct them. Twenty-five years later we have the American Automobile Association on record saying we don't need more regulations because litigation pressure is enough to protect people from what you like to call a 'secret game of automobile roulette.' Maybe the only thing that can end this is a bipartisan movement in Congress for regulations that'll make it too costly to cover up mistakes that can kill people."

"I hear you, Hike, but I also think we need a campaign to make the federal government enforce some of the most important safety regulations already on the books."

"For example?"

"Let's start with federal law requiring carmakers to advise NHTSA within a reasonable time of a defect that relates to motor vehicle safety. Is there anything that fits that definition better than a car spontaneously racing out of control and overpowering the brakes until it crashes? We know that car companies have received thousands of credible runaway car reports, most of which have never been reported to NHTSA."

"If you were NHTSA's administrator, Tom, what would you do about that?"

"Do you remember what NHTSA did about Toyota's so-called 'sticky pedal' problem?"

"Didn't it hit Toyota with about 50 million dollars in civil penalties for not immediately reporting sticky pedals?"

"Exactly; and the worst a sticky pedal can do is interfere with deceleration when pressure on the accelerator is released."

"Do you recall whether there was any evidence of sticky pedals causing accidents?"

"If there was, Hike, I'm not aware of it. Of course, there are hundreds of well-documented cases of sudden accelerations ending in a terrible crash."

"So your point is that NHTSA could have forced the industry's hand by aggressively seeking civil penalties every time it learned about a credible sudden acceleration report that wasn't reported to the government within a reasonable time."

"Exactly; and what did these political hacks do instead? They let Volkswagen of America decide which reports the government would even be allowed to see at a time when Audi 5000s had a sudden acceleration rate several times greater than any other company."

"Based on the evidence, do you think a recall back in the '80s could have ended this unmitigated calamity?"

"Yes; and that's why NHTSA's failure to initiate a recall is disgraceful. The regulations are crystal clear *that unsafe vehicle performance is a defect that authorizes a safety recall.* From the beginning, drivers, passengers, and witnesses outside the car have been reporting the most dangerous vehicle behavior imaginable."

"So those reports were enough to order a recall?"

"I'm not the only one who believes that. The Ford Motor Company in 1979 created a 75 million dollar reserve to cover a sudden acceleration related safety recall."

"How do you know the reserve was specifically for sudden accelerations?"

"Because the report specifically says that the reserve was created to cover a recall for sudden accelerations like those being reported at the time about the Audi 5000."

"How did you get your hands on a smoking gun like that?"

"There was a class action in California pertaining to an electronic component called a thick film ignition module. The gutsy judge handling the case ordered Ford to turn over the records of a senior management group called the Technical Affairs Committee and, voila! Molly or JoEllen found a report describing the 75 million dollar recall reserve."

I could see Hike was pondering this and waited for his response.

"It seems to me," he began, "that the same logic about a performance-based recall applies to uncontrolled accelerations that are still destroying lives. Why not ask a federal court in D.C. for an injunction requiring that NHTSA initiate a performance-based recall based on all the evidence you've developed? As far as I know, that strategy has never been tested."

"That's an interesting idea, Hike, but who is going to do it? We're too busy with work on these individual cases to take on something like that."

"There are plenty of experienced lawyers out there who so far have taken a pass about sudden accelerations. If NHTSA isn't willing to follow the law, it's high time trial lawyers stop being cowed by tort reformers and start challenging the kind of criminal concealment this agency has encouraged."

"I agree; and the email I sent you earlier today certainly supports your argument."

Here's what I was referring to:

> Around noon on Monday 11/12/12, my wife was making a left turn from a dead stop onto Highway 441 here in Gainesville, Florida. She noticed her SUV speeding up to 45 mph. After a pause, the van accelerated to over 80 mph as she frantically tried to stop the car, but it did not respond. She even tried the emergency brake to no avail. She went through shifting gears to either neutral or park; she's not sure which due to the frantic situation. The SUV slowed and she pulled over to the side of the highway and called me in tears . . . . MDX towed the car to Gatorland Acura, and they said they never had this problem and asked whether this was the first time this had happened. Yes, this was the first time. The dealer called me today and said no codes came up on the computer. Gatorland Acura said on Friday an engineer from Acura would come and look at the SUV. We are reluctant of course to trust driving this vehicle again . . . .

"When I read your email, Tom, it occurred to me that you should encourage readers who've experienced a sudden acceleration, or know someone who has, to get their story to you by email at tom@thomasjmurraylaw.com. Can you imagine what might happen if you were to send several hundred similar emails to major media outlets and members of Congress?"

"Since we're on a roll," I chortled, "I could also shower the White House with the same emails. But," I sighed, "do you really think that might end this travesty?"

"Not by itself; but if the media were to get behind such an effort, it might provide the world with a good example of how the free flow of information in a democracy can become a force that even a powerful industry and corrupt government agency cannot ignore indefinitely."

As you ponder these "big ideas," keep in mind the admonition of Tony Lee quoted in the headnote to Chapter Eighty: "COULD BE YOUR FAMILY, COULD BE YOU;" and with that, let us find out how the Ford Motor Company reacted to Betsy Benjaminson's "bomb."

CHAPTER 95

# FORD RESPONDS TO *CORPORATE COUNSEL*

## FORD TAURUS IS INVESTIGATED FOR STICKY THROTTLES

The National Highway Traffic Safety Administration is investigating whether about 310,000 Ford Taurus and Mercury Sable models from the 2000-3 model years should be recalled because the vehicles' throttles might stick, according to a report (PDF) posted on Friday to the agency's web site. The agency said its investigation of the Tauruses was prompted by 50 complaints from owners about unintended acceleration involving the 3-liter, 4-valve Duratec V-6 engine, but not the 2-valve version, which uses a different design.

*The New York Times Wheels*, October 26, 2012

**DAVID HECHLER ALSO TALKED WITH MOLLY, WHO SHARED WITH** *Corporate Counsel* some of our experiences in Ford cases:

> The main battleground has been the courts, where plaintiffs have made slow progress convincing juries and judges that electronic malfunctions are real. Translating the evidence into a winning formula hasn't been easy. Proving a circumstantial case rarely is. "We have the burden of proof, and we should," says Molly O'Neill, who works with the dean of sudden acceleration trial lawyers, Tom Murray of Sandusky, Ohio. "But you cannot open up the car and show what went wrong. That's the nature of electronics."
>
> Before one of Murray and O'Neill's biggest wins, a trial judge ruled that their expert couldn't mention EMI, which was an important part of their explanation of how the accident happened. In the *Daubert* hearing, the judge [Naomi Buchwald] said she was concerned that the expert's findings couldn't be replicated in tests. They later won *Jarvis v. Ford* on appeal in 2002, in a decision written by Sonia Sotomayor before she was elevated to the U.S. Supreme Court. Murray says it is one of the first successful challenges to the electronics in a car's cruise or throttle control. Yet, for EMI, it was another argument lost in translation.
>
> ***
>
> Asked to respond to criticism of its company, Ford offered a full-throated defense of its regulator. "NHTSA has investigated alleged unintended accelerations many times over many years and has concluded that driver error is the predominant cause of these events. NHTSA's work is far more scientific and trustworthy than work done by personal injury lawyers and their

> paid experts." The email statement concluded: "Ford has reviewed its own data and determined that its vehicles are not affected by the problems experienced by Toyota owners."

Notice how, instead of relying on the engineers who designed its by-wire electronics, Ford imitated a contortionist by hiding behind a regulatory agency firmly ensconced in its hip pocket. Although *Corporate Counsel's* readers couldn't have known that NHTSA had to invent reasons for shifting the blame to drivers, one wonders how many of its readers were bemused by Ford's "full-throated defense of *ITS REGULATOR*."

For my part, Ford's reflexive attack on "personal injury lawyers" is among the best left-handed compliments I have received in fifty years at the bar.

We have come to the penultimate chapter in this saga of corporate cruelty and government corruption. Throughout these pages, I have suggested that "pedal misapplication" as the cause of sudden accelerations is a myth concocted by carmakers and perpetuated by the Department of Transportation and NHTSA. Now let's find out whether I may have overstated my case.

CHAPTER 96

# LAND OF MAGICAL THINKING

**FAMILIES OF CRASH VICTIMS FILE LAWSUIT AGAINST TOYOTA**

**LAWYER SAYS UNINTENDED ACCELERATION CAUSED FATAL 2009 CRASH.**

Four people died when a Toyota Highlander crashed head-on into a midsize sedan on Route 202 near the Peterborough-Jaffrey town line in 2009. Witnesses told police the SUV seemed to be out of control, traveling at high speeds and swerving in and out of the breakdown lane. Attorneys are blaming "sudden unintended acceleration," a problem that prompted a series of recalls from Toyota three years ago at about the same time of the crash . . . Driving the Toyota was Dr. Stephen Lagakos, a Harvard University professor. His passengers included his wife and mother, who were also killed, along with the driver of the other car.

*WMUR.com*, October 12, 2012 (updated)

**A QUESTION RUNNING THROUGH THESE PAGES IS WHETHER NHTSA** sold out to the car industry in the 1980s, and then stubbornly concealed that its 1989 industry-wide study blaming drivers was an invention devoid of empirical or scientific support? Although I knew that proving a tacit collaboration between a powerful industry and the federal government wouldn't be easy, I could never have imagined that in the end it would be NHTSA that would provide clinching proof that its studies and reports blaming drivers are both slanderous and a national disgrace.

Following the 2010 Congressional hearings, NHTSA commissioned a study by a team of human factors experts who reported their findings in a report entitled "Pedal Application Errors" published in March of 2012. We were struck immediately that the study was conducted by a group of human factors experts from NHTSA's Office of Behavioral Safety Research. Although they had no technical background for a study relating to sudden acceleration, we wondered whether these behavioral scientists might have come up with something we had overlooked. We discovered, however, that they had relied heavily on the work of one Richard Schmidt, whose numerous papers purporting to explain why pedal errors cause sudden accelerations have made him a "go-to" witness for car companies, and whose work has also been cited by NHTSA. When I promised in Chapter Fifty-Nine that we would eventually meet someone who has been paid good money to peddle nonsense on behalf of carmakers, I had Schmidt in mind. Here is how NHTSA's McMath denial in 1999 approvingly summarized the basis for Schmidt's conclusion that drivers accidentally cause cars to suddenly speed out of control:

Schmidt concluded that pedal placement errors rarely involve "conscious choice," and drivers involved in a sudden acceleration crash are therefore frequently not aware of their errors in foot placement:

> Once unintended acceleration is initiated, a serious contributing factor is the failure to detect and correct the foot placement error, mainly because of lack of effective feedback from the well-learned, essentially automatic foot movements. The onset of the unintended acceleration may produce a startled reaction compounded by severe time stress, placing the individual in a state of hyper-vigilance [panic] in which information-processing activities necessary to take effective action are seriously disrupted.

Notice Schmidt's logic: Drivers are so accustomed to pushing on the right pedal that when they push on the wrong pedal they don't realize it because of a lack of "effective feedback"; and when the car unexpectedly begins to move, they're suddenly stricken with an attack of "hyper-vigilance" that turns the car into an unguided missile. In other words, because people sometimes can't tell the difference between a high hard brake pedal and a low soft gas pedal, they can be turned in an instant into a hyper-vigilante behind the wheel of a speeding, two ton machine. Although we found Schmidt's theory strange, it was not until we were retained in a case pending in Cook County, Illinois, that I had an opportunity to grill him about the basis for a theory he had been propounding for many years. I began the deposition on November 22, 2011 with an elementary question:

**Q:** Does the term sudden acceleration have a distinct meaning to you?

**A:** I used the NHTSA definition . . . which fits an uncommanded full throttle situation from a stop or near stop after shifting from park to a drive gear, with a perceived brake failure.

***

By conflating "uncommanded full throttle acceleration" with "a perceived brake failure," Schmidt's definition implicitly posed whether there is *credible evidence anywhere that drivers accidentally floor* the accelerator pedal and keep it there in the belief the car is rapidly accelerating because of a brake failure. Did Schmidt have the answer?:

**Q:** Is it your position or hypothesis that in these occurrences . . . the driver mispositions his or her foot over the accelerator pedal?

**A:** Yes.

**Q:** In this hypothesis, does the driver misposition his or her foot . . . over the accelerator pedal before he begins the shifting movement?

**A:** I would say simultaneous with . . . .

**Q:** Does the driver misposition his foot before or after . . . the shifting process begins.

**A:** Well, that's why I say contemporaneously, both of those things are operating together. I don't know exactly what the timing is, but they both generally operate together.

**Q:** Explain how, in your hypothesis, the shifting during this misposition.

**A:** Well, the driver gets into the car, and perhaps mispositions in the car because he has just sat down anew in the vehicle. And then in an attempt to get the car going, he has to do two things. One is put his foot lightly on the brake, and two, shift out of park into drive or reverse . . . .

**Q:** Is it your hypothesis that it is during the process of moving the foot to the brake pedal that the foot gets mispositioned?

**A:** Yes.

***

Notice that in Schmidt's hypothetical sequence, the foot never touches the brake pedal, which raises the obvious question how momentarily mispositioning one's foot on the gas pedal could lead to a sudden, unintended acceleration, particularly in a car with an automatic shift interlock?

**Q:** Now, I'm sure as part of your research, you've looked into whether drivers typically put their foot on the brake pedal during start up or during the shifting maneuver, whether or not the car has a shift lock; have you researched whether drivers typically place their foot on the brake pedal during startup procedures?

**A:** I really haven't done any research to answer that question directly, but certainly from complaints about unintended acceleration, that's what the driver says he does.

**Q:** I think we can agree that typically, in these sudden acceleration cases, the driver says he got in the car, put his foot on the brake at startup; that's a rather standard version of the allegations made by drivers, isn't it?

**A:** Yes it is.

***

I was now ready to find out exactly what basis Schmidt had for his theory:

**Q:** So in the classic sudden acceleration, the driver makes a series of mistakes. He mispositions his or her foot, he then pushes on the gas pedal enough to cause wide open throttle acceleration, he persists in that mistake for some period of time, depending on the circumstances, and then,

in many cases, at least, a crash occurs; is that a good profile of what happens?
**A:** I think I heard you say that the driver puts his foot on the accelerator pedal and immediately generates full throttle.
**Q:** Yes.
**A:** That's not what I think.
**Q:** What do you think?
**A:** Well, *what I think is the driver intends to put his foot lightly on the brake, but his foot goes to the accelerator instead. So the pedal application is a light one.*
**Q:** Ok.
**A:** Not full throttle at all.
**Q:** Ok.
**A:** And then subsequent to shifting into drive or reverse, the car starts to move, the driver attempts to stop the car by pushing on the brake, but is on the accelerator instead, so the car goes a little faster.
**Q:** Ok.
**A:** And so he pushes again, and so on and so on until you have a full throttle event. It's not my view that the driver initially puts his foot on the accelerator in a full throttle way, not at all.
**Q:** In other words, he doesn't go pedal to the metal immediately?
**A:** No.
**Q:** It's a progressive series of actions on the part of the driver?
**A:** I think in the classic case, yes, that's right.

***

I could hardly believe my ears. It was obvious that if a driver intended to put his foot lightly on the brake pedal, but his foot went to the accelerator instead, he/she wouldn't be able to move the gear lever from park if the car had a shift-lock device; and since virtually every automobile manufactured in the past twenty years has had this device, Schmidt's hypothesis as a practical matter ruled out pedal misapplication for any sudden acceleration that began at gear engagement; and, since the vast majority of uncommanded throttle activations in today's cars do not begin "from a stop or near stop after shifting from park to a drive gear," Schmidt's theory was also irrelevant as an explanation for currently occurring sudden accelerations.

Furthermore, the contradiction between a progressive series of actions by a driver causing a car to gradually accelerate on one hand, and Schmidt's definition of an "uncommanded full throttle acceleration from a stop or near stop after shifting to a drive gear," on the other hand, was so patently obvious that I decided it was time to give Schmidt enough rope with which to strangle his theory, which quickly led to a land of magical thinking:

> **Q:** What information did you use, Dr. Schmidt, in formulating your hypothesis?
>
> **A:** Well, one would be *sort of doing a thought experiment*, assuming the hypothesis that the car did it and that the car malfunctioned in some way that predicts the unintended acceleration thing. But that also has the drawback that it requires two, at least two, malfunctions of the car to occur at the same time and to fix themselves afterwards. That data tends to refute the hypotheses that talk about a car being at fault.

***

A thought experiment?? There's certainly nothing wrong with thought experiments, which have led to some of the greatest achievements in human history because they asked the question "what causes a certain thing to happen?" In this case, however, the critical question has always been what are the possible causes of this automotive behavior? Had NHTSA asked itself that question and taken the trouble to learn even the rudimentary facts about electronics, it would have known enough "to ask carmakers the right questions about their electronics, and to *recognize when their responses were dangerously inadequate or misleading*." As for Schmidt, it struck me that he must have bypassed this crucial question and focused exclusively on the failure of vehicle inspections to find physical evidence of a defect. My hunch proved correct:

> **Q:** You say for a sudden acceleration to have been caused by some kind of malfunction, there have to be two malfunctions in the car at the same time, is that right?
>
> **A:** At least two, yes.
>
> **Q:** At least two. What are the minimum two?
>
> **A:** One of the two has to be something wrong with the fuel delivery system, the acceleration system. Number two is the brakes have to fail . . . .
>
> **Q:** What in your thought experiment needs to go wrong with the fuel delivery system?
>
> **A:** Well, I have no idea about that . . . . I'm not an engineer. Secondly, I don't really know what aspect of the fuel delivery system is claimed to have failed. All the driver knows is that something failed and the car went into wide open throttle . . . .
>
> **Q:** You took at face value what the drivers said, and then, as I understand it, tried to determine scientifically whether those reports were valid or not.
>
> **A:** Right, in the sense that *the thought experiment* that we referred to here a minute ago is the idea that vehicles don't fix themselves.

***

What Schmidt had done was now clear. Because he had no idea what might cause a car to spontaneously race out of control, he had assumed that because "vehicles don't fix themselves," the fact that inspections didn't find a defect meant there was no defect. But that was like a doctor reasoning that because hearts don't fix themselves, a patient had not suffered a heart attack. In any event, Schmidt's logic shows that in the land of magical thinking, blissful ignorance of how things work on planet Earth can be useful; and because the behaviorists who wrote NHTSA's 2012 report were smitten with Schmidt's work, they drew upon it to concoct this variation of his theory:

> Under extreme stress, a panicked reaction may occur when a person attends indiscriminately to minor and major threats, frantically searching for a way to escape a perceived hazard. This contemporarily impairs cognitive functioning, resulting in impulsive and often poor and dangerous choices. People may freeze, appearing to take no action at all, when they are actually attending to multiple cues in rapid succession without being able to make an effective response. *This is a 'hyper-vigilant' state*, characterized by these causes: a strong, startling stimulus, perception of this stimulus as life-threatening, in the sense that a solution must be found immediately. In unintended acceleration events, the strong stimulant is the unexpected, violent acceleration often accompanied by loud sounds. The driver may perceive this as life-threatening, invoking fear for self, passengers, and other drivers or pedestrians. A sense of imminent danger makes it important to find a solution. Information processing is impaired as the driver's distracted by what is happening in

the environment; he or she *does not identify the solution, i.e. to move the foot to the brake, because the driver 'knows' the foot is on the brake, so assumes the brakes have failed.* [Italics added.]

Although I don't know whether hyper-vigilantes may exist elsewhere in the cosmos, I do know we have yet to find evidence of their existence on planet Earth. It is the soul of irony, therefore, that a group of academics hired to provide cover for NHTSA managed to concoct a knockoff of Schmidt's work that captures the parade of horrors that follows a sudden, uncommanded vehicle acceleration. In fact, it's hard to imagine anything more unexpected, life threatening, and terrifying than having one's car violently accelerate out of control with the engine roaring. Anyone in whom this wouldn't "invoke fear for self, passengers, and other drivers or pedestrians" has ice water in his/her veins.

Although I was quite sure that Schmidt's "thought experiment" meant we would never encounter him again, I didn't want to conclude the deposition without offering him every chance to cite proof for his theory. As it happened, he had recently co-authored a paper entitled "Cars Gone Wild" that carefully analyzed the often studied North Carolina State Crash Data covering thousands of accidents following which drivers admitted having made a pedal error. If there was proof anywhere to support Schmidt's "thought experiment," this is where it would most likely be found.

In "Cars Gone Wild", Schmidt and his colleagues analyzed 2,000 accidents described in this crash data and uncovered "39 classic unintended acceleration events":

**Q:** Please tell us how many of the 39 drivers . . . admitted to making some kind of pedal error?

**A:** The driver never admitted making a pedal error.

**Q:** Why would all of the 39 drivers deny a pedal error, when so many of the other drivers in the North Carolina study admitted a pedal error?

**A:** I'm not positive about the answer to that. In one sentence, that's sort of typical of the phenomenon, unintended acceleration, classic unintended acceleration where the driver makes a pedal misapplication and continues to believe that his foot was on brake, and that the brake failed, when, in fact, his foot was on accelerator . . . .

***

Although Schmidt's response begged the question I had asked, it didn't matter because it was now clear that the only basis for his "thought experiment" was between his ears. But I still wanted to give him every chance to defend his theory:

**Q:** I know your hypothesis; now I'm interested in . . . having you tell us about any empirical or scientific research you can point to that would indicate, or explain, why drivers who are involved in a classic sudden acceleration would universally deny that they had made a pedal error . . . . drivers never admit this or virtually never admit this, true? . . . We can agree that the data shows that there's nothing unusual in the fact that none of the 39 drivers in the Carolina study admitted a pedal error?

**A:** That's right.

**Q:** . . . Now your hypothesis is, they don't know they made a pedal error?

**A:** Yes.

**Q:** So they don't admit it.

**A:** Well, yes, I really believe they don't know they made a pedal error . . . .

**Q:** OK.

**A:** And they continue not to know that after the episode is over when they describe it.

How about that? Thousands upon thousands of people of all ages, educational backgrounds, and experiences, have sent their cars wildly out of control, failed to realize it, continued doing it until the car crashed, and thereafter remained unaware of what they had done. When Schmidt, who has a Ph.D. in psychology, couldn't cite a single source to explain why people readily admit pedal errors following other kinds of accidents, but universally deny causing a sudden acceleration, I knew it was time to end the deposition.

And so 22 years after NHTSA exonerated the car industry and shifted the blame to drivers, it turns out there was nothing more substantial to back up this slur against drivers than a "thought experiment." That might not be quite so outrageous were it not that the bureaucratic functionaries who oversaw this travesty left behind government reports that are still being used to cheat terribly injured people of compensation. But since we live in a country with the most advanced legal system in the world, the question remains what can be done to correct this grotesque desecration of truth and justice?

CHAPTER 97

# "LITIGATION PRESSURE" AND THE FUTURE OF AUTOMOTIVE SAFETY

"[C]orporations have no consciences, no beliefs, no feelings, no thoughts, no desires. Corporations help structure and facilitate the activities of human beings, to be sure, and their 'personhood' often serves as a useful legal fiction. But they are not themselves members of 'We the People' by whom and for whom our Constitution was established . . . ."

Dissenting opinion of
U.S. Supreme Court Justice John Paul Stevens in
*Citizens United v. Federal Election Commission.*

**WE'VE SEEN THAT THE CAR INDUSTRY IS ON RECORD THAT IT PREFERS** "litigation pressure" to government regulations. Fortunately for anyone who drives or gets near automobiles, the American legal system is wonderfully equipped to honor this preference. That's why I will encourage every lawyer to read this book and help the car industry along with a healthy infusion of "litigation pressure." Here are some possibilities:

- Class actions.

Toyota's agreement to pay $1.1 billion to cover diminished market value of its models caused by adverse publicity surrounding its sudden acceleration crisis is a good example of what "litigation pressure" can accomplish. For a company with a $40 billion cash reserve, however, that was only a slap on the wrist. But it was also only the tip of a gigantic litigation iceberg. For example, there are several hundred sudden acceleration lawsuits pending just against Toyota. Since I am involved in many of those cases, I will only say that we are continuing to uncover evidence that we hope will help the decision-makers in Tokyo to appreciate that "litigation pressure" in this country includes punitive damages. Perhaps when that sinks in, Toyota will decide to embrace the benefits offered by "litigation pressure" and offer fair settlements in these pending cases.

A class action similar to the one against Toyota has recently been filed against the Ford Motor Company. Since I am also involved in that case, I will only say that my colleagues and I are determined to also help Ford appreciate the benefits "litigation pressure" can have for the long range good of the company.

Finally, as regards class actions, Toyota and Ford are not the only companies whose models with throttle-by-wire electronics are experiencing sudden accelerations. Don't be surprised, therefore, if you read about similar class actions intended to spread the benefits of "litigation pressure" more evenly across the industry.

- Personal Injury and Wrongful Death Suits.

Modern discovery allows trial lawyers to drill deeply with surgical precision into a large corporation's best kept secrets. In fact, virtually everything in this book is based on testimony and evidence obtained through discovery, which raises a particularly tragic aspect of this story that I touched on earlier. During the 1980s, lawyers shied away from sudden acceleration cases because vehicle inspections invariably failed to find evidence of a defect that could explain this automotive behavior. When the federal government in 1989 ruled out electronics and blamed drivers, it became almost impossible to find a lawyer willing to accept a sudden acceleration case. In fact, had Sam Sero not discovered that power was supplied to the cruise control servo at ignition, it is unlikely that my firm would have accepted the *Manigault* case in 1995, six years after NHTSA published its disastrous industry-wide study. Even then, however, our involvement would have ended had Ford made a half-way decent settlement offer instead of removing the sound from a videotaped braking demonstration. When Judge Anthony Calabrese found that the Manigaults had been defrauded of a fair trial and issued a scorching 25-page Order, Clarence Ditlow sent a copy to a producer at NBC *Dateline*, Steve Eckert, which resulted in an hour-long documentary seen by nearly eight million people. One thing then led to another and by the time the *Manigault* case was finally resolved, we had been drawn into cases around the country that eventually produced the materials on which this book is based. In short, for want of a fair settlement offer in *Manigault*, the battle to keep the truth about sudden accelerations concealed became a war the car industry is now slowly but surely losing.

None of this, however, changes the fact that thousands of people and families have been deprived of justice by cynically dishonest government reports that carmakers have used to effectively slam the courthouse door in the faces of people victimized by their negligence. But as the truth about runaway cars continues to emerge, the time is right for all good men and women at the bar to respect the car industry's preference for "litigation pressure," rather than government regulations, by joining a campaign to help carmakers get their throttle control electronics right.

- Other Possibilities.

All states have consumer protection laws that are generally being underutilized when it comes to unsafe cars. In recent years, we have uncovered proof that late model cars that have already suddenly accelerated are much more likely to do so again. Because this vehicle behavior is always dangerous, owners of these cars and their families are not only at an increased risk of being seriously injured, their cars cannot be sold without either disclosing their sudden acceleration history or running the risk of being sued by someone injured as a result of a similar malfunction. While it is not known how many people now find themselves in this situation, the data we are uncovering suggests that there are thousands of car owners who, because of this predicament, have a particularly compelling basis for requiring manufacturers to repurchase these cars. In fact, a class action on behalf of these owners might be just the kind of "litigation pressure" the car industry is yearning for.

These are obvious ways lawyers can respond to the car industry's preference for litigation. The urgent need for a "litigation pressure" campaign is underscored by the following statement in a report recently published by the National Academy of Sciences:

> "It is troubling that the concerns associated with unintended acceleration evolved into questions about electronics safety that NHTSA could not answer convincingly, necessitating a request for extensive technical assistance from NASA . . . . As more complex and interacting electronics systems are developed, the

prospect that vehicle electronics will be suspected and possibly implicated if unsafe vehicle behavior increases."

The NAS report stands as a warning of things to come if "litigation pressure" doesn't convince carmakers that telling the truth about their electronics makes better business sense than keeping their dealers, customers, and the public in the dark. My hope is that this book will convince lawyers and non-lawyers alike to do their part in getting this across to the boardroom heavyweights who run these companies, always keeping in mind that *"it could be your family, it could be you."*

*About the Author*

*Tom Murray is a nationally recognized trial lawyer and legal educator. While he has written extensively for legal publications, this is his first book intended for a general audience. Tom and Ann Murray, who have seven children and 14 grandchildren, live in Huron, Ohio.*